The First-Generation

College Experience

Amy Baldwin, M.A.

Pulaski Technical College

PEARSON

Boston ■ Columbus ■ Indianapolis ■ New York ■ San Francisco ■ Upper Saddle River
Amsterdam ■ Cape Town ■ Dubai ■ London ■ Madrid ■ Milan ■ Munich ■ Paris ■ Montreal ■ Toronto
Delhi ■ Mexico City ■ Sao Paulo ■ Sydney ■ Hong Kong ■ Seoul ■ Singapore ■ Taipei ■ Tokyo

Editor-in-Chief: Jodi McPherson
Development Editor: Jennifer Gessner
Editorial Assistant: Clara Ciminelli
Vice President, Director of Marketing: Margaret Waples
Marketing Manager: Amy Judd
Production Editor: Annette Joseph
Editorial Production Service: Omegatype Typography, Inc.
Manufacturing Buyer: Megan Cochran
Electronic Composition: Omegatype Typography, Inc.
Interior Design: Omegatype Typography, Inc.
Photo Researcher: Annie Fuller
Art Director: Linda Knowles
Cover Designer: Susan Paradise

Library of Congress Cataloging-in-Publication Data

Baldwin, Amy
 The first-generation college experience / Amy Baldwin.
   p. cm.
 Includes bibliographical references and index.
 ISBN-13: 978-0-13-707123-4 (pbk.)
 ISBN-10: 0-13-707123-X (pbk.)
 1. College student orientation—United States.   2. First-generation college students—United States—Case studies.   I. Title.
 LB2343.32.B247 2012
 378.1'98—dc22

                                                      2010052048

Printed in the United States of America

10 9 8 7 6 5 4 3 2 1   WEB   15 14 13 12 11

www.pearsonhighered.com

ISBN-10: 0-13-707129-9
ISBN-13: 978-0-13-707129-6

The College Experience

I believe everyone has a story worth telling. My story is that I am a mother, a teacher, and a student. These three roles have been a part of who I am since my earliest memories. While other little girls played house, I played school, giving homework and telling my "students" (either agreeable neighbors or silent stuffed animals) to be quiet and pay attention. When my older sister went off to her first day of school, I begged to follow, and I gathered my "school supplies" and stuffed them into a bag. Although I was the youngest child, I mothered the neighborhood kids as early as 10 years old when I started babysitting. My teaching career started a little earlier—in 3rd grade—when I was asked to help my friend Jennifer master fractions. I continued my career throughout junior high and high school by tutoring in English, giving swimming lessons, and teaching art.

Nothing, though, prepared me for teaching at the community college. The first class I ever taught was both frightening and exhilarating. It was the first time in my life that I realized what I was doing was *exactly* what I should be doing with my life, but it was also the first time that I felt completely and utterly out of my league, ignorant, even downright dumb. I am sure my students have felt the same way—eager and excited to start a new chapter in their lives, but also concerned about the unknown. Speaking of unknown, I felt I knew nothing about how to be an effective teacher with first-generation students, and it was obvious that I needed to use what I knew about being a student to learn who my students were and what they really needed. Along the way, I discovered that being a nurturer for the abilities and talents that graced my classroom was a fitting role for me as well. How proud I am of the very ones who started their college career unsure of their abilities and who grew in confidence as they marked success after success.

Because I always love learning new things, I have now come full circle and am a student in a doctoral program. I am experiencing similar situations as my students—balancing a full-time job, a family, and college classes and worrying whether or not I can do it all. It's sometimes a struggle to get everything done, but I have used my experience to learn more about how my students feel and what they need in terms of content and support. I have a greater appreciation of their previous experience, their time, and even their levels of frustration when they find themselves stressed out!

It is because of these experiences that I continue to provide what I believe is the best information in the most concise way to college students who fill a variety of roles themselves and who have to make it all work while they are pursuing a degree. I hope you find this book helps make your journey a little easier—at the very least, know that you are not alone in your experiences and that you can do it!

Brief Contents

Contents

PART I: MOVING IN

Chapter 1   YOU FIRST   1

Chapter 2 — YOUR COLLEGE 24

Chapter 3 — RELATIONSHIPS 48

PART II: MOVING THROUGH

Chapter 8   WRITING, RESEARCHING, AND PRESENTING   160

Chapter 9   STUDYING AND TESTS   184

PART III: MOVING ON

Chapter 10   STRESS AND HEALTH   208

Chapter 11   NEXT SEMESTER   230

Chapter 12   A CAREER AND A LIFE   254

Preface

What Is a First-Generation Student Like?

What is a typical first-generation student like? Well, a "typical" student anywhere is hard to find; they are men and women, all ages, from all walks of life and with inspiring stories to tell about how they made their way to college. To see for yourself, walk into the student center or pass by a study area, and you may see students getting acquainted like the four new friends we are about to meet. They may be first-generation students—students who have formed a study group—talking about how they chose to attend the college.

For Laura, 31, the decision to enroll was not difficult despite the fact that she is the first person in her family to attend college. She does have a good friend who went to college while he raised a family and worked, and he served as a role model for her when she made the decision. She chose her local college because of the learning support they offer and the flexible scheduling. She shares with the group that after her youngest son started kindergarten, she enrolled because she envisioned something better for herself and her future. Not knowing what she wanted to do, she took classes that interested her and fulfilled the requirements for an associate of arts degree. At the end of last semester, she was inspired by her teachers to pursue social work, and she now has a "thirst for knowledge." With the help of counselors and instructors and the learning support staff, she is managing a learning difficulty and enjoys the fact that she serves as a role model of her own to her children when she sits down to study and complete assignments.

Michael, 42, is also a first-generation college student. Although he served in the military and has a wealth of work experience and knowledge, he lacks a degree and a career that he could call his life's purpose. Most of the men and women in his family have entered the military rather than go directly to college. Although they know from their work in the military that a college degree can be valuable to employers, none other than Michael have decided to try it out. Michael tells the study group that his girlfriend convinced him to check out the nursing program at the local college because graduates always find high-paying jobs and are known for being well prepared and successful. However, before Michael can gain acceptance into the nursing program, he has to complete a developmental math course, which is why he has asked his fellow students to form a study group. Michael has learned quickly that he can be more successful if he studies with others. His girlfriend has certainly provided the support he needs to make this huge step to change his life, and now he is realizing that so many others at his college have similar backgrounds and are willing to help him.

Juanita, 18, is the youngest of the group, but she is the most experienced first-generation student at the table, because she has been taking concurrent classes through her high school for over a year. Juanita's high school counselor first told her about the program providing college-level classes for high school students to earn college credits while still in high school.

As Juanita explains to the study group, she chose to take concurrent classes because she wants to earn a master's degree, and the sooner she can reach her goal, the more time she will have for a family and a career. However, she admits that it has been challenging to keep up with the demands of her classes, and her parents, who are excited about being able to send their first child to college, don't always understand the kind of pressure she is under. She is expected to read, write, and study more than she did in her high school classes that were not taught at the college level. Luckily for her, she tells her new friends, her family is only a cell phone call away if she needs additional support.

Evan, 20, is by definition a first-generation student. Although his mother got a certificate in computer programming and his father attended one year of college, he is the first with the goal of a four-year degree. Always up for a challenge, Evan says he chose the local college because of its reputation for rigorous classes that will prepare him for an engineering career. He plans to complete his associate of science degree first, because he can apply for a scholarship when he transfers if he keeps his grades up. Evan also reveals that he made good grades in high school and could have attended a four-year university out of state. However, he likes what his college has to offer and prefers the thought of sitting in small classes that offer individual attention rather than getting lost in a sea of 200 students listening to a lecture.

These stories are representative of the backgrounds and challenging situations of first-generation students. What do all these people have in common with you? They have discovered that an education is key to realizing dreams and achieving goals even if they are the first in their families to make the decision to get a degree. They know, as you do too, that the first step to a satisfying career and a life filled with possibilities is enrolling in college.

No doubt, you have your own story as to why you are attending a college for the first time in a long time or as the first in your family, but the common denominator you share with your classmates and the students who share their stories in this text is that you all took an important step to improving your lives through education. With guidance, determination, and hard work, you will succeed in your quest to move from first in college to first in class. As you read the student stories that start each chapter, you will learn more about the challenges and triumphs that each student faces during the semester. You will also have the opportunity to reflect and write about your own story as you move from first in college to first success.

ACKNOWLEDGMENTS

A very special thank-you to the following people for helping me during the process of writing this book: Kyle, Emily, and Will; Sande Johnson and Jennifer Gessner; Amy Judd; Peggy Valdez-Fergason; and the instructors and administrators who provided valuable feedback during the process. Thanks also to the reviewers of this book: Sutonia Boykin, LaGuardia Community College; Mo Cuevas, West Texas A&M University; Jennifer Guerrier, Valencia Community College; James Mendoza, Tacoma Community College; Yolanda Reyna, Alto College; David Rodriguez, San Antonio College; Ethel Schuster, Northern Essex Community College; Karla Thompson, New Mexico State University; Peggy Valdez-Fergason, Community College of Denver; and Robert Blu Vela, Austin Community College.

Introduction to Faculty

"Sí, se puede," which means "Yes, you can" or "Yes, it can be done" in Spanish, was a phrase used by Cesar Chavez and the United Farm Workers almost 40 years ago, and it was also seen in campaign ads and billboards during the 2008 presidential election. It is a fitting message for the optimism that has recently taken hold of higher education, based in our realization that we can do something for students who have historically not been successful at college. These students are often referred to as first-generation or first-in-family students who need the basic information that is often missing from other books of tips for student success. They need, in other words, a textbook that helps them make those first steps that will turn into first successes.

According to Marcy (2004), "Contemporary students are more ethnically and racially diverse and come from a wider range of socio-economic backgrounds than at any time in history. They face more life pressures and bring with them a greater array of life experiences than our original systems ever imagined" (p. 207). Nonetheless, it is no secret that the American higher education system has not always adapted its learning methods and support systems to help the very students who have the most to gain from an academic credential. However, with recent studies that have focused on students of color, first-generation students, developmental students, and low-income students and with recent national, regional, and collegewide initiatives to narrow achievement gaps and improve the success of these students, the ones who were once labeled "at risk" are now able to reap the benefits of new ways of serving their unique needs.

We know, for instance, that when we intentionally engage African American and Hispanic students through active learning and cocurricular activities, they achieve

> personal, social, and academic gains that were greater than their White counterparts' as a result of putting more effort into class assignments, involving themselves in class discussions, and using college services such as the library and computer technology. (Greene, Marti, & McClenney, 2008, p. 517)

We also know from studies (Saenz, Hurtado, Barrera, & Yeung, 2007) that first-generation students are more likely to work while in college and more likely to be influenced in their academic decisions by family. Armed with information from such studies, yes, we can improve the higher education experience for many students.

With these ideas in mind, you will notice that this book, *The First-Generation College Experience*, is not like any other student success text. It is for the student who needs a little extra attention and support to have a firm footing in the academic world. It is about helping those students who have felt disenfranchised, disengaged, and disappointed by the educational system to empower themselves with the knowledge and the skills necessary to imagine and realize a new future. It is also a book about change, specifically transformation, or the intentional process by which we help students change as individuals, as scholars, and as citizens of their communities.

To that end, each chapter contains the following features with the focus on basic information or the "what, when, and where" for being successful in college.

WHAT will support students

■ **It's All Relative:** Acknowledging the enormous influence our students' families have on their academic success, these tips help students create ways to incorporate family support into their academic plans.

■ **It's in the Syllabus:** Examining aspects of a syllabus reminds students to review one of their most important documents in college—the "contract" between their instructors and themselves.

■ **Your Terms of Success:** Because many first-generation students are unfamiliar with the terms that are unique to the college setting, this feature provides a handy overview of common words they will encounter as well as their meanings.

■ **Think about It:** Famous quotes can help students consider another way to view the chapter's topic.

■ **Integrity Matters:** Moving beyond just thinking about how integrity plays a role in a student's academic life, this feature also provides an opportunity to reflect on integrity issues.

■ **Tech Tips:** Students need information about the immediate technological support their colleges offer as well as current technology that can assist students in their educational goals.

WHEN will students relate to the material

■ **Student Stories:** Beginning each chapter and elsewhere throughout the book, the stories of four new students on the journey through college are presented to show how different types of first-generation students will benefit from this book.

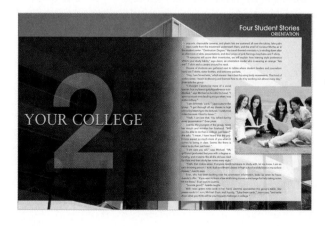

■ **Reflection, Critical Thinking, and Collaboration Exercises:** Exercises appear after each section within the chapters to offer students opportunities to stop, think, and synthesize the information they have read.

■ **PLUS Exercise:** The final in-chapter exercise asks students to reflect on the student story at the beginning of the chapter and to give advice for making good choices.

WHERE can students apply what is being learned

- **From College to University (with University Portfolio):** This connection for students who plan to transfer from a community college to a four-year university provides opportunities to apply concepts and plan for the move.

- **From College to Career (with Career Portfolio):** This connection for students who plan to move into the world of work right after college helps students plan for their careers.

- **Stories of Success:** Diverse success stories from first-generation graduates allow students to imagine themselves as empowered individuals after college.

- **Path of Discovery Journal Entry, Chapter Review Questions, Case Scenarios, and Research It Further:** These end-of-chapter activities allow students to think about concepts in depth, practice what they have learned, and apply their knowledge to new situations.

These features, as well as the practical and basic information within chapters, are designed with the first-generation student in mind to encourage reflection and critical thinking. We know that many first-generation students need help and support that traditional students may not need. This book gives them the foundation they need to build on their first successes.

REFERENCES AND RECOMMENDED READINGS

Gabriel, K. F. (2008). *Teaching unprepared students: Strategies for promoting success and retention in higher education.* Sterling, VA: Stylus.

Greene, T. G., Marti, C. N., & McClenney, K. (2008). The effort-outcome gap: Differences for African American and Hispanic community college students in student engagement and academic achievement. *The Journal of Higher Education, 79*(5), 513–539.

Kuh, G., Kinzie, J., Schuh, J. H., Whitt, E. J., et al. (2005). *Student success in college: Creating conditions that matter.* San Francisco: Jossey-Bass.

Marcy, M. B. (2004). When diversity and dollars collide: Challenges for higher education. *Innovative Higher Education, 28*(3), 205–218.

Saenz, V. B., Hurtado, S., Barrera, D., & Yeung, F. (2007). *First in my family: A profile of first-generation college students at four-year institutions since 1971.* Los Angeles: HERI.

Tinto, V. (1994). *Leaving college: Rethinking the causes and cures of student attrition.* Chicago: University of Chicago Press.

Watson, L. W., Terrell, M. C., & Wright, D. J. (2002). *How minority students experience college: Implications for planning and policy.* Sterling, VA: Stylus.

Introduction to Students

You made it! You have taken the first steps to a college education, and for that, you should feel a sense of accomplishment. It is no easy task to apply for admission, enroll in classes, and find your way around campus, but you have obviously completed those steps successfully. Getting your course supplies, such as textbooks and notebooks, too, is a feat worth congratulations. Now is the time to take a moment and think about why you are here and what you hope to achieve.

W. Edwards Deming, professor and industrial consultant, once said, "It's not enough to do your best. You must know what to do and then do your best." Obviously, from your commitment to take the first step into college, you have the desire to do your best. Now you just need the tools to help you know what to do so that you can do your best in college, in a career, and in your life.

With that thought in mind, this book is designed to help you learn what you need to do to accomplish your goals by providing you with basic information about college expectations, academic strategies, and life management skills. This book is intended for the students who are the first in their families to go to college and for the students who are thinking for the first time in their lives that they want something better for themselves, something that includes getting a college education. If that is you, then you will find this book to be a valuable resource as you take those first steps.

To help first-time students like you on the path to success, this book is arranged around three sections that focus on getting somewhere: "Moving In," which provides information about transitioning into college smoothly; "Moving Through," which offers strategies and tips for getting through your academic requirements successfully; and "Moving On," which helps prepare you for the life you want after completing your education. You will also find, before the chapters begin, a quick primer on financial planning, titled "Finances First." It is never too early to start thinking about paying for college and managing your money while you are here.

The student stories that begin each chapter allow you to consider what life will be like for you now that you are in college. You will get to know Juanita, 18, who is dependent on her family for support; Laura, 31, a single parent who has a learning disability; Michael, 42, who has an accomplished military career but no previous college education; and Evan, 20, who has many ambitions but no clear path to success. These stories will help you see others meet the same challenges you will surely face as a new student, and it will also help you see how others may experience college for the first time.

Other features that you may find helpful as a first-time student include "It's All Relative," which provides information about issues related to family and gives you the opportunity to create a plan for managing your family relationship. Studies have shown that for many students, family is their first priority, and recognizing the role it plays in students' lives is important to helping those students achieve success. "Your Terms of Success" provides a list of terms you may not be familiar with as a first-time student that will help you navigate your way through college. Likewise, "Tech Tips" explains how to easily access information about how technology can and will be used in college. Whether you are technologically savvy or a beginner, you will benefit from seeing how technology can be applied to help you succeed.

"Integrity Matters" will remind you of one of the core values of higher education, doing what is right even if no one is watching, and will offer opportunities to explore ways to act with integrity, a good habit to build on during college. "From College to University" (with Portfolio) and "From College to Career" (with Portfolio) will help you create a plan for life after college, whatever path you take after your current college experience. Finally, each chapter ends with a story of success, a story about a real person who, much like you, started college with dreams of big things and made those dreams come true. Use their stories for inspiration when you need it.

The entire book has been written with your best interests in mind. May it serve you well as you take those first steps toward your future!

One of the greatest challenges for first-generation students isn't meeting the academic expectations of college; it is handling the financial issues that come into play when you get there. Some students choose to go to school full time and not work whereas others juggle a job—either part time or full time—while going to school. No matter what their financial situations, many are adding the expense of going to college to their other obligations, or they are using grants, loans, or scholarships to cover costs.

As you know by now because you successfully enrolled in college, investing in your future takes more than courage; it also takes some cash or at least access to funds to cover the costs. Unfortunately, as Catherine Rampell (2009) recently reported for the *New York Times*, the costs of college continue to rise and will likely increase with each passing year. So what can you do? The first step, and the reason this section precedes the actual chapters in the book, is to become financially literate. There are many resources available that can help you learn more about how to become financially fit. The next step is to create a plan for staying on a budget and for anticipating expenses in the future. The following section provides you with a brief overview of both steps.

ESTIMATING College Costs

Estimating what you are going to spend for your college education is a great first step to understanding your financial situation, and it will help you with budgeting. Because this is your first time in college, it will be helpful to see what you can expect to spend as you work on and complete your degree. Unfortunately, college tuition and fees are only part of the costs involved in earning a degree. No matter what you pay for tuition and fees, you will pay only a fraction of the actual costs of educating one student. Colleges make up the difference through taxes, state and federal money, and gifts and donations.

To determine your estimated costs, you will need to get very specific about what you will need during the semesters you plan to attend. The following list is only a suggestion of possible supplies (because specialized programs may require other materials): textbooks, notebooks/binders, computer/laptop, backpack, paper (for notes), paper (for printing), pens/pencils, calculator, computer software, thumb drive, stapler, hole puncher, ruler, and supplies for labs or certain classes such as drawing. Create a list of what you know you will need and then write down how much you think each item will cost. You will use this estimation when you create a budget.

In addition to supplies and tuition, you may also find other costs associated with going to college. For example, your transportation costs may increase as you go from home or work to campus and back. You may also discover that you need regular, reliable Internet access that will create an additional monthly cost. Costs for parking or day care may also have to be factored in. Especially for first-generation students, unexpected costs such as these can be an awakening to investments of money and time that weren't covered during new student orientation. There may well be additional expenses that you may encounter. You will want to talk with students who have been at your college for a few semesters or recent graduates to determine what else may be needed. These same students may also provide you with some cost-saving ideas as well.

CREATING a Budget

In order to manage these costs while balancing your other financial obligations, creating a budget will help you stay on track. A budget doesn't have to be a headache. In fact, it is relatively easy to make a budget. The hard part is following it. First, you need to establish a customized budget sheet. Figure 1 shows a sample budget form that you can start with. In the first column, you will estimate your income and expenses. The middle column will be used to record actual amounts for income and expenses. Record any differences in the marked column by subtracting the actual amount from the estimated amount. For example, if you estimate that you earn about $1000.00 a month, but this month you earn $1092.56, the difference is $92.56. If you earned $997.36, then the difference is –$2.64.

Once you determine the categories that fit your lifestyle, you will need to gather all the bills and paystubs that you have and add up your expenses and income. It is a good idea to review at least three months' worth of bills to get an accurate picture of your expenditures. If you have any bills that are paid less frequently than once a month, then you will need to convert them to a monthly expense. For example, if you pay $240 for car insurance every six months, your monthly expense is $40 ($240 divided by six months).

One key to an accurate budget that helps you track your spending is to be honest about your expenses. That means you must write down everything you spend, even the money for snacks or supplies. You may find that you spend $25 a week ($100 a month) on items that are unnecessary. The more you can track unnecessary items, the better you can control your spending.

After you get an accurate picture of your income and expenses, you can start setting short-term and long-term financial goals. Because you are in college and probably trying to keep expenses to a minimum, you may think that creating and working toward financial goals will be a difficult undertaking until you have a job with a steady income and secure future. However, you can start setting small short-term goals now. For example, your first short-term goal could be keeping a monthly budget and making adjustments periodically.

FIGURE 1 Sample Budget Form

Category	Estimated Amount per Month	Actual Amount per Month	Difference
Income			
Source 1 (wages/salary)			
Source 2 (scholarship, financial aid, etc.)			
Source 3 (alimony, employee tuition reimbursement, child support)			
Total Income			
Expenses			
Mortgage/rent			
Utilities			
Car payment/transportation			
Insurance			
Groceries			
Household items			
Clothing			
Gas			
Car maintenance			
Cellular phone/pager			
Eating out			
Entertainment			
Health care (medications, doctor's visits, etc.)			
Credit cards or loans			
Total Expenses			
Net Income (Total Income minus Total Expenses)			

Another short-term goal could be to gather all the documents about your financial aid and keep them organized until after you graduate. Meeting these two goals will help you reach larger goals down the road.

You should also write down your long-term financial goals. One of these goals could be financial freedom and security. However, in order to reach that long-term goal, you will need to make a list of other goals and start working toward them. Be sure to include long-term goals that prepare you for retirement and the unlikely event of disability and unemployment.

Don't Take Credit

Credit cards can be very tempting when you are in college because they are so easy to use and the offers pour in just about every day. The reality of credit cards, however, is that they can

TABLE 1 Credit Card Payments

Month	Previous Balance	Interest	Balance + Interest	Payment	Remaining Balance
Month 1	$1,000.00	$14.17	$1,014.17	$20.00	$994.17
Month 2	$ 994.17	$14.08	$1,008.25	$20.00	$988.25
Month 3	$ 988.25	$14.00	$1,002.25	$20.00	$982.25
Month 4	$ 982.25	$13.92	$ 996.17	$20.00	$976.17
Month 5	$ 976.17	$13.83	$ 990.00	$20.00	$970.00
Month 6	$ 970.00	$13.74	$ 983.74	$20.00	$963.74

cause big financial problems, leading to debts that are sometimes difficult to pay off. Think about this: You don't want to start a new career after college that pays a good salary only to send a substantial portion of it to a credit card company.

In case you are still enticed to use a credit card, think about this sobering information. If you were to charge $1000 on a credit card that charges 17% interest and only pay $10 a month, you will be accruing more in interest than you will be paying each month. And that is only if you do not charge anything else!

Table 1 shows that paying twice as much—$20—each month for six months only reduces the balance by $36.26—after paying $120. Unfortunately, some students have many more thousands of dollars of credit card debt, and with the current interest rates, it is no wonder that students can find themselves in an endless cycle of charging and paying minimums. If it is at all possible, put the cards away until you are out of college, and then use them wisely.

Practice Good Financial Habits

A good financial plan is only as good as the degree that you stick to it. The following tips can help you increase your financial literacy muscles, especially if you exercise them regularly:

- Read all financial statements each month.
- Compare financial statements with your recording of expenses and income.
- Separate bills from other mail.
- Create a schedule for paying bills.
- Sign up for online payment plans if available and if it is easier to pay in this way. Unreliable Internet access and various email addresses will make it difficult to keep up with online bills.
- If you have a credit card, use it for emergencies only.

- Try to put back a small percentage of your income each month for unexpected expenses. For example, for every $100 you earn, put $5 (5%) in an emergency savings account. Create a goal to increase your savings percentage.
- Keep up with the changes in tuition and fees at your college.

Protect Yourself

Budgeting and creating a plan are not enough to make sure that you are on firm financial foundation because you will also need to protect yourself from the various scams that can do more harm than just draining your bank account. If anyone you do not know contacts you through email or by phone to ask you to send money or provide a bank account number, delete the email or hang up the phone. Thousands of well-meaning people get scammed this way by providing access to their bank accounts, only to find out that their money is gone and their credit is ruined. If the information sounds too good to be true or doesn't seem "right," it quite possibly is a scam.

LEARN More

There are numerous resources available for you to explore financial matters further. There are many local, state, and federal government programs that can provide free information and counseling if you are interested in getting your finances on track. The best defense is good information about your situation and your possibilities. For starters, you can—and should—request a free credit report. A request form from the Federal Trade Commission is available at www.ftc.gov/credit. You can also find a local (and usually free) financial help center that provides workshops and counseling for people who want to know more about their financial situation. You can find these agencies online or in the phone book. Don't forget that your local library and bookstore offer many good resources on money management and financial matters. Start with a good book, such as *Personal Finance for Dummies* (Tyson, 2009), that defines common terms and provides basic information. Remember that the best way to protect your financial future—and to secure the hard work that you are doing in college to get a better job—is to empower yourself with knowledge about what you have and what you want to do with it in the future.

REFERENCES

Rampell, C. (2009, October 20). The skyrocketing costs of attending college. *New York Times*. Retrieved November 24, 2009, from http://economix .blogs.nytimes.com/2009/10/20/the- skyrocketing-costs-of-attending- college/

Tyson, D. (2009). *Personal Finance for Dummies* (6th ed). New York: Wiley.

Supplemental Resources

INSTRUCTOR SUPPORT – Resources to simplify your life and support your students.

Book Specific

Online Instructor's Manual This manual is intended to give professors a framework or blueprint of ideas and suggestions that may assist them in providing their students with activities, journal writing, thought-provoking situations, and group activities. The test bank organized by chapter includes: multiple-choice, true/false, and short-answer questions that support the key features in the book. This supplement is available for download from the Instructor's Resource Center at www.pearsonhighered.com/irc

Online PowerPoint Presentation A comprehensive set of PowerPoint slides that can be used by instructors for class presentations or by students for lecture preview or review. The presentation includes all the graphs and tables in the textbook. The presentation contains bullet point PowerPoint slides for each chapter. These slides highlight the important points of each chapter to help students understand the concepts within each chapter. Instructors may download these PowerPoint presentations from the Instructor's Resource Center at www.pearsonhighered.com/irc

Online Clicker Questions PowerPoint slides created specifically for use with Clicker systems that can be used by instructors in class lecture situations to assess students' collective knowledge of key concepts through multiple-choice questions for each chapter. The presentation includes content from the textbook, with multiple-choice assessments in PowerPoint slide format for each chapter. They highlight the important points to help students understand the concepts, and allow instructors to seamlessly use with any Clicker system. Instructors may download these PowerPoint presentations from the Instructor's Resource Center at www.pearsonhighered.com/irc

MyTest Test Bank Pearson MyTest offers instructors a secure online environment and quality assessments to easily create print exams, study guide questions, and quizzes from any computer with an Internet connection.
Premium Assessment Content
  • Draw from a rich library of question testbanks that complement the textbook and course learning objectives.
  • Edit questions or tests to fit specific teaching needs.
Instructor Friendly Features
  • Easily create and store questions, including images, diagrams, and charts using simple drag-and-drop and Word-like controls.
  • Use additional information provided by Pearson, such as the question's difficulty level or learning objective, to help quickly build a test.
Time-Saving Enhancements
  • Add headers or footers and easily scramble questions and answer choices all from one simple toolbar.
  • Quickly create multiple versions of a test or answer key, and when ready, simply save to Word or PDF format and print!
  • Export exams for import to Blackboard 6.0, CE (WebCT), or Vista (WebCT)!
Additional information available at www.pearsonmytest.com

MyStudentSuccessLab Are you teaching online, in a hybrid setting, or looking to infuse exciting technology into your classroom for the first time? Then be sure to refer to the MyStudentSuccessLab section included in the coming pages of this Preface to learn more. This online solution is designed to help students build the skills they need to succeed at www.mystudentsuccesslab.com

Other Resources

"Easy access to online, book-specific teaching support is now just a click away!"

Instructor Resource Center — Register. Redeem. Login. Three easy steps that open the door to a variety of print and media resources in downloadable, digital format, available to instructors exclusively through the Pearson/Prentice Hall 'IRC'. www.pearsonhighered.com/irc

"Choose from a wide range of video resources for the classroom!"

Prentice Hall Reference Library: Life Skills Pack (ISBN: 0-13-127079-6). Contains all 4 videos, or they may be requested individually as follows:
- *Learning Styles and Self-Awareness*, 0-13-028502-1
- *Critical and Creative Thinking*, 0-13-028504-8
- *Relating to Others*, 0-13-028511-0
- *Personal Wellness*, 0-13-028514-5

Prentice Hall Reference Library: Study Skills Pack (ISBN: 0-13-127080-X). Contains all 6 videos, or they may be requested individually as follows:
- *Reading Effectively*, 0-13-028505-6
- *Listening and Memory*, 0-13-028506-4
- *Note Taking and Research*, 0-13-028508-0
- *Writing Effectively*, 0-13-028509-9
- *Effective Test Taking*, 0-13-028500-5
- *Goal Setting and Time Management*, 0-13-028503-X

Prentice Hall Reference Library: Career Skills Pack (ISBN: 0-13-118529-2). Contains all 3 videos, or they may be requested individually as follows:
- *Skills for the 21st Century – Technology*, 0-13-028512-9
- *Skills for the 21st Century – Math and Science*, 0-13-028513-7
- *Managing Career and Money*, 0-13-028516-1

Complete Reference Library—Life/Study Skills/Career Video Pack on DVD (ISBN: 0-13-501095-0).
- Our Reference Library of thirteen popular video resources has now been digitized onto one DVD so students and instructors alike can benefit from the array of video clips. Featuring Life Skills, Study Skills, and Career Skills, they help to reinforce the course content in a more interactive way.

Faculty Video Resources
- Teacher Training Video 1: *Critical Thinking*, ISBN: 0-13-099432-4
- Teacher Training Video 2: *Stress Management & Communication*, ISBN: 0-13-099578-9
- Teacher Training Video 3: *Classroom Tips*, ISBN: 0-13-917205-X
- Student Advice Video, ISBN: 0-13-233206-X
- Study Skills Video, ISBN: 0-13-096095-0

Current Issues Videos
- ABC News Video Series: *Student Success Second Edition*, ISBN: 0-13-031901-5
- ABC News Video Series: *Student Success Third Edition*, ISBN: 0-13-152865-3

MyStudentSuccessLab PH Videos on DVD (ISBN: 0-13-514249-0).
- Our six most popular video resources have been digitized onto one DVD so students and instructors alike can benefit from the array of video clips. Featuring Technology, Math and Science, Managing Money and Career, Learning Styles and Self-Awareness, Study Skills, and Peer Advice, they help to reinforce the course content in a more interactive way. They are also accessible through our MSSL and course management offerings and available on VHS.

"Through partnership opportunities, we offer a variety of assessment options!"

LASSI—The LASSI is a 10-scale, 80-item assessment of students' awareness about and use of learning and study strategies. Addressing skill, will, and self-regulation, the focus is on both covert and overt thoughts, behaviors, attitudes, and beliefs that relate to successful learning and that can be altered through educational interventions. Available in two formats: Paper ISBN: 0-13-172315-4 or Online ISBN: 0-13-172316-2 (access card).

Noel Levitz/RMS—This retention tool measures Academic Motivation, General Coping Ability, Receptivity to Support Services, PLUS Social Motivation. It helps identify at-risk students, the areas with which they struggle, and their receptiveness to support. Available in paper or online formats, as well as short and long versions. Paper Long Form A: ISBN: 0-13-512066-7; Paper Short Form B: ISBN: 0-13-512065-9; Online Forms A,B & C: ISBN: 0-13-098158-3.

Robbins Self Assessment Library—This compilation teaches students to create a portfolio of skills. S.A.L. is a self-contained, interactive library of 49 behavioral questionnaires that help students discover new ideas about themselves, their attitudes, and their personal strengths and weaknesses. Available in Paper, CD-Rom, and Online (Access Card) formats.

Readiness for Education at a Distance Indicator(READI)—READI is a web-based tool that assesses the overall likelihood for online learning success. READI generates an immediate score and a diagnostic interpretation of results, including recommendations for successful participation in online courses and potential remediation sources. Please visit www.readi.info for additional information. ISBN: 0-13-188967-2.

Pathway to Student Success CD-ROM
The CD is divided into several categories, each of which focuses on a specific topic that relates to students and provides them with the context, tools, and strategies to enhance their educational experience. ISBN: 0-13-239314-X.

The Golden Personality Type Profiler
The Golden Personality Type Profiler™ helps students understand how they make decisions and relate to others. By completing the Golden Personality Type Profiler™ students develop a deeper understanding of their strengths, a clearer picture of how their behavior impacts others, and a better appreciation for the interpersonal style of others and how to interact with them more effectively. Using these results as a guide, students will gain the self awareness that is key to professional development and success. ISBN: 0-13-706654-6.

"For a truly tailored solution that fosters campus connections and increases retention,
 talk with us about custom publishing."
Pearson Custom Publishing—We are the largest custom provider for print and media shaped to your course's needs. Please visit us at www.pearsoncustom.com to learn more.

STUDENT SUPPORT –
Tools to help make the grade now, and excel in school later.

"Today's students are more inclined than ever to use technology to enhance their learning."
Refer to the **MyStudentSuccessLab** section of this Preface to learn about our revolutionary resource (www.mystudentsuccesslab.com). This online solution is designed to help students build the skills they need to succeed.

"Time management is the #1 challenge students face." We can help.
Prentice Hall Planner —A basic planner that includes a monthly & daily calendar plus other materials to facilitate organization. 8½ × 11.
Premier Annual Planner—This specially designed, annual 4-color collegiate planner includes an academic planning/resources section, monthly planning section (2 pages/month), weekly planning section (48 weeks; July start date), which facilitate short-term as well as long-term planning. Spiral bound, 6 × 9. Customization is available.

"Journaling activities promote self-discovery and self-awareness."
Student Reflection Journal—Through this vehicle, students are encouraged to track their progress and share their insights, thoughts, and concerns. 8½ × 11. 90 pages.

"The Student Orientation Series includes short booklets on specialized topics that facilitate greater student understanding."
S.O.S. Guides help students understand what these opportunities are, how to take advantage of them, and how to learn from their peers while doing so. They include:
   • Connolly: *Learning Communities* ISBN: 0-13-232243-9
   • Hoffman: *Stop Procrastination Now! 10 Simple and SUCCESSFUL Steps for Student Success* ISBN: 0-13-513056-5
   • Jabr: *English Language Learners* ISBN: 0-13-232242-0
   • Watts: *Service Learning* ISBN: 0-13-232201-0

For Students!

Why is this course important?

This course will help you transition to college, introduce you to campus resources, and prepare you for success in all aspects of college, career, and life. You will:
- Develop Skills to Excel in Other Classes
- Apply Concepts from College to Your Career and Life
- Learn to Use Media Resources

How can you get the most out of the book and online resources required in this class?

Purchase your book and online resources before the First Day of Class. Register and log in to the online resources using your access code.

Develop Skills to Excel in Other Classes
- Helps you with your homework
- Prepares you for exams

Apply Concepts from College to Your Career and Life
- Provides learning techniques
- Helps you achieve your goals

Learn to Use Media Resources
- **www.mystudentsuccesslab.com** helps you build skills you need to succeed through peer-led videos, interactive exercises and projects, journaling, and goal setting activities.
- Connect with real students, practice skill development, and personalize what is learned.

Want to get involved with Pearson like other students have?

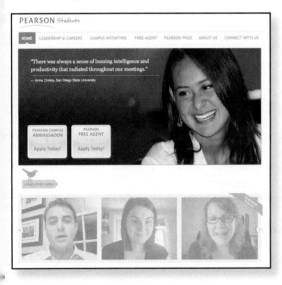

Join www.PearsonStudents.com
It is a place where our student customers can incorporate their views and ideas into their learning experience. They come to find out about our programs such as the **Pearson Student Advisory Board**, **Pearson Campus Ambassador**, and the **Pearson Prize** (student scholarship!).

Here's how you can get involved:

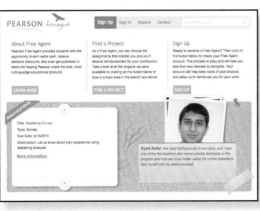

- Tell your instructors, friends, and family members about **PearsonStudents**.
- To get daily updates on how students can boost their résumés, study tips, get involved with Pearson, and earn rewards:

  [f] Become a fan of **Pearson Students on Facebook**

  [t] Follow **@Pearson_Student on Twitter**

- Explore **Pearson Free Agent**. It allows you get involved in the publishing process by giving student feedback.

See you on **PearsonStudents** where our student customers live. When students succeed, we succeed!

PEARSON
mystudentsuccesslab ™

Succeed in college and beyond!
Connect, practice, and personalize with MyStudentSuccessLab.

www.mystudentsuccesslab.com

MyStudentSuccessLab is an online solution designed to help students acquire the skills they need to succeed. They will have access to peer-led video presentations and develop core skills through interactive exercises and projects that provide academic, life, and career skills that will transfer to ANY course.

It can accompany any Student Success text, or be sold as a stand-alone course offering. To become successful learners, students must consistently apply techniques to daily activities.

How will MyStudentSuccessLab make a difference?

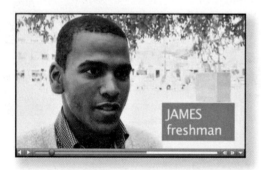

Is motivation a challenge, and if so, how do you deal with it?
Video Presentation — Experience peer led video 'by students, for students' of all ages and stages.

How would better class preparation improve the learning experience?
Practice activities — Practice skills for each topic — beginning, intermediate, and advanced — leveled by Bloom's taxonomy.

What could you gain by building critical thinking and problem-solving skills in this class? **Apply (final project)** – Complete a final project using these skills to create 'personally relevant' resources.

APPLY
Calendaring for the Term
Overview: This "final" activity has students use the syllabus for your course to plan their work in this class for the term. As part of the activity, they're provided a calendar template that can adjust to any start and end date, so no matter what length your course is, this template will work. Then, students are instructed to find all the key dates in your syllabus and calendar sufficient time to complete all assignments or prepare for all tests. Once complete, students submit the calendar to your dropbox for grading.
Grading Rubric Suggestions:
A grade: All important dates are included and clearly specified. Dates should be based on your syllabus but typically include reading assignment due dates, exams and projects to withdrawal dates and extra credit activities. In addition, for each due date, students also calendar adequate time to study, read or otherwise prepare to meet their responsibilities for your course. [Note: To gauge adequate time, estimate 2-3 hours of study for each credit hour. So, for a 3-credit course, students should plan on 6-9 hours of study per week.]
B grade: All but 10-20% of the important dates are included. For each due date on the calendar, sufficient time is allowed for studying, reading, or other preparation and/or 10-20% of the dates have insufficient time for studying, reading, or otherwise preparing.
C grade: Twenty-five percent of the important dates are missing and/or 25% of the dates aren't calendared with sufficient time to prepare for them.
D Grade: Fifty percent of the key dates are missing and/or aren't calendared with sufficient time to prepare for them.
F Grade: Most or all key dates are missing and most or all aren't calendared with sufficient time to prepare for them.

As an instructor, how much easier would it be to assign and use MyStudentSuccessLab if you had an implementation guide?
Instructor Guide – Describes each activity, the skills addressed, an estimate of student time on task, and a grading rubric for the final Apply activity.

MyStudentSuccessLab Feature set:
Topic Overview: Module objectives.
Video Presentation - Connect: Real student video interviews on key issues.
Practice: Three skill-building exercises per topic provide interactive experience and practice.
Apply - Personalize: Apply what is learned by creating a personally relevant project and journal.
Resources: Plagiarism Guide, Dictionary, Calculators, and Assessments (Career, Learning Styles, and Personality Styles).
Additional Assignments: Extra suggested activities to use with each topic.
Text-Specific Study Plan (available with select books): Chapter Objectives, Practice Tests, Enrichment activities, and Flash cards.

MyStudentSuccessLab Topic List -
1. Time Management/Planning
2. Values/Goal Setting
3. Learning How You Learn
4. Listening and Taking Class Notes
5. Reading and Annotating
6. Memory and Studying
7. Critical Thinking

8. Problem-Solving
9. Information Literacy
10. Communication
11. Test Prep and Test Taking
12. Stress Management
13. Financial Literacy
14. Majors and Careers

MyStudentSuccessLab Support:
• **Demos, Registration, Log-in** - www.mystudentsuccesslab.com under "Tours and Training" and "Support."
• **Email support** - Send an inquiry to MyStudentSuccessLab@pearson.com
• **Online Training** - Join one of our weekly WebEx training sessions.
• **Peer Training** - Faculty Advocate connection for qualified adoptions.
• **Technical support** - 24 hours a day, seven days a week, at http://247pearsoned.custhelp.com

PERSONALIZE THE EXPERIENCE WITH

PEARSON LEARNING SOLUTIONS

FOR STUDENT SUCCESS AND CAREER DEVELOPMENT

The Pearson Custom Library Catalog

With Pearson Custom Library, you can create a custom book by selecting content from our course-specific collections. The collections consist of chapters from Pearson titles like this one, and carefully selected, copyright cleared, third-party content, and pedagogy. The finished product is a print-on-demand custom book that students can purchase in the same way they purchase other course materials.

Custom Media

Pearson Learning Solutions works with you to create a customized technology solution specific to your course requirements and needs. We specialize in a number of best practices including custom websites and portals, animation and simulations, and content conversions and customizations.

Custom Publications

We can develop your original material and create a textbook that meets your course goals. Pearson Learning Solutions works with you on your original manuscript to help refine and strengthen it, ensuring that it meets and exceeds market standards. Pearson Learning Solutions will work with you to select already published content and sequence it to follow your course goals.

Online Education

Pearson Learning Solutions offers customizable online course content for your distance learning classes, hybrid courses, or to enhance the learning experience of your traditional in-classroom students. Courses include a fully developed syllabus, media-rich lecture presentations, audio lectures, a wide variety of assessments, discussion board questions, and a strong instructor resource package.

In the end, the finished product reflects your insight into what your students need to succeed, and puts it into practice. Visit us on the web to learn more at www.pearsoncustom.com/studentsuccess 800-777-6872

Now Available!
A 'one-stop shop' for student success.

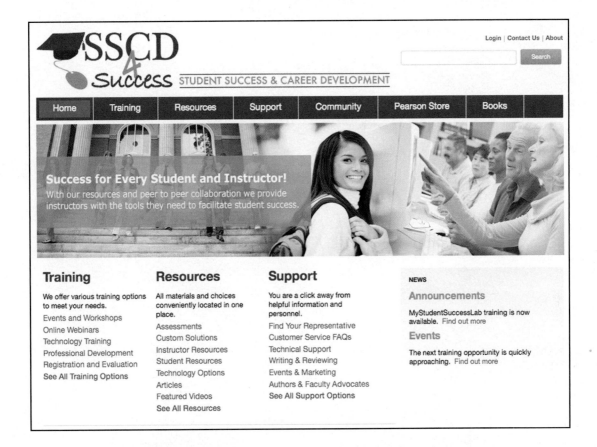

This website offers a compilation of Pearson's training, resources, and support options all in one convenient place.

We provide variety of **Training** options to meet your needs. Events and Workshops around the country as well as Online Webinars. MyStudentSuccessLab Technology training is available too.

A wealth of **Resources** are available to address a range of interests, including assessments, online catalog, customized solutions, Instructor Resources, and Student Resources. Technology is addressed, whether you're teaching online, hybrid, or just need an engagement tool.

For **Support**, always contact your local sales professional, however, the SSCD Team is here to help anytime including Customer Service, Technical Support, Editorial, Events, Marketing, Specialists, and Faculty Advocates.

Welcome to the **Pearson SSCD Online Community** where we connect, empower, and renew with one another. Regardless of your institute origin, teaching background, or experience level, we strive to ensure there are resources available to support our mission—infusing success for EVERY student and instructor!

www.pearsonhighered.com/sscd4success

1
YOU FIRST

uanita calls her mother for the second time in two hours. She often finds her mother's voice and advice exactly what she needs to hear. She has just created her schedule, visited with her advisor, and now is looking for where her classes will be. If there is one thing Juanita does well, it is preparing to make a good first impression.

"Call me," she texts to her mother. Juanita's mom calls immediately. Despite the fact that neither Juanita's mother nor father attended college, her mother always seems to know what to say to keep Juanita on track.

"Do you think I can do this? I just discovered one of my classes is in a building on the other side of campus. Even on a nice day, I don't know if I can make it in the 10 minutes I have between classes."

"Juanita," her mother says with softness and fatigue in her voice, "you always overthink these things. I know you like to be prepared, but things will be different, including how you are going to manage getting to classes in different buildings. It's not high school."

Juanita doesn't know if her schedule is right for her. The classes seem different from the dual enrollment classes she took in high school; even though it seems the expectations and workload are the same, the different students of varying ages are something for her to get used to. Only a few of her friends are attending with her, and she didn't see any of them a few weeks ago when the college offered campus tours for incoming students. Now, the only time she "sees" them is on their websites where she can view their latest pictures.

"Yeah, but I didn't have to make a life decision in high school. It made me nervous when my advisor asked me to choose a degree plan," she replies, biting her nails.

"You did choose electrical engineering, just like we talked about, right?" her mother asks.

"Well, I wanted to talk to you about that. I saw a flyer about careers in the health field. I showed my advisor and she said I could make a really good salary right after I graduate and it wouldn't take as long as a degree in engineering," Juanita says.

"But you don't like working with people who are sick, Juanita. Don't you want to build things instead? You were always building things in the backyard, growing up," her mother responds.

Juanita feels the conversation going in the same direction it always does, and she moves from biting her nails to chewing her cuticles.

"Juanita, you need to make a decision really soon. You need to get through as soon as you can and get a good job that will pay enough to support you. If not, I don't know if I can support you for much longer," says her mother.

Hearing this causes Juanita's stomach to harden because she knows that her father will not be able to work much longer and her mother will have to take care of him. When that happens, there may not be enough money to stay in college. Because of the classes she has taken in her high school's dual enrollment program, Juanita could graduate with an associate's degree next year, but if she doesn't get a scholarship to continue her education, she may not be able to transfer to a four-year university. Now she is thinking seriously about a degree that takes less time and can get her into a good career fast.

"You can't afford mistakes, Juanita," says her mother. "I will be proud of you whatever you decide, but make a choice and stick with it."

Juanita knows her mother is right. She has a goal of getting a degree—and nothing will keep her from that—but she is not sure how to make the right decisions between today and the day she graduates.

As she winds her way down the hill and to the campus center food court, she tells her mother good-bye and promises to pick up a prescription on her way home. She resolves to make an appointment with her advisor and think about what she should do.

In this CHAPTER

This chapter is devoted to you first because knowing who you are will help you lay a solid foundation on which to build success. Starting with understanding yourself seems like the easiest of subjects, but getting to the point of really knowing yourself will take time. You are now a college student and your journey will be an exciting one, but it will also be one in which you will find yourself changing, growing, and defining or redefining who you are and who you want to be.

More specifically, after completing this chapter, you will be able to do the following:

■ **Discover your story.**
■ **Set your goals and create a mission statement.**
■ **Determine your learning style preference.**
■ **Develop your support system.**

YOUR STORY

The question "Who are you?" sounds easy to answer. You may start by listing a variety of characteristics. For example, you are a male, age 25, married, father of a son, an electrician, and a Native American. Or you are a single female, age 19, part-time sales assistant, full-time student, and mountain climber. But what are you beyond those labels? Where have you been? What are you doing now? Where are you going and where do you want to be? Now the questions get a little more difficult and take more time and thought to answer. The point is that you need to have some idea of who you are, or at least an idea of where you want to be, when you begin college.

Maybe you can say that you don't know who you are yet, but you hope that enrolling in classes and pursuing a degree will help you come to a better understanding of who you are. Don't worry, though, if you cannot immediately articulate the essence of you. This question—"Who are you?"—and the possible answers have been intriguing human beings for thousands of years. In his book *Who Are You? 101 Ways of Seeing Yourself* (2000), Malcolm Godwin explores the ways that we have tried to answer this question. From body types to ancient Indian mysticism to workplace dynamics, there are numerous ways you can learn more about what and how you think. The ultimate goal is to know yourself and your environment well enough to reach your goals.

Of course, who you are will change, maybe dramatically, as you take classes, encounter new subjects, and research interesting topics. But taking the time now to think and reflect about yourself will help you map your course throughout the college experience and beyond—returning to work, raising a family, attending another college, having a fulfilling career. This chapter assists you in understanding who you are by helping you identify what you know and how you learn. This chapter also aids in your decisions about who and what you want to be while helping you make the transition into college.

Your Background

To discover your story—and to write your future—you will need to consider where you began. Your background, which includes your family, your culture, and your experiences, will serve as a foundation for creating a life. Think about your personal history and how it has shaped who you are. Also, consider how your family has influenced you as well—what beliefs have they instilled in you? What is their attitude toward your college aspirations? Who you are and how you have developed will be part of your value system as well as part of the foundation for setting goals for future achievements. If you have had great support and good educational experiences, you may find envisioning your future degree rather easy. However, if you have had substantial challenges in your life, you may need more support and resources to see that you can indeed be successful. No matter what your background—and to be a first-generation student means you have a unique life story and a wonderful opportunity to be successful—your college will give you the chance to write a life story that includes a college education.

Think **ABOUT IT**

He who knows others is learned; he who knows himself is wise.

—Lao-tzu, *Tao te Ching*

Your Values

Part of your life story will include your value system. Values can be inherited from your parents, or they can come from what your culture, religion, or ethnicity regard as important. Values can also be formed from both positive and negative experiences. For example, a value of yours may be honesty, which means that you try to be truthful and straightforward in most situations and that you expect others to be honest with you. If you value hard work, then you strive to do your best in your life. If a friend has treated you with compassion, you may value sensitivity to others. On the other hand, if you have been discriminated against in the past, you may now value open-mindedness in others.

The importance of knowing and understanding your values is that this knowledge can help you set realistic goals. If you value a satisfying career, for instance, you will set goals supporting that value. Therefore, you will probably investigate careers and fields that are challenging and interesting. If you value a stable financial future, you will set goals that enable you to earn enough money to provide for your needs and wants. If you value your family, you will make spending time with them a priority. Your values should be a true reflection of who *you* are and what *you* believe.

Think about Juanita's conversation with her mother. Her mother wants Juanita to consider electrical engineering, perhaps because she values financial stability and success or career prestige. What if one reason Juanita hesitates at choosing a major and career path is that she values a career that helps the human condition? What if she also wants to learn more about how we recover from illness? If she decides to adopt her mother's values and ignore her own, what kind of future can you envision for her? Although her mother's intentions may be well meaning, Juanita will have to compromise herself in order to meet her parents' goals for her, and she will probably suffer some regret in the future.

Does this example mean that you should ignore others who have helped you figure out what you want to be? Certainly not. But you should pay attention to what you want when you do get help with your educational and career goals. Be open to others' suggestions, but make sure you feel comfortable with your final decision. Those who truly want you to succeed will be proud of you when they know you have achieved your heart's desire, not theirs.

Integrity MATTERS

Staying true to your values is part of integrity. If you try to please others or adopt their values when you do not completely agree with them, you will lack integrity. This may not be an issue for you until you are tested on those values.

For example, you may have been raised with the value of staying true to your ethnic or cultural heritage, even at the expense of meeting someone new or experiencing a new culture. Now that you are in college, you may find that you are exposed to a variety of ethnicities and cultures and that you enjoy and appreciate learning more about other perspectives and lifestyles.

YOUR TURN

Have you ever taken on someone else's values that were not truly a reflection of your own? • Why did you? • What was the outcome? • What did you learn about yourself?

_____

_____

_____

_____

Your Dreams

As you consider your goals, you will also want to think about your dreams. What do you want to do that you have not written down because you feel it is too far-fetched? There are many stories of people who denied their dreams and took jobs that provided them with financial security and prestige, only to discover that their lives were not fulfilled because those were not their values.

Why don't more people follow their dreams? First, they may not know what they are. Second, these same people may be scared. Following what one's heart wants often contradicts what one's head is saying. Third, some people need to make the "safe" choice first before they feel confident that they can fulfill their dreams. In other words, they may need to take a job that pays well so that they can save money to fulfill their dreams at a later date.

Although you may not be able to drop everything right now and follow your heart, you should at least start thinking about what you really want to do with your life as you plan your college degree.

Reflection
EXERCISE 1.1

What is the dream that has brought you to college? How does earning a college certificate or degree help you achieve that dream? ■

YOUR GOALS and MISSION STATEMENT

To fulfill your mission in life, you will need to have a plan. Setting goals and achieving them will put you on the path to fulfilling that mission. If you are not used to writing down tasks for the day or voicing your plans for the future, you will need to start working on making lists and talking about what you want to be and do.

From your list of values and your mission statement, you will be able to formulate goals that support both what you believe in and what you want for yourself. The fact that you are reading this book is evidence that you are someone who has set a goal and is working toward achieving it. Also, the fact that you are in college says that you value education as a means of improving your life. You may have overcome many obstacles to get where you are today. You may have faced pressure from your family and friends to join the workforce on graduating from high school rather than go to college, or you may have gotten negative feedback from others when you decided to stop working, or stop working as much, to get a degree.

Nonetheless, realize that setting and achieving goals is not as easy as writing them down and crossing them off. You will encounter obstacles, some of which may threaten to knock you off course. Flexibility and determination are the keys to achieving your goals despite setbacks.

Your Mission Statement

Mission statements are declarations of what people or institutions believe in and what they hope to accomplish. Mission statements, then, are usually broad strokes of the overall picture of what you want to accomplish. Values are the foundation of a mission statement. If you are unsure of your values, then your mission statement will not be easy to understand and follow. Thus, you need to know what you value before you can write a mission statement.

As you meet your goals and learn new things, your mission will likely change and your mission statement will need to be revised. The following is an example of a mission statement that you can use as a model for writing your own.

Sample Personal Mission Statement

My mission is to have a fulfilling personal and professional life that allows me to meet new people, take on new challenges, and have flexibility in my schedule. As a mother and wife, I want to have a close relationship with my family, acting both as a caregiver and as a role model. As a teacher, I will be dedicated to providing students with the best possible education to prepare them for a four-year university curriculum as well as for the demands of the world of work.

Setting Goals

To build on your mission statement—and to fulfill that mission in the process—you will need to set goals that you can achieve. A goal is something that you work toward—it may be to learn how to cook macaroni and cheese, to quit a bad habit, or to write a novel. Whatever your goals, they should be reasonable and attainable in the time frame that you have assigned. For instance, if you want to lose 10 pounds in one week, you may need to rethink the time in which you would like to achieve your goal. A more reasonable goal would be to lose 10 pounds in four months. Reasonable goals are more likely to be met.

As you begin to think about your goals, consider dividing them into long-term goals and short-term goals. Certainly, one of your long-term goals is to earn a degree. This goal may take one year or more, depending on how many degree requirements you need to complete or how many other responsibilities you may have. Short-term goals that contribute to the long-term goal of earning a degree include completing your classes successfully, studying for exams, or working on research papers.

When you make your list of goals, consider the following guidelines:

- Make your goals attainable and reasonable.
- Break larger goals into smaller goals that will lead to fulfillment.
- Think of setting goals in these time frames: 1 week, 1 month, 1 semester, 1 year, 5 years, 10 years.
- Regularly review your goals and make changes as necessary.

Because it is difficult to plan 10 years into the future, make a list of goals that are tied to the near future. For instance, if you want to own your own business in the next 10 years, think about how to structure your short-term and long-term goals by looking at examples like the following:

Long-Term Goal (10 Years)
- Run a successful landscape design firm.
- Provide landscaping for low-income properties.

Long-Term Goal (5 Years)
- Work for a landscape design firm.
- Continue community service and encourage coworkers to participate.

Long-Term Goal (3 Years)
- Complete my associate's degree in landscape design and management.
- Continue community service work.

Short-Term Goal (9 Months)
- Complete two semesters of landscape design classes.
- Continue working at the garden center.

- Plant and maintain my own flower and vegetable garden.
- Participate in a community service project that landscapes low-income properties.

Short-Term Goal (1 Semester)
- Complete the classes that will count toward my degree.
- Look for a community service project that landscapes low-income properties.

Short-Term Goal (1 Month)
- Help a friend plant new trees.
- Attend a local lecture on seasonal planting.
- Begin research for a final paper on plant diseases.

Short-Term Goal (1 Week)
- Study for my classes.
- Apply for a job at a garden center.
- Weed and fertilize the backyard.
- Take a hike in the park.

No matter what you want to achieve, be sure that you write down all your goals and review them every few months to assess your progress. Henriette Anne Klauser has made a career of helping people write down their dreams and goals so they can finally realize them. In *Write It Down, Make It Happen: Knowing What You Want and Getting It!* (2001), Klauser states, "Writing down your dreams and aspirations is like hanging up a sign that says 'Open for Business.' . . . Putting it on paper alerts the part in your brain known as the reticular activating system to join you in the play" (p. 33). In other words, the process of writing down your goals tells your brain to start paying attention to your ambitions and makes you aware of opportunities to achieve them.

Managing Your Goals

You will see this suggestion throughout this book: To accomplish anything, set goals by writing them down. Even something as simple as spending two hours preparing for class should be written down as a goal for the day or week. Goals must be manageable, however. Too many goals and you could become overwhelmed at the thought of meeting them all, or you may feel like a failure for not accomplishing everything. Avoid the temptation to overschedule and be realistic about how long it will take to complete your goals for the day or week. Too few goals and you will likely feel like a rudderless ship, easily veering off course.

Once you have written down your goals, communicate them to your coworkers, family, and friends. Enlist them to help you meet your goals, especially if you need to schedule time to study and complete assignments. For example, tell them that you must have the evenings free of distractions, or make arrangements with them to have a weekend or weekday to yourself to study. Don't assume that because they know you are in school they will also know you need extra time and personal space to get your work finished. Managing your time will be much easier if your priorities and goals are concrete, realistic, and communicated to those around you.

Staying on Track

As you work toward your goals, make an effort to eliminate anything that keeps you from focusing on them. If you think you don't have time to accomplish two short-term

TABLE 1.1 Activities That Contribute to or Distract from Your Goals

Activities That Contribute to Your Goals	Activities That May Distract You from Your Goals
Practicing correct car maintenance allows you to get to school and work safely.	Socializing excessively depletes the time and energy you have to focus on your goals.
Exercising allows you to remain healthy and reduce stress.	Mindlessly watching TV may not contribute to learning.
Proper eating and sleeping will keep you healthy and reduce stress regularly.	Using drugs and alcohol is dangerous and keeps you from focusing on goals.
Reading the newspaper keeps you informed, helps improve reading skills, and contributes to learning.	Sleeping and eating irregularly creates stress, which inhibits the ability to reach goals.

goals during the week, examine where you have been spending your time and eliminate the activities that do not contribute to your goals.

If you watch seven hours of television a week and aren't achieving your short-term goal, whether to become more informed, to relax, or any other sought-after result, then spend that TV time doing something that does contribute to your goal. In addition to meaningless activities, anything that distracts you and is unnecessary in your life should be eliminated, including a habit that is destructive or dangerous, such as taking drugs. In fact, making a goal of staying healthy (e.g., eating right, exercising, de-stressing your life) is not only a good goal in itself, achieving it will help you achieve your other goals.

If you are unsure whether your activities contribute to your goals, take a few minutes to list what you have done this week and determine how each activity has supported or not supported one of your goals. Table 1.1 gives some examples.

Managing Your Priorities

A discussion of values and goals cannot be complete without also talking about priorities. Simply stated, a priority is something that is important at the moment. Today your top priority could be studying for an exam, but later in the day, it could be taking care of a sick child, which means that studying will have to come second if at all. Priorities, by their very nature, can change weekly, if not daily or even hourly.

Your actions also reflect your priorities. If you say that your first priority is to pass your classes this semester but you spend all your spare time playing basketball with friends, then your social life as well as a little exercise is really your top priority. You must make sure you know what your priorities are and take action to satisfy them. You may also need to express your priorities to others so that they can help you stick to them.

STAYING MOTIVATED

One of the hardest parts of setting goals is maintaining the momentum to achieve them. There will be times in your academic career when you will feel overwhelmed by the responsibilities you have, and you will feel unsure of your ability to handle it all. When you feel weighed down by all that you have to accomplish for a particular week or day, try to calm down first. If you can, talk with a friend, an instructor, or a counselor and explain your frustration and stress. Sometimes an instructor who knows you are feeling overwhelmed by expectations in a course will help you find resources to keep on track. A friend may also volunteer to help by studying with you.

To stay motivated and resist the temptation to give up because of the stress, review your short- and long-term goals. Is there anything you can change to make your goals more reasonable or attainable? Have you allowed enough time to achieve them? Revising your goals or your time line may be necessary to keep yourself on track.

Finally, think positively about yourself and your progress. Many students before you have successfully juggled a job, classes, and a family. That is not to say that they did not doubt themselves along the way or suffer any setbacks. The difference between these students and those who were not successful is that they persevered because they believed in themselves more often than not. Tell yourself that you can get through stressful times.

Collaboration EXERCISE 1.2

Working within a small group, exchange mission statements with each other. Using a classmate's mission statement, write down two long-term goals and four short-term goals that would be appropriate for the classmate based on his or her mission statement. Share your predictions with the group and discuss how well they matched your classmate's actual goals. ■

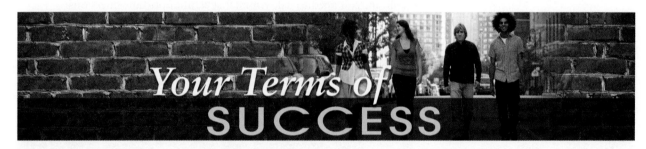

Your Terms of SUCCESS

WHEN YOU SEE . . .	IT MEANS . . .
Background	The experiences you have had that make up who you are.
Learning style preference	The learning style that you prefer or the one in which you learn best.
Long-term goal	A goal that will take a month, a semester, a year, or several years to complete.
Mission statement	A statement in which you describe how your values and goals will create your life's mission.
Motivation	What keeps you moving toward your goal.
Multiple intelligences	Learning style preferences, or "intelligences," that include bodily/kinesthetic, intrapersonal, and naturalistic.
Priority	Something that is important at a particular moment.
Short-term goal	A goal that takes an hour, a day, or a week to complete.
Value	What you believe in.
VARK	Learning style preferences distinguished according to four categories: Visual, Aural, Read/Write, and Kinesthetic.

Even the most dedicated student cannot do it all alone. In fact, behind every successful college graduate is a good support system, usually comprising family, friends, and community members. It is no secret that succeeding in college will take more than just studying hard—you will need to surround yourself with people who encourage you to do your best. There will be times when you need others for academic, emotional, and even financial support. Recognizing who in your circle of friends, family, and contacts will be your best resources is part of the process of creating a support system that will inevitably be part of your college success.

Your Family

Whether you live with your parents, you are a parent, or you are somewhere in between, your family is an important part of who you are and what you will become. Your family has influenced your values and beliefs, and your family members may be a part of the reason you have enrolled in college. For many students, staying in college and being successful depends on the support of family. If your family will be an important part of your life as you pursue a degree, then you will need to consider how they will support you and what you need to communicate with them about the time commitments of studying and taking classes that may reduce your time with them. As you begin your first semester in college, you need to ask yourself several important questions:

- Who in my family will support my decision to attend college?
- What types of financial support can I expect?

It's All RELATIVE

The definition of a first-generation student is one whose parents have not completed a bachelor's degree. In some cases, students with a parent who has achieved a certificate or associate's degree can still be considered first generation.

Your family's educational experiences will affect your attitude toward obtaining a degree yourself. In some cases, you may be following in your family's footsteps (especially those who have achieved degrees or other markers of distinction), or you may be blazing a new trail for future family members.

YOUR TURN

Has anyone in your family gone to college? • What kinds of education have your family members completed? • What is your family's attitude toward a college degree? • How have their experiences and educational attainments affected your desire to get a college degree?

_____

_____

_____

- What kinds of emotional support can I expect?
- How may my relationships change with my family?
- What can I do to communicate my needs while I am in college?

Answering these questions early and communicating your feelings at the beginning of the semester will make it easier for you to keep the lines of communication open in the long run. If you don't feel comfortable talking face to face with your loved ones, you could write a letter. At the very least, getting your thoughts down on paper first can help you polish what you want to say before you say it. Figure 1.1 provides a sample letter you can use for ideas to write your own family.

Giving yourself the time and space to complete your work for your college classes will be essential to making a successful transition.

Fotolia

Your Friends

Another important part of your support system is friends. You may not be able to choose your family members, but you have more choice as to which friends will be positive influences on your college experience. If you have friends who have also attended or are attending college, you will have a great opportunity to connect with each other on this common pursuit. Even if you do not attend the same college, you can develop a support system with them based on your similar experiences. You can share advice and study strategies as well as a shoulder to lean on when you feel stressed. Knowing that a friend is also pursuing college success can often give you the motivation to continue working hard.

FIGURE 1.1 Sample Letter to Family

Dear Family,

I want to first thank you for encouraging me to attend college. I am very excited and a little nervous, but because you have been so supportive of my decision, I know that I have a good support system to be successful. I do, though, want to let you know what you can expect as I take college classes. First, I will have to spend time at the college going to classes, meeting with my professors, and studying. I may not be able to participate in all the family activities and responsibilities that I used to because of tests, papers, and lab assignments. I may also not be available to help you in the ways that I did in the past because I will be devoting most of my time to school. However, when I do get breaks between semesters, I will do my best to use that time to reconnect with you. Remember that this won't be forever—I will be graduating before we know it.

I also hope that I can count on you if I need someone to talk to. Encouraging me to continue during the times I get a little stressed will help me feel as though I can do it. Your understanding that I am doing something valuable and good for my future is important to me.

Sincerely,

You

Although friends, especially those who are in college too, can provide a solid support system, not all friends, just as not all family members, will be a positive influence as you work toward your certificate or degree. Those who are not supportive may be very open about their anger, jealousy, or disappointment that you are pursuing a different path than theirs; others will be more subtle. Some friends may fear loss of time together or even replacement by new friends. In some cases, you may discover that your values no longer match your friends' ideas, which may signal a time to lessen your contact with them.

For sure, you will be busier than previously, and keeping in touch will be more difficult. Letting friends know that you may not be able to give them as much time as in the past can help you create some necessary distance. Of course, there is always the option of being upfront and honest about any lack of support. Telling certain friends that you need positive relationships while you are in college may be the message they need to hear to change their attitudes toward your exciting endeavor. If they still don't get the message, it may be time to eliminate them from daily contact.

Your Community

There are a variety of places you can look for support as you make your way through college. Your community may offer support to college students such as you. Check out your local community center to see whether they offer workshops on time management or study skills; the local library may sponsor book clubs or study groups. Area churches, temples, and synagogues may provide financial support for students in need. Most communities support residents' goals to go to college and earn degrees because of a feeling that as more residents achieve college degrees, the greater will be the likelihood that the community improves. A gesture as simple as offering a discount for college students at a local store is a sign that the area businesses recognize and value students' hard work in college. Local community leaders may also be willing to provide internships or mentoring sessions for students who could use extra advice and guidance throughout college. See what your community has to offer, or start your own community support group.

Critical Thinking
EXERCISE 1.3

Who is part of your support system so far? Are they mostly family or friends? Make a list of people and describe what kind of support they provide. Is it financial? Emotional? Academic? Spiritual? ■

YOUR LEARNING STYLE PREFERENCES

Knowing your learning style preferences provides a foundation for understanding yourself in other aspects of your life. Information about what you like and dislike, how you relate to others, and how you work most productively will furnish direction for achieving your goals and, as Gordon Lawrence (1995) states in his book *People Types and Tiger Stripes,* lead you to make "dramatic improvements in the effectiveness of [your] work" (p. 5). (See the Appendix for Neil Fleming's VARK learning styles inventory, which focuses on four learning style preferences: Visual, Aural, Read/Write, and Kinesthetic.) In the next few pages, you will complete a personality preference inventory, which can help you see an aspect of who you are. Looking at your values, dreams, mission statement, and goals in light of your learning style can work to create a more complete picture of who you are and how to get where you want to go.

TABLE 1.2 Learning Style Preferences, Majors, and Careers

Learning Style Preference	College Majors	Careers
Visual	Art, graphic design, drafting, architecture, interior design	Art teacher, artist, graphic designer, architect, interior designer, stylist
Aural	Music, communications, counseling	Musician, music educator, marketing director, public relations director, counselor
Kinesthetic	Sciences, sociology, computer technology, culinary arts, massage therapy	Nurse, doctor, therapist, networking specialist, computer technician, chef, massage therapist

Although learning preferences are not necessarily directly linked to college majors or careers, you can easily see that your learning style preference will come into play when you choose your major and your career. Kinesthetic learners, for example, may be drawn to majors or careers that allow them to move about or use their bodies to complete tasks. Landscape design, auto body repair, culinary arts, and nursing are just a few college degree programs that would appeal to kinesthetic learners. Review Table 1.2, which lists possible majors and careers for some learning style preferences, but note that it is not considered an exhaustive list. Also, some majors and careers may speak to more than one learning style preference; for example, an advertising executive who writes, edits, and directs commercials may rely on almost all the learning style preferences on a daily basis as she creates commercials and ads for clients. For sure, she will need to work individually, with peers, and with her boss on different aspects of a project, and she may find that she is needed to complete tasks at different times of the day, even late at night when filming continues long after the typical workday ends.

Harvard psychologist Howard Gardner is well known for his theory of multiple intelligences, which is another term for "what we know, understand, and learn about our world" (Lazear, 1991). Gardner has created eight categories of how we can know and learn.

Verbal/linguistic intelligence is evident in people who can use language with ease; they enjoy reading and writing and may be journalists, novelists, playwrights, or comedians. The logical/mathematical intelligence is demonstrated by an ease and enjoyment with numbers and logic problems. People who have a strong leaning in this intelligence like to solve problems, find patterns, discover relationships between objects, and follow steps. Career choices for logical/mathematical thinkers include science, computer technology, math, and engineering.

The visual/spatial intelligence is characterized by anything visual—paintings, photographs, maps, and architecture. People who have a strong visual/spatial sense are usually good at design, architecture, painting and sculpture, and map making. The bodily/kinesthetic intelligence focuses on body movement. It is found in people who enjoy using their bodies to express themselves. Obvious career choices for this intelligence include dancing, sports, and dramatic arts. Musical/rhythmic intelligence encompasses

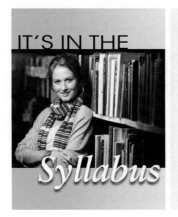

mental proficiency with the rhythms of music and hearing tones and beats. People who have strong musical/rhythmic intelligence may use musical instruments or the human voice to express themselves. Career choices for this intelligence include all types of musical performance.

How you relate to others and yourself is part of the interpersonal and intrapersonal intelligences. People with strong interpersonal intelligence relate strongly with others. They read others' feelings well and act with others in mind. Intrapersonal intelligence centers around the ability to understand oneself. People who possess intrapersonal intelligence know how and why they do what they do. Naturalistic, the eighth intelligence, refers to people who enjoy and work well in an outdoor environment. Naturalistic people find peace in nature and enjoy having natural elements around them.

Learning Preference Inventory

There are numerous ways to see yourself and understand your behavior in certain situations, and many education specialists and psychologists have provided theories on how we take in and process information. They have developed different inventories and personality profiles to enhance your understanding of yourself. As you will discover in Chapter 5, the learning process is somewhat complex; it involves more than just our preferences in how we create knowledge, because there are many factors that influence our ability to take in and process information.

Theories about the two hemispheres of our brain, known as the left brain and the right brain, have given us insight into how people think, learn, and see the world. People who have strong left-brain tendencies are more likely to be logical, to see parts rather than the whole, and to prefer to do activities step by step. They are also more analytical, realistic, and verbal than their right-brained companions. The right-brain tendency shows up in a preference to see the whole picture rather than details, to work out of sequence, and to bring ideas together. Surveys available online can indicate which hemisphere is dominant in your brain.

The Myers-Briggs Type Indicator (MBTI), on the other hand, is a personality assessment that provides you with information about how you prefer to think and act. For example, one dimension of the personality test asks you how outgoing or extroverted you are in certain situations or how reserved, or introverted, you are in social settings. These questions indicate whether you are extroverted (E) or introverted (I). Like brain hemisphere inventories, the MBTI can be found in books or online sources. Samples of the complete inventories are also available.

Other inventories, such as both the Dunn and Dunn Learning Styles Assessment and the PEPS Learning Styles Inventory, focus not only on how a person prefers to take in information, but also on social and environmental learning preferences. These types of inventories provide a thorough view of how you like to learn, whether it is the temperature of the room, the amount of light and sound, or an inclination for moving about as you learn.

Regardless of which learning theory leads you to greater personal insight, as stand-alone models they are somewhat insignificant unless you *use* the information to benefit actual learning. The purpose of the learning plan inventory in Figure 1.2 is to provide

FIGURE 1.2 Learning Plan Inventory

TIME OF DAY PREFERENCE

Read each statement and circle the number on the scale that best represents you
(1: Least like me—5: Most like me)

	SCALE				
1. I feel most energized in the morning.	1	2	3	4	5
2. My energy level soars late at night.	1	2	3	4	5
3. I get more accomplished in the afternoon.	1	2	3	4	5
4. I concentrate best before noon.	1	2	3	4	5
5. Late at night is my most productive time.	1	2	3	4	5
6. Afternoon is the best time for me to complete important tasks.	1	2	3	4	5
7. I wait to do projects until I have had a full night's sleep.	1	2	3	4	5
8. I prefer to start and complete projects after I have completed everything else I need to do for the day.	1	2	3	4	5
9. I feel best about working on a project if it occurs between getting started for the day and ending the day.	1	2	3	4	5

INTAKE PREFERENCE

Read each statement and circle the number on the scale that best represents you
(1: Least like me—5: Most like me)

	SCALE				
1. When I am trying something new, I like to "see" it in my head before doing it.	1	2	3	4	5
2. I can understand a concept best when I hear it explained.	1	2	3	4	5
3. I don't really understand something unless I do it or experience it myself.	1	2	3	4	5
4. I explain my ideas best by talking through them.	1	2	3	4	5
5. I figure out what I think about a topic by experiencing it firsthand.	1	2	3	4	5
6. I like to draw what I'm thinking so others will understand.	1	2	3	4	5
7. When trying to get from one place to another, I am most confident when I have already traveled there.	1	2	3	4	5
8. When trying to get from one place to another, I am most confident if I can see the route I need to take.	1	2	3	4	5
9. When trying to get from one place to another, I am most confident when I am told the directions by someone who has been there before.	1	2	3	4	5

(continued)

FIGURE **1.2** Continued

SOCIAL LEARNING PREFERENCE

Read each statement and circle the number on the scale that best represents you
(1: Least like me—5: Most like me)

SCALE

1.	I work best alone.	1	2	3	4	5
2.	I feel comfortable asking my boss or professor questions when I'm not sure what to do.	1	2	3	4	5
3.	I rely on friends or coworkers to help me complete work or figure out what to do when I am stuck on a task.	1	2	3	4	5
4.	I need little interaction with others to complete a task.	1	2	3	4	5
5.	I'm most comfortable working in groups on a project.	1	2	3	4	5
6.	I'm most at ease working on a task that my supervisor monitors closely.	1	2	3	4	5
7.	I can get group projects completed faster than when I work alone.	1	2	3	4	5
8.	I am more confident when my boss or professor gives me constant feedback as I complete a project.	1	2	3	4	5
9.	When others interfere with a project I am working on, I get little done.	1	2	3	4	5

TASK MANAGEMENT PREFERENCES

Read each statement and circle the number on the scale that best represents you
(1: Least like me—5: Most like me)

SCALE

1.	I enjoy thinking up and starting new projects.	1	2	3	4	5
2.	It is easy for me to complete important tasks.	1	2	3	4	5
3.	I like to be spontaneous when I work on a project; I go wherever the mood takes me.	1	2	3	4	5
4.	I like to have a detailed schedule before I begin a project.	1	2	3	4	5
5.	I like to have a general idea of the main goal and then discover what needs to be done as I work toward the goal.	1	2	3	4	5
6.	I like to consider the steps to a project first before thinking about the overall picture.	1	2	3	4	5
7.	I need to know what the end goal is before I begin a project.	1	2	3	4	5
8.	I am considered creative.	1	2	3	4	5

FIGURE **1.3** Learning Plan Categories

Time of Day Preferences: morning, afternoon, night

Intake Preferences: visual, auditory, kinesthetic

Social Preferences: individual, peer(s), mentor (professor, expert, leader, etc.)

Task Management Preferences: logical/analytical, spontaneous/creative you with a basic understanding of the factors that influence your learning preferences, which you can use to create an individualized and flexible learning plan for the various tasks and assignments that you will experience in college. Ultimately, greater personal understanding and self-knowledge leads to action, and this learning plan inventory provides you with not only information about how you prefer to learn but also a roadmap for completing tasks and goals successfully by applying your preferences.

The inventory in Figure 1.2 is adapted from the models just discussed, and the statements will help you discover your learning style preferences in four areas: time of day, intake, social learning, and task management (see Figure 1.3).

To complete the inventory in Figure 1.2, read the statements in each category and circle the number that corresponds most closely to your degree of identification with the statement. The number 1 means the statement is least like you whereas the number 5 means that the statement is most like you. You will calculate your answers after the inventory.

USING TECHNOLOGY TO GET AHEAD

Your college website may provide information about schedules (when you can take classes), courses, and career choices that are available based on the types of certificates and degrees that the college offers. All of these pieces of information tie into your learning styles preferences. You may choose class times based on when you best learn (if you have some choice in your schedule); you may choose classes, especially electives, based on how you prefer to learn; and you may choose a degree and subsequent career based on your overall preferences. Look for additional information that can help you connect your learning style preference to completing your degree.

Calculating Your Score

For each learning preference category, write the numbers you circled for each statement in the calculation tables in Figure 1.4. Then add up the numbers for each type of question. The higher numbers will indicate your strongest preferences.

Afterward, complete Figure 1.5, labeled "My Learning Preferences." You will use this information to complete your own learning plans.

Transitioning into college means that you will be spending more of your time studying and attending classes.

Learning Plan in Action

Table 1.3 shows a learning plan in action for a student who works best at night, is both a strong visual and auditory learner, performs best with peers, and prefers to break down assignments into manageable parts.

There are many ways of viewing yourself and creating a plan of action for your work in college, but no single inventory, assessment, or work plan will reflect the exceptional person you are or your unique circumstances; in other words, no matter which inventory you take or what you learn about how you prefer to learn, the results are not the final verdict on your abilities and potential.

The goal then of this learning plan is to provide you with an adaptable, flexible model for putting your learning style preference into action. It also gives you a roadmap for accomplishing the many goals that you will set for yourself. Additionally, it can serve as a place to start when faced with situations that require you to work outside your learning preference comfort zone. For example, what will you do, as a morning learner,

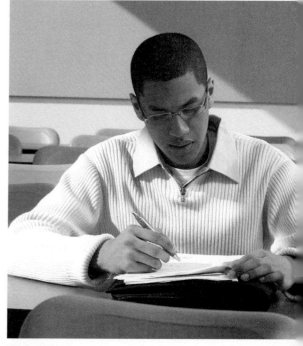

Thinkstock

FIGURE 1.4 Calculation Tables

Time of Day Preference

Morning	Night	Afternoon
1. ____	2. ____	3. ____
4. ____	5. ____	6. ____
7. ____	8. ____	9. ____
Total ____	Total ____	Total ____

Intake Preference

Visual	Auditory	Kinesthetic
1. ____	2. ____	3. ____
6. ____	4. ____	5. ____
8. ____	9. ____	7. ____
Total ____	Total ____	Total ____

Social Learning Preference

Individual	Mentor	Peer
1. ____	2. ____	3. ____
4. ____	5. ____	6. ____
9. ____	8. ____	7. ____
Total ____	Total ____	Total ____

Task Management Preference

Spontaneous/Creative	Logical/Analytical
1. ____	2. ____
3. ____	4. ____
5. ____	6. ____
8. ____	7. ____
Total ____	Total ____

when faced with completing an important project late at night? Or how will you, as an individual learner, fare when required to collaborate with classmates on an assignment?

One way to move outside your learning preference comfort zone is to take time to reflect on how you would act in such situations and consider how you will meet similar challenges to those portrayed in this book, especially involving the characters whose stories begin each chapter; for example, you have already met Juanita and have learned more about her relationship with her family. In the next chapter, you will read about all four characters and their experiences with orientation.

FIGURE 1.5 My Learning Preferences

Time of Day	
Intake	
Social	
Task Management	

Although the characters are fictional, representative of the many different first-generation college students, their stories ring true because they are based on real-life situations that you may face as well. Reflecting on who you are and how you will get where you want to go will help you create your own story of success.

Learning Styles and Career Choices

Discovering your learning style preference and personality type will definitely help you set realistic short-term and long-term goals. For example, discovering that you have a read/write learning preference and work well with deadlines and staying organized may confirm that your long-term goal of being a writer will work well with who you are and how you learn and work. However, identifying your style and type should not limit your choices or keep you from working on areas of your learning style and personality that may be weaker or get less attention. If you are a strong visual learner but are taking a class that relies on listening effectively and critically, you should

Reflection EXERCISE 1.4

What have you learned so far about yourself? What information in this chapter has been most helpful to you in discovering how who you are will help you succeed in college? ■

TABLE 1.3 Learning Plan Example

Learning Task: Study for biology midterm	
Time of Day	Night—after dinner
Intake	Visual and auditory—review notes and talk through them with study group
Social	Peers—biology study group
Task Management	Logical/analytical—go in order of the chapters and work with classmate who can help me

(Personality + Learning Style = Understanding Situations)

Think about Juanita's uneasiness with setting a goal to complete a certain degree. She is 18 and feels as though she will have to live with her decision the rest of her life no matter what she chooses. Using what you have learned from this chapter, what advice would you give her? How can she be sure, if she can be sure at all, that her current goals will prove worthwhile in the future? What if they do not?

Now, considering your own learning style, personality type, and special circumstances, what would you do in her situation?

use that opportunity to become a better listener, to improve your aural learning style preference by following listening tips like the ones found in Chapter 7. Likewise, if you work better alone and have a strong kinesthetic learning style preference, choosing a career as a computer technician may play to your strengths. However, you may also find yourself working with others collaboratively and communicating frequently in writing and verbally.

Therefore, whatever your learning style strengths and personality preferences may be, consider how other styles and types will factor into your short-term and long-term educational goals. Then look for opportunities to strengthen those less-developed sides of your learning and personality so that you can become a more well-rounded person, comfortable in a variety of situations.

From College to University

WHAT YOU KNOW AND HOW YOU LEARN WILL CHANGE

The transition from a community college to a four-year university can be relatively smooth if you are willing to apply some of the ideas in this chapter to your new environment and your new challenges. First, consider that your definition of who you are will change by the time you transfer, perhaps dramatically. You will likely be more confident in your abilities and you will be better able to handle the stress of juggling numerous responsibilities. Second, your values may also change after your semesters at a community college; if you were unsure of what you valued before, you may finally have a clearer picture of your belief system. On the other hand, you may be more confused than ever about what you believe after studying different religions, psychological theories, and social ideas. Because higher education values inquiry and research, no matter what shape your values are in by the time you transfer, you will find support as you struggle to make sense of it all at both the community college and the four-year university.

Third, just as your knowledge of yourself and your values will have changed, your goals will go through a transformation. Although your main goal of graduating with a four-year degree will still be in sight, you will notice that you have already met some of your smaller goals. You have probably become more organized. Perhaps you have successfully completed an associate's degree. Just the fact that you are ready to transfer credits means that you have accomplished some necessary steps to fulfilling the rest of your goals.

Finally, you will be able to revise your statements about who you are because of the changes you have experienced after taking classes at a community college. You may even be able to include a career choice in your statement. Also, you may know yourself better through application of the learning styles discussed earlier. However, you will need to be prepared to adapt to different teaching styles and new pressures after you transfer.

Now, to prepare yourself for the next step, you will need to revise, preferably on paper, your mission and values statements. You will also need to realize that you may have to adapt the learning styles that you have felt most comfortable with—or to explore and use new styles—at your four-year school.

Building Your University Portfolio 1

Find someone you know (or ask your professor for the name of a former student) who has transferred to a four-year university and ask how his or her self-view has changed, if it has, since transferring to a university. Have learning style preferences changed or been reinforced? Has his or her mission and goals changed? If so, how?

_____

_____

_____

_____

From College to Career

GOALS AND A MISSION WILL HELP YOU SUCCEED

Many businesses rely on creating mission statements, strategic plans (long-term goals), and operational plans (short-term goals) to chart a course for their success. Because you have experience writing your own mission and goals, you will be able to contribute to your company's planning because you understand how the company's values underlie its mission and how its goals create its road map to success. Your experience in goal setting will also help you to write departmental or personal goals. If you understand how values, mission, and goals fit together, you will be better able to create goals that are explicitly linked to the focus of your workplace.

Building Your Career Portfolio 1

Contact someone whose career is similar to what you want to do. Ask how goal setting affects his or her job. Does the person's company have a mission statement and long-term goals? What advice does he or she have about managing priorities? How does the person stay motivated to meet current goals and make new ones?

_____

_____

_____

_____

First Voices

**From janitor at a community college to Ph.D. in philosophy:
First-generation student is transformed by college experience**

Kelsey Wood,
Ph.D., Instructor
of Philosophy

When I was finishing high school, I didn't think that I would become a first-generation college student. My father was a construction worker—an electrician—and my mother was a secretary. They both worked full time, and they did their best, but they couldn't afford to send me to college, so I left my small town in Texas and moved to Dallas. I got a job as a janitor, working all night at a community college and taking classes there during the day.

There were some dedicated instructors at that community college, and I received some good grades, and eventually I got a job there as a tutor for courses in English as a second language. I made friends with some of the immigrant students I was tutoring. Like them, I was also struggling to work and to be a student at the same time, so sometimes we helped each other out with things like car repairs and rides to class.

Before I transferred to a university, I went to community college for three years. At a community college in Dallas, Texas, I learned the most important thing I know, namely, that learning transforms our lives. Once I graduated from my community college, I eventually earned a Ph.D. in philosophy.

Today I am an instructor at a community college because a community college changed my life—a college made up of ordinary people like me: people from the big city and people from small towns, people from around the world, people who agreed sometimes and disagreed a lot, people who worked together to learn and to share what was learned.

Based on my community college experience, the common purpose we share here is the commitment to equal opportunity in education. Because learning gives life purpose and meaning, equal opportunity in education can be more than a remote ideal.

PATH OF DISCOVERY
Journal Entry

Name and describe three people or situations that changed your life. What did these people or situations teach you about your values, priorities, motivations, or goals? How have they changed you?

CHAPTER REVIEW QUESTIONS

1. How do your values and background affect your goal setting?
2. Why do some people have trouble reaching their goals?
3. What steps can you take to manage your priorities effectively?
4. How does your learning style and personality preference affect goal setting?

CHAPTER 1 CASE SCENARIOS

1. Peter has started college, but he is not sure what he wants to do. In fact, he is afraid to tell his parents that he wants to be a dental hygienist because his parents want him to take over the family business. Neither of his parents went to college, and they don't understand why any of their children would want to work outside the family business. Peter values loyalty to his family—he has been through many challenges that have strengthened his relationship with his parents—but he also has a strong interest in working in the health field. Peter's ultimate goal is to be a dentist, but he thinks that working as a hygienist first would be a way to make sure that he has what it takes. What advice would you give Peter? What should he do to make sure his goals are met?

2. Serena, a single parent, has started her first semester in college, but she also works full time in a law office. Her sister keeps Serena's twin boys while she works, but she sometimes has to miss work when her sister cannot look after them. Serena wants to get a four-year degree and eventually go to law school, but she feels as though it will take too long if she doesn't start now. She is motivated by time and money. She wants to hurry and get her degree, and she wants to be financially independent so that she can take care of her boys. She works very hard, but she doesn't have any other family or friends who can help her. To add to her obstacles, her sister is not supportive of Serena's desire to get a degree and improve her life. Serena's sister thinks that she has all she needs and shouldn't "mess it up by going to college and getting all kinds of crazy ideas." What advice would you give Serena? What have you learned about setting goals and managing priorities that would help Serena? What have you learned about overcoming challenges that might encourage her?

RESEARCH IT FURTHER

1. During the Middle Ages (A.D. 500–1500), the terms *sanguine, phlegmatic, choleric,* and *melancholic* were used often to describe people. Research these descriptions further and then determine a suitable category for each of your classmates.

2. Choose a long-term career goal and research the necessary qualifications to accomplish it. For example, if you would like to be a network administrator, check your college catalog for degree requirements and look on the Internet for job descriptions that include the kind of degree and work experience you would need. List any other necessary skills for this career.

3. Using the key term "mission statements," search the Internet for college and business mission statements. Print at least three different mission statements and determine the similarities and differences. Report your findings to the class.

References and Recommended Readings

Beals, M. P. (1994). *Warriors don't cry.* New York: Pocket Books.

Dickerson, D. J. (2000). *An American story.* New York: Anchor Books.

Fleming, N. (2009). VARK Learning Style Preferences. Retrieved Oct. 19, 2009, from www.vark-learn.com.

Glass, L. (1997). *Toxic people: 10 ways of dealing with people who make your life miserable.* New York: St. Martin's.

Godwin, M. (2000). *Who are you? 101 ways of seeing yourself.* New York: Penguin.

Klauser, H. A. (2001). *Write it down, make it happen: Knowing what you want and getting it!* New York: Simon & Schuster.

Lawrence, G. (1995). *People types and tiger stripes* (3rd ed.). Gainesville, FL: CAPT.

Lazear, D. (1991). *Seven ways of teaching: The artistry of teaching with multiple intelligences.* Palatine, IL: Skylight Publishing.

Myers-Briggs Type Indicator. (2008). Retrieved May 15, 2008, from www.myersbriggstypeindicator .co.uk.

Rodriguez, R. (1982). *Hunger of memory: The education of Richard Rodriguez.* New York: The Dial Press.

Smiley, T. (2006). *What I know for sure: My story of growing up in America.* New York: Anchor Books.

YOUR COLLEGE

2

Passports, disposable cameras, and plastic leis are scattered all over the tables; fake palm trees rustle from the movement underneath them; and the smell of coconut fills the air in the student center. "Destination: Degree," the travel-themed orientation, is winding down after an afternoon of skits, presentations, and door prizes of pink flamingo keychains and T-shirts.

"If everyone will score their inventories, we will explain how learning style preference affects your study habits," says Jason, an orientation leader who is wearing an orange "Ask me!" T-shirt and a camera around his neck.

Dozens of students are gathered next to tables where student leaders and counselors hand out T-shirts, water bottles, and welcome packets.

"Hey, I am 'kinesthetic,' which means I learn best by using body movements. That kind of makes sense. I teach kickboxing and learned how to do it by working out almost every day," Evan tells the group.

"I thought I would be more of a social learner, but my learning style preference is individual," says Michael as he rubs his head. "I spent so much time leading troops when I was in the military."

"I am definitely 'aural,'" Laura says to the group. "I got through all my classes in high school by listening to the lectures. I rarely took notes because I liked to listen."

"Yeah, I can see that. You talked during every presentation!" Evan jokes.

Juanita, the youngest of the group, twists her mouth and wrinkles her forehead. "Will you be able to do that in college, just listen?" she asks. "I mean, I have heard that the professors expect so much more of you when it comes to being in class. Seems like there is more to do than just listen."

"I am sure you will," says Michael. "My girlfriend graduated last year with a degree in nursing, and it seems like all she did was read for class and then study her notes every night."

"Yeah, that makes sense. If anyone needs someone to study with, let me know. I am an early morning person. I took dual enrollment classes in high school and did best in my earliest classes," Juanita says.

Evan, who has been looking over his orientation information, looks up when he hears Juanita's offer. "If you want to learn a few kickboxing moves in exchange for help taking notes, let me know," Evan says to Juanita.

"Sounds good!" Juanita laughs.

With neon green note cards in her hand, Jasmine approaches the group's table. She passes cards to Laura, Michael, Evan, and Juanita. "Take these cards," Jason says, "and write down what you think will be your biggest challenge in college."

"If anyone wants to exchange a home-cooked meal for some babysitting while I study, let me know, too," says Laura, continuing the conversation. "Balancing family, a job, and college full-time," she prints on the card.

Michael writes his down: "Worried I am too old to go back to school. Can't teach an old dog new tricks." Juanita writes, "Not sure what degree or career I want," and Evan records, "Meeting new people."

As the four of them hand in their cards, they gather their backpacks and the college planners they received when they signed in for orientation.

Michael gives the group his number before they leave. "I know Laura is the talkative one, but give me a call if you ever need anything. Good luck to everyone!" he says.

In this CHAPTER

Evan, Laura, Michael, and Juanita will soon discover the expectations of college, and after participating in orientation, they should be well prepared to handle the changes they may encounter from their previous roles and routines: Evan has worked full time for the past two years; Laura has been a stay-at-home mother; Michael has been in the military; and Juanita has just graduated from high school. Just as these four students have been oriented to college life, the purpose of this chapter is to introduce you to this new culture, to reveal the truths about higher education, to debunk the myths, and to prepare you for meeting the challenges that you will inevitably face. This chapter also provides you with information about what this new environment will look like and what you can expect in terms of communication between the college and you.

More specifically, after completing this chapter, you will be able to do the following:

- **Identify the transitional issues of going to college.**
- **Describe the expectations of college.**
- **Explain the processes of college.**
- **List and define the resources on campus.**

TRANSITION and TRANSFORMATION

This is an exciting time as you transition into college life. The definition of *transition* means a change, a modification, and you will find that going to college creates a change in you—and not just in your schedule and your workload. You will find that your concept of yourself will change, your relationships will change, and your outlook on your future will change. Each of these changes will require an investment of your time and reflection to make it happen. At the end of your college experience, you will find yourself *transformed* into a new person. You will most likely be more thoughtful and more confident about your abilities; most certainly, you will be more aware of what it takes to earn a degree. However, this change or transformation won't be easy; the following discussion on transitioning from where you are now to where you want to be will give you a better understanding of what you need to do to make change happen.

Think ABOUT IT

"If we can transform ourselves, we have the potential to change the world.

—**Laura van Dernoot Lipsky**"

For some students, the move from high school to college seems fairly simple—both require reading, writing, testing, and attending class. Students who are taking the step from work to school may also see some similarities between their jobs and classroom work—both require working hard, keeping motivated, and following the rules. If the differences between high school or work and college are that similar, then why do so many college students have difficulty making a successful transition?

The answer to that question can be given by the instructors who see smart, competent students have trouble adjusting to the climate and culture of college because they do not understand what is expected of them. In other words, in order to be successful, students must know how they should be preparing beyond the questions on the next test; they need to know how college works and how to navigate through not only their courses, but also the common challenges that they will face as they work toward a degree or certificate.

Table 2.1 illustrates some of the differences and similarities between high school, a full-time job, and college. Notice that the greatest differences occur between high

Reflection EXERCISE 2.1

Create a list of 10 expectations of your instructors that you have discovered so far this semester. Divide your list into expectations that you feel you can meet and those that may be challenging for you. ■

TABLE 2.1 Differences between High School, Full-Time Work, and College

High School	Full-Time Work	College
Attendance is mandatory in order to meet requirements; at least 6 continuous hours are spent in class each day	Attendance is mandatory in order to stay employed; at least 8 continuous hours are spent at work each day	Attendance is possibly not mandatory; different amounts of time are spent in class and between classes each day
Very little choice in what classes you take and when you take them	May have little choice in work assignments and when the work is to be completed	More flexibility in when you work on assignments and how soon you complete them before the due date
Moderate to no outside work necessary to be successful	Moderate to no overtime work necessary to complete job duties	Substantial amount of outside work to complete assignments and to be successful
Teachers check homework and keep you up to date on progress; they will inform you if you are not completing assignments and progressing well	Supervisors check completion and quality of work at regular intervals; they will inform you if you are not meeting the standards for the position	Professors choose whether to check all homework or provide feedback on progress at regular intervals; they may not inform you if you are not meeting the standards of the course
Teachers review material and expect that you remember facts and information	Employer provides basic information and expects that you use it to complete the job effectively	Professor presents concepts and theories and expects that you evaluate the ideas, synthesize the ideas with other concepts you have learned, and develop new theories
There are frequent tests over small amounts of material with opportunities for grades to be raised if needed	There are employee improvement plans to allow you to improve your ratings if needed	There are standards and grading criteria, often allowing only a few chances (through infrequent testing/assignments) to meet them

school and college. There are some similarities between a full-time job and college, although there are also distinct differences.

HIGHER EDUCATION, HIGHER EXPECTATIONS

No matter whether you are enrolled at a community college or a four-year university, the expectations of higher education will be higher for you. It is worth noting the differences between the two so that you understand how you will be able to meet the expectations no matter where you are. The degree programs at community colleges are shorter than at universities, usually requiring one or two years, but the reality is that you may need to take more time to complete a degree program if you plan to enroll as a part-time student. Also, if you need developmental or remedial classes before you can start on the required curriculum, completion of the program will be delayed. The degree programs at universities, on the other hand, are usually called "four-year" programs because earning a bachelor's degree takes a minimum of 8 semesters of full-time status (at least 12 credit hours per semester). However, it most students take more than four years to complete a bachelor's degree.

Both university and community college classes and degree programs are demanding. Instructors who teach in the technical, industrial, and business fields are expected to graduate students who can pass licensing exams, which means the standards in the class must be high. Likewise, students who intend to transfer to four-year universities after they complete their general education requirements would not be successful if the courses they took at the community college were not challenging. Universities also want

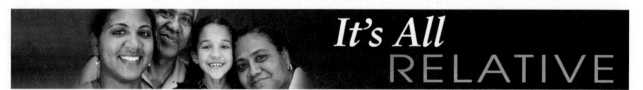

It's All RELATIVE

Smooth transitions and true transformations will affect your relationships. Your family and friends will either be supportive or worry that changes will mean they are less connected to you. It is very common for first-generation students to feel a little stress in their relationships as they grow because of their educational experiences.

Consider what it will take from your family for you to change into a college-educated person. Will you need their support 100%? Or will you be able to transition with minimal support or assistance? Recognizing who will be part of your "transition team" will help you determine whom to call when you need support.

YOUR TURN

Who are the people in your life who will embrace your transformation into a college-educated person? • How will they support you? • Who seems less supportive of you? • Why do you think their support is questionable?

_____

_____

_____

to prepare students for entering the workforce or graduate program; thus, they provide high expectations to make sure their graduates are successful beyond college. Community colleges want well-prepared and successful graduates; thus, it is in their best interest to provide courses that require the best work from their students.

Go for the Gold by Remembering SILVER

Making a successful transition will not only include comparing where you have just come from (home, work, or another institution of learning) to college life, but it will also involve breaking down the experience into parts that you can master. To remember what you need to start and end well, remember this simple acronym: SILVER. This stands for Supplies, Instructors' Expectations, Learning, Vocabulary, Effort, and Responsibility.

Supplies, or "The Right Stuff"

Making sure you are adequately prepared for the journey you are about to take is the first step in being successful. You wouldn't head out on a trip to unknown lands without a map, proper gear, and plenty of food and water! Think of your college supplies as part of your survival gear, too. The most important items that you will need at the beginning of the semester are required textbooks and course materials. You can find out what books and materials you will need either through the bookstore or through your professors. Usually an exact list of course materials is included in your syllabus. In high school, books and course materials are provided for each student, but in college, you will be responsible for obtaining and purchasing your own materials—and you will need to do that before or at the very beginning of the semester. Trying to get by without the textbook or required calculator or software can seriously hurt your chances of success and is not recommended. If you find yourself unable to acquire or buy needed materials, then you will need to talk to your instructor immediately to ask about alternative arrangements.

In addition to books and materials, you may also need access to a computer. Your professors will expect that you have a working knowledge of how to use one. If you do not have the skills needed, then seek help from computer lab technicians, special computer classes, and classmates. Having the necessary computer skills as well as regular access to a computer will be integral to your success. Most colleges provide computer labs, email accounts, and printers for student use, but the hours may be limited, they may be crowded at busy times during the semester, and you may have to pay for the pages that you print.

Other "right stuff" items include paper (for both note-taking and printing purposes), pens, a dictionary, a writing handbook, and a thesaurus. As you take more classes, you may need specialized reference books and supplies, such as a graphing calculator, to help you study and complete assignments. A good, sturdy backpack that allows you to carry all your books and notebooks will also be essential. Because you will not have a locker or place to store your things between classes, you will have to find a bag that holds up to the task of carrying heavy materials over a period of weeks. One other item that new students need, which is becoming more essential each year, is a portable storage device that will hold your computer files and allow you to access them at any computer. Thumb drives, also known as flash drives and pin drives, are increasingly popular because they hold a large amount of data and are easy to carry.

Instructors' Expectations

In addition to your supplies, knowing and meeting your instructors' expectations will make a great foundation for success. One essential expectation that instructors have is preparation—yours. You should be ready *before* you get to class by reading the assigned pages or completing the homework. Instructors who prescribe these tasks expect students to prepare—they may even administer quizzes to ensure that students have prepared—and to ask questions about anything they do not understand. Instructors may assume that if you don't ask questions or participate in a discussion, you understand the assignment. They may also hold you accountable on exams for the assigned reading that has not been discussed in class.

Another expectation is that out-of-class assignments must be typed; in fact, unless otherwise stated, assume that all outside assignments should be word-processed, because they are easier to read and look more professional. If you don't know how to use a word processor, now is the time to learn; relying on others to word-process your work could put you at a disadvantage. You may not be able to control when the person will complete the work, which can make you miss assignment due dates.

Instructors also expect college students to be able to access technology regularly and use it competently. What this means is that your professor will expect that you have consistent access to a computer and the Internet. She will also assume that you have an email account and can send emails—even messages with attachments—successfully. If you lack these skills and equipment, you will need to find out where you can access a computer on campus or off campus and make sure that you have the ability to use it properly.

One last expectation—but not the only one left—is that instructors expect you to use their office hours, the time they are scheduled to be in their offices, to meet with them if you have any questions or need anything. This is a time not only to address any concerns you may have about your progress, but it is also a wonderful chance to get to know your professors better.

Learning

Taking responsibility for your learning is the cornerstone for college success, and in college you will be actively involved in the learning process. Being an *active* learner means that you are no longer a passive participant in your education, listening to a lecture or reading recreationally. Instead, college classes require that you participate in your own learning by reading actively and critically (see Chapter 6), by listening actively and critically (see Chapter 7), by completing assignments, by working with other students, and by making connections between the courses you are taking and your life. Active learners also seek out more information about topics and look for ways to improve their understanding of concepts by finding help when needed. In essence, active learners make their education a top priority.

One of the most important shifts in thinking about your learning experience in college is realizing the various ways and places that learning and student support can take place outside the classroom. In Chapter 5 Michael will face his fear of asking for help by seeking help in the tutoring center, and as he discovers, the classroom is not the only place meaningful learning experiences happen! Professors routinely direct students to learning labs, tutors, or supplemental instruction to help bolster the learning that takes place in the classroom. Consider, then, that classroom learning is only a fraction of the time and activity making up your college experience. In fact, if you follow the standard model for using the number of hours you are in class to determine how many hours a week you should spend studying, class time is only one-fourth of the time you should be devoting to learning. The rest of that time, of course, will be spent preparing for class, but it can also be used working one-on-one with a tutor or reviewing notes and studying with a group. That means that 75% of your college time should be for activities that contribute to your learning when you are in class.

Vocabulary

With a new environment comes a new language. It won't be too long before you are talking about an AA, BS, GPA, and FERPA all at one time. Knowing what terms mean when they are used will make communication clearer. For example, do you know what a credit hour is? It is the unit of measurement that colleges use that usually equals the amount of time you are in class each week during a 16-week semester. What about FERPA? This acronym stands for Family Educational Rights and Privacy Act, and it is important to know because it determines who can access and discuss your grades or other official records. In college, if you are age 18 or over, only you can discuss your grades with a professor. If others, such as a spouse, parent, or employer, want to know how you are doing, then you can allow them access to that information by letting a college official know. The Your Terms of Success feature provides some of the critical vocabulary you will need in college.

Effort

The comedian and writer Woody Allen once said, "Eighty percent of success is showing up." Definitely, in college classes, you can't be successful unless you attend regularly. College professors may not take attendance or make an issue of students who are not present; however, it is still your responsibility to attend. If you are receiving financial aid through grants or loans, your attendance may be important to continued funding in the future. Some colleges even require students to pay back funds received if they fail to attend classes regularly.

Irregular attendance will not only mean missed lectures and jeopardized financial aid, but also result in missed information about assignments, tests, and grading. Especially in courses that build on concepts (such as math, foreign languages, and writing), your lack of attendance can lead to problems with successfully doing assignments and performing on tests later in the semester.

If you miss a class or intend to miss a class, you should mention this to your professor. Although you may not need a doctor's excuse, you should be prepared to justify your absence, especially if you have missed an exam. Most professors, though, may not care why you were absent or may not distinguish between excused or unexcused absences. Instead, they will simply insist that you find a way to come to class and keep up with the work.

Attending class is just part of the effort you will put forth; you will also need to produce quality work. Writing a paper and turning it in is only part of the requirement. You also have to adhere to the standards of the course. If your professor asks for a 10-page paper that argues a contemporary topic and uses five sources, you must follow those guidelines. In some instances, you may receive no credit for completing an assignment if you have not followed the requirements.

Spending more time to complete an assignment *usually* translates to better quality, but this is not always the case. For example, someone who types 30 words a minute will need less time to produce error-free assignments than someone who "hunts and pecks" at the keyboard. The quality of your work is what you will be graded on, not the number of hours you spend doing it.

Responsibility

No doubt you already juggle numerous responsibilities, and going to class and studying are just more tasks that you must complete each week. Handling your responsibilities skillfully will take a positive attitude, respect for yourself, and maturity. Laura knows how important being responsible for herself and her son is. She has spent many years relying on herself and a few family members to meet her responsibilities. Obviously, as a student she has the responsibility to take notes, study for tests, and attend classes regularly. But she also has the responsibility to ask questions when she doesn't understand or to resolve any conflict that may occur.

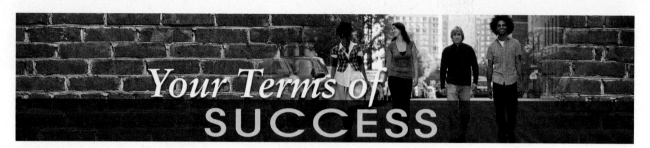

Your Terms of SUCCESS

WHEN YOU SEE . . .	IT MEANS . . .
AA	Associate of Arts; a degree program offered by community colleges consisting of about 60 credit hours; usually transfers to a four-year institution as part of the core curriculum.
AAS	Associate of Applied Science; a degree program offered by community colleges consisting of about 60 credit hours; usually does not contain as many core courses as an AA and is not designated for transfer, but is intended for students who will enter the workforce after graduation.
Academic integrity	Doing honest work on all assignments and tests.
AS	Associate of Science; a degree program offered by community colleges consisting of about 60 credit hours; usually transfers to a four-year institution as part of the core curriculum; emphasizes science courses.
BA	Bachelor of Arts; a degree program offered by four-year institutions consisting of about 120 credit hours.
BS	Bachelor of Science; a degree program offered by four-year institutions consisting of about 120 credit hours.
Core curriculum	Also called general education requirements or basic courses; the common courses that almost all students who earn a bachelor's degree complete.
Corequisite	A course that can be taken at the same time as another course.
Course objectives	The goals of a course.
Credit hour	The unit of measurement colleges use that usually equals the amount of time you are in class each week during a 16-week semester.
Degree plan	A list of classes that you must complete successfully in order to be awarded a degree.
FERPA	Family Educational Rights and Privacy Act; federal law that regulates the communication and dissemination of your educational records.
GPA	Grade Point Average; each earned grade is awarded grade points that are multiplied by the number of credit hours taken; dividing total grade points (quality points) by total credit hours results in the grade point average.
Grading criteria	The standards by which an assignment is graded.
Prerequisite	A course that must be taken before one can take another course.
Quality points	The points determined by a grade point multiplied by the credit hours for a course; used to calculate grade point average.
Syllabus	The contract between an instructor and a student; provides information about the course content, course objectives, grading criteria, and course schedule.

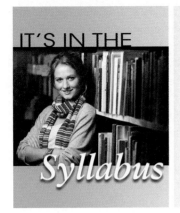

IT'S IN THE *Syllabus*

What are your instructors' expectations? Look at your syllabus for each class you are taking and determine what each one expects of you. Are you supposed to do the majority of your work outside of class? Are you expected to be responsible for completing a group project?

What kinds of supplies are you required to have for each class? Will you need computer access to complete assignments? How will you purchase or access the required supplies?

With responsibility also comes maturity, which is the foundation for many of the other components of college culture. Without a mature attitude and outlook, the other parts are unattainable. Even simple, seemingly obvious actions can help you present yourself as a dedicated, mature student—for example, paying attention during lectures, presentations, talks by guest speakers, and videos. Although this sounds self-evident, it is sometimes forgotten after the first few weeks of the semester. Work on looking toward the front of the room and avoiding distractions. A common barrier to paying attention, besides staring out the window, is doing homework in class. Instructors frown on students who use class time to study for other classes or complete assignments that were due at the beginning of class. Just remember that the instructor sees what you are doing—that you are not paying attention—and will make note of it.

Small but important actions that convey maturity and readiness to meet college expectations include staying for the duration of the class, limiting off-topic conversations with classmates, refraining from eating or participating in distracting activities, and getting ready to exit class only after the instructor has dismissed everyone. One everyday activity that causes big problems in class is the use of cell phones, headsets, and other electronic communication devices. In some classes, such as a chemistry lab, the distraction can be dangerous. Some colleges have strict policies forbidding the use of cell phones and pagers in class. There may be exceptions, however. For example, if you work in a field that requires your immediate attention in the event of an emergency or if you have a gravely ill family member, ask whether you may leave these electronic devices turned on. If your college does not have a policy, turn off your cell phone and pager in class anyway. Students who answer social calls in class appear immature and unconcerned about their education.

A more important way to demonstrate maturity in college is to understand and appreciate constructive criticism from your instructor. When you receive advice or comments about your work or progress in the course, look at it as an opportunity to learn more about yourself and the expectations of college. The instructor's job is to educate you and help you learn more about the world; it is not the instructor's job to undermine those efforts by cutting you down.

Any new experience may seem overwhelming at first until you realize how many people are there to help you.

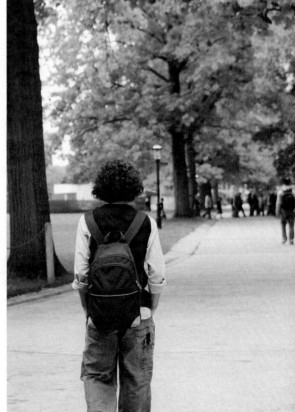

Jupiter Images/Getty Images

Although it is a great confidence builder, positive feedback does not necessarily challenge you to do better or indicate where you can improve. Be open to the challenge of receiving constructive criticism about the quality of your work. It takes a mature person to value constructive criticism and learn from it and to remember that your professors, counselors, and advisors want to help you be successful, so they will often set high standards that they know you can achieve.

Chapter 3 discusses diversity and relationships in depth, but it is worth mentioning here that dealing with diversity, conflict, and controversy takes a certain level of maturity. Effectively meeting any challenge to your belief system or values will demand that you act with integrity and openness. Because the purpose of getting an education is to stretch your mind and expand your ideas, you will need maturity to help you put all that new information into perspective.

Controversial Content

For the most part, college will be a straightforward experience—you will learn the expectations and when you meet them, you will be successful. There are, though, other aspects of college culture that may be uncomfortable or even shocking to you. All colleges value diversity, whether in the student body population or in the backgrounds of its faculty. Most definitely, you will find diversity in ideas and theories among the subjects that are offered, which may challenge your beliefs and values. Still other subjects may contain material that you find disrespectful, offensive, distasteful, or disturbing. Besides the reading and discussing of controversial issues, your college may produce student and faculty work that contains language, images, or situations that you find offensive.

What should you do if you encounter college "culture shock"? First, remember that the purpose of college is to provide you with a wider worldview and understanding of diversity—even if that diversity involves different ideas and theories. Second, remember that you have the right to an opinion and a feeling about what you encounter in college. There is no reason you should hide your feelings or attitudes about what you are learning and experiencing. With this said, the third point to remember is that with your right to an opinion, you also have an obligation as a college student to examine your previously held beliefs and evaluate how they are being challenged in your courses or as you participate in college activities. You also have the responsibility to appreciate that there is more than one way to view an "offensive" idea or image. Figure 2.1 provides a list of possible subjects that could be controversial to you or other students.

Critical Thinking
EXERCISE 2.2

As part of learning outside of class, professors expect you to visit a tutor if you need additional practice or help. Nonetheless, students may not always take advantage of the assistance offered. What could the college do to encourage more students to get help with their classes? ■

HOW COLLEGE WORKS

Now you know what to expect and what is expected of you in college, but knowing a few other customary practices will help you go from being a "tourist" to a "native." The following information will provide you with a better understanding of how college works beyond what happens in the classroom.

Schedules

First, it is helpful to note that colleges organize class time around semesters or terms, which can be as short as 4 weeks, usually during the summer, or as long as 16 weeks.

FIGURE 2.1 A Sample of Possible Controversial Subjects

The existence of God, higher being

Conservatism and liberalism

Nudity in art, photography

Sexuality, including homosexuality and adultery

The creation of the universe

The theory of extraterrestrial life

Evolution

The beginning of life

Scientific investigation and experimentation (stem cells, cloning)

Socioeconomic theory

Many colleges have at least four semesters: fall, spring, first summer term, and second summer term; the summer terms are shorter than the fall and spring terms. Other colleges organize the academic calendar around 10- or 11-week terms. If you are unsure how many weeks the semester is, count the number of weeks from the first day of class until the last day of finals. You can find the information in the college catalog or in the course outline of your syllabus.

College classes are scheduled on different days during the week. This arrangement may differ significantly from your high school schedule. In college, you may take classes once a week, as is the case for evening or night classes, or you may take them on Mondays, Wednesdays, and Fridays or just Tuesdays and Thursdays. Usually, colleges do not offer classes on Friday nights, so if you take classes for the evening, you will take them either once or twice a week, Mondays through Thursdays.

Exceptions to this schedule occur during shortened terms such as summer semesters or intersessions in which you may go every day during the week. Also, you may have a lab or special class that meets only once a week but is tied to another class such as biology or chemistry. The best advice for new students is to read the schedule of classes carefully before registering, and as always, ask an advisor, counselor, instructor, or fellow student if you have trouble reading your schedule.

Colleges award credit hours (remember this term from earlier in the chapter?) based on how many hours a week you are in class during a regular semester (summer or intersession terms will double or quadruple the number of hours a week as compared to a regular semester). Thus, a three-credit-hour class will require that you spend about 3 hours in class per week—some classes may last only 50 minutes three times a week. Exceptions do exist: Labs are often worth one credit hour, but they may meet for more than one hour one day a week.

Figure 2.2 shows a typical schedule of a full-time student. Notice the "TR" under the "Days" column; "T" stands for Tuesday and "R" for Thursday. Thus, the biology class meets both Tuesday and Thursday whereas the lab meets on Thursday only. As noted, labs and other special classes may meet for more than one hour a week, but they are usually worth only one credit hour. Although the classes in this schedule meet two-and-a-half hours each week, they are given three credit hours. Three hours is often an approximation of the time spent in class.

FIGURE 2.2 16-Week Class Schedule

Fall 2012 (16-Week) Schedule

Course ID	Course Name	Days	Time	Credit Hours
ENGL 030	Composition Fundamentals	MWF	8:00–8:50 A.M.	3.0
BIOL 110	Biology	TR	8:00–9:15 A.M.	3.0
BIOL 112	Biology Lab	R	9:25–11:25 A.M.	1.0
MATH 034	Intermediate Algebra	MWF	10:00–10:50 A.M.	3.0
COLL 101	Freshman Seminar	TR	12:15–1:30 P.M.	3.0
Total Hours				13.0

If the schedule in Figure 2.2 reflects a 16-week semester, this student will spend over 40 hours in class for the semester. During summer or intersession terms, you will spend about the same number of hours in class, but you will attend class more often and for a longer period of time.

Because Figure 2.3 is a schedule for a 4-week term, the classes meet for more than three hours a week. In this case, students meet for 10 hours a week for 4 weeks, which will equal 40 hours or the equivalent of the total number of hours a three-credit-hour class will meet during a 16-week term.

Grades

What is a discussion about college expectations without mentioning grades? For sure, grades are an important part of your education, and at the same time they are unimportant. How can something be both important and unimportant? Grades are important because they often reflect your level of achievement on an assignment or in a course; they are also important for obtaining and maintaining scholarships and financial aid. Additionally, grades are important to family, friends, and employers who may be supporting you financially and emotionally. Many people view grades as a reflection of a level of success. For instance, most of the people you ask would view a student who has straight A's as someone who is smart and successful. Earning good grades can motivate you to do your best and give you more confidence as you earn them.

Although good grades feel great when you earn them, grades are not always an indication of your success or lack of success in mastering a subject. James M. Banner, Jr.,

FIGURE 2.3 4-Week Class Schedule

Summer 2012 (4-Week) Class Schedule

Course ID	Course Name	Days	Time	Credit Hours
MATH 101	College Algebra	MTWRF	8:00–10:00 A.M.	3.0
ENGL 101	Composition I	MTWRF	10:10–12:10 P.M.	3.0
Total				6.0

Your college transcript, which includes your grade point average, can reveal more than just the grades you earned in courses. It can also disclose academic integrity issues, should you have them. For example, some colleges make notations on students' transcripts if they have failed a class because of plagiarism or cheating. Sometimes referred to as "FX" grades, these marks can be evidence that a student did not follow academic integrity policies.

In some cases, these marks can be deleted from transcripts if the student successfully completes an academic integrity workshop or successfully completes a certain number of semesters without any other violations.

YOUR TURN

What is your college's academic integrity policy? • How does the registrar's office designate failing grades that are due to academic integrity violations? • Are there any programs at your college to help students understand and follow the academic integrity policy?

_____

_____

_____

and Harold C. Cannon (1999), in their book *The Elements of Learning,* define grades as follows: "Grades are evaluations of your work, not of your character or intelligence. You may be a wonderful person but a failure as a biologist. You may find it impossible to do satisfactory work in history but may excel in all other subjects" (p. 160). Banner and Cannon assert, therefore, that grades have limitations. They are a necessary part of evaluation, much as you are evaluated on your job. However, as Banner and Cannon point out, grades do not show the whole picture of who you are. Grades, then, are only part of the story of your education.

If grades only sometimes indicate a level of success in a course and sometimes not, what are you to do? How will you know when to worry about your grades and when to concentrate on learning the material? The purpose of this chapter is to help you answer these questions for yourself by explaining how professors grade and how you can make good grades in college. The chapter also discusses what you can do to deemphasize making a good grade and increase your attention to mastering the material of the course. This is not to say, however, that grades are never important. They are significant because they are a way to describe the work you have done in a class. However, grades alone are not the magic carpet to success in college; they are only part of the story of your achievements. Your goal should be to strike a balance between caring about your grades and caring about improving your skills and increasing your knowledge.

As stated earlier, college professors grade a student on his or her ability to meet the standards of the course or of a particular assignment. Effort is definitely a necessary part of earning good grades—and you will earn the respect of your professor and fellow students by demonstrating an intense effort to master the concepts of a class—but it is only one part of achieving success in a course. College professors expect you also to meet the

FIGURE 2.4 — Grading Criteria for an A Paper

- An excellent introduction with engaging hooks, setup, plan for essay, and/or main idea
- An original, significant thesis that offers insightful interpretation or thought
- An inventive and logical organizational plan
- Smooth and varied transitional expressions, phrases, and sentences that provide unity and coherence
- Strong conclusion that ends the essay effectively
- Expressive, clear style with sophisticated sentence structure and word choice
- No more than three major grammatical errors

standards, sometimes called *grading criteria*, of the course. Figure 2.4 shows a potential set of criteria for a college-level paper. In this case, the criteria are for an A paper.

Knowing how your college assesses student performance is a start to improving your overall outlook on grading. The following is a typical grading scale in college:

100–90	A
89–80	B
79–70	C
69–60	D
59–0	F

Some colleges may use a plus or minus next to a letter grade such as A– or C+. Usually, colleges that allow for pluses and minuses will also alter the grading scale to designate the different grades. Here is an example of a grading scale that includes plus and minus grades:

100–94	A
93–90	A–
89–87	B+
86–84	B
83–80	B–

Each semester, the registrar will calculate your grade point average, or GPA, and post it to your transcript. Because the calculation of your GPA requires a little mathematical skill, it is important to know how your registrar figures it. Hours are the number of hours you are in class each week. As discussed previously, classes are usually worth three credit hours. Science or specialized classes that have labs usually carry four credit hours. Depending on the course and the program, credit hours can be as many as six or as few as one. To know how many hours a course carries, check the description in the college catalog, because some classes meet for more hours a week than they are worth in terms of credit. Letter grades carry a point value called *quality points*. Table 2.2 shows how many quality points each letter grade is worth.

TABLE 2.2 — Grades and Quality Points

Letter Grade	Quality Points
A	4
B	3
C	2
D	1
F	0

Courses that are designated developmental or remedial usually do not figure into your grade point average, so they do not carry any quality points. If you audit a course or receive AP (Advanced Placement) or CLEP (College-Level Examination Program) credit for a course, you will not receive quality points either. In other words, although you receive credit on your transcript for taking the course or taking an equivalent of the course, the class will not factor into your grade point average. Before you figure your GPA, you will need to figure your grade points for each class (see Table 2.2). You arrive at your grade points by multiplying the quality points for the grade you received by the number of hours the class is worth. For instance, if you took a four-hour class and you made a B, then you will multiply 4 (hours) by 3 (quality points for a B).

Evan is taking 15 hours (five 3-hour courses) this semester; if he receives an A, B, and three C's, then his grade would be calculated as shown in Table 2.3.

Finally, divide the grade points total by the hours total (39/15). Evan's GPA would be 2.6.

TABLE 2.3 GPA Calculation Table

Hours	Grade (Quality Points)	Grade Points (Hours × Quality Points)
3	A (4)	$3 \times 4 = 12$
3	B (3)	$3 \times 3 = 9$
3	C (2)	$3 \times 2 = 6$
3	C (2)	$3 \times 2 = 6$
3	C (2)	$3 \times 2 = 6$
15 Hours		39 Grade Points

Collaboration **EXERCISE 2.3**

Working within a group, discuss why you think attendance is important to success in college. Besides information and assignments, what can students miss when they do not attend class regularly? ■

COLLEGE RESOURCES

Now that you have a better understanding of college culture and what is expected of you, it is time to examine how your college looks. Getting to know the layout of the campus and the people who work there is important to understanding the culture. For example, knowing where to go when you need to use a computer will make your ability to complete an assignment a little easier. Finding your professor's office may save you time and stress when you need to talk to him about an upcoming test. Of course, the more you are on campus, the better able you will be to find people and places that will help you no matter what you need.

Knowing where to go to find services and people is only part of learning about your college. Another important aspect is finding and using the information that the college produces for students. College publications are a great place to find information about courses, programs, scholarships, activities, and policy changes. It is important that you regularly read these publications in order to stay up to date with what is going on.

The Campus

Find a map of your campus and study it for a few minutes. How many buildings does it have? How much parking space? How much "green" space or landscaping? Are there any unique features to your campus that make it an inviting and exciting place? Familiarizing yourself with your campus is probably the first activity you did when you enrolled in classes. If you have not taken a tour or simply walked around the campus,

FIGURE 2.5 Campus Layout Checklist

Building or Area	At My College	Not Sure
Student center or union		
Library		
Bookstore		
Administration building		
Theater or auditorium		
Snack bar or food court		
Athletic training facilities (indoor or outdoor)		
Science labs		
Technical and industrial training facilities		
Computer labs		
Separate divisions (such as technical and industrial, computer information systems, allied health, business, and general education)		
Individual departments (such as accounting, drafting, welding, and natural sciences)		
Student parking		
Benches and tables for meeting outside		
Quiet study space inside		

do so within the first few weeks of the semester. Locate the library, the student center, student parking, the bookstore, the business office, and the registrar's office—just to name a few destinations.

The more you know about your campus's layout, the easier it will be to find what you are looking for when you need it most. Using your map of the campus or your memory, check off in Figure 2.5 the types of buildings or departments within buildings that you know are present at your college.

If your college has more than one campus, familiarize yourself with the layout of other college property. You may have to travel to a satellite campus to take a test or to pick up materials for a class. If you have the time and the other campus is not too far away, ask for a tour. At the very least, familiarize yourself with any of the items you marked "not sure" in Figure 2.5.

College Catalog

The college catalog is an essential document during your academic career. All the information that you need to apply for financial aid, to choose courses, and to graduate is contained in the catalog. You will also find out what you are required to do to complete a degree. The academic calendar is usually placed at the beginning of the catalog. There you will find the dates for registering, dropping courses, and taking final exams.

It is important to read and keep your college catalog because if the college changes any requirements of your degree program, you will be able to follow the guidelines that were published the year you began the program. For instance, if you are working on an office management degree and you have taken three semesters of courses so far, you will not necessarily have to adhere to new requirements that are made at a later date.

Student Handbook

The student handbook, which provides you with specific information about student conduct, academic standards, and services, is another valuable publication. Usually, the handbook contains descriptions of career services, the bookstore, computer labs, and financial aid offices. Academic information including probation and suspension for misconduct and qualifications for making the dean's list can also be found in the student handbook. Most schools view the student handbook as a legal document that outlines what students can do in certain situations, so be sure to read it closely and keep a copy at home or in your book bag.

College Newspaper

College newspapers differ from the college catalog and student handbook in that students are usually the ones who are responsible for the content. Within a college newspaper, you will find articles about upcoming events; reports on changes on the college campus; editorials on important student issues; profiles of programs; and advertisements for used books, performances by musical groups, and anything else that students want to announce. The college newspaper is also a forum to explore controversial topics and to discuss sensitive issues.

Newspapers always need students to interview, write, edit, and publish. If you are interested in working for the newspaper, contact the editor or visit a journalism or composition professor.

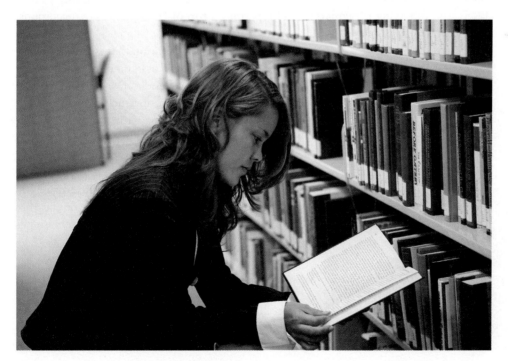

Getting familiar with the library and other services on campus and online will be essential to your transitioning smoothly.
Fotolia

Bulletin Boards

Even with the increased use of the Internet, the bulletin board is still an important way to get a message to students. Found all over campus, bulletin boards usually advertise used books, needs for roommates and part-time jobs, and upcoming campus events. Bulletin boards within academic buildings often announce four-year university programs, summer workshops, and other types of academic activities.

It's in the Syllabus

Anything that professors hand out in class is a communication tool. The syllabus is one of the most important documents that you will receive in class, so be sure to read it carefully. In the syllabus you will usually find the following information:

- Instructor's name; office location, phone number, and hours open to students; and email address
- Prerequisites for the course
- Course description from the catalog
- Textbook information
- Course objectives, or what you will accomplish by the time you finish the class
- Course content, or what topics will be covered throughout the semester
- Assignments and due dates
- Grading criteria
- Attendance and late work policies
- Academic integrity statement (which also appears in the student handbook)
- Disability accommodations policy
- General policies for classroom conduct

The syllabus is considered a contract between the student and the instructor. This means that not only will the syllabus describe what is expected of you during class, but it will also discuss what you can expect from the instructor. Both of you—student and instructor—will be bound by what is stated in the document. Reading the syllabus closely and following it regularly will keep you on top of class policies, expectations, and assignments.

USING TECHNOLOGY TO GET AHEAD

There are numerous websites that provide information about succeeding in college. The College Board has many tips for new-to-college students that can help them navigate financial aid and studying. There are even websites devoted to specific groups of students such as first-generation and Latino college students. There are GPA calculators, too, that can help you calculate your grades. All of these resources are at your fingertips and can greatly enhance your education.

Other essential information that is handed out in class includes directions to assignments, photocopied readings, study questions, and notes. Regard anything that is given to you by the instructor as important, even if you are told, "This won't be on the test."

You should also consider the grades and written comments you receive as communication from your instructors. Be sure to read any comments or suggestions that are written on papers and exams, ask questions if you don't understand them or they are illegible, and save all feedback until the semester is over.

Put It Online

The college's website is where you can find the most current information about classes, academic programs, and contact information for professors. It is easier to update information on a website because it doesn't involve printing and distribution, so it is more likely to provide the most accurate information. College websites usually list phone numbers and email addresses of professors and deans, which makes contacting them easier.

In addition to general information about degrees and departments, your college's website may give you access to professors' syllabi and assignments. This provides a good opportunity to investigate what courses you want to take based on the course objectives and assignments.

Campus Organizations

Campus organizations or student groups are another part of college life you will want to learn more about. Depending on how large your college is and how involved the students are, you may find a variety of student organizations and clubs in which to participate. Even if your time is limited, consider getting involved in some way. You may be able to get on an email list or a social networking site to keep up with events and meetings—if you cannot make those same events and meetings every time. Campus organizations include, but are not limited to, student government, student leadership programs, and clubs focused on certain interests (e.g., gay, lesbian, bisexual, and transgendered issues; political action; community service; academic honors and distinctions; religious or spiritual development; and career exploration). Getting involved will help you transition to the college and provide immediate connections with students, faculty, and staff.

Reflection
EXERCISE 2.4

The information you have already received will help you navigate college more smoothly. Organize the different sources of information by type and answer the following questions: What information have you received by email or the Internet? What information have you received from an advisor? Finally, which kinds of information are most useful to you and why? ■

PLUS
EXERCISE 2.5

(Personality + Learning Style = Understanding Situations)

Let's consider Laura's challenge in college: balancing work, family, and college. As she confirms in orientation, she is an aural learner. From what you have learned in Chapter 2, what should Laura know about transitioning to college full time that will help ease her mind? What resources could help her be successful?

Now, considering your own learning style, personality type, and special circumstances, what will you do to make the transition to college easier? What have you learned from the chapter that will make the transition smooth for you? ■

From College to University

THE CHANGES IN CULTURE AND COLLEGE SERVICES

If you are moving from your community college to a larger, more diverse university, you may experience a slight culture shock despite the semesters you already have under your belt. In addition to a bigger campus with more buildings to find and more students to meet, you may find that a university seems more impersonal. Many students who transfer from a smaller community college complain that professors do not seem to care about them personally and that they lack the support and guidance they received at their previous school. Transfer students also note that expectations increase—and their grades decrease—especially as they move into their majors and begin working toward a career.

Culturally, you should expect that your new university will offer more activities and groups than your smaller community college. You also should expect some kind of adjustment period as you get used to your new professors' expectations of you. Statistically, transfer students do experience a slight drop in GPA. This drop, however, is not necessarily an indication that they were not properly prepared for transfer by their community college.

All in all, the culture shock you experience when transferring to a four-year university will depend on how much bigger and how much more different the school is from your community college. Just remember that whatever differences you notice, there are people at the four-year school who can help you deal with the adjustment. Seek out counselors, advisors, faculty, and students to help make your transition smoother. Your campus map and list of faculty and administrators will point you in the right direction.

Building Your University Portfolio 2

Find someone you know (or ask your professor for the name of a former student) who has transferred to a four-year university and ask him or her what the expectations are for junior- and senior-level classes? How much work is expected outside of classes? What kinds of supplies (e.g., a laptop, Internet access) are recommended or necessary? What resources are available to help students transition?

_____

_____

_____

_____

From College to Career

HOW THE CULTURE WILL CHANGE AGAIN

Just as you had to adjust to college culture, you will have to make a new adjustment to the workforce if you have never held a full-time job. When starting your first job out of college, you will experience a period of getting used to the way the office or business works. You will encounter new terms, new methods of doing things, and new people. In addition, you will experience working in groups or teams to accomplish tasks, and you will be expected to communicate orally and in a written format. You may also rely more heavily on electronic mail and computers to do your work. Certainly, integrity will be an important part of your working experience. There will be less supervision and more expectation that you do the work you say you will do.

Paying attention to how others act on the job can alleviate any anxiety that you may feel. Just as you made friends and found mentors in college, you should look for others who can offer guidance and help as you learn the ropes of a new career. Also, think about how you adjusted to college and use the same strategies to make your new working environment seem less foreign and more comfortable.

Building Your Career Portfolio 2

Contact someone in a career that is similar to what you want to do. Ask that person how it felt to transition from college or a training program into the career. Were there rules and expectations that he or she had to figure out? How did this person adjust? Was there a support system to help with the transition?

_____

_____

_____

_____

First Voices

STORIES OF SUCCESS FROM COLLEGE GRADUATES

**Getting involved on campus set student's path to success:
Education major found involvement key to learning**

Jackie Connelly,
Elementary Education,
B.S., Preparatory Math
Instructional Assistant

Most of my best memories in all of my college years are from the different ways I have been involved at my community college.

Although more affordable than a university, tuition was very expensive! Scholarships were necessary in order to help ease the burden. I had a state-funded scholarship that covered 75% of my tuition and a scholarship for playing in the symphonic band and woodwind choir. I also had a scholarship for being a "Hispanic Achiever" that helped me get through my first year. I always had money reimbursed to me and used it to buy textbooks!

Since I was "just" at a community college, I did not think there would be any student activities. Because of this, my first year in college was dull since I only attended classes and worked off-campus. In the summer, I learned how wrong I was and jumped at the opportunity to make my college experience more enjoyable by getting involved with the student government association. I also joined other great campus organizations like Valencia Volunteers, which promotes community service, and Phi Theta Kappa, an honor society. Most important, I began working on campus as a preparatory math tutor. I never knew how much I liked math until I started working on campus. Since graduating from Valencia, I continue to work there as a preparatory math tutor and lab assistant. These jobs have provided so much practical experience and inspired me to pursue a minor in mathematics education to supplement my elementary education studies.

My decision to get involved has greatly shaped who I am today, as well as my future. The best advice I could give to anyone beginning an educational journey is to get involved! The lessons learned outside of the classroom are unexpected and priceless.

PATH OF DISCOVERY
Journal Entry

What is your experience so far with college culture? What has been the biggest difference you have experienced between high school or work and college?

CHAPTER REVIEW QUESTIONS

1. What differences exist between high school and college or a full-time job and college?
2. Name and explain five different characteristics that professors will expect from you as a college student.
3. How and why do colleges grade?
4. What types of documents and communication can you expect in college? What are their purposes?

CHAPTER 2 CASE SCENARIOS

1. In Jennifer's literature class, she is reading Tim O'Brien's *The Things They Carried*. Although she understands that the book is about the Vietnam War, she doesn't know why she has to read a book that contains so much profanity and graphic images of death. She has made an appointment to speak to her professor about the reading assignment because she wants to get out of reading a book that is so depressing and discomforting. What advice would you give Jennifer before she speaks to her professor? Predict what the outcome of the talk will be and what the consequence of the discussion will be on Jennifer's college career.
2. Ja-Ling is taking a biology class. One of her assignments is to create a group presentation on an assigned topic. Her group's topic is the theory of evolution, a theory that Ja-Ling finds fascinating; however, when she meets with her group to prepare for the presentation, two of her group members express deep concern that they are being asked to study something that they don't believe in. They refuse to help with the project even though they know their lack of participation will lower the whole group's grade. What should Ja-Ling do?

RESEARCH IT FURTHER

1. Find the University of South Carolina's (USC's) Carolinian Creed on the Internet. Using USC's creed as a basis, write your own creed that would fit your college's values. Is there anything that you would revise or add to USC's creed?
2. Find a map of your college and determine what building or landmark is the geographical center of the campus. Then write a short paper on how that building is an appropriate "center" of your college. Questions you may want to consider include the following:

What does the building house—a library? A classroom for the engineering department? A student center? What does the building symbolize? If you were to design a display or piece of art that reflects the "center" of the college, what would it look like?

3. Interview a college employee about his or her job and how it fits into the college's structure. Present the information about the person and the job to your class.

References and Recommended Readings

Banner, J. M., Jr., & Cannon, H. C. (1999). *The elements of learning.* New Haven, CT: Yale University Press.

The College Board. (2008). *Succeeding in college: What it means and how to make it happen.* Plano, TX: Author.

Dabbah, M. (2009). *Latinos in college: Your guide to success.* Scarborough, NY: Consultare.

Newport, C. (2005). *How to win at college: Surprising secrets for success from the country's top students.* New York: Broadway.

Nist-Olejnik, S., & Patrick Holschuh, J. (2007). *College rules!: How to study, survive, and succeed in college.* Berkeley, CA: Ten Speed Press.

Watkins, B. D. (2004). *Everything you ever wanted to know about college: A guide for minority students.* Camillus, NY: Blue Boy Publishing.

3

RELATIONSHIPS

"Evan, are you going to be around later today? I may need some help," Michael asks his new friend and study group partner. Michael stayed after orientation to exchange numbers with Evan and, since then, they have talked a few times on campus and on the phone.

One reason Michael felt an instant connection with Evan that first day was that Evan is a lot like him—athletic, driven, and still unsure of himself as a college student. From his experience in the military, Michael knows how to deal with diversity; he has met all kinds of people from different countries and backgrounds.

"Sure, man," Evan says. "Maybe you can help me, too. I have to move some furniture for my aunt this weekend. You think you can lend me a hand?"

Michael paces outside the library and drops his backpack on the wall before he sits down next to it. Although he has been through the college orientation, he is still getting used to the college experience. His philosophy professor, for example, has a very different view of the world and challenges her students to question their own views. Sometimes the debates get heated and he forgets that he is there to learn, not to get angry and shut down. His political science instructor does not agree with him on the responsibility and roles of state governments, but he does allow Michael to share his military experiences and is respectful of Michael's point of view.

"Are you sure you can use help from an old man like me?" Michael asks. Michael has never thought much about being 42 until some students he is working with on a group project said something about his being "too old" to work with.

"You may be old, man, but I'm pretty sure you can bench press more than me," Evan says as he laughs.

"Maybe when I was your age, but not anymore," Michael says. "Seriously, though, I have this group project, and, well, my group keeps meeting without me, and I have to do well on this project."

"Ah, c'mon," Evan says. "I would make you the leader of my group. I've heard you debate others and win! You are fierce in an argument."

"I think that is part of the problem, too. I ran into a guy in the class and he said he saw two people in my group meeting in the library and working on the project when I was able to meet, but no one even called me," Michael says. "I don't know, maybe I come on too strong, offend people."

"So what do you need from me? Need some boxing tips?" Evan asks.

"Do you think if I talked to the professor that she would reassign me to another group or tell me to deal with it?" asks Michael.

"Man, what do you have to lose by asking?" Evan replies.

One of the easiest parts of college can be the hardest for busy college students. The easy part to making friends and forging relationships is that people are everywhere—in class, computer labs, and the library—and everyone shares at least one thing—college—in common. As Michael will discover, getting to know those around you is essential to your well-being and happiness while you are working on your degree. The hard part, however, is making the time to cultivate relationships. As a community college student, you most likely have other activities that fill your schedule outside of class: work, family, hobbies, church, and friends. Part of this chapter's purpose is to show you the benefits of starting and maintaining strong relationships with people on campus.

In addition to making friends and connections with people in college, this chapter also discusses diversity as an issue to be explored and appreciated. You will certainly notice that the people you encounter in college are from a variety of backgrounds and you will most likely meet numerous people who have differing values, goals, opinions about politics and religion, and ways of leading their lives. An important component of being an educated individual is understanding that college is, in part, about learning to listen to others, understanding their points of view, and appreciating them in the larger context of humanity. This chapter, then, presents you with several categories of diversity—to be sure, there are as many categories as there are people—to explore and discuss with your instructors, class-mates, and others. There is also discussion of instances in which a lack of appreciation for others' differences can lead to prejudging them, or worse, discrimination. All of these topics will help you create and maintain mutually respectful relationships with others while broadening your own appreciation of diversity and encouraging others as well.

More specifically, after completing this chapter, you will be able to do the following:

- **Describe the different types of people and their roles on your campus and list the benefits of cultivating relationships in college.**
- **Explain the importance of appreciating diversity.**
- **Discuss how stereotyping, prejudice, and discrimination are related.**
- **Understand the process of resolving conflict in relationships.**

YOUR RELATIONSHIPS in COLLEGE

Research has shown that getting to know at least one person, no matter who it is, on your campus will increase the likelihood that you will stay in college and complete your degree (Kuh et al., 2005). Whether it is the janitor or a career counselor, getting to know someone beyond just her name, title, and face is to your advantage while you are in college.

You have probably noticed already that there are many people who work at a college—and most of them are there to support and guide you through your college experience. Equally important to understanding where buildings and services are located is knowing who does what on your campus. It will save you time to know, for example, that getting copies of your transcript involves speaking with someone in the registrar's office or that checking on loan applications will include contact with a financial aid officer. These people and many others are charged with the task of helping you succeed each semester you are in college, and it will make your transition from either high school or the world of work much easier if you are familiar with the various common jobs on campus.

Professors

There may be no one more important to your college and possible future career success as your professors. They do not just provide you with access to content and support you as you think critically about the subject matter; they also can be mentors and resources as you complete your degree and start a career. One way to start out on the right path to a good relationship is to greet each professor with a smile and a "Hello" when you see her in and out of class. College professors see their relationships with students outside of class as part of their advising and mentoring duties. For many instructors, their students are not only people in their classes, but they are also potential graduates from their programs or transfer student success stories. Being friendly in and outside of class is a great way to start on the path to a strong, valuable relationship during your college career (and maybe even after)!

Another way to start developing meaningful relationships with your professors is to appreciate the diversity of disciplines, personality types, and teaching styles among them. For sure, you will not love every class (although we professors wish you could), every teaching style, and every personality that you will encounter in college. When you take pleasure in the class and the instructor, enjoy every minute of it; when you don't, use the experience to keep focused on what you want: a college degree. Also realize, however, that what you "don't like" at first may just be a first impression that will not necessarily continue throughout the course. Sometimes students' initial experiences in a class are uncomfortable, but those same experiences may later come to be ones appreciated as leading to meaningful insights about the course topic as well as themselves.

Because each instructor's expectations in terms of class preparation and policies regarding attendance, late work, and make-up exams will differ, be mindful that the rules that applied in one class may be different in another. Relationships built on acknowledgement of others' boundaries (in this case, professors' expectations and policies) as well as respect and integrity are stronger and more authentic than more superficial interactions. To cultivate a solid relationship with your professor, make the most of his office hours. Office hours are best used for questions about material that was previously covered, assignments and policies that were previously explained, and anything else that does not pertain to the day's lecture or in-class activity. Sometimes students only see office hours as a time to discuss a problem; office hours should be used for positive visits as well—stopping by to say "Hello" or to follow up on an idea that sparked your interest in class are great ways to strengthen a relationship.

It would be a perfect world if there were no conflicts in your interactions with your instructors. However, there may be a time in your college career when you don't feel as though you have a strong, respectful relationship. If you experience conflict with a professor, be sure to discuss the issue as soon as possible—and in private. Use "I" statements to explain your perspective rather than "you" statements. For example, saying

"I am confused about what our exam will cover" is better than saying "You were confusing when you talked about the exam." Using "I" statements also underscores your control over your actions and reactions during the conflict. Look, too, for common ground that can help you manage the conflict maturely and respectfully.

A good relationship for its own sake is perfectly acceptable, but also remember that professors can provide a link to other opportunities beyond the classroom. You will most likely turn to a professor when you need a recommendation letter for student activities, scholarships, internships, and jobs. Getting to know at least one professor well will give you an advantage when you want to move forward in your college career. Professors in your certificate and degree program are usually tied closely to the business and industry in which they teach. Thus, a good relationship with a professor in respiratory therapy, for example, may lead to a job opportunity in the field. A professor who teaches a general education course, one designed for transfer to a four-year university, may work closely with a professor in the same discipline at the local university. She may know about special scholarships or helpful people to contact once you have completed your degree.

Although a good relationship with your professors is a key to enjoying your education experience, remember that professors are not equals in the relationship and still must challenge you to learn and stretch your concept of yourself and others as well as evaluate you during and at the end of the term. It will be important for you to understand boundaries in relationships, as discussed later in the chapter.

Advisors, Counselors, and Learning Support Staff

In addition to professors, some of the most important relationships that you will forge during college will be with people whose sole job is to make sure you succeed. Counselors and advisors will be key people in your academic career, so be sure to take the time to get to know these individuals. Tutors, mentors, and other support staff can also play important roles in the success of your college experience.

Advisors

Your advisor may be the first person you encounter at college. An advisor explains to you what courses you should take, how many hours you should schedule per semester, and how to plan ahead. An advisor works for you; it is his or her job to see that you complete your degree as smoothly as possible. You may be lucky enough to have the same advisor throughout your college career. In that case, regular contact will help keep the lines of communication open. If you have a different advisor each semester, you may wish to find one person on whom you can rely to act as a regular advisor. That person may be a former professor or a counselor who has advised you in the past. The goal is to find someone on campus who has an interest in your education beyond one semester.

Counselors

You should take the opportunity to get to know at least one counselor on your campus. Whether it is a career counselor or a disability counselor, make it a point to schedule an appointment while you are in college. Getting to know counselors is a great way to obtain more information about the school and its services. For example, a career counselor may inform you of a career fair or recruiting day. He can also help you prepare a résumé and practice interviewing. Counselors for students with personal issues are another valuable resource for you. Even if you do not need personal counseling, you may benefit from a relationship with someone who does it professionally. This type of counselor can give you tips for managing stress and dealing with difficult people, just to name a few experiences you may have in college.

Tutors, Mentors, and Student Leaders

In addition to the key people already mentioned, a variety of other people work or volunteer their time to help students achieve their academic, career, and personal goals. For example, working one on one with a tutor in a learning assistance lab can provide you with a unique relationship, because a tutor can really get to know what your learning needs are and how to help you fulfill them. A tutor can be a great resource for understanding the material for a class because he is often a student himself or has just recently taken the class.

Student or peer mentors are other helpers you can find on your college campus who can be instrumental in keeping you on track to success. Peer mentors are usually current students who have been successful in their classes and are willing to provide support to new students who may need extra encouragement to navigate the choppy waters of the first few semesters. Peer mentors may give you advice for studying, for choosing a degree, or for balancing family, work, and college. And just think—if you are also successful, you may be a great peer mentor for a student who is just like you when you started!

Finally, you may come in contact with student leaders, whether in special clubs, associations, or student government. Unlike peer mentors, whose primary role is to work one on one with learners, student leaders work with both students and the college or organization to provide leadership in certain areas. For example, you may encourage a student government representative to ask college officials for more family-friendly activities that you can attend with your children. If administrators agree, then the Student Government Association may work with you and other students to find out which activities are best and you may even help organize an event to get more students involved.

Classmates

Getting to know your classmates can make the difference between struggling all alone and meeting new challenges with a like-minded support group. Who else can relate to the challenge of studying for a chemistry final exam than the students in the class with you? Think about it: Your classmates may be a majority of the people who populate your college campus. You may get to know well only three or four professors throughout your college career, but you have the potential of meeting and working with hundreds of students.

In addition to sharing experiences with your fellow students, you can also rely on them as study partners or emergency note-takers if you can't be in class. Another benefit to making friends with classmates is that you can learn about other classes, instructors, and degree programs from them. Their firsthand knowledge could help you choose the best classes and the most promising programs.

Getting to know your classmates can be relatively simple, especially because you will be sitting close to them during each class. Here are a few tips for creating lasting relationships with fellow students:

- Introduce yourself to those sitting around you. It may be helpful to arrive early and start conversations with other students.
- Exchange phone numbers or email addresses with classmates who seem reliable and trustworthy. You may need to call someone if you miss class. Offer to study

with someone. Not only will you help a classmate, but you will also help yourself learn the material.

- Keep in contact with friends even after the semester is over. Although you may not share classes anymore, you still can study and offer support to one another.

Family and Friends

Entering college will be a new experience not only for you, but also for your family and friends, especially if they have not gone to college. Communication, then, will be the key to weathering any changes in your relationships. They need to know how you feel about going to college, and they need to be aware that you will be going through changes while you are there. Surely you will be experiencing changes in your outlook on life, your belief in yourself, and your attitude toward the future.

When these changes occur, people around you may react differently. Some will be supportive and excited that you have created personal goals and are achieving them. A few, however, may react negatively, possibly jealous of your success or your new "lease on life" because they either did not have the same opportunities or squandered the chances that they did have. Others who react negatively may be insecure about themselves and feel "dumb" around a person in college; these same people often fear that once the college student graduates, he or she will leave them for a "better" spouse or friend. Also, there are parents who do not want to acknowledge that their children

It's All RELATIVE

Your family and friends will continue to be important to you as you meet new people at your college and learn many new things. However, you may find that your family's values do not always match the values of others. The challenge will be in strengthening your connection to your family (if that is what you want) and being open to new people who may differ greatly from those you have known all your life.

Sharing with your family what you are learning is a good way to open the lines of communication, but you will need to determine both what and how much you want to share. Nonetheless, sharing with them what you are learning and whom you are getting to know will ease their minds that they are not losing you as a close family member. Likewise, you may want to ask them questions about what they are learning (on the job or raising a family) and whom they are meeting each day. The goal is creating an environment in which you all value each other's experiences, no matter how different they may be from your own.

YOUR TURN

What have you learned so far that you would be willing to share with your family? • What topics are "off limits" with your family? • What is your plan for keeping the lines of communication open about the different ideas and people you are learning more about?

_____

_____

_____

are grown adults who are and should be making decisions on their own; parents are also often worried that their children will be exposed to value systems and beliefs that are very different from what they taught. Whatever the reasons that the people around you react to the changes you experience, be comforted by the fact that you will survive, and better yet, you will have more of an understanding of the *diversity* of opinions that you will encounter. Learning how to deal with different people in college will allow you to apply what you learn to your personal relationships.

Reflection
EXERCISE 3.1

What relationships on campus have you cultivated so far? What challenges might you have in getting to know tutors, student leaders, and mentors? ■

EXPLORING DIVERSITY

An exciting part of college is that you will meet and work with people from different age groups and backgrounds. Unlike a traditional university, at your college you may be part of a study group that includes a grandparent, home-schooled teenager, veteran, administrative assistant to a dean, full-time detective, and minister. Because of this variety, college students need to be especially sensitive to others' values and perspectives, which is one of the purposes of diversity.

A simple definition of *diversity* is "difference" or "variety." Another term heard when diversity is discussed in a college setting is *multiculturalism*. Although the two words have different implications, they often have the same motivation—to expose the community to a variety of ideas, cultures, viewpoints, beliefs, and backgrounds.

When people talk about diversity, they usually mean diversity in race, gender, ethnicity, age, and religion. Colleges that want to promote diversity on their campuses often look for opportunities to hire and enroll people from different backgrounds than the majority of the campus population. They do this with the belief that diversity enriches the educational experience for all because it exposes faculty, staff, and students to new ideas and challenges our preconceived notions of the world around us.

Gender and Sexual Orientation Diversity

The latest educational statistics show that almost two-thirds of the college student population across the country is female. In the past few decades, women have enrolled in college in record numbers. It may seem strange to think that several decades ago, there were far fewer women in college, especially in law and medical schools. No doubt, you will encounter gender diversity at your college, and what this means for you is that you will have plenty of opportunities to work with both men and women and explore any preconceptions you may have about the differences between the sexes. You may have to pay more attention to society's assumptions about gender and be more attuned

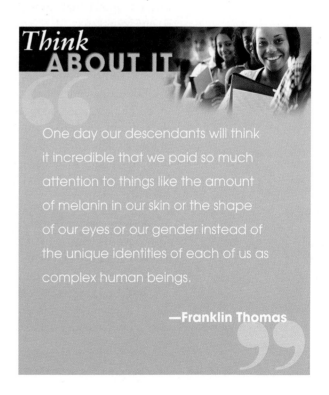

Think
ABOUT IT

One day our descendants will think it incredible that we paid so much attention to things like the amount of melanin in our skin or the shape of our eyes or our gender instead of the unique identities of each of us as complex human beings.

—Franklin Thomas

to how language, art, and the sciences, among other disciplines, perpetuate gender stereotypes.

Sexual orientation is another type of diversity that you will more than likely encounter in college if you have not already. Homosexuality and bisexuality are just two categories of sexual orientation diversity. Organizations such as the Human Rights Campaign (www.hrc.org) strive to educate others about discrimination that can—and does—occur because of the stereotypes and prejudice that exist regarding sexual orientation. Why should you know more about sexual orientation as a part of diversity? Sexuality is part of the human experience, and one purpose of higher education is to help you better understand and appreciate your own and others' human experience. Recognizing sexual orientation as a category of diversity gives you a more complete picture of humankind.

Sexual Harassment

Colleges and universities as well as many workplaces have been aggressively educating students and employees about recognizing and preventing sexual harassment for decades. Sexual harassment, by legal definition, refers to a superior, or a person in power, sexually harassing a subordinate, or a person with less power than the harasser. College and employee policies often broaden the definition, however, to include any unwanted sexual advances that create an uncomfortable situation or hostile environment. This broader definition means that, in college, a student can sexually harass another student or a student can sexually harass a professor—or any other scenario that involves students, prospective students, and employees and guests of the college. To further round out the definition, women can sexually harass men and people can experience sexual harassment from colleagues of the same sex.

Despite educational programs for new students and required seminars for employees, colleges—like any place where people live and work—are not immune to instances of sexual harassment. According to Katz (2005), the American Psychological Association surveyed female graduate students about their experiences in college. The survey results found that 12.7% of female students experienced sexual harassment and 21% avoided taking certain classes for fear of being sexually harassed. Surveys about sexual harassment in the workplace paint a dimmer picture, with 31% of female employees and 7% of male employees claiming to be sexually harassed at work.

Educating yourself about the seriousness of sexual harassment, your college's policy on the subject, and common behaviors often considered sexual harassment are steps in the right direction to minimizing incidents. For sure, sexual harassment is no laughing matter, and a review of your college's statement on the matter will reveal the college's discipline policy for those who sexually harass others. Some college policies list the following behaviors as sexual harassment:

- Offensive jokes or comments of a sexual nature
- Requests or demands for sexual favors in return for favorable treatment or rewards (e.g., a good grade)
- Unwanted physical contact or assault
- Showing or distributing sexually explicit materials to others
- Posting sexually explicit images or websites in college-owned online course management systems or emailing those images or links to websites from college-owned computers

Although not always considered sexual harassment if material is not distributed to others, accessing sexually explicit websites with college-owned computer hardware and software may be prohibited conduct that will result in disciplinary action on the part of the college and possible criminal charges.

As with all forms of diversity in which possible problems can arise, be sensitive to others; treat everyone you meet on campus with respect; and be honest with others if you feel uncomfortable in a situation or with certain conversational topics.

Racial, Ethnic, and Cultural Diversity

Over the last 20 years, colleges have embraced and developed multicultural studies in response to the past emphasis on "white, male, Western" history, ideas, and culture. Cultural and racial ignorance at its worst has led to the deaths of millions of people all over the world. Understanding and appreciation for the diversity in culture and ethnicity create connections between people who have much to learn from each other. Figure 3.1 provides you with tips that can help you better appreciate diversity.

Generational Diversity

The idea that our parents' generation is vastly different from our own, which will be greatly different from our children's generation, is considered a fact of life. One unifying viewpoint among the generations is that different generations view the world differently.

You will, no doubt, encounter generational diversity at your college and in the world of work—more so than in generations past. According to the Department of Education's website (2010), the growth in certain age groups will continue to rise: "From 2006 to 2017, NCES projects a rise of 10 percent in enrollments of people under 25, and a rise of 19 percent in enrollments of people 25 and over."

What is a "generational cohort" and what does it mean for your college and work experience? According to Ron Zemke, Claire Raines, and Bob Filipczak, in their book *Generations at Work: Managing the Clash of Veterans, Boomers, Xers, and Nexters in Your Workplace* (2000), a generational cohort is a group of the population that was born within a certain period of time, that marked as important some of the same world events, and that hold certain common values. In their book, the authors recognize and

FIGURE 3.1 Tips for Appreciating Racial, Ethnic, and Cultural Diversity

- Work to eliminate all racial, ethnic, or cultural stereotypes or slurs from your thoughts and vocabulary. Stop yourself before you speak and ask, "Is this a stereotype or could it be offensive to some?"

- Racial, ethnic, and cultural jokes, images, and cartoons are insensitive at best, harassment at worst. Avoid making fun of others' heritage. Be sensitive to others' backgrounds.

- Learn more about your heritage and culture.

- Strive to learn more about cultures that are new and different to you.

- Participate in college and community cultural celebrations.

- Attend seminars, guest lecturers, and artistic performances about different cultures and countries.

- Do not tolerate others who exhibit racial and cultural insensitivity. If you don't feel comfortable saying something to them, then avoid them and similar situations in the future.

TABLE 3.1 Generations, Birth Years, and Core Values

Generation	Birth Years	Core Values
Veterans	1922–1943	Dedication, sacrifice, patience, respect for authority
Baby Boomers	1943–1960	Health and wellness, optimism, personal growth
Generation Xers	1960–1980	Diversity, fun, self-reliance, global thinking
Nexters or Millenials	1980–present	Civic duty, morality, street smarts

describe four generations that can be found in the workplace (and college for that matter). These generations are defined and described in Table 3.1.

Each of the generational groups, the authors contend, holds certain values that influence how they work with others and how they achieve personal success. The diverse core values and attitudes can create enriching experiences for generations that work together, or they can be a cause of conflict for those who do not understand and appreciate fellow students and coworkers of a different generation. Misunderstanding generational differences at its worst can become ageism, which is discriminating against someone because of his or her age. The key with generational diversity—as with all types of diversity—is to learn more about yourself and others and appreciate the differences.

Other Kinds of Diversity

Learning to work well with others, regardless of how different they are from you, and complete tasks as a team is an important skill to develop in college.

Dealing successfully with diversity includes more than working well with people from different national, religious, or political backgrounds, or with different abilities or disabilities; you will also need to consider the diversity of attitudes and work ethics. For example, not everyone you meet in college or in your career will value the same things you do. What will you do if you work with people whose values conflict with your own? What will you do if the differences between your own and others' work ethics cause conflict?

You will get the opportunity to experience these differences in class when you are assigned a group project or presentation. Even if you all are the same gender, race, religion, and age, you will still find that each of you is different and has different expectations and opinions of the assignment. Being able to work with others, regardless of their learning and work styles, is a skill. The more you are exposed to diversity, the more you will be able to handle and appreciate the differences between you and everyone you meet.

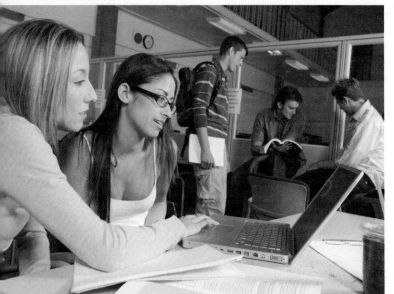

Fotolia

TABLE 3.2 Teaching Styles

Teaching Style	Description	Tips for Success
Lecture	Professor talks for the majority of the class; a brief outline may be included; questions are limited or discouraged; usually very structured	Practice good listening skills; record lectures with permission; take good notes during class and review them frequently
Discussion	Professor poses a question and requires students in the class to answer and build on an idea or theme	Practice good listening skills; record theme or question for the discussion; note repeated ideas; record essence of each person's contribution; participate in discussion
Project	Professor bases class learning on projects; provides instruction for assignment; assigns roles; monitors progress	Make connection between project assignment and course objectives; ask for feedback during project to make sure you are progressing; refer to course materials for extra help
Problem solving	Professor poses or writes a problem on the board; walks through solving the problem	Break process down into steps; identify any step that is unclear; ask for extra practice and feedback if needed

Teaching Styles Diversity

You will encounter many different teaching styles. It has been said that most professors teach the way they learn best, but there are college instructors who use a variety of teaching methods to encourage student learning. You will be more successful if you can identify each teaching style and understand how to adapt to it. Gone are the days of saying, "I just can't learn in her class. She doesn't teach the way I need her to." Like the people who must work together in groups with sensitivity to one another's personalities, you, too, will need to identify your learning style and how it will fit into your professor's teaching style. Ideally, your instructor will recognize that his students have different learning style strengths and adapt his material to those learning styles, but not everyone you will encounter in college will vary his teaching style to meet your needs. Your best bet is to be ready to learn no matter what the teaching style.

To help you recognize the different methods of teaching, Table 3.2 contains a description of each and tips for making the most of the different types of classroom instruction.

Critical Thinking EXERCISE 3.2

There are some communities and groups around the world that believe a "pure" (no diversity) group, race, or community is ideal. What would be the benefits of being in a group that valued "sameness"? What would be the drawbacks? ■

FIGHTING HATE

To understand the problem of hate in our world, all you have to do is open a newspaper or click on the latest news story online. Hatred for others because of skin color, religious beliefs, or sexual orientation has fueled violence and discrimination all over the world. Whether it involves millions of people being slaughtered in a third-world country or one person being beaten up for his beliefs, the remedy to begin combating hatred is the same: learning to understand others and appreciate diversity. To do that, we must confront the very ideas and processes that lead people to greater acts of hatred.

Stereotypes

Stereotyping is an oversimplified opinion of someone or something. We often use stereotypes to make quick decisions every day. When choosing a checkout line, we may make a quick decision as to which is the fastest based on the people in line and what they have in their carts. When playing outfield on a softball team, we may stereotype the smaller players as weaker hitters, which will cause us to move closer to the infield. Parents also encourage children, who have difficulty making complex decisions, to stereotype strangers in order to protect themselves. Although these stereotypes are not necessarily harmful, they can create problems for us. Our superficial analysis may put us in the slowest checkout line; we may move so close to the infield that the smaller player hits the ball over our heads; we may confuse children about the characteristics of a stranger, making it difficult for them to trust adults.

Stereotypes can serve a purpose in the short run, but as the examples illustrate, stereotypes do not take into consideration all the facts. For the most part, stereotypes keep us from having to think about the complexity of issues, leaving us unable to appreciate the beauty of diversity. In essence, stereotypes are shorthand for evaluating situations and making decisions, but if used repeatedly, they can become prejudice and discrimination.

Prejudice

Prejudice is literally "pre-judging" a person or situation without knowing the facts. Prejudice is often based on stereotyping, showing how stereotyping can easily become negative. Let's take a seemingly harmless example of stereotyping that can result in prejudice: If you assume that all smaller softball players are weak hitters, then you may take that stereotype a bit further by disliking playing with smaller players because they don't make the game very challenging.

Like stereotyping, prejudice is a judgment based on little or no information or misinformation about a person or subject. In other words, it is based on ignorance or lack of correct information. That is why education is so important—you can avoid prejudging people or situations by learning about them and making decisions based on *knowledge* rather than ignorance. Although we cannot always avoid stereotyping, we can eliminate prejudice and subsequently eradicate discrimination by making the decision to learn about others.

There are a variety of ways we can categorize and classify ourselves and others. Understood as one way of knowing ourselves better, these types of diversity are helpful tools. If they are used to stereotype and then make judgments about people based on these stereotypes, then the categories become means to discrimination.

Sexist Attitudes

The increased number of women in college has changed the culture to be more sensitive and inclusive to women, but stereotypes and prejudice about females still exist. However, sexism is not limited to prejudice against women. Men, too, can suffer from sexist attitudes that are based on stereotypes.

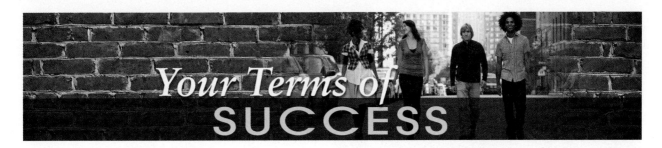

Your Terms of SUCCESS

WHEN YOU SEE . . .	IT MEANS . . .
Administrator	A person who manages staff at a college.
Advisor	A person who works with students to provide guidance and planning for a degree.
Ageism	Discrimination toward a person in a certain age group.
Counselor	A person who advises students on personal, academic, or career matters.
Diversity	A state of difference; variety.
Due process	Formal procedures designed to protect a person's rights.
Faculty	A person or persons who teach.
Homophobia	Irrational fear of homosexuals.
Instructor	A person who teaches.
Mentor	A person who provides advice or guidance.
Peer mentor/peer leader	A person of equal status who provides advice or guidance.
Racism	Hatred of a race; discrimination toward a person of a certain race.
Sexism	Hatred of a gender; discrimination toward a certain gender.
Sexual harassment	Unwanted or offensive sexual advances, usually by a person in a superior position.
Tutor	A person who provides academic support.

Homophobia

Sexual orientation prejudice often takes the form of homophobia, or fear of homosexuals. Homophobia is sometimes born out of ignorance of sexual orientation diversity, and sometimes it comes from a person's own background and values.

Racist Attitudes

Racist attitudes can be obvious or subtle. People can hold racist views, like all other prejudices, and not realize that they are being intolerant of others. Asking people of other races what kinds of racism they experience is one way to understand what they perceive as prejudice. Monitoring your own words, actions, and attitudes is another way to be more sensitive to other races and cultures. You may think you don't mean any harm by what you say or do, but the recipients of your ideas may not always agree.

Ageist Attitudes

As you read earlier in the chapter, different generations have different values and viewpoints. An environment in which people from different generations work closely together can be exciting or tense, depending on how much people are willing to recognize, understand, and appreciate their generational differences. Problems arise, though, when people have prejudicial attitudes about a certain age group. We usually think that ageist attitudes stereotype mainly older people, but younger people can also experience prejudicial views directed at them.

Discrimination

Discrimination occurs when an action is taken on the basis of a prejudice. If, for instance, you decide that you do not want to play softball against teams with smaller players because you believe they are not as fun as teams with bigger players, then you have discriminated against smaller players and their teams. Because of recent laws and lawsuits, colleges and other places of business are sensitive to discrimination issues and spend substantial time and resources educating employees about the subject. It will be an important part of your education to understand how

Integrity MATTERS

The underlying factor of integrity in a relationship is trust. If you can trust others, then you will be better able to learn, grow, expand, and improve yourself. If you do not have trust, then you may shut yourself off from others and experiences that are new to you. Trusting others takes time—it isn't an overnight event. Give people reasons to trust you and then deliver on your promises. Likewise, put your trust in others, giving them an opportunity to prove themselves trustworthy.

A specific part of trust in relationships is reliability or, expressed another way, doing what you say you will do. If your classmate asks you to take notes for him on days he cannot be in class and you fail to do so each time, then you lack reliability. Your classmate will not be able to trust you to help him. If you agree to take notes knowing that you may not be able to do it, then you are not being honest—with him or yourself.

YOUR TURN

How have you demonstrated that you are trustworthy? • What was the effect? • In what areas of your life could you trust others—or even yourself—more? • What can you do to improve trust?

_____

_____

_____

and why people discriminate so that you can be prepared for similar problems stemming from prejudice, which is why this chapter spends a considerable amount of time on this subject.

Sexism, racism, and ageism are the most common types of discrimination in the workplace. Even though most organizations strive hard to eliminate overt discrimination, other types of prejudice can often appear in everyday situations. For example, a coworker may declare that she won't hire anyone from a certain college because she believes that all its graduates are more interested in partying than working. Your boss may state his disdain for people from a certain part of the country and then refuse to promote an employee who is originally from the same area. Although you may not be able to change everyone's mind, you should be attuned to these more subtle, and sometimes acceptable, forms of discrimination and make an effort to eliminate them.

Collaboration
EXERCISE 3.3

Working in a group, choose one of the groups noted previously who often encounter prejudice and discuss how the college or the community can help people appreciate this type of diversity. What events could help the community learn more about fighting hate or more about celebrating diversity? ■

RESOLVING CONFLICT

While you are in college, you may find yourself in a conflict that must be resolved in order for you to be successful and satisfied. The conflict can arise with a family member, a classmate, or even a professor. How you handle the conflict may have long-term consequences that directly tie to your ability to complete a degree. Oftentimes, a minor conflict, such as miscommunication or a misunderstanding, can easily be resolved. Other times, the disagreement may be larger than you can handle with a calm conversation.

Creating Boundaries

Because you will be surrounded by a diverse group of people, it may be difficult for you to create and maintain the traditional boundaries that exist between students and their counselors, professors, administrators, and learning support staff. It almost seems contradictory, but boundaries may be necessary at the same time that you are getting to know others. Why should you refrain from close relationships with professors

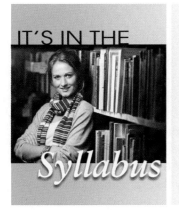

IT'S IN THE
Syllabus

What are your professors' office hours? Where are their offices located? How do they prefer to be contacted when you have a question?

What are the expectations regarding meeting with your professors? Should you only meet with them when you have a problem? What other reasons would you have to meet with them?

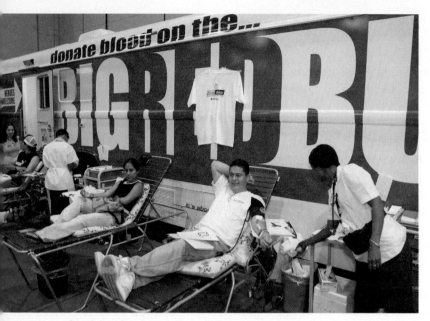

Participating in activities on campus and volunteering for worthy causes are great ways to meet new people.

Jeff Greenberg/PhotoEdit

and advisors when you need them to get to know you if you are to ask for a referral or recommendation?

For one, some colleges discourage intimately personal relationships between professors and students, just as many companies prohibit the same type of overly friendly relationships between supervisors and employees, because such relationships can be problematic. For example, intimate relationships can result in perceived or actual unfair evaluation or treatment. Because a professor is considered a superior, the college views the professor's role as one of authority and power. Many sexual harassment policies and laws are built on the imbalance of power between a person in authority and a subordinate.

Another possible problem is that other students may see the relationship as favoritism and feel as though they are being treated unfairly. Additionally, sexual relationships between students and college personnel are sometimes strictly prohibited at colleges. If you have not already done so, check your student handbook regarding your college's policy about relationships between students and faculty. Ultimately, you will need to make the decision that is best for you and your situation as to how friendly you should be with faculty or other college officials.

If you get along well with your professor and genuinely enjoy her company, then your best move is to respect the professor–student relationship while you are in class. You can do this by meeting your professor during her office hours on campus and keeping conversations focused on your progress in your classes and your career plans. You can then continue the friendship after you have finished the semester and have no intentions of taking another class with that professor again. Some friendships between professors and students are long-lasting, so consider cultivating them once the class is over.

When a Problem Arises

A time may arise when you have a problem in one of your classes. If it does, you can be assured that the college's employees will work with you to resolve it. There are, however, rules and procedures regarding how to resolve a problem at a college. Knowing and following these procedures will ensure that any problem is handled appropriately and quickly.

The first step to resolving a conflict in class is to define the problem. Is it a communication problem? Is it a problem with the course material? Is it a problem with the course standards? Once you have defined the problem, your next step is to discuss the problem with the person involved directly. If the problem is with your instructor, make an appointment during her office hours to discuss the issue. If you are emotional—angry, upset, nervous—wait until you have calmed down to meet. Your goal in talking with the instructor is to resolve the conflict.

For the process of conflict resolution to work, you will need to complete the first two steps. Starting at the

Reflection
EXERCISE 3.4

From what you have learned about diversity, how can you make changes in your interactions with others that will show that you value and appreciate diverse peoples and situations? ■

top will only delay resolution. If you are not satisfied with the result or if you feel the problem has gotten worse, not better, move to the next step: talking to the department chair or dean. You will no doubt be asked if you have met with the instructor. Again, your goal at this step is to resolve the issue. Occasionally, the instructor may be called in to help reach a resolution. Staying calm and focused on resolving the conflict will be to your advantage. In the event that the problem is not solved at this level, your last stop is with the dean of students or vice president for instruction.

Tips for Lasting Relationships

As discussed at the beginning of the chapter, college students often have a harder time cultivating friendships because of their busy schedules and because they do not typically spend four years with the same group of people. What else can you do to forge relationships in college?

Leave time in your schedule to talk with friends or meet with instructors. If you must leave directly after class to get to work, you will not be as successful in cultivating important relationships. One way to ensure that you connect with your professors is to make an appointment with them during the semester to ask questions or get feedback on your progress. Your ulterior motive is to cultivate a relationship with them. Also, be sure to approach conflict as an opportunity to learn more about yourself, and always act with integrity. Lasting relationships are built on trust and doing what is right.

PLUS EXERCISE 3.5

(Personality + Learning Style = Understanding Situations)

Consider Michael's dilemma with his classmates. Although he is outspoken in class, confronting another person one on one is not his strength and because he is not sure if his study group is shutting him out intentionally, he doesn't want to make the situation worse. Also consider how as a visual learner what he sees or visualizes has a greater effect on him. Using what you have learned from this chapter, what advice would you give him for approaching the situation? How can he combat the stereotypes that some in his group seem to have or that he has about others?

Now, considering your own learning style, personality type, and special circumstances, what would you do to resolve a conflict with your classmates about working together on a required group project? How would you deal with any stereotyping, prejudging, or discrimination in the group? ▮

From College to University

THE RELATIONSHIPS YOU FOSTER NOW WILL OPEN DOORS AFTER TRANSFER

Your relationships with advisors, counselors, and professors should yield more contacts at your new school. Advisors and counselors will be able to recommend certain programs and administrators. Professors will be able to put in a good word with the people they know at your transfer school, which may mean extra consideration for admission into a program or for a scholarship.

Those same relationships may also prove fruitful if your advisors, counselors, or professors have inside knowledge of little-known internships and aid, or if they know about deadline extensions and special transfer scholarships. The closer your relationships, the better able you will be to use your connections to make a smooth transfer.

Advisors, counselors, and professors can also provide advice about the particular challenges you may face once you have completed the move.

Building Your University Portfolio 3

Contact a professor you have this semester and ask what she needs to know about a student before she writes a letter of recommendation. Write the information you learn below or in your portfolio.

_____

_____

_____

_____

_____

_____

_____

From College to Career

DEALING WITH DIVERSITY IS A KEY TO SUCCESS ON THE JOB

We sometimes think that once we reach our ultimate educational goal and have started our dream career, we will be magically transported to a world in which everyone gets along. Unfortunately, we are brought back down from the clouds as early as the first day on the job.

Certainly, you will never stop needing to make positive connections with others or to redefine the relationships you already have. You will also encounter diversity on a daily basis and will have to rely on what you have learned in college (and life in general) in order to consider others' feelings, beliefs, and attitudes. What you have learned in college about other cultures, time periods, and philosophical and political ideas should provide you with well-rounded views that will make it easier to work with and appreciate your diverse coworkers.

Building Your Career Portfolio 3

Contact someone in a career that is similar to what you want to do. Ask about the kinds of diversity he or she encounters as part of the job. What advice about appreciating diversity would this person give others who want to enter the same field? Record the person's answers below or in your portfolio.

_____
_____
_____
_____
_____
_____
_____

First Voices

STORIES OF SUCCESS FROM COLLEGE GRADUATES

From small town to big results: College graduate finds himself and so much more in college

Jason Henry,
M.A., Student
Services Specialist

Even though I am a first-generation college graduate, I never had to think much about whether or not I would go to college—I just always knew I was going! I was raised in a small town located in the Bible Belt of the South. I had a loving and well-intentioned family but they never quite "got" me. I realized I was gay when I was very young and I knew that my only ticket out of my hometown was college. I intentionally chose a school as far from home as possible but still in-state for tuition purposes.

While in college I discovered I could be myself, be free. It was something I had never experienced before. I took classes that challenged the ways in which I perceived the world such as sociology, speech communication, philosophy, and sexual identity, among many more. I was involved in every student organization I could find. I quickly became president of the Student Activities Board and top student senator in the Student Government Association, as well as a member of the debate team. These organizations taught me leadership skills, the importance of critical thinking, and networking with others. Soon, the dean of students encouraged me to consider graduate school and a master's degree in student development where I could help other students just like me succeed in college. When I graduated with my bachelor's degree I was bestowed with one of the university's highest awards given to student leaders.

Since earning my master's degree I have gone on to work in community colleges. I coordinate new student orientation, serve as an academic advisor, and teach college success classes. I have received numerous awards for excellence and dedication to student success. Going to college was the very best thing I ever did. I owe all my success to taking classes that challenged the ways I viewed the world, participating in student organizations, and getting to know my campus leaders.

PATH OF DISCOVERY
Journal Entry

Reflect on how the information about diversity and relationships in this chapter has made you think about how you have treated others in the past. What mistakes have you made? What have you done well in terms of treating others with respect? What will you do in the future?

CHAPTER REVIEW QUESTIONS

1. Name and explain four different categories of diversity.
2. How will you use what you have learned in this chapter to start and improve relationships with people on campus? Whom will you seek out and why?
3. What strategies can you use to deal with difficult people?
4. Whom on your campus will you need to get to know to be successful?

CHAPTER 3 CASE SCENARIOS

1. Jonathan has been raised in a very religious household. He believes that homosexuality is wrong, and he is struggling with an assignment in one of his classes in which he must write about the issue from a sociological perspective. The professor cautioned the students that they must be objective in their papers, but Jonathan doesn't think he can. What should Jonathan do?
2. Marie has been married for 14 years. She and her husband have twin girls who are 12. Since Marie started college, she has noticed that her husband seems less interested in her and what she is learning in her classes. He has started belittling her desire to earn a degree. Although he first encouraged her to enroll at the nearby community college branch in their town, he now seems to be against her continuing there. Marie has been discouraged by his reaction and is thinking about not enrolling next semester. What would you tell Marie to do?
3. One of Willis's professors has missed three night classes in a row without telling the students beforehand and without providing a plan to make up the missed material. Willis really needs this class for his major in business, and he is worried that he won't be successful in subsequent classes. He is also worried that if he complains to the instructor, his grade will be lowered in retaliation. Because he may have to take the professor again later, what should he do?

RESEARCH IT FURTHER

1. Review the section on teaching styles and determine what styles might be missing. Interview classmates in different courses to get ideas for other teaching styles. Write your own descriptions of the new styles and provide tips for being successful in those classes.
2. What does your college do to promote cultural appreciation on the campus? Collect examples of the college's promotion of multiculturalism and determine what, if anything, the college could do to enhance racial, ethnic, and cultural sensitivity and understanding.
3. What is your college's policy regarding relationships between students and faculty? In addition to reviewing your student handbook, interview students, faculty, and administrators about their opinions on faculty–student relationships.

References and Recommended Readings

Department of Education. (2010). Retreived December 16, 2010, from http://nces.ed.gov/fastfacts/display.asp?id=98.

Katz, N. (2005). Sexual harassment statistics in the workplace and in education. Retrieved July 5, 2005, from http://womenissues.about.com/cs/sexdiscrimination/a/sexharassstats.htm.

Kuh, G., Kinzie, J., Schuh, J. H., Whitt, E. J., et al. (2005). *Student success in college: Creating conditions that matter.* San Francisco: Jossey-Bass.

Zemke, R., Raines, C., & Filipczak, B. (2000). *Generations at work: Managing the clash of veterans, boomers, xers, and nexters in your workplace.* New York: Amacom.

TIME and ENERGY

4

Pouring her fourth cup of coffee at 11:00 P.M. Laura searches for the history paper assignment that she copied from the board. It's due at 9 A.M. tomorrow. She sinks into her chair at the kitchen table to go through her backpack one more time and debates whether to call a classmate for help. As she begins to tremble from the caffeine, her mind races. Is it too late to call? Will he know how to help her? Laura doesn't normally procrastinate about her schoolwork, but her middle child has been sick for two days and she's been home caring for him and taking him to doctor's appointments. Because of her dyslexia, Laura has taken good notes during class. Her study routine includes recording each lecture, listening to each one repeatedly, and then writing and rewriting what she hears. For information that her professor emphasizes as important, she rewrites her notes in red. Although she still can't find the assignment with the specific requirements, she does have her lecture notes to work with to begin the paper.

At midnight, she is still working. Despite another cup of coffee, she is tired and her eyes begin to water. She listens to the recorded lecture in which her professor introduces the assignment.

Three hours, two more cups of coffee, a bag of spicy corn nuts, a 68-ounce fruit-flavored sports drink, and one rerun of "Judge Judy" later, Laura's paper is finished. As she prints her final copy, the printer begins to screech loudly and stops with her last page clutched in its mouth. The ink light blinks at her like her mother's pointing finger, saying, "You shouldn't have waited to the last minute, Laura Leigh. This is what happens when you procrastinate."

Frantic, she rips the page from the printer and shakes the ink cartridge in hopes of getting the last page printed before she hits the bed. When she presses print, the first three words barely appear on the page before the ink completely disappears. The only thing she can do is to save her paper to a thumb drive and hope that tomorrow provides her with a solution.

Exhausted, she shuffles to bed. She sets her alarm an hour earlier so that she can call her mother to come over and watch her son. Before her head reaches the pillow, she remembers a flyer she found for the campus computer lab, which opens at 7 A.M. This may be the solution she was hoping for if she can get to the campus early.

After several hours of deep sleep, Laura has a renewed determination to get the assignment finished and submitted. Because she gets to campus early, she is able to print off the remaining page in the computer lab—thanks to some help from the lab assistant. As she slides into her seat in her history class, she pulls her completed paper out, looks it over one more time, and turns it in. It may not be her best work, she thinks, but it is finished.

"I will return your papers next week," says her professor. He turns to write on the board and says, "In the meantime, you may want to get started on your next paper assignment on Greek culture."

Laura reaches into her backpack, replaces her pen with a red marker, and writes "IMPORTANT" at the top of the page as she copies the assignment from the board.

In this CHAPTER

Laura feels the effects of "life getting in the way" as she manages her time and keeps her energy up. Would you have done the same as Laura? Is there anything you would have done differently, either during the episode or before it happened? To help you answer these questions, this chapter focuses on different time management options that can help you stay on task and handle tough situations throughout your college career. It also spends time explaining how maintaining your energy is part of your time management strategy. Your goal in reading this chapter will be to find the most appropriate method for you to keep time and energy in balance with one another.

More specifically, after completing this chapter, you will be able to do the following:

- **List college-related activities that will need to be considered when you create a time management plan.**
- **Describe different time management strategies that you can use to build your time management plan.**
- **Explain the interconnection between time management and energy management.**
- **Identify reasons for procrastination and create a plan for eliminating it.**

IS TIME on YOUR SIDE?

Is it surprising that the number one biggest challenge reported by college students is time management? Why do so many students identify time management as an area they need more help with? One answer may be that many of them are adding another responsibility to their busy lives. Another answer could be that they are now expected to do things they haven't done before or haven't done for a long time. Being a student demands more than just showing up for class. There is plenty of work to do outside of class—at home, in the library, on the computer, and in study groups. Being aware of how you will need to spend your time versus how you actually spend it and choosing the most personally effective strategies will not only help you complete more tasks in a *timely manner* but will also help you minimize the stress that comes from trying to juggle many responsibilities.

The benefits of managing time effectively include not only getting tasks completed, but also experiencing the success of accomplishment. Darwin B. Nelson and Gary R. Low (2003), in their book *Emotional Intelligence: Achieving Academic and Career*

Excellence, state that "[a]n important by-product of good Time Management is a feeling of self-control—we are managing our responsibilities, not being managed by them" (pp. 100–101). In other words, managing your time effectively will help empower you to take control of your life and what happens in it. You will certainly feel more in control of your time after you complete this chapter!

Getting Organized

The first aspect to consider when it comes to managing time and stress is getting organized. Seems like a simple idea, but think about how much time you have wasted before when you couldn't find something or how you missed an important event because you didn't write it down. Nothing is more stressful than knowing you could have done better if you had been organized! Getting organized for success, however, doesn't have to take a lot of money and time. If you use a few simple strategies, you can save yourself both time and energy in the long run. To help get organized, think of the three S's (supplies, space, and same time): getting the right *supplies* (including a calendar), keeping your *space* clean and organized, and checking your "to do list" or calendar at the *same time* each day.

Supplies for Success

Pens, pencils, calculators, paper, notebooks, and thumb drives, oh my! In addition to books, lab manuals, and computer supplies, there are many other items you will need in college to get organized and complete assignments. What you *need* will depend on what you are taking and your instructors' expectations. What you *want* to get in addition will depend on your preferences and budget. At the very least, a good, sturdy backpack that can accommodate all your books and notebooks—and that doesn't break your back—should be high on your supply list.

Many a good student has fallen victim to "assignment amnesia." This occurs when otherwise smart students believe they can remember all of their assignments and appointments without writing them down or consulting their syllabi and course outlines. Fortunately, there are measures you can take to prevent an attack of assignment amnesia, such as using a calendar or device like a cell phone that keeps track of your assignments and to which you can also add all the other tasks you need to complete from your personal, professional, and college life.

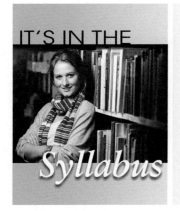

IT'S IN THE
Syllabus

What are the supply requirements listed in your syllabus for each class (e.g., textbook, notebook, graphing calculator)?

What are the supply requirements that are needed but not listed in your syllabus for each class (e.g., printer ink, copy paper, thumb drive)?

For a paper calendar, you have many different types from which to choose. Once you determine the type that works best for you—a monthly, weekly, or daily calendar—make a habit of writing down your tasks, no matter how big or small. Here is an example of a typical list of a day's activities for a student like Laura:

Thursday
- Make appointment to have oil changed
- Pick up medicine for Terry
- Take Phillip to baseball
- Study for history quiz on Friday
- Read 30 pages for English
- Get book from library

A typical monthly calendar, such as in Figure 4.1, allows you to see several weeks at once so that you can remain aware of upcoming events, but often there is little space on a monthly calendar to write down detailed information such as the daily activity list just shown.

A weekly calendar allows you to see an entire week at a glance, as in Figure 4.2. A weekly calendar provides room to write out details of each activity; however, it is often difficult to anticipate what you must do the next week.

Daily calendars like Figure 4.3 usually provide the most space to write your day-to-day tasks and appointments. However, this kind of calendar may be the most difficult to work with if you need to plan ahead. Because you have no visual cue for the rest of the week or month, you may overlook important events or be surprised by them. A daily calendar works best if you are extremely organized and can plan ahead effectively; alternately, use it in addition to a monthly calendar.

FIGURE 4.1 Monthly Calendar

Sunday	Monday	Tuesday	Wednesday	Thursday	Friday	Saturday
					1	2
3	4	5	6	7	8	9 picnic—noon
10	11 work late	12	13	14	15 pay bills	16
17	18	19	20	21 play rehearsal 7:00	22	23
24	25 nutrition exam	26	27	28	29	30 birthday party

FIGURE 4.2 Weekly Calendar

Monday	Tuesday	Wednesday	Thursday	Friday	Saturday	Sunday
8:30 Work 2:00 Geology 3:00 Trig. 5:00 Pick up dinner 7:00 Study for Accounting	9:00 English 11:00 Acct. 6:00 Help sister with painting	8:30 Work 2:00 Geology 3:00 Trig.	9:00 English 11:00 Acct.	8:30 Work 2:00 Geology 3:00 Trig. 7:00 Movie with friend	8–10 Clean house 3–4 Exercise 6–11 Study	3–8 Work on paper

Space Considerations

The right stuff and the ideal calendar are just the first steps to managing your time well; there is more you must consider. To manage your time most effectively and efficiently, create a clutter-free space where you can study and complete assignments. If you don't have a place in your house or apartment that you can call your own,

FIGURE 4.3 Daily Calendar

Monday March 12, 2012	
7:00	Wake up, shower, get ready for school
8:00	Drive to school, arrive early and study in the library
9:00	College Algebra
10:00	English 2
11:00	Study for Biology exam
12:00	Eat lunch and review notes for College Algebra
1:00	Biology—EXAM!!
2:00	Drive to work
3:00	Work
4:00	
5:00	

a comfortable chair or seat at the kitchen table may be all that you can spare. Make sure it is comfortable and quiet and has adequate space for books, notebooks, and other supplies. It has to be a place where you *want* to be or it will be difficult to go there to stay on task.

Same Time, Same Place

A good system for writing down your daily tasks and establishing a place to complete your assignments are a good foundation to managing your time well and reducing the negative effects of stress. However, there is one last tip: Create a routine. In other words, every evening write down your goals for the next day and every morning review what you need to do for the day. Knowing what to expect for the day will make surprises less likely. As you complete each task, scratch it off the list. You will get the satisfaction of a completed job and can focus on the next task.

IT'S TIME for COLLEGE

As you have already discovered, going to college is about learning new ways of doing things and adjusting to different expectations and experiences. It is worth knowing, too, that your college is a time-conscious place. The classes are set on semesters or terms; classes meet at specific times and days during the week; there are certain dates that you can enroll in classes and talk to the people who work there; and there are other special dates such as financial aid deadlines and tuition payment due dates that help keep your college running smoothly. Without the college's effective time management strategies, you would not be able to get the classes you need and the degree you want!

It is important, then, to be aware of how the college manages its own time, and the best place to start is the academic calendar. You will be able to find this on your college's website or in the college catalog. The academic calendar will provide many important dates including, but not limited to, the following:

- Deadlines for registering and filing financial aid forms
- Date for the beginning of classes (or instruction)
- Drop/add dates for changing your schedule
- Due dates for tuition payment
- Withdrawal dates for leaving college before the semester is over
- Registration dates for the next semester
- Holidays or breaks within the semester and between semesters
- Last day of classes (or instruction) and finals week

As with other activities throughout the semester, being aware of the dates on the academic calendar will help you have a smooth semester and guide you to prepare for the next one.

In addition to the academic calendar, there are other out-of-class activities that you will need to be aware of as you plan your time during the semester. Your instructors will have office hours, or days and times they will be available in their offices, that are listed in the syllabus. These hours are for you to make an appointment to see your

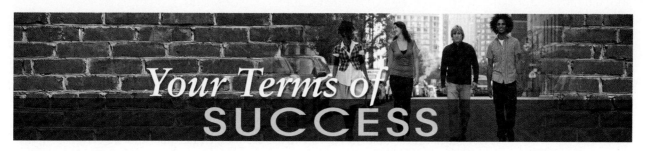

Your Terms of
SUCCESS

WHEN YOU SEE . . .	IT MEANS . . .
Academic calendar	The college's calendar that provides important dates throughout the semester. May include due dates for tuition payments and dropping classes.
Add/drop dates	The dates on your academic calendar when you can add or drop a class from your schedule. Usually occurs within the first week of classes.
Class schedule	Your schedule of classes for the semester.
Course calendar/course outline	Your instructor's calendar that provides important dates throughout the semester; may include due dates for projects and tests.
Daily calendar	A calendar that shows one day at a time.
Due date	The day that an assignment must be completed and turned in.
Energy zapper	An activity or person that lowers your energy levels.
Finals week	The week scheduled in the academic calendar in which final exams will be held. Your class meeting time may change during this week.
Last day of instruction	The date on the academic calendar that shows when the last day of the regular class meetings will occur. Usually comes before finals week.
Monthly calendar	A calendar that shows one month at a time.
Office hours	The hours your instructor is in her office and available to meet with students. Your instructor's office hours can be found in the syllabus.
Procrastination	The act of delaying an activity.
Reenergizer	An activity or person that increases your energy levels.
Student study day	A date on the academic calendar in which no classes or final exams are held. It is intended for students to have a day of studying before the week of finals begins.
Time management	A strategy for controlling how you use your time.
Weekly calendar	A calendar that shows one week at a time.
Withdrawal date	The date on the academic calendar showing the final day that you can withdraw from all of your classes. When you withdraw from classes, a "W" will be added to your transcript next to the classes from which you withdrew.

instructor if you need help on an assignment, want to get to know her better, or would like to talk about your progress in the class. You will also want to be aware of the hours of such services as the library, tutoring center, and computer labs. Last but not least, most colleges have student life activities that provide entertainment or additional educational opportunities, and they also offer career and community activities that give you the opportunity to connect and network with others. The business hours of different services on campus as well as the dates for special events may be found on your college website, in the college catalog, in the student newspaper, or on bulletin boards around campus.

Making Time for Classes

How much time should you devote to classes? Some first-time students seriously underestimate the amount of time needed to prepare for a class, study for tests, and complete assignments. Unfortunately, they often realize their error only when an assignment is due or a test is given. A common formula for calculating the amount of study time is to multiply the number of credit hours for the course by three. For example, a demanding class that carries three credit hours and meets three times per week for 1 hour each time will require 9 hours per week of out-of-class work. These 9 hours plus the 3 hours in class means you will spend a total of 12 hours studying and attending that one class each week. Multiply 12 hours by four classes and you will have a 48-hour college work week. Add 40 hours of work on the job and you will be spending 88 hours per week working on your job and your classes!

Other classes may take a little less time, and you may be able to spend only 2 hours for every 1 hour you are in class, which would mean that you will spend 6 hours plus the 3 hours you are in class for a total of 9 hours each week. Either way, you will be spending anywhere from 36 to 40 hours a week if you are taking 12 credit hours a semester. This, of course, is assuming you are taking a 16-week course. For shorter terms, such as 4 weeks, you will be spending much more time in and out of class.

Looking at Table 4.1 can be overwhelming for students, especially if they work more than 25 hours and take more than 12 credit hours per semester. A full-time student who also works full time can expect to spend half the hours in every week working on classes or her job (and that doesn't include time to sleep)! Studies have shown that the reality of how much time students spend outside of class is much lower than the recommended number of hours, but students often find that how much time they spend varies from semester to semester, depending on what kinds of classes they take.

TABLE **4.1** Student's College and Work Schedule

Responsibility	Contact Hours per Week	Outside Hours per Week	Total Hours per Week
College Algebra	3	6–9	9–12
Composition 101	3	6–9	9–12
US History	3	6–9	9–12
Reading	3	6–9	9–12
Work	25		25
			TOTAL: 61–73

FIGURE 4.4 Laura's Monthly Calendar

Sunday	Monday	Tuesday	Wednesday	Thursday	Friday	Saturday
7:00–10:00 Study	6:30–7:30 Get ready for school	6:30–7:30 Get ready for school	6:30–7:30 Get ready for school	6:30–7:30 Get ready for school	6:30–7:30 Get ready for school	7:00–10:00 Clean house, shop
10:00–11:00 Go to church	7:30–7:45 Travel to work	7:30–7:45 Travel to work	7:30–7:45 Travel to work	7:30–7:45 Travel to work	7:30–7:45 Travel to work	10:00–11:30 Soccer
11:15–12:30 Lunch with parents	8:00–12:30 Work	8:00–12:30 Work	8:00–12:30 Work	8:00–12:30 Work	8:00–12:30 Work	11:30–12:15 Lunch with team
12:45–3:45 Study	12:30–1:15 Eat lunch and run errands	12:30–1:15 Go to doctor's appointment	12:30–1:15 Eat lunch with friend	12:30–1:15 Eat lunch and walk 1 mile	12:30–1:15 Eat lunch and study	12:15–2:00 Run errands
3:45–5:45 Do yard work	1:15–4:45 Work	1:15–4:45 Work	1:15–4:45 Work	1:15–4:45 Work	1:15–4:45 Work	2:00–6:00 Go to library and do research
6:00–7:00 Eat dinner	4:45–5:00 Travel	4:45–5:00 Travel	4:45–5:00 Travel	4:45–5:00 Travel	4:45–5:00 Travel	6:00–7:00 Fix and eat dinner
7:00–8:00 Walk 3 miles	5:00–5:45 Eat dinner and study	5:00–5:45 Eat dinner and study	5:00–5:45 Eat dinner and study	5:00–5:45 Eat dinner and study	5:00–7:00 Eat dinner with friends	7:00–9:00 Study
8:00–10:00 Do laundry, get ready for next week	6:00–9:30 Classes	6:00–9:30 Classes	6:00–9:30 Classes	6:00–9:30 Classes	7:00–9:30 See movie	9:00–10:00 Answer email and watch TV
10:00 Go to bed	10:00 Go to bed	10:00 Go to bed	10:00 Go to bed	10:00 Go to bed	10:00 Go to bed	10:00 Go to bed

To see how the recommended study hours look when they are scheduled throughout the week, check out Laura's calendar in Figure 4.4. She works a full-time job 40 hours a week and is in class 12 hours each week.

Given Laura's schedule shown in Figure 4.4, will she be able to find the 48 hours she needs to attend and study for college classes? If she were to add 2 hours a night after class—assuming that she felt like studying after a long day—she would study an additional 10 hours during the work week, leaving 22 hours and 15 minutes of studying to be completed in her "spare time."

Look at the calendar again. In order to reach 48 hours of studying and class, where will Laura include additional study time? Will she need to study every waking moment that she is not at work, in class, or taking care of herself and her other responsibilities? If she cannot devote that much time to her college classes, would Laura need to take fewer classes, ask for help with home responsibilities, or cut back on her hours at work?

FIGURE 4.5 One-Hour-a-Day Time Management Plan

Day of the Week	Time	Assignment	Completed	
Sunday	3:30–4:30 P.M.	Read Chapter 5 and take notes while reading. Review notes after reading the chapter once.	Yes	No
Monday	7:00–8:00 P.M.	Review reading notes as well as class notes. Define all vocabulary terms that are key to the chapter and that are unfamiliar.	Yes	No
Tuesday	11:15–12:15 P.M.	Answer study questions that accompany the chapter	Yes	No
Wednesday	8:00–9:00 P.M.	Create sample test questions on flash cards and write the answers on the back.	Yes	No
Thursday	7:00–8:00 P.M.	Complete homework questions for the chapter.	Yes	No
Friday	5:30–6:00 A.M. 3:30–4:00 P.M.	Review flash cards.	Yes	No
Saturday	3:30–4:30 P.M.	Rewrite notes from the entire week of class. Include any material that was assigned in the reading but not covered in class.	Yes	No

Despite what some may think, Laura doesn't have to give up her dream to be in college, but she will need to rearrange her schedule. Without doing so, she will not be able to meet the demands of her classes. However, she can feel some comfort in knowing that getting up a little earlier, multitasking, and using her weekends for studying at longer intervals can be short-term changes to her schedule.

But What Do I Do?

The question sometimes arises as to what you should be doing for those 6 to 9 hours for each class every week. First, you will need to read any assigned material *before* class. Another activity that will need to be part of your outside study time is reviewing your notes from class and, by working with a classmate, filling in any information gaps that you were not able to get. Rewriting your notes after the discussion of the chapter or topic is another very important way you can spend an hour for the week. Of course, you will need to budget time to complete assignments, such as review questions at the end of a chapter or a research project.

The plan in Figure 4.5 is for *one* college class. If you have more than one, you will need to add an hour each day of the week for each three-credit-hour class that you are taking.

Even with the best intentions, many students, however, opt to cut back on studying because other activities, such as running errands and participating in their children's activities, are necessary parts of their lives and cannot be eliminated or rearranged. Realistically, you may be able to cut back on studying in some classes at slower times; however, you should not eliminate study

Think **ABOUT IT**

" The great dividing line between success and failure can be expressed in five words: "I did not have time."

—Franklin Field "

hours for all classes throughout each semester. Your best bet is to recognize that taking college classes is a tremendous time commitment and to work your other responsibilities (except maintaining your health) around them as best you can. You won't always be able to put college as your first priority, but you will need to make a conscious effort to put studying near the top of your list most of the time.

Analyzing Your Time

Recognizing that we all have the same number of hours, analyzing your time is another step to effective time management. Tim Hindle (1998), in his book *Manage Your Time*, suggests keeping a time log of your day that is divided into 30-minute increments (p. 9). Separate from your calendar, the purpose of a 30-minute time log is to help raise your awareness of what you are doing throughout the day. You can make your own time log like the one in Figure 4.6 to keep up with one day's worth of activities, but be sure to give yourself time to write down your activities either every few hours or at the end of the day. Keeping an eye on how you spend your time will help you make realistic time management goals and will keep you from wasting too much time or miscalculating how long it takes you to complete tasks.

Asking "Where did the time go?" and "What do I do with my time?" is a start to analyzing your time. You will also need to analyze your time management skills—or how well you use your time wisely to meet your goals and stay healthy in the process, such as with the assessment in Figure 4.7 that asks 10 questions about your time management abilities.

FIGURE 4.6 Time Log Example

Time	Wednesday's Activities
7:00 A.M.	Get ready for classes; eat breakfast
7:30 A.M.	Review notes for business class
8:00 A.M.	En route to school
8:30 A.M.	Business Communications
9:00 A.M.	Class, continued
9:30 A.M.	Class, continued
10:00 A.M.	See advisor to plan next semester's classes

Scheduling time to relax and recharge is just as important as scheduling your class work.

Thinkstock

FIGURE 4.7   Personal Time Assessment

Circle the number (1–Never, 2–Sometimes, 3–Usually, 4–Always) that best describes your experience.

Statement	Never	Sometimes	Usually	Always
1. I arrive to class prepared.	1	2	3	4
2. I review my notes within 24 hours of class.	1	2	3	4
3. I spend my time on campus taking care of personal business, talking with professors, studying, or doing research.	1	2	3	4
4. I have study goals, and I achieve them each week.	1	2	3	4
5. I feel prepared for tests.	1	2	3	4
6. I spend enough time on writing assignments.	1	2	3	4
7. I get enough sleep each night.	1	2	3	4
8. I spend some time each week doing something I enjoy.	1	2	3	4
9. I have enough time to take care of most of my personal needs.	1	2	3	4
10. I get support from others to help me meet my educational goals.	1	2	3	4
Score each column.	_____	_____	_____	_____
Total:		_____		

Score Range	Meaning
40–32	You do a good job of managing your time. For the most part, you are satisfied with how you manage your time and what you accomplish each week.
31–26	You are doing a good job managing your time for most activities. Identify your weaker areas and create a plan to improve time management in those areas.
25–19	You may be dissatisfied with your time management and find only a few goals are met each week. Review what you are doing right with some of your time and make a plan that will draw on your time management strengths.
18 or less	You may feel as though you are not meeting the majority of your goals during the week. An honest look at your goals, your necessary activities, and your priorities is needed.

Back-Dating Time Management Plan

If there is one piece of advice that experienced students want to pass along to new students to help them manage their time better, it is that even though they sound the same when spoken aloud, the words *due* and *do* don't mean the same thing. Starting the night before a project is due may create more stress than is necessary. Therefore, the method

FIGURE 4.8 Back-Dating Time Management

Sunday	Monday	Tuesday	Wednesday	Thursday	Friday	Saturday
		1	2	3	4	5
6	7	8 1:00 P.M. Receive paper assignment	9 6–7:30 P.M. Choose paper topic; brainstorm or freewrite on topic	10	11 9–10:30 P.M. Reread brainstorming list; create a draft outline	12
13 3–5:00 P.M. Write first draft of paper	14	15 11–12:00 noon Visit writing lab for assistance with paper	16	17	18 8:30–10:30 P.M. Write second draft of paper, incorporating tutor's advice	19
20 3–4:30 P.M. Write final draft of paper	21	22	23 8–9:00 P.M. Edit and finalize paper; print out on quality paper; place in backpack	24 2:00 P.M. Turn in paper	25	26
27	28	29	30			

of creating "do" dates before your assignment is "due," or back-dating assignments, is essential if you are going to create habits of completing work successfully. For example, let's say you have a career exploration paper due on the 24th of this month (see Figure 4.8). In order to build enough time into your schedule, you can use a calendar to divide the possible steps to completing your paper and fill in the calendar according to the time you have to work on the paper. When back-dating assignment tasks, remember to provide adequate time between tasks so that you can reflect on the work that you have done and approach the assignment with "fresh eyes" each time.

Critical Thinking
EXERCISE 4.2

What do you see as your greatest time management strengths? What are your time management weaknesses? What will you do to build on your strengths while also addressing your weaknesses? ■

Just as important as managing your time is managing your energy. Think about this scenario: You have all weekend off from work and your spouse has taken the kids to visit the grandparents. Therefore, you have 48 hours of complete solitude to write a research paper that is due on Monday. Sounds ideal, doesn't it? But what if you have the flu for those two days? Does the time mean anything when you don't have the energy to do any work? What if, instead of having the flu, you pulled two double shifts and haven't slept more than 5 hours in two days? Will you be able to use your free 48 hours productively or will you need to take care of yourself?

Time, in other words, is only valuable if you have the energy to use it well. Thus, you need to be aware of how you feel, how energetic you are, and how willing you are to use your time wisely. To determine when during the day you feel the most energetic, place an X in the appropriate column for each time of day in Figure 4.9. If you work nights and sleep during most of the day, create your own box with the times you are awake.

In addition to the time of day, your energy levels rise and fall during the week. Do you find yourself tired on Monday mornings, but full of energy on Fridays? Or do you feel worn out by Thursday evenings, but rejuvenated on Sundays? Depending on your work, school, and personal schedules, you will find that you have regular bursts of energy at certain times of the week. To determine which days of the week you feel most energetic, write an X in the appropriate columns in Figure 4.10.

Identifying Time and Energy Zappers

Despite your best efforts in managing your time and energy, there will be times when you find your best laid plans are interrupted by needy people and last-minute changes in plans. A few distractions during the day can be a nice break from the mundane tasks

FIGURE 4.9 Time of Day Energy Levels

Time of Day	High Energy	Neutral	Low Energy
6:00 A.M.			
8:00 A.M.			
10:00 A.M.			
12 noon			
2:00 P.M.			
4:00 P.M.			
6:00 P.M.			
8:00 P.M.			
10:00 P.M.			
12 midnight			

FIGURE 4.10 Day of Week Energy Levels

Day	High Energy	Neutral	Low Energy
Sunday			
Monday			
Tuesday			
Wednesday			
Thursday			
Friday			
Saturday			

of going to school and working or caring for a family. However, if they take so much time away from your studies that you can't seem to keep up with the pace of your classes or they stress you out, you will need to find ways to eliminate or at least lessen the frequency of intrusions like the following:

- People who want your attention and time but who don't really need it
- Interruptions such as unnecessary phone calls
- Fatigue and illness
- Personal problems
- Mindless television watching
- Internet surfing that serves no purpose
- Continuous "chatting" online
- Playing video or computer games
- Inability to say no
- Procrastination
- Poor organization
- Inability to concentrate because of learning difficulty, medication, or stress

Now is the time to block out the zappers. You won't be able to afford the time that they waste, and you will need to be proactive in getting rid of them. Some will be easy to reduce or get rid of, such as playing video games or hanging out all day with friends; others will be more difficult, such as learning to say no to people or eliminating procrastination. The key to getting rid of energy and time wasters is to take on the easiest ones and work on the others through goal setting. Of course, one person's time waster is another person's stress reliever. If you find that playing a video game or going to a movie with friends is necessary to refresh yourself before tackling other important tasks, schedule it as part of your weekly routine. When those activities keep you from finishing others, it may be time to reassess how often you do them.

One way to help manage your energy is by becoming aware of activities that relax you when you are stressed or that allow you to refill your energy reserves. In Figure 4.11, place an X in the appropriate column next to each activity—or in both columns if warranted, or neither. Use this chart when planning your time, scheduling activities that rejuvenate you or help you recharge when you need more energy. If an activity helps you wind down, you may want to schedule it after you have completed major tasks.

FIGURE 4.11 Time and Energy Relaxers and Reenergizers

Activity	Relaxer	Reenergizer
Watching television		
Spending time with family or friends		
Pleasure reading		
Doing housework		
Exercising (light to moderate)		
Gardening		
Talking on the phone		
Writing		
Cooking		
Shopping		
Napping		
Participating in a hobby		
Surfing the Internet		
Organizing closets, drawers, files		
Enjoying a nice meal		

Integrity MATTERS

Sometimes doing what is easiest, even if it not the right thing to do, seems like the best way to manage time effectively. For example, a student who does not have enough time to finish a paper may be tempted to download one from the Internet, use someone else's previous work, or ask someone else to write it. Such an action certainly allows the student to turn in a paper on time, but it is not the way to act with integrity. In fact, such a short cut actually *shortchanges* the educational process. A student who "saves time" by not doing her own work for a class risks more than not learning from the assignment; she may find herself in serious academic jeopardy when the professor confronts her with the evidence that she did not do her own work.

YOUR TURN

In what ways have you saved time by not doing something or not doing it right? • How did you feel about not completing the task or by not completing it to the best of your ability? • What have you learned about acting with integrity and managing your time?

_____

_____

_____

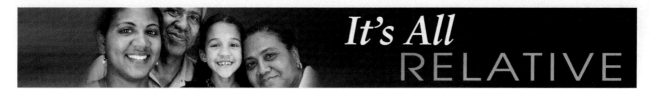

It's All RELATIVE

Your family may be one of the main reasons you are in college. Making time for them will be another task you will have to schedule if they are an important part of your life. Communicating with them about your class schedule and your time management strategies will help them understand when you are sometimes too busy to do the things that you used to do. In fact, the more you communicate what you have to do and remind them why you are in college, the more likely they will understand when you have to stay focused on your school work.

In addition to telling them what your schedule will be like, you will also want to schedule time with them throughout the semester. As you know from reading about other obligations, making time for what is important to you—in this case, your family—requires that you actually write down when you will spend time with them.

YOUR TURN

What do you want to communicate with your family about your schedule this semester? • Is there any time of the semester that you may not be able to give them as much attention as you have in the past? • Is there any time in the semester that you can schedule special time with them? • If so, write down your answers below.

_____

_____

_____

Running Low on Time and Energy

There will be times when you find that goals for the day or week are still left on your list, but you don't have the time and energy reserves that you hoped to have. Sometimes life throws us a curveball, and our beautiful plans are mangled if not completely destroyed. If you find yourself in such a situation, then you will benefit from changing goals and priorities quickly and eliminating unnecessary items from your "to do" list. For example, perhaps you had planned to bake a friend a birthday cake from scratch, but you don't have two hours to do it. What can you do? How about buying a cake on the way to your friend's house? The outcome is still the same: Your friend has a cake for his birthday. Or you hoped to get all the bills paid by the end of the day, but you don't have the time and energy left. Pay the bills that are due the soonest and complete the task the next day.

There will be some days when you just can't do it all. You may find that you cannot read the assigned chapter in your sociology class the night before. If this happens to you—and it will at some point in your college career—then create a back-up plan as you did with the birthday cake. Avoid giving up completely if you run out of time or energy; do something, even if it is just a little bit. Can't get to the library to start looking for sources for your research paper? Create an outline or a task list instead, and go to the library the next day. Do something that keeps you moving forward, but don't give up. You will have more energy and time the next day to complete new tasks.

Collaboration EXERCISE 4.3

Working within a group or with another classmate, describe the types of activities that can zap students' time and energy; then create solutions for managing them. Present your ideas to the class. ■

What if Laura had started her assignment early and all she had to do was print it out before heading to bed at a reasonable hour? Certainly, her stress levels would be much lower and her work would most likely be her best. Not all students manage their time wisely all the time, but procrastination does not have to be a necessary part of going to college.

Procrastination Pitfalls

Postponing an activity or task, whether because you think it will not take too long to finish or you find more interesting activities to do, can have serious consequences. For example, if you put off researching your legal terminology paper until the night before, you might find that the library has closed early or that access to online databases is down. You may even discover, like Laura, that your computer is not working or your printer is out of ink. Underestimating the amount of time needed is another serious consequence of procrastination. Writing a paper may have taken you a few hours in high school, but in college, it may take you days if not weeks to do the research, drafting, and revising that is expected of college-level work. At the very least, you will not be able to get any help you may need if you wait until the last minute. Professors won't be available, classmates may be completing their own work, and tutors may be booked up with appointments.

Procrastination then can be a barrier between you and success; for sure, it can cause you unnecessary stress. Managing your time and planning ahead will, however, minimize the likelihood that you will procrastinate.

Procrastinator Types

To break the cycle of procrastination, it may be helpful to consider why you procrastinate and what that says about who you are. Nike's slogan "Just do it!" sounds simple, but it doesn't work for everyone. Determining your procrastinator type will help you find the solution that works best for you. For example, do you procrastinate in certain classes? Do you procrastinate when faced with certain types of assignments? What reward do you get for not doing the work ahead of time? Some students crave the rush of doing an assignment at the last minute. They believe that the only way to motivate themselves is to hear a clock ticking down the hours or minutes left. Others are afraid of failing or not doing well on an assignment. This fear makes starting an assignment overwhelming. Still others just have too much to do every day, and they cannot find time because they have set up their lives

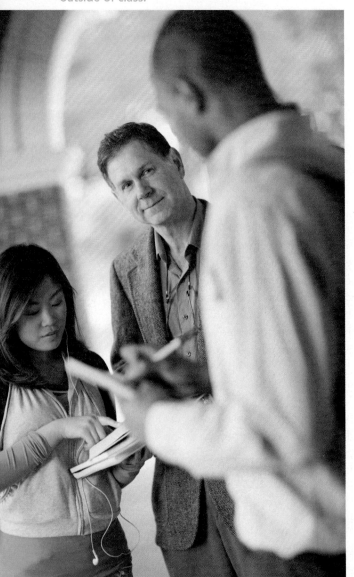

Schedule time to work with your classmates and talk with faculty and advisors outside of class.

Fuse/Getty Images

TABLE 4.2 Procrastinator Types

Adrenaline Addict	The adrenaline addict craves the rush he feels when he waits until the last minute. Without the faster heartbeat, he can't seem to get motivated to complete any assignment. He finds doing assignments in small chunks well before they are due bores him to tears. If he's not completely exhausted after the process, he gets no satisfaction in the work he has done.
Fearful Loafer	The fearful loafer worries what will happen when she completes the assignment. Will she pass? Will she fail? Will she have forgotten something important to include? Will her professor like her work so much that she will be expected to perform at that level all the time? It does not matter what scenario the fearful loafer dreams up, it will make her worry too much to get started on time, and she will wait until the last minute when she has to face her fears.
Stretched-Thin Slacker	The stretched-thin slacker wants to complete assignments on time, but he has too many assignments, too many activities, and too many responsibilities to get it all done. Instead of focusing on completing one task, the stretched-thin slacker takes on more to avoid handling what he has.
Paralyzed Perfectionist	The paralyzed perfectionist always wants to do her best, but when she doesn't think she can do her best, she doesn't want to do anything at all. The paralyzed perfectionist won't even start unless she knows the end product will be her best work ever.

so that there is no time left for college work. Finally, there is the person who feels that anything worth doing is worth doing perfectly. The trouble comes when they cannot complete an assignment perfectly, so they choose not to do it at all. Table 4.2 provides more details for the four types of procrastinators just described. Think about what type you are and which strategies you would use to break the procrastination cycle.

Eliminating Procrastination

A few quick and fast tips can help you eliminate the urge to procrastinate. Remember, these are habits that must be used every day you have something to do. Practice one or more of them any time you feel the need to put off until tomorrow something that has to be done today.

- *Write down what you must do.* Use your back-dating time management strategy to make a time line for your project. Break the task apart into smaller chunks that each take 30 minutes to an hour to complete.
- *Just do it, no matter how you feel.* Start right here, right now, and don't think about finding a better time to begin.

Reflection EXERCISE 4.4

Do you procrastinate? If so, which type of procrastinator are you? What can you do differently to eliminate procrastination while in college? ◼

Tech TIPS

USING TECHNOLOGY TO GET AHEAD

Technology such as cell phones, video games, and the Internet can provide opportunities to avoid doing your college work. Instead of limiting access to them, use them instead to help you manage your time. Cell phones have timers, alarms, and calendars that can keep you on track. The Internet can connect you to friends through social networking sites to provide a support group for your classes. Video games (or other fun activities) can be your reward for completing assignments on time.

(Personality + Learning Style = Understanding Situations)

Let's revisit Laura's dilemma. She is an aural learner and introverted; she also takes longer to complete assignments because of her dyslexia; and she has to juggle family and college because she is a single parent. What time and stress management strategies can she use the next time that she has an assignment due?

Now, considering your own learning style, personality type, and special circumstances, what would you do to avoid the stress of completing an assignment the night before when you find yourself challenged by unexpected events? ▨

■ *Reward yourself.* When you complete a particularly difficult project, give yourself a special treat—an extra hour of sleep, a favorite television show, or some time with friends.

■ *Keep the end in mind.* Remind yourself of the reason that you are in college and think about how this project supports that goal. For example, that research paper will make you a better communicator at your future job.

■ *Leave it to the pros.* Write a list of pros and cons for doing the project on time and then for *not* doing it on time or at all. Decide which list you can live with.

■ *Look in the mirror.* Review Table 4.2 on procrastinator types. Once you determine why you procrastinate, you will become better able to make changes in your habits.

From College to University

HOW TO HANDLE THE NEW PRESSURES ON YOUR TIME

A good time management strategy that works for you will serve you well when you transfer to a university. Yes, there will be more work and more expected of you when you get closer to completing a bachelor's degree, but there may also be less direction from professors. They will assume you have solid time management skills. The more you practice now, the better you will be able to handle even more restrictions on your time. Additionally, there will be more for you to do as you work toward completing a four-year degree. You may find yourself participating in a career-related club, interning to get experience for your résumé, talking to professors about graduating, and putting together applications for jobs.

Try out a few strategies and find what works, but also talk to students who have already transferred to find out what new expectations you will encounter.

Building Your University Portfolio 4

Contact a friend or an acquaintance who is attending a four-year university or who has just recently graduated. Ask him or her what time management strategies work best for the increased demands on time. Be sure to ask what additional activities you will be involved in once you transfer. Record your friend's advice here or in your portfolio.

_____

_____

_____

_____

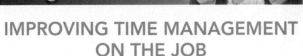
IMPROVING TIME MANAGEMENT
ON THE JOB

If you decide to go directly from college to work, or back to work, your time and stress management skills can be the difference between a dreaded job and a life-fulfilling career. Time management will be even more important on the job because your actions will affect more people. Just as in moving from college to university, the more you practice good time management skills, the more likely you will be able to complete assignments on time. Beware, though, that on the job, the stakes will be much higher than they were in college. Using a calendar and writing down daily tasks will help you keep on top of your "to do" list. There may be times when you won't be able to manage your time as effectively as you wish, but if you can be honest and speak up quickly, you may be able to save others' time as well.

Building Your Career Portfolio 4

Contact someone in a career that is similar to what you want to do. Ask about the demands on his or her time. What was surprising about the amount of time needed to complete tasks? Does he or she have much control over how much time to spend on certain tasks? What advice can this person give you about time management? Record the advice here or in your portfolio.

_____

_____

_____

_____

First Voices

STORIES OF SUCCESS FROM COLLEGE GRADUATES

A dream comes true after a few setbacks: First-generation student fulfills his dream after enrolling at a community college

At the early age of about ten, I knew I wanted to be a video game designer. However, as time went on, I slowly thought that dream would never come to pass. Next thing I knew, I was in high school, in my _third_ ninth-grade year. Without a care in the world and not really thinking about graduating high school, or my dream, I began to accept what had become of me. It was during this time, I realized I needed to step up and pursue my dream again.

Miles Morton,
Webmaster and
Game Developer

I completed that year of high school. I went to summer school and started the next school term in the eleventh grade. I was beginning to feel alive and proud of myself. I graduated high school a year late in 1997.

It wasn't until 8 years later in the year 2005 when I decided to go to college. I worked very hard on my education and in my second semester I started working as a work-study, maintaining the school website. I graduated from National Park Community College (Arkansas) in May of 2007, with my associate's degree in Computer Information Systems with an emphasis on computer programming. In August of 2007, I was hired on full time as the webmaster of the college. I began working on my bachelor's degree in Software Engineering from the University of Advancing Technology within the same month.

In March of 2009, a friend and I went to the Game Developers Conference in San Francisco, California. It was a dream come true. On returning home, we started our own game development studio, Augutron Interactive, LLC (http://augutron.com). My dream has finally come true.

PATH OF DISCOVERY
Journal Entry

What energizes you the most? What could you do for hours and not notice that time has passed? Describe the activity and discuss why you think you find so much pleasure in the activity that you don't mind spending time doing it.

CHAPTER REVIEW QUESTIONS

1. What activities and responsibilities will you have to manage while you are in college? How will managing your time help you stay on top of these tasks?
2. Name and describe two time management strategies. List the advantages and disadvantages of each.
3. How are time and energy connected? What activities zap your time and your energy and what can you do to eliminate the amount of time and energy they take from you?
4. What are the different reasons for procrastinating? What strategies are available to eliminate procrastination?

CHAPTER 4 CASE SCENARIOS

1. Janice has been doing very well in her classes. She has been able to manage her time wisely and adjust her schedule any time something unexpected has come up. However, Janice has had a hectic week. Her boss expects her to stay late for the week to finish a special project, she has an important exam on Thursday evening, her daughter has been sick with a stomach virus, and her husband has been out of town for the last two weeks. Her goal is to take care of each problem without jeopardizing her job, her grade, or her daughter's welfare. What do you recommend? Is it realistic to think she can take care of each of her problems?

2. George has a 20-page research paper in his abnormal psychology class due at the end of the semester. The professor has asked for an annotated bibliography, an outline, and a rough draft to be turned in at the same time as the final draft. George is feeling overwhelmed. Help him map out a plan of action so that he can fulfill his requirements without unnecessary stress.

3. Barbara has been sick for two weeks and has fallen behind in her classes. She is worried that she won't be able to catch up or that she will not be allowed to make up her work. What should she do?

4. Glenn is a constant procrastinator. He feeds on the adrenaline that runs through his veins when he waits until the last minute to complete an assignment. The last time he did this, for a computer programming class, he ended up failing the assignment because he ran out of time and was exhausted for three days because he had stayed up 36 hours straight. Glenn really wants to break his bad habits. What advice can you give him to help him manage his energy and time effectively?

RESEARCH IT FURTHER

1. Keep a journal of how you spend your time for the next 7 days. Write down how long you spend on each activity. Make sure you are honest and that you write in your journal every few hours. Then, create a report for your class as to how you spend the majority of your time.

2. Create a survey that asks your classmates how they cope with stress. Once you collect your data, report the results to your class and determine which stress relievers are healthy and which are unhealthy.

3. Brainstorm the different ways that students can relieve stress in unhealthy ways. Then, search the Internet or library resources for information about the effects of these unhealthy activities.

4. Create a "toolbox" for students who are plagued by procrastination. Make the toolbox creative and fun.

References and Recommended Readings

Dodd, P., & Sundheim, D. (2005). *The 25 best time management tools and techniques: How to get more done without driving yourself crazy.* Chelsea, MI: Peak Performance Press.

Hindle, T. (1998). *Manage your time.* New York: DK Publishing.

Leland, K., & Bailey, K. (2008). *Time management in an instant: 60 ways to make the most of your day.* Franklin Lakes, NJ: The Career Press.

Nelson, D. B., & Low, G. R. (2003). *Emotional intelligence: Achieving academic and career excellence.* Upper Saddle River, NJ: Pearson.

Sibler, L. (1998). *Time management for the creative person: Right-brain strategies for stopping procrastination, getting control of the clock and calendar, and freeing up your time and your life.* New York: Three Rivers Press.

5
LEARNING, MEMORY, and THINKING

ichael can shoot the cap off a bottle of beer at 100 yards; he can hike 12 miles in a hot sandstorm with 30 pounds of equipment on his back; and he can build a jungle gym out of scrap wood for his two nieces. What Michael can't do, he thinks as he rubs his head, is understand algebra. He shifts his backpack to his other shoulder and looks at the sign on the door. He is in the right place—the tutoring center—but he doesn't know if he really belongs here.

Inside the student center, Michael sits back down on a chair outside the large window that overlooks the lot where his truck is parked, and he opens his math notebook where he has scrawled a few notes from the last class.

The order of operations is F-O-I-L: first, outer, inner, last. "But after that, I don't know what to do," he thinks to himself.

He writes on the red cover of his note-book, "F-O-I-L. F-O-O-L. F-A-I-L." He just knows that he will fail the class because he can't keep factoring polynomials and solving absolute value equations straight. If his professor would just slow down and allow students to "get it" before moving on to the next unit, he wouldn't feel so stressed. It doesn't help his nerves to know that when another student asked the professor to slow down, he told the class that they needed to get a tutor if they couldn't keep up.

"Isn't teaching me algebra *his* job, not a tutor's?" Michael asks the bulletin board that lists the tutoring center's hours. He notices that in 30 minutes, the tutor for algebra will be leaving and his hope of getting any help will be over. Before he decides to leave, his girlfriend Michelle calls him.

"Will you be home by the time I get off work?" she asks. "I need you to pick up something for dinner."

"Unless I can understand my algebra homework, I don't know when I will be home," he jokes.

"Did you do what I told you? Did you see Tamara in the tutoring center?" she asks.

"I'm standing right in front of it. But I can't make myself go in. It reminds me of being put in the 'dummy class' in junior high school because I couldn't get fractions," he tells her.

Michael's teenage difficulty in learning coupled with his military background makes it difficult for him to seek help on his own. By the time he got to high school, he was able to slide by, and in the military his superiors ordered everything he did. It is strange for him to complete homework that is not turned in or to get help from a peer who has only recently completed the class and is 20 years younger than he. Plus, he has accomplished so much in his life on his own that he feels awkward asking someone for help. If he can't do it on his own, he thinks, maybe he can't do it at all. His girlfriend's voice shatters the silence.

"Michael, do you remember when I struggled through biology? I wanted to be a nurse so much, but I didn't think I had what it took if I couldn't pass one of the first classes," she says.

"Yeah, I do. I remember helping you study before tests."

"Do you remember how much better I did after I went to the tutoring center? I found someone who helped me take better notes and organize my studying time. Plus, she helped me figure out a study strategy that helped me deal with the huge amount of written material I had to remember for the tests."

Michael doesn't say anything in response, but remembers how she struggled. He feels a little guilty that he can remember that he tried to get her to quit school once because she seemed so stressed out all the time and never wanted to do fun things with him. Glad that she stuck it out, Michael suddenly feels competitive. If she can make it through biology and become a nurse, he can surely get through algebra—and with a better grade.

Michael pulls out a square of gum, a habit he developed after quitting smoking two years ago, and responds to Michelle.

"This may be the only time I will say this," he jokes, "but you are right. I need to see what kind of help I can get. I'll call you before I leave."

With a little more confidence, Michael digs around in his dusty backpack, grabs his calculator and a mechanical pencil, and walks through the double swinging doors into the tutoring center.

In this CHAPTER

Michael's story illustrates a typical situation in which a student struggles with learning on his own. For Michael, remembering the order of operations in algebra is part of his challenge. He is also unsure of reaching out for help to supplement what he can do on his own. Many other new students ask the same questions: "Isn't my professor supposed to make sure I master the material in class?" and "If I have trouble keeping up with the work, does this mean I will never be successful?" Experienced students know that most of the required work and learning expected of them will occur *outside* the classroom, and that often means working with others, either in a study group or at a tutoring center, to be successful *inside* the classroom.

To help you improve your learning, no matter where it happens, this chapter focuses on the latest brain research as it relates to learning and memory. It also explains the importance of active learning. Finally, the different types of thinking that will be required of you are explored at the end of the chapter.

More specifically, after completing this chapter, you will be able to do the following:

- **Describe the stages of learning.**
- **Label the process of memory.**
- **Define the processes of creative, analytical, and critical thinking.**
- **Explain the problem-solving process as it relates to critical thinking.**

THIS IS YOUR BRAIN in COLLEGE

Seems like there are dozens of bumper stickers and T-shirts that broadcast what people are born to do. "Born to Run," "Born to Shop," and "Born to Boogie" are just a few that you may see. But could you add "Born to Learn" to the list? All of us, researchers say, are indeed born to learn. Babies do it without giving the process any thought. The process is simple: The more you do something, say Angus Gunn, Dr. Robert W. Richburg, and Dr. Rita Smilkstein (2007), the more you create connections in the brain that not only help you remember how to do something, but also help you get better at whatever it is you are learning to do. These brain researchers call this process "growing dendrites," referring to the "tree-like" structures on the ends of neurons, or nerve cells in the brain. The more you practice something, the more those dendrites grow, improving the connections between the neurons in your brain. See Figure 5.1 for an example of what a brain cell looks like.

FIGURE 5.1 Dendrite

The Learning Process

The good news about brain research is that spending more time actively learning a subject can translate into deeper learning, and a positive attitude toward challenging learning environments will enable you to learn more. In their book, *Igniting Student Potential*, Gunn, Richburg, and Smilkstein divide learning into six stages that begin with being curious and motivated to learn something new, move to practicing and refining the new skill, and then end with mastery of the skill. Table 5.1 provides an overview of the learning stages. If you think about anything that you are good at, you should recognize the same process that you went through to get better and better at it. We often recognize the need to practice sports and musical instruments, but sometimes we don't make the same connections with other skills such as writing, reading, and math. Michael would feel more confident about seeing a tutor if he realized that learning algebra is a process that involves time for practice. How much time is needed will be different for different people, but brain researchers contend your skills will increase just as your dendrites will grow.

What happens when you can't get motivated to learn a new skill and make it past the first stage in learning? Dr. Carol Dweck (2006) refers to people who lose interest when learning "get[s] too challenging—when they are not feeling smart or talented" as having a "fixed mindset" (p. 22). People who "thrive when stretching themselves" have a "growth mindset" (p. 22). In her book *Mindset: The New Psychology of Success*, Dweck asserts that people with a fixed mindset believe that they are either born smart or not, that there is no changing their "fixed" state of intelligence. People with a growth mindset, on the other hand, believe they can develop talents and skills; even if they fail at a task, they see it as an opportunity to learn more and improve on what they know about the task.

TABLE 5.1	Six Stages of Learning a New Skill
Stage 1	*Motivation.* Responding to stimulus. Not knowing how to do it or how it works, just trying it.
Stage 2	*Beginning Practice.* Doing it ("practice, practice, practice"), learning from one's own mistakes. Starting to get the feel for it.
Stage 3	*Advanced Practice.* Increase of skill and confidence through more practice, more trial and error, getting comfortable.
Stage 4	*Skillfulness.* More practice, doing it one's own way, deviating from the norm, taking risks, creativity, branching out. Building understanding, skill, and confidence.
Stage 5	*Refinement.* Activity becoming second nature, creativity, learning new methods, strong satisfaction.
Stage 6	*Mastery.* Increased creativity, broader application, teaching it, continuing improvement, expertise.

Source: Adapted from Smilkstein, R. (2003). *We're born to learn: Using the brain's natural learning process to create today's curriculum.* Thousand Oaks, CA: Corwin Press. Used with permission.

In the story at the beginning of the chapter, you learned that Michael knows how to do many things, which no doubt came from a belief that he could improve on his skills; however, he seems to have a fixed mindset about algebra. Sometimes one bad experience or several in a row can influence how we see ourselves as learners and masters of a skill. Dweck wants us to know that believing in our ability to learn will result in learning and mastery of whatever task we set our "growth" minds to.

Learning in College

How does the information about brain research and learning translate to what you are doing in college? It may be helpful first to identify where, how, and with whom learning can take place. If you think about a clock face in which the big hand is pointing to the 12 and the little hand is pointing to the 3, you can see that for a three-credit-hour class you will be spending 3 hours per week learning in the classroom (see Figure 5.2). As stated in Chapter 4 this means that you will need to spend three times 3 hours learning outside of class.

You could easily spend those 9 hours a week per class reading the textbook and studying your notes. However, you will probably have to engage in a variety of other activities as part of learning, such as researching and writing papers, completing homework, visiting with your professor outside of class, studying with a classmate or in a group, or working with a tutor.

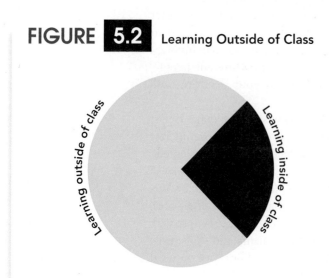

FIGURE 5.2 Learning Outside of Class

Learning outside of class

Learning inside of class

Why do you need to do all of that to learn when listening in class, taking notes, and reviewing them before the test worked before? The answer is that in college, you will be responsible for more than just memorizing material and restating it on a test or in a paper. Instead, you will be asked to apply (use information in a new situation), analyze (break information down into its parts and examine it), synthesize (create new information based on what you have learned), and evaluate (judge the information), and you will be graded on your ability to do all of those activities well.

THE MEMORY GAME

You will be more likely to remember what you have learned when you have moved it from short-term memory to your long-term memory. Memory is divided into two types—short-term memory and long-term memory. When you meet someone for the first time, you will keep that person's name and face in your short-term memory; in fact, according to Harvard psychologist George Miller (2008), you can only store five to nine items in your short-term memory. If you try to put too many items in there, you will find that some of them slip away. Try this by glancing at the following list for 30 seconds. Then cover up the list and write down the words you remember in the space provided; the words do not have to be in the order that you see them.

cup	paper	pencil	magnet	ruler	scissors
spoon	towel	tape	apple	knife	straw

_____

_____

How well did you do? If you remembered five to nine items, then you can consider your memory average. It takes some work, though, to transfer information from your short-term memory to your long-term memory.

Figure 5.3 shows what areas of the brain are used in memory. Your long-term memory is responsible for storing information like names and dates as well as skills such as

IT'S IN THE

Syllabus

By rereading your professors' syllabi and by considering your experiences so far, determine how much time you will need to spend outside of class to meet the goals of each course you are taking. Which classes will require the most amount of time? How will you be spending that time?

What other kinds of learning expectations are there? Considering Table 5.1, Six Stages of Learning a New Skill, what stages will you need to go through?

FIGURE 5.3 Brain Map

Prefrontal cortex

Cerebellum

tying your shoe. People can have well-developed memory storage for images and words (visual), sounds (aural), and processes (kinesthetic).

In the article "Remember This," Joshua Foer (2007) states, "It's hard for us to imagine what it must have been like to live in a culture before the advent of printed books or before you could carry around a ballpoint pen and paper to jot notes" (p. 49). We could add cell phones that take pictures and record video and voice to the list of technologies that keep us from having to remember every single detail of an event. All of these options for creating artificial memory are what Mary Carruthers, author of *The Book of Memory*, refers to when she states that "[a]ncient and medieval people reserved their awe for memory. Their greatest geniuses [are the people] they describe as people of superior memories" (in Foer, p. 49).

Today the information is at our fingertips and we don't have to memorize the ever-increasing amount of information that is generated daily. But memory played a significant role in ancient and not-so-distant history. Those who could remember significant events, poetry, and songs were revered for their gifts of memory. In many cultures, remembering was essential to surviving and thriving. People remembered the stories of celebrated heroes and the markings of poisonous plants. They couldn't just type key terms into a search engine and learn about them at their convenience! Nonetheless, we still need to continue to develop and improve our memory because it is an integral part of learning.

Mnemonic Devices

Mnemonic devices are memory aids or strategies that help you remember items, concepts, or a series of events. Usually, mnemonic devices are *not* used for deep learning, but there will be times during college that remembering the names, for example, of all the bones in the body or all the constitutional amendments must be accomplished before deeper learning can happen. Thus, you may find yourself using mnemonic devices as part of your learning process.

Let's go back to the word list and figure out how you could remember all of the items. Ancient Romans are credited with being able to remember significant amounts of information by using the Roman Room or loci method. This visualization technique can be useful when trying to remember a string of seemingly unrelated items or complex material that needs to be pulled together.

To create a Roman Room, visualize a familiar place, such as a room in your house. If your room is connected to other rooms, then you will have more "places" to put ideas. When you visualize your room, pay particular attention to the items that are already in the room, such as furniture or favorite pictures, and unique details, such as peeling paint. The more vivid the visualization, the better able you will be to remember the items you place there.

To see the Roman Room or loci method in action, take another look at the list.

| cup | paper | pencil | magnet | ruler | scissors |
| spoon | towel | tape | apple | knife | straw |

Can you place these items in your kitchen? Put the straw in the cup and place it in the cabinet. Tape the paper on the front of the cabinet. Place the towel on the counter next to the apple, spoon, and knife. Then, put the pencil, ruler, magnet, and scissors in the drawer.

Take 30 seconds to visualize this room or create your own Roman Room with the items listed. Then cover up both the list and the description of the room and see how many you can remember. Write the words in the space provided here.

_____

_____

_____

_____

_____

Did you remember more words this time? If not, then visualization strategies may not be the only type of mnemonic device you need to help you remember lots of information. There are other mnemonic strategies that may benefit different learning style preferences. Acrostic sentences and acronyms are just two methods that may help students with a read/write learning style preference.

Take the first letters of items in a series to form sentences that help you remember the items and their order—acrostic sentences. For example, music students remember the order of the treble clef staff—E, G, B, D, F—with the sentence "Every Good Boy Does Fine." To recall the order of biological groupings used in taxonomy, just remember "Kids Prefer Cheese Over Fried Green Spinach" (Kingdom, Phyllum, Class, Order, Family, Genus, Species).

Take the first letters of items in a series to spell a new word to create acronyms. Examples of acronyms that we use every day include AIDS (acquired immune deficiency syndrome), SADD (Students Against Drunk Driving), REM (rapid eye movement), and SCUBA (self-contained underwater breathing apparatus).

Although there are too many words in our list above to create an acronym, you can create an acrostic sentence (or two) with the letters of each word. Because the order of the items is not important, feel free to rearrange the letters to make your sentence(s).

C P P M R S
S T T A K S

Despite being a little more difficult to compose than acronyms and acrostics, rhymes and songs are another type of mnemonic device that often appeal to aural learners. Who doesn't remember "Thirty days hath September . . ." and "In 1492, Columbus sailed the ocean blue"? Again, simple information works best for these memory strategies. It will take more work to remember the economic effects of Columbus's discovery of the New World.

Think
ABOUT IT

The true art of memory is the art of attention.

—Samuel Johnson

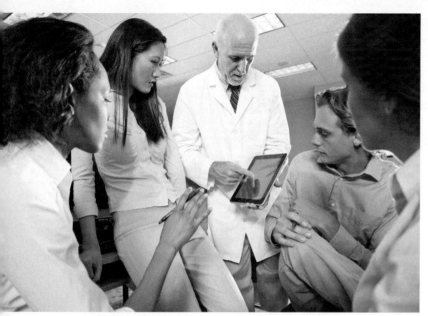

No matter what your degree plan or class, you will use creative, analytical, and critical thinking in and out of the classroom to complete assignments and solve problems.

Shutterstock

Memory Strategies

When you have the time to explore the variety of memory strategies, try them out until you find the one that works best for the subject matter and your learning style. However, many students need a memory strategy that works quickly when they are cramming before a test. Those students may be successful in remembering information when they get to the test the next day, but the possibility of their remembering it weeks, months, or even a year later is slim. That is why professors and tutors discourage students from cramming—it may work some of the time, and it is better than not studying at all for a test, but it often produces significant anxiety and stress, and the material is less likely to be in your long-term memory when you need it later.

With that warning, there will be times, nonetheless, when despite your best intentions, you will need a fail-safe memory technique to help you remember key concepts in a short period of time. One method, called *chunking*, was developed by Dr. George Miller (2008), the same person who discovered that the human brain can only hold "seven, plus or minus two" items in short-term memory. Chunking is similar to the Roman Room or loci method in that items are grouped together to allow the brain to make connections, making it easier to recall the information later.

To see chunking in action, consider the following 10-digit number:

5114796210

It may be easier to chunk the numbers the way a phone number is divided:

511-479-6210

You probably don't realize that you chunk any time you memorize a phone number or Social Security number. In other words, you are taking the seemingly random numbers and putting them together in groups. The goal in chunking is to reduce a large number of items into only five to nine items. To practice this mnemonic technique, use the following list of key terms. First, however, make sure that you know the definitions of each term. Record your definition next to each item in the list:

Acrostic _____

Acronym _____

Chunking _____

Cramming _____

Loci method _____

Long-term memory _____

Mnemonic device _____

Rhyme _____

Roman Room _____

Short-term memory _____

Teaching others _____

Next, group the items together logically. Then complete the chunking with the remaining terms. For example, one way to group some of the terms could be in a sentence: **Mnemonic devices** are strategies for remembering and they include **acrostics, acronyms, rhymes,** and **Roman Rooms.** How else could the terms be grouped together? Use the spaces below for your ideas.

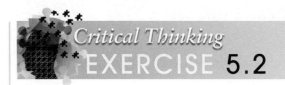

After reviewing the mnemonic devices, determine which ones would work best for you and use them to create a memory strategy study sheet that would help you remember the major ideas in this entire chapter. ■

- _____
- _____
- _____

THINK about IT

Think about it. Three simple words that you have probably heard many times, but have you ever thought about how you are thinking? The term for thinking about thinking is *metacognition*, or the act of being aware of your own thought processes. So far in this book, you have thought about what you value, how you spend your time, what college culture is, and how you relate to others. You have also been asked to think about what you are reading and learning in the reflection and critical thinking exercises or the end-of-chapter questions and ideas for further research. In fact, this book has been designed so that instead of passively taking in the information, you are actively engaged in thinking it through and creating knowledge.

The same activities that have brought you to this point in the book are the types of endeavors you are currently practicing in your classes as well. You are moving beyond only taking information in to send it back out in the same form for a test or paper. Instead, you are building creative, analytical, and critical thinking skills with each course. Strong critical thinking skills will set you apart in the classroom and the workplace: You will be better informed, because you will know to seek out the information you need; you will make better choices, because you have thought through all the possibilities; and you will continue to improve on your chosen solutions, because you will understand that evaluating your conclusions is the key to making better future choices.

Creative Thinking

Creative thinking, or the act of creating ideas for solving problems, is an integral part of education. Without creative thinking, there would be no inventions, new formulas, breakthroughs in technology and science, new art movements, advances in design and architecture—the list is endless. Without creative thinking, there would be no electricity, no indoor plumbing, no automobiles, and no zippers in our clothes. Just getting to your classes would be a totally different experience.

In *Creative Problem Solving*, Robert Harris (2002) contends that creative thinking is a skill, a process, and an attitude (pp. 1–2). In other words, creative thinkers are not born with special powers of the imagination; they just use their imaginations more

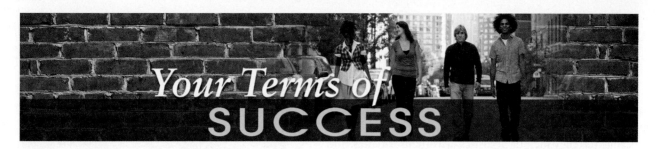

Your Terms of
SUCCESS

WHEN YOU SEE . . .	IT MEANS . . .
Acronym	An abbreviation in which the first letters create a word; AIDS is an acronym for Acquired Immune Deficiency Syndrome.
Acrostic	A mnemonic device in which the first letter of each word in a sentence stands for information or a process; Please Excuse My Dear Aunt Sally is an acrostic for the order of operations: Parentheses, Exponents, Multiplication, Division, Addition, and Subtraction.
Advanced practice	Doing an activity with more skill.
Analytical thinking	Breaking apart information and examining its parts.
Beginning practice	Doing an activity, learning from mistakes.
Cerebellum	Region of the brain that controls sensory perception and motor skills.
Chunking	A method for remembering information by grouping it together in small chunks.
Cramming	A method of studying that involves trying to remember large amounts of material in a short amount of time.
Creative thinking	Thinking that involves generating ideas.
Critical thinking	Thinking that involves reviewing information for accuracy, authority, and logic before considering it useable.
Dendrite	The branch at the end of a neuron.
Loci method	A mnemonic device that uses spatial relationships; information to be remembered is associated with a location or objects within a location.
Long-term memory	Memory that lasts longer than a few days.
Mastery	Doing an activity with expertise.
Metacognition	Thinking about thinking.
Mnemonic device	A method of remembering information.
Neuron	A cell in the nervous system.
Prefrontal cortex	A region at the front of the brain where complex thinking is believed to occur.
Refinement	Perfecting an activity that has become second nature.
Roman Room	Another term for loci method.
Short-term memory	Memory that lasts only for a few hours or a few days.
Skillfulness	A demonstration of an ability to complete a task.

regularly than others. The good news is that you can learn to think creatively by following some basic guidelines.

- *Improve your imagination.* Find ways to keep your mind sharp and your imagination flourishing. Turning off the TV and picking up a book is an easy way to stimulate your imagination. If you enjoy kinesthetic activities, create something to get your mind active.

- *Think in all directions.* Thinking in all directions means that you consider ideas that have worked before, have not worked before, have worked for other problems, and have not been paired with another idea. Some of the most creative ideas have taken ordinary solutions and reapplied them to other problems. Creative thinking demands that all angles be considered as you generate ideas.

- *Suspend judgment.* For creative thinking, evaluation is not necessary—save it for critical thinking and problem solving. The focus should be on getting ideas down, not on judging them for their practicality or judging yourself as not capable of being creative. "There is no wrong answer" is a common phrase at this point to keep you generating thoughts.

- *Keep it up.* One main difference between people who think creatively and those who choose not to is perseverance, or the determination to see ideas through—and to keep generating them when the ones you come up with don't work.

Harris states, "Creative thinking creates the ideas with which critical thinking works" (p. 5). To improve your critical thinking and problem-solving abilities, you will need to consider the guidelines listed, find ways to practice them, and maintain your curiosity and a positive attitude.

USING TECHNOLOGY TO GET AHEAD

Improve your thinking skills by visiting the numerous websites that are dedicated to brain games. Logical puzzles, word games, and visual tricks are all accessible with a little searching. Look also for memory games, which can help you strengthen your memory muscle.

Critical Thinking
EXERCISE 5.3

This chapter uses several figures to illustrate key concepts: a neuron, a pie chart, and a brain map. Review each one and determine which is most helpful in conveying the information and which is least helpful. Redraw the least helpful figure to add or delete information to make it more effective in communicating the information. ■

Analytical Thinking

Analytical thinking involves breaking down a subject and examining its parts. Students who learn about computer processing or automotive technology use analytical thinking so that they can understand how a machine works. When they master how the parts work together, they are able to diagnose problems that may occur within the processes. The same is true for students learning about the processes in the body: They use analytical thinking to determine how muscles work or how the lungs are supposed to function. Students of literature use analytical thinking to break apart short stories or poems to determine what effect the setting has on the characters or what effect language has on the tone of the text.

Anyone who has tried to figure out why an event has happened (e.g., How did I run out of money before payday?) has used analytical thinking. Just as with any skill, however, it takes practice to become better at seeing the parts of a process or a whole unit and determining how the parts work together to create a unified result. To develop your analytical skills, you can apply the following guidelines:

- *Break down a whole into its parts.* Ask yourself, "What are the pieces that create the entirety?" Try this by examining a dollar bill. What are the different images on the front and back?

- *Examine each part for a unique function.* If you are still looking at the dollar bill, determine what function each part has on the bill. Does it convey important information about how to use the bill? Does it represent a significant event in history?

- *Organize parts by function.* What elements can be grouped together? How did you determine which groups to create? For example, are there words, images, or numbers that can be grouped together?

- *Explore the meaning behind the parts.* If possible, find out more information about how each part functions or its meaning. In the case of the dollar bill, you can learn more about the pyramid on the back and what it means or more about the objects in the eagle's talons.

- *Reexamine the whole in light of its parts.* Look back at the whole and determine what you have learned from examining the parts. Do you have a better understanding of how all the parts work together? For example, how do all of the parts of the dollar bill come together to make one statement about our nation?

Critical Thinking

The term *critical thinking* is difficult to define, although it has a long tradition. Critical thinkers such as Socrates and Thomas Aquinas, to name only two, have had a tremendous effect on the way we think about the world. But what makes them critical thinkers? Sherry Diestler (1998), in her book *Becoming a Critical Thinker,* defines a critical thinker as "someone who uses specific criteria to evaluate reasoning and make decisions" (p. 2). In other words, someone who thinks critically does not take information at its face value; instead, the information is reviewed for accuracy, authority, and logic before it is considered useable.

Chapter 6 discusses how to read critically, and that certainly is a start to making informed decisions about what you read, but you will also use critical thinking in other parts of your everyday life. Sometimes you are faced with an important decision, and you will need to use critical thinking in order to make the best choice.

To illustrate the importance of using critical thinking skills, consider this first scenario: Michael receives an email message from a friend who claims that she has sent him a virus unknowingly. Her email message instructs him to search for the offending file and delete it immediately. Unaware of any problems that are usually associated with viruses, he searches for the file and finds it, exactly where his friend said it would be on his computer. Michael's friend is a trustworthy person and he values her advice, so he deletes the file. He gets an email message the next day from her apologizing for sending him a hoax. Thus, he has deleted a perfectly normal file on his computer.

Now, consider this second scenario: Juanita sends Evan a link to a pop-up blocker because she knows that he hates those annoying intrusions while surfing the Internet. Because Evan has been deceived by free software before, he decides to search several reputable sites that are devoted to reviewing new software. Evan finds that the pop-up

You can't be a true critical thinker without maintaining integrity in the process. To think critically with integrity you will need to be fair in your judgments and represent others' views as accurately as possible. Critical thinkers know that every viewpoint has a counterargument that is equally valid, and critical thinkers with integrity acknowledge those other viewpoints without misrepresenting them.

Critical thinkers who have integrity also do not shortcut the process of examining and judging an idea. The reward is the assurance that their final conclusions are fair.

YOUR TURN

If your professor asked you to write a paper on affirmative action defending the practice although you did not agree with that position, how would you consider the topic critically and with integrity to the learning process and your own beliefs?

_____

_____

_____

blocker is a fraud; clicking on the link that Juanita has sent would flood his computer with pop-up advertisements of questionable origins.

In the first scenario, two people, at least, have been deceived by what appears to be legitimate and helpful information. Who doesn't want to rid her computer of a potentially dangerous virus? Unfortunately, Michael and his friend did not question the information. In the second scenario, however, Evan has encountered false claims before and realizes that he must check out every piece of information that comes to him, regardless of the friendly source. Evan is a critical thinker whose analysis led him to review the information he was sent and to search for authoritative sources providing reliable information he could use to make a decision about what action to take.

As the Information Age evolves, critical thinking skills are not just advantageous; they are essential to survival. Not only do you need to possess these skills, but you also need others to possess them as well so that you will not constantly have to evaluate every piece of information that you receive. Can you imagine a world in which everything that you read is suspect and there is no sure way of finding out what is true and accurate and what is not? For people who do not think critically, that imagined world is a reality.

Problem Solving

Problem solving relies on critical thinking as well as creative and analytical thinking. In order to think critically to solve a problem, you will need to go through a process, whether within a group or as an individual. Remember that the more minds working on a problem, the more likely that all sides of the problem can be addressed, which may make the solution better. Although you may not always have an opportunity to work in a group on a problem, you may be able to ask others for their advice during the process.

The process of using critical thinking to solve a problem can be broken into a series of steps.

- Clearly identify the problem.
- Brainstorm possible solutions to the problem. *This is where creative thinking comes in.*
- Analyze the possible solutions for their viability. *This is where analytical thinking comes in.*
- Think through each solution and determine the benefits and drawbacks to each. *Creative and analytical thinking at play here.*
- Choose the solution that potentially works the best. *This is where critical thinking comes in.*
- Evaluate the solution after it is in place. *Critical thinking again.*

Step 1: Identify the Problem

Sometimes we assume we know what the problem is, and we try to fix it only to find out that our solution doesn't work because we were fixing the wrong problem. Consider a crying baby who last ate two hours ago. You may assume that the baby is still hungry and wants more to eat. When you try to feed the baby, he rejects the food. Now what? Is the baby not hungry? Have you offered something the baby doesn't like? Is the baby sick, too hot, too cold, tired? You can imagine how much time and energy you will spend trying to find the solution to the problem.

Identifying the problem's cause is the first logical step before you can begin to solve it. If you do not identify the cause—or at least eliminate possible causes—before starting the next step, either you won't solve the problem or you might create a whole new problem to solve.

Step 2: Generate Ideas

Once you identify the cause of the problem, this is the point where creative thinking will kick in. When you generate ideas, there are no rules except not to eliminate any

Learning material in short sessions over time is more effective than a long cramming session the night before an assignment is due.

Fotolia

It's All RELATIVE

Good critical thinking and problem-solving skills will be crucial to maintaining a good relationship with your family while you are in college. There may be times that you need to solve a problem between you and a family member or when your skills can help another solve his or her own issue.

Learning to identify the problem first will be important because there could be many reasons for the problem in your family. Unclear expectations or a lack of communication about the changes in your schedule or time commitments can be the root of a problem. Extra stress (and less sleep) may also contribute to conflict.

Once you have identified the actual cause, then you can use the additional five steps to solve the problem.

YOUR TURN

What problem do you need to solve in your relationship with family members? • What do you think are the causes of the problem? • If you are not sure of the cause, how will you work to identify it?

_____

_____

_____

ideas because they are too far-fetched or too odd. The goal for this step is to get the ideas recorded, and the more you can think "outside the box," the more likely you are considering all possibilities.

When generating ideas, consider using brainstorming, freewriting, clustering, and role playing (if you are able to work with another person) to get ideas flowing. This is a good time to use your learning style strength to stretch your imagination.

Step 3: Assess the Possibilities

More creative and analytical thinking will help you break down the different ideas at this stage. What are the different parts of the possibilities? Are there any that are impossible, impractical, or illogical? Determine the least viable solutions are and eliminate them from the list.

Step 4: Think through Solutions

Thinking through each solution will involve exploring its benefits and drawbacks. Consider the possibilities, but don't completely discard any at this point. You may need them after you evaluate your final solution and find it to be ineffective.

Step 5: Choose the Best Solution

When choosing the best solution, consider the effects of the solution. Will it cause another problem? What kind of emotional, physical, and financial investment will it take? What will you need to do to implement the solution correctly? Creative thinking to consider all sides of the implementation of the solution will be needed before you make a final decision. Analytical thinking can help you put all the possibilities in a table format so you can examine the consequences.

Collaboration
EXERCISE 5.4

Working in a group, discuss some issues on your campus that need to be solved. Use the critical thinking process to develop a viable solution. Share your ideas with the class. ■

Step 6: Evaluate the Solution

The final stage of problem solving is evaluation. The ability to evaluate allows you to use what you have learned in the process of solving the problem to solve other problems. Ask yourself whether the problem was adequately resolved. Did the solution only partly solve the problem or was it a complete solution? What, if anything, would you do differently if you experience the same problem again?

Putting Critical Thinking into Practice

What do you do in the following situations?

- You have an exam at 9:00 A.M. and you get into your car at 8:20 to get to class on time. Your car won't start.
- You need a math tutor to help you get through elementary algebra successfully. The tutoring center's hours are not convenient for you because you work every evening that the center is open late.
- You are worried that you may not be able to purchase your textbooks for next semester because the bookstore's prices are higher than you had anticipated.

If your car won't start and you have to get to an exam, would you be likely to give up and go back into the house, hoping that you can make up the exam? If you cannot find a tutor for elementary algebra, would you plod through the course and pray that you make it? If you are not able to afford textbooks next semester, would you see how far you can get without buying them? What are the other possible solutions to these problems? If you use the critical thinking steps for problem solving, you may realize that there are other alternatives, or possible solutions, to your predicaments.

Here are one student's problem-solving steps for the first scenario:

1. *Clearly identify the problem.* I have two problems. The first is that my car won't start, and the second is that I need to get to school to take an exam.

2. *Brainstorm possible solutions to the problem.* To address my more immediate problem, getting to school to take my test, I can do one or more of the following:
   - Call a friend to pick me up.
   - Call a cab to take me to school.
   - Take a train or bus.
   - Call my instructor to ask about taking a make-up exam.
   - Run to school.
   - Walk to school.

3. *Evaluate the possible solutions for their viability.*
   - Call a friend. I can get Jessica to pick me up, but she will then be late for work.
   - Call a cab. It will cost $20 and I won't be able to get to school until 9:15 A.M.
   - Catch a train or bus. There are no trains available. I don't know the bus schedule and will have to walk 1.2 miles to get to the bus stop.
   - Call my instructor. She may not allow me to make up the exam; I may not be able to get a message to her.

- Run to school. I am not in shape to make it all the way.
- Walk to school. The distance to school is 3.5 miles. It will take me at least an hour to get there, which will give me only 30 minutes to take my exam.

4. *Think through each solution and determine the benefits and drawbacks to each.* I have eliminated walking to school and catching the bus. I am left with three possible solutions: (1) Call my friend Jessica to pick me up; (2) call a cab; and (3) call my instructor about making up the exam.

- *Option 1:* The benefit of calling Jessica is that she is a friend and would help me out. I would also be able to make it to the exam on time. Drawbacks to calling Jessica is that she would be late to work if she took me to school and I would still have trouble getting to work.
- *Option 2:* The benefit of calling a cab is that I would definitely get to school. A drawback is that it would cost me $20, which I don't need to spend. Also, I wouldn't be able to get to school until 9:15. And how would I get to work after my classes?
- *Option 3:* The benefit of calling my instructor is that I could explain why I could not make it to class, and she might be sympathetic to my dilemma. Another benefit is that she might allow me to make up the exam. A drawback is that I might not be able to get a message to her that I am having car trouble, or she might not allow me to make up the exam.

5. *Choose the solution that potentially works the best.* My solution is to call my friend Jessica because it is the easiest solution. I won't have to pay to get to school, and I can get there on time. She may, though, be irritated at me for asking for a favor at the last minute. Then again, she may be very glad to be able to return a favor for me.

6. *Evaluate the solution after it is in place.* After Jessica takes me to school, I will be able to evaluate whether or not the solution worked. If Jessica can get me to school on time without being late for work, then the solution will be a success. If she has trouble picking me up or if she gets mad at me because I have made her late, then I will have to consider other solutions if I have car trouble again.

PLUS EXERCISE 5.5

(Personality + Learning Style = Understanding Situations)

Let's revisit Michael's dilemma. He is a visual learner and extroverted with friends but introverted when he is around people he just met. Michael prefers structured learning environments in which he is told exactly what he needs to do and what he needs to study. What learning and thinking strategies can he use to improve his learning and retention both in and out of the class?

Now, considering your own learning style, personality type, and special circumstances, what would you do to feel comfortable about keeping up with your classes and studying when you are challenged by the material? ■

From College to University

DIFFERENT TYPES OF THINKING WILL BE NEEDED TO CONTINUE YOUR LEARNING

When you transfer to a university, you will continue to use creative, analytical, and critical thinking skills. In upper-level classes, your professors will move away from knowledge and comprehension to synthesis and evaluation. You will spend more time doing research and determining whether the sources you find are reliable and accurate. You will also use those sources to support your own new ideas, developed through creative thinking, about current issues in your major. All in all, you will be more responsible for the depth and breadth of your education, and strong thinking skills will help you deepen your learning.

Building Your University Portfolio 5

Find someone you know (or ask your professor for the name of a former student) who has transferred to a four-year university and ask him or her what kinds of thinking are involved in upper-level (junior and senior) classes. Is there more analytical, creative, or critical thinking expected?

_____

_____

_____

_____

From College to Career

HOW CRITICAL THINKING WILL BE USED ON THE JOB

Critical thinking on the job is essential to a rewarding and successful career. Your employer, no matter what your position, will value your ability to think critically and solve problems, and you will value the work you do if you are allowed to use those skills to improve yourself and your environment.

How will you use critical thinking on the job? There will be, no doubt, countless opportunities to think critically at work. You may be asked to think critically about a problem in order to solve it. For example, you may realize that the office does not run efficiently and you have evaluated ways to improve the flow of work. No matter how you arrive at thinking critically on the job, keep the steps to problem solving handy.

As you have read in this chapter, critical thinking is a process, not an end. Once you have solved a problem, new issues will arise that require critical thinking. To improve yourself and your progress on the job, you will have to be committed to thinking critically.

Building Your Career Portfolio 5

Contact someone in a career that is similar to what you want to do. Ask what kinds of thinking dominate his or her daily tasks. Does this person need to be creative each day? Does he or she need to analyze on a usual basis? Does this person need to draw conclusions and evaluate every day? What thinking skills does he or she consider the most important?

_____

_____

_____

_____

First Voices

Adult student returns to start a new life: Credits developmental classes with firm foundation

John Byers,
B.S., Manager of
Student Activities

Ten years ago I was a 42-year-old newbie to the college experience. Working in construction, I'd fallen off a roof, broke my back, and developed a tumor in my spine, which kept me from returning to my profession. Starting down the college path was one of the most intimidating experiences of my life. I had worked in construction for 27 years, raised two children, built a home, and never thought I'd ever go to college.

I didn't know what to expect when beginning college. I hadn't opened a textbook in over 24 years. Fortunately, my fears were quickly put to rest once I got to know my instructors and embraced their guidance, knowledge, and encouragement. My first teacher in English 101, Sabrina Swartz, was one of the exceptional ones who took me under her wings and helped lay the foundations of my academic skills.

I was blessed to have many other great instructors who provided encouragement and direction; however, some were not so engaging. My approach was to absorb all the knowledge possible, no matter what the teaching style.

My developmental classes were key to my success. They instilled in me the confidence to start my new life and career. With the support of my wife (now of 32 years), I focused on my studies and got involved in numerous clubs and committees on campus.

As I took advantage of every opportunity that came my way, I forged ahead in my commitment to my academics and received numerous awards, including the All-Ohio Academic Award. I graduated from Bowling Green State University with a 4.0 and a bachelor's of science in technology at the age of 50.

Putting myself into every opportunity that came my way helped me not only to gain valuable knowledge but opened many doors to new experiences and networking contacts at the college and in the community. This led to my current job as Manager of Student Activities at Owens Community College and then receiving the college's highest employee achievement award, The Mount Everest Award.

PATH OF DISCOVERY

Journal Entry

How will practicing critical thinking steps affect your future decisions? Do you think you will be better prepared to solve problems and make better choices or do you think you will be more confused about the choices you have?

CHAPTER REVIEW QUESTIONS

1. What has recent brain research told us about learning?
2. In what ways will you be expected to learn in college?
3. Define creative and critical thinking and compare and contrast these approaches to understanding.
4. Identify and describe the six steps of critical thinking/problem solving.

CHAPTER 5 CASE SCENARIOS

1. Joan has been named a student ambassador for her college. One of her duties is to help prepare fall orientation for new students. The advisers have told the ambassadors that last year students rated orientation low because they had to wait in long lines to get registered and the information they received was too detailed and difficult to comprehend. Joan and her fellow ambassadors have been asked to create a new way of providing orientation to students. What process will the group need to follow to create a successful program for new students?
2. Sidra wants to earn money for college tuition next year, but she doesn't have the time to work 40 hours a week. Sidra's creative thinking process results in the following ideas: sell blood, tutor classmates, tattoo herself with a local company's logo and charge them for advertising, sell items on the Internet, work as a telemarketer, or house sit for friends and family members. Explain what steps she needs to follow in order to determine the most viable solution.
3. Kenya has decided to apply for a loan forgiveness program that will pay all her tuition as she completes a degree in computer networking. The loan forgiveness program requires that she find a job in networking within 3 months of graduation or she will owe the full amount of her loans. After she completes a year of her degree program, she learns that the job market for networking specialists does not look promising for the next 5 years, which may mean she will have great difficulty finding a job when she graduates in a year. What should Kenya do?

RESEARCH IT FURTHER

1. Using the key terms "critical thinking" and "creative thinking," search the Internet for tips for improving critical and creative thinking skills. Make a table of the different tips and present the information to your classmates.
2. Create a survey to distribute to fellow students that asks them to describe the top concerns on campus. Report your results to the class and choose one to solve through the critical thinking process.
3. Interview faculty members in different programs on your campus and ask them to provide a critical thinking scenario that a graduate of their program would encounter on the job. Ask them to work through the problem to a feasible solution. Share the different problem-solving scenarios with the class and ask them to compare and contrast the solution processes.

References and Recommended Readings

Diestler, S. (1998). *Becoming a critical thinker: A user friendly manual* (2nd ed.). Upper Saddle River, NJ: Prentice Hall.

Dweck, C. (2006). *Mindset: The new psychology of success.* New York: Random House.

Foer, J. (2007). "Remember this." *National Geographic, 212*(5), 32–55.

Gunn, A. M., Richburg, R. W., & Smilkstein, R. (2007). *Igniting student potential: Teaching with the brain's natural learning process.* Thousands Oak, CA: Corwin Press.

Harris, R. (2002). *Creative problem solving: A step-by-step approach.* Los Angeles: Pyrczak Publishing.

Miller, G. (2008). The magical number seven, plus or minus two: Some limits on our capacity for processing information. Retrieved March 10, 2008, from www.musanim.com/miller1956.

6
READING

E ven though he can bench press hundreds of pounds, Evan feels weak when he thinks about his "to do" list this week for his classes:

To Do This Week

- 54 pages of genetics with pictures and boxed stories about scientists and experiments on DNA from biology textbook
- 72 pages of aviation mechanics with diagrams of interiors of airplanes, graphs, and dozens of drawings of different parts of a plane from aviation textbook
- 213 pages of an autobiography that has to be read in addition to the textbook
- 3 pages of an article that has be summarized and critiqued

When Evan was in high school, he didn't have to read much to get by—and he barely got by—but now his instructors not only expect it, they demand that he keep up with his reading. Between quizzes, required discussion, writing assignments, and tests, Evan is discovering that college without reading is like kickboxing without sore muscles.

All of his reading assignments swim in his head as he heads to the learning assistance lab to get help with the writing assignment for the article he has to read. When Michael heard Evan was having trouble with a reading and writing assignment, he told him about the center.

"Evan, I know exactly what you need to do. I just got help with my algebra homework, and the tutor explained it in a way that I could get it. It works. Just try it," Michael had said earlier in the week.

"It's not that I don't know what to do," Evan says to the tutor. "I just don't like to read. It's boring. I would rather run laps all day than sit down and read. And there is so much of it. It's insane," he says.

The tutor laughs at his last remark. "It does seem like a lot at first," she says, "but you will get better at reading the more you do."

"I don't think I want to get *that* good at it," Evan jokes. He pulls out his assignment from his freshman seminar class; the reading assignment is to find an article about college students and write a summary and critique.

"Once you find the article you want, read the article first for meaning. Check out the title, the publication information, the date," the tutor says, "and once you begin reading, stop after every paragraph, at first, and see if you can summarize the author's ideas. When you can sum up what the article says, then you can read the article critically."

"I think I am getting this, but what am I going to do about the chapters and the book I need to read?" Evan asks.

"Just follow the same process. It works for other types of reading," says the tutor.

Evan knows that like sports, you only get better with practice and by challenging yourself with harder exercises.

In this CHAPTER

Whether you love to read or you find the activity to be a challenge, reading will be an integral part of your education in college. Can you imagine getting a degree and *not* reading a page? Technology may have changed the way we read and how we incorporate written information, but it has not changed the importance of reading in becoming an educated individual. This chapter addresses the different reading strategies for sharpening your reading skills, whether you are reading books, magazines, e-books, or Web articles.

More specifically, after completing this chapter, you will be able to do the following:

- Identify college-level reading expectations.
- Define active reading and critical reading.
- Describe methods for improving reading skills.
- Explain different reading strategies.

COLLEGE READING EXPECTATIONS

If death and taxes are unavoidable parts of life, then reading is an inevitable part of college and lifelong learning; fortunately, reading is more enjoyable and more profitable than death and taxes. The bottom line is that you will not be a successful student if you do not read assigned and supplemental material regularly. Likewise, it will be difficult to practice lifelong learning after college without reading on a regular basis. As previous chapters have mentioned, reading class handouts and college publications as well as your textbooks is essential to success in college. Reading is important to your college education and lifelong learning for many reasons; the following are just a few incentives for making reading an integral part of your daily college work:

- Reading provides you with basic information that you can use to create knowledge of a subject.
- Reading improves your understanding of others and the world around you by exposing you to new viewpoints, ideas, and cultures.
- Reading helps you understand yourself, which will assist you in making better life choices.

Despite this, it must be acknowledged that some students just do not enjoy reading because of bad experiences in school or due to learning difficulties. For these students, reading can be a challenge to academic fulfillment. Professors would be ecstatic if all their students read well and enjoyed all the assigned reading material. More realistically, students find some reading dull and difficult to comprehend, and they long to read something "exciting." The not-so-good news is that until you get into classes that pertain to your major or career choice, you may feel that the assigned reading is unin-

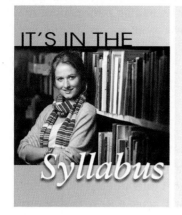

IT'S IN THE

Syllabus

Review your syllabi and determine how many pages (approximately) you are required to read each week for ALL of your classes. Do some classes require more reading than others? Which ones? Are some of the reading assignments harder than others? Which ones?

How do you plan to handle the reading load this semester? Do you expect to keep up with the readings? Why?

teresting, but the good news is that there are ways to improve your comprehension *and* enjoyment of the reading assignments.

In addition to the subject matter that you will encounter in college reading, you will also find the reading load to be greater than in high school or in most jobs. If you are taking four three-credit-hour classes, you can expect to read more than 100 pages a week if each professor assigns a chapter from the textbook. This number does not reflect full-length novels, supplementary articles, required periodical subscriptions, reserved library materials, online resources, and your own notes from class—all of which may be part of your weekly reading load. The truth about college reading is that there will be plenty for you to read and that you will also be held accountable for not only reading, but comprehending and thinking critically about the material.

Information Literacy

Along with the increased reading load, your professors will also expect you to be an information literate student. That means that you not only know how to read well, but you also know how to find information and use it effectively and ethically. This chapter discusses critical reading later, and you will also read more about researching in Chapter 8, but it is worth introducing the concept as part of the expectations for reading in college. The American Library Association's website (2010) defines *information literacy* as the ability to do the following:

- Determine the extent of information needed
- Access the needed information effectively and efficiently
- Evaluate information and its sources critically
- Incorporate selected information into one's knowledge base
- Use information effectively to accomplish a specific purpose
- Understand the economic, legal, and social issues surrounding the use of information, and access and use information ethically and legally.

Their website www.ala.org provides even more information about how information literacy is used on college campuses. For sure, to become truly

USING TECHNOLOGY TO GET AHEAD

Some of the material available online, such as e-books, is also available in audio formats. If you have trouble reading or prefer hearing information read aloud, look for audio files of the information. Some publishers provide additional podcasts that accompany their textbooks and provide summaries of the material; some e-books and databases have audio files of the material in which the works are read by a computer; and software such as JAWS allows students who need assistance with reading to hear what is on a computer screen.

information literate, you will need to become proficient at finding information, read that information thoroughly, assess the value of the information, and use it effectively in a presentation, paper, or other assignment.

What to Do with a Reading Assignment

The majority of your reading in college will most likely be assigned by your instructors. When you first get a reading assignment, you will need to spend a little time preparing to read, which will help you maximize the benefit from the time that you have available. No doubt, in the first week of classes, you will be given handouts, syllabi, and chapters to read in your textbook. How do you manage it all without falling behind and feeling overwhelmed at the start of the semester? First, remember that all written material that your professors give you needs to be read. You will be held responsible for it immediately or at a later date; therefore, you will need to create a process for reading and remembering what you have read.

No matter how big or small the assignment, treat the reading seriously. In other words, make a conscious effort to read and remember important information. A positive attitude about the reading assignment will help make the other steps easier to complete. Before you begin reading, you will also want to organize assignments according to size, importance, and date of completion; start with the most important documents first, and then work your way down the stack. Shorter assignments can be completed first unless their due dates are far off.

To increase your chances of reading effectively, set a definite time and place to read. Just as you would set a time to study or go to work, you will need to schedule time to read, preferably at the same time each day. Finding a comfortable, quiet area to read is also important because it will put you in the mood to focus on what you are reading. Equally important to setting a definite time is to establish routine breaks from reading. Get up, walk around the room, get a drink of water, and get the circulation going in your legs again. Taking breaks in which you physically move around the room will help your concentration and keep you from falling asleep.

In addition to finding the right place, consider setting a purpose for reading. Learning to understand and set purposes for reading will make the assignments easier to comprehend and complete. For example, if your reading purpose is to improve your understanding of networking, then when you sit down with the textbook for your computer networking administration class, you are in the right frame of mind. Conversely, if your reading purpose is to be entertained when you read a chapter in economics, you may be disappointed and less receptive to remembering what you have read.

As noted in previous chapters, writing down goals is the first step to realizing them. The same holds true for reading. If you want to increase your reading speed, vocabulary, and understanding of the material, you should do more than give them passing consideration. Set specific, concrete goals for individual assignments or the whole semester. An example of a reading goal could be to increase the number of pages you can read in one sitting or to learn five new words a week and use them.

Finally, take care of yourself throughout the semester as you do your assigned work. You won't be able to read effectively if you are overtired, hungry, or sick. Don't try to force yourself to read if physical or psychological issues distract you. Too much sugar and caffeine and too little sleep can make reading more difficult; so can certain medications and emotional distractions. If you cannot concentrate, return to the material when you are feeling better, although sometimes you will just need to dig in and get it done regardless of how you feel.

FIGURE 6.1 Sample Reading Log

Title of Text or Chapter _____

Number of Pages _____

Author _____

Class _____

Instructor _____

Date Reading Should Be Completed _____

Estimated Time to Complete _____

Reading Goals _____

Actual Time to Complete _____

Reading Goals Achieved   YES   NO

Skimmed   YES   NO   PARTIALLY

1. What is the reading about?

2. What did I learn from the reading?

3. What questions do I still have about the reading?

4. What difficulties, if any, did I have while reading?

New Vocabulary Words and Definitions:

Another way to prepare to read effectively is to start a reading log that will help you focus your reading goals and prepare you to read actively. Figure 6.1 provides a method for reading effectively as well as critically. The first two questions at the bottom of the log support active reading whereas the last two ask you to think critically about what you have read.

Reading in the Disciplines

The following strategies for reading in the disciplines show just a sample of the material you may encounter in college.

Math

Take your time in reading both the written information and explanations as well as the visual representations of problems and steps for solving them. Reading assigned chapters *before* you get to class will help you check your reading comprehension.

Literature

You may find you have more reading in literature classes—novels, short stories, plays, and poetry. Start early with these long reading assignments and take notes along the way. Depending on the complexity of the literature, you may need to read the work a few times, especially poetry, and sound each word out. Although sounding out individual words, or subvocalization (see "Reading Difficulties" section), is often considered a reading difficulty, it may be necessary to slow down and read short pieces of literature aloud. Also, pay attention to details when reading fiction and poetry.

Languages

The goal in reading in a foreign language is to improve your comprehension first. Use a dictionary the first time you encounter new vocabulary and work on improving your speed.

Sciences

Reading in the sciences will take time and focus as you encounter new concepts and processes. Look for visual representations of the content in your textbook.

Social Sciences

Large amounts of assigned material will be part of any social science class. Start reading the chapters early and look for key ideas. People and their theories or their actions (in history) will be key components of the reading. Learning the who, what, when, and where of the material will make it easier to remember.

Reading Difficulties

For some students like Evan, no matter how much they want to read well, the activity is difficult. Dealing with reading difficulties can make a short reading assignment seem like climbing Mount Everest and can make it hard to stay motivated. The following paragraphs describe some common reading difficulties that students experience. It is not intended as a comprehensive list, nor is it intended as a diagnosis for problems that you may experience. If you think you may have a reading difficulty or a learning disability, you should see your college counselor for a proper diagnosis. Your college's counseling services should also provide you with resources that will help alleviate any problems you may experience because of a learning difficulty.

Some reading difficulties are more bad habits than disorders. Subvocalization, or pronouncing each word in your mind as you read, is one bad habit that some readers engage in. Reading the same words or sentences over and over again, or regression, is another bad habit of some readers. Improving your reading speed, or the rate at which your eyes move across the page, often eliminates the reading habits that slow you down. Moving a finger, pen, or pencil to follow the text as you read can also slow down your reading speed. Unless you are stopping to take notes along the way, eliminate the use of an instrument to keep your eyes moving. Finally, poor concentration can negatively affect how quickly you read. In some cases, poor concentration is part of a larger issue that may be diagnosed by a health professional. If poor concentration is just a bad habit, then you can work toward improving concentration by eliminating distractions and following the suggestions outlined in this chapter.

Dyslexia is a neurological disorder that makes it difficult for a person to comprehend and recognize written words; it may also cause trouble with writing and spelling. According to the International Dyslexia Association (2009), 15 to 20% of all students have dyslexia, and most people with dyslexia have average or above-average intelligence. The good news about dyslexia is that many students have learned to cope with the disorder and succeed in college and careers.

Attention deficit disorder (ADD) or attention deficit hyperactivity disorder (ADHD) is a behavioral disorder that causes a person to have difficulty in paying attention. Reading can become just another obstacle that someone with ADD or ADHD must overcome. In order to work through any difficulties that ADD/ADHD may cause, you will need to contact your counseling center. As with dyslexia, ADD/ADHD can be managed so that your reading skills get sharper.

Some reading difficulties are actually the result of vision problems. A regular eye exam can determine whether your difficulties are caused by the need for corrective glasses or contacts. If you think your vision is the reason that you have difficulty reading words, get your eyes checked by a doctor. You may want to stop first at your college's health clinic, if one is available, for a screening. Also, take advantage of any health fairs that are offered on your campus where you can get a free screening that may pinpoint the problem.

Reflection
EXERCISE 6.1

How much reading do you expect to do each week while you are taking classes in college? What difficulties, if any, do you anticipate in completing the reading? How are you prepared for the expectations? ■

READING ACTIVELY and CRITICALLY

Active reading, a term that you may hear often in college along with *active listening*, means that you are fully engaged in reading by focusing your mind and body on the activity. Many first-time students read passively rather than actively and do not fully concentrate on the material. Just reading the words is not enough for college classes. Instead, you must be a part of the process by making sure you comprehend what you are reading.

Critical reading is another term that you will hear frequently in college. Some students may think that critical reading means having a negative reaction to what they have read, but it actually involves a series of steps to react and respond to the reading—either positively or negatively, depending on the material. Your end goal in critical reading is to question and evaluate the material, not to take it at face value. Critical reading, as well as active reading, is a skill that will take practice to develop. The following sections provide specific strategies for improving both skills.

Skimming and Scanning

You may already be familiar with the terms *skimming* and *scanning* as they pertain to reading. Skimming is reading material quickly and superficially, paying particular attention to main ideas; use this method of reading when you first get a reading assignment because it can help you get a feel for the material, how long it is and how difficult it will be to read. In order to skim a text effectively, you should read the first and last paragraphs and the main headings of each chapter, as well as the first and last sentences of remaining paragraphs; of course, if time is a factor, you can delete some of the steps or add more, such as reading the first and last paragraphs

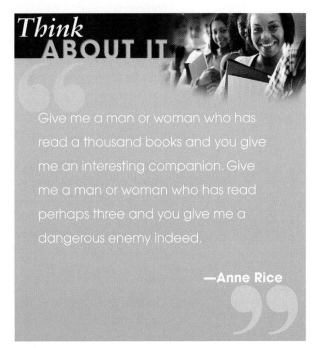

Think
ABOUT IT

Give me a man or woman who has read a thousand books and you give me an interesting companion. Give me a man or woman who has read perhaps three and you give me a dangerous enemy indeed.

—Anne Rice

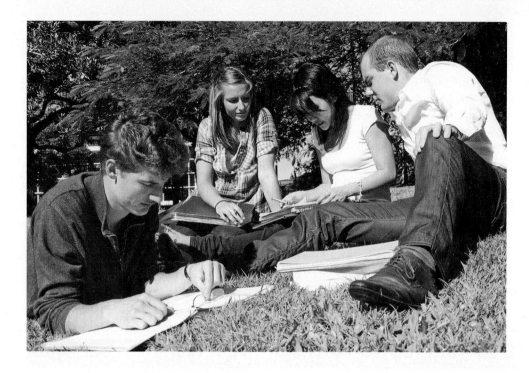

of each section. Ideally, skimming should be done before in-depth reading. However, sometimes skimming may be the only chance you have to read the material. If this is the case, be sure to pay attention to the major headings of each section and the first and last paragraphs of the sections. Don't be surprised, though, if you miss major ideas that are sandwiched in the middle.

Although it now has a meaning similar to skimming, scanning is a method of reading that has traditionally meant "examining a text closely." Nonetheless, some reading experts define *scanning* as looking quickly for a specific item or topic as you would scan a phone book for someone's name or a dictionary for a particular word. Scanning also includes examining the table of contents and index of a book to narrow your focus and prepare you to find what you are looking for. Just as with skimming, scanning requires that your eyes move quickly over a page. However, the difference is that you know what you want to find and will slow down once you find it. Scanning is particularly useful when reviewing sources to use for a paper. You can determine rather quickly if the source pertains to your topic or not. Once you scan, you can then skim or read the text actively.

Breaking Down the Material

As stated earlier, part of scanning a text includes examining its parts. Certain pages of a book or article hold valuable information for deciphering its purpose. Students who want to "hurry up" and read the meat of the assignment often overlook some of the most important parts: The title, author, table of contents, chapter titles, introduction, section headings, headnotes, bibliography, and index are wonderful and revealing components of a piece of writing.

Title

The title of an article or book will give you a clue as to what it is about. For instance, the title of this book is *The First-Generation College Experience* because the information within it reflects the unique needs of first-generation students, not other types of students at institutions of higher education. When reading any material, take time to think about the significance of the title of the work you are reading and go back to the title to look for additional meaning once you have completed the whole text.

Author

Knowing something about the author of a text can be just as important as what he or she has to say. Because of their reputations, some authors lend credibility to their words whereas others instantly make readers suspicious of their motives. If you recognize the author's name, then you should have a good idea of what the text is about. The more you read, the more you will encounter writings by certain people, from whom you will begin to anticipate certain viewpoints.

Table of Contents

Most books have a table of contents that shows how the book is organized, listing the chapters as well as any subsections that appear in the chapters. The table of contents also contains the beginning page number for each chapter or section. Familiarizing yourself with the table of contents will make it easier to find information when you need it.

Introduction

Sometimes overlooked, the introduction can provide all the information you may need to determine whether a particular book is what you want. When researching a topic, you can decide whether a book will be a good source for you by reading the introduction. Introductions typically tell the reader what the whole book is about, the unique features you will find, and which viewpoint is supported.

Chapter Titles

The titles of chapters are a good indication of what you can expect to read within the book. Chapter titles also help you locate information more quickly. Can you imagine trying to find information from this book about taking notes without any chapter titles? You would have to scan each chapter until you found it.

Section Headings

Section headings work in the same way as chapter titles. They indicate how the material is organized and they give you a sneak peek of what is to come.

Headnotes

The text that appears at the beginnings of sections or before essays that explains or briefly summarizes what you are about to read is called a *headnote*. Headnotes can provide biographical information about the author or can indicate the essay's main points.

Bibliography

A bibliography, or list of references or works cited, usually appears at the end of an article or a book, right before the index. Literally, a bibliography is a list of books that the author has read or used in preparing the text. This section of a book or article is often overlooked, but actually contains a wealth of information for the reader. If you want to learn more about a topic that the author briefly mentions, you can look at the bibliography to see what other books are listed about the subject. Also, if you are doing research on a topic and need instant access to a list of more sources, an author's bibliography can supply you with potential material.

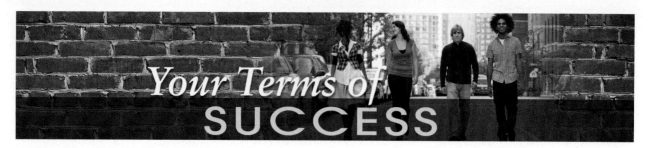
Your Terms of SUCCESS

WHEN YOU SEE . . .	IT MEANS . . .
Active reading	Reading to remember and understand; reading with a purpose.
Bibliography	A list of books or other sources.
Comprehension	The ability to remember and understand.
Context clues	Hints of a word's meaning by how it is used in a sentence.
Critical reading	Reading to evaluate and to question.
Dyslexia	A learning disability that makes it difficult for a person to read, spell, or listen effectively.
Headnote	The information that appears at the beginning of a work; often contains background information on the material or the author.
Index	An alphabetical list of subjects or terms that appear in a book; placed at the end of the book.
Information literacy	The ability to determine if information is needed, to access the information, to assess the usefulness of the information, and to incorporate the information ethically and responsibly.
Introduction	The beginning paragraph or pages of a text.
Section titles	The titles that appear within the sections of a chapter.
SQ3R	A reading strategy that stands for Survey, Question, Read, Recite, and Review.
Subvocalization	Sounding out individual words while reading.
Table of Contents	A list of the chapter titles and section headings in a book; appears at the beginning of a book.

Index

One of the last elements of a book is its index, which is an alphabetical list of major ideas or words that are keyed to the pages on which they appear. If you need to find that information on note taking, for instance, you can use the index to pinpoint the exact page. Indexes are especially helpful in research when you are evaluating sources to see whether they contain material about your subject. For example, if you need some information on Lorraine Hansberry and have located a book on African American playwrights, you can look for her name in the index to see whether she is mentioned in the book. If she is not listed in the *H*'s (for Hansberry), then you know that the book is not a good resource for you.

You are probably thinking that this process seems time-consuming and unnecessary, especially if you do not have much time to spend reading anyway. Yes, the process takes

FIGURE 6.2 Questions for Critical Reading

- Who is the author? What is his or her background? What makes him or her knowledgeable about this subject? Does he or she have any bias toward the subject?
- What is the audience for this material? Are the length, vocabulary, and organization of the information appropriate for the audience?
- Are there any factual errors? Does the author misrepresent information or oversimplify it?
- Does the author say anything that seems confusing?
- Do the author's examples support her overall point? If not, which ones do not support her main point? Why don't they support it?
- Does the author leave anything out of the information?
- What else would you like to know about the subject?
- What questions do you have about the information that the author did not answer?
- Overall, how do you rate the reading?

time, but the more you do it, the less time it will take because you know what to look for. Also, your reading speed and comprehension will improve, which will mean that you can complete all your assignments more quickly.

Questioning

Once you have actively read assigned or researched material, your next step will be to read it critically. In most cases, this will mean rereading the material, especially if it is short. Be sure to allow yourself plenty of time for this activity. At this point in the critical reading process, you do not necessarily need to answer the questions you raise—you will just want to look for places within the material where you want to know more, need clarification, or disagree with the author's conclusion.

Questioning the author to find his or her purpose in writing the material is the first place to start. If the material comes from a certain source, whether a magazine or newspaper or blog, you will also want to question the source's purpose. Questions to ask include whether the author is an authority. Is he or she credible? Is there an agenda or bias in the writing? By considering the source, you may ask, "What is the purpose of presenting this material?" If it comes from a newspaper, does the material aim to inform, persuade, or present one side of a debate? If the material comes from a blog or an anonymous website, does the material intend to serve as reliable information, or is it only someone sharing his or her observations with no intention of providing accurate information? See Figure 6.2 for more examples of questions to ask. Writing these questions in the margins of the text or using a notebook for your questions is a good start to reading critically.

Evaluating

Another important element of critical reading is evaluating what you have read for its credibility and usefulness; it is also a part of information literacy. By asking the questions suggested in the preceding section, you can use the answers to determine the

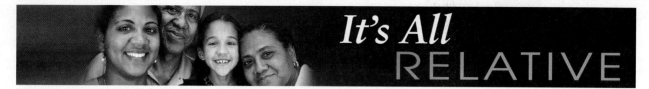

It's All RELATIVE

As you begin to read more in college, you may find that your conversations with your family change. For example, you may be aware of how you talk with family members or what words you use to express yourself. Communicating in a new way may bring your closer to your family and a feeling of belonging or it may push you apart, especially if they feel confused by your new vocabulary and topics of conversation.

As you improve your vocabulary and reading comprehension, be sure to acknowledge how this new side to you will fit into your family's expectations of you. You may find yourself sharing and teaching others in your family about what you are learning, too, or you may decide to hold back.

YOUR TURN

Do you feel comfortable talking with your family about what you are learning? • Do you change how you talk and what you say when you are with them? • Do you feel a better connection with others now or do you feel more distance? • Explain.

_____

_____

_____

reliability of the information. For example, if you ask about the author of an article on diet and exercise and you find out that the person has a Ph.D. in health and has conducted research on eating healthy foods and exercising, you may conclude that the author is credible and therefore the information she provides is reliable. You can also use evaluation to determine whether material has a bias or presents only one side of an issue. If the website, for instance, uses inflammatory language, ignores counterarguments, or fails to mention any other explanation or reason for its conclusions, then it may be unreliable. There is so much data at our fingertips that anyone who accesses information will need to use evaluation to determine whether it is actually useful.

Collaboration
EXERCISE 6.2

Working within a group, discuss how you use active and critical reading for this class. Then, choose another class and discuss how you use active and critical reading. Are the processes any different? If so, why? If not, why? ∎

DEVELOPING YOUR READING SKILLS

Whether you are an expert reader or in need of extra practice, you will definitely strengthen your reading skills while you are in college. The key to improving your reading skills is regular practice in reading assigned material such as textbooks, articles, and websites—really anything that your professors require or suggest that you read. The following section provides tips for developing those skills as you read.

Building Your Vocabulary

Increasing your vocabulary is another benefit to reading regularly. Some students get sidelined when they read because they encounter unfamiliar words; few students take the time to look up words that they don't know, and they subsequently miss out on learning new ideas or understanding the intent of the author. It is well worth your time to look up words when you read, but there are some methods you can use to decrease the time you spend flipping through your dictionary.

The first method for learning new vocabulary words is to look for context clues in the sentence. Many times you can figure out what the word means by how it is used in a sentence or by the words that surround it. Consider the following sentence:

> Students often use context clues to *decipher* the meanings of unfamiliar words.

If you didn't know that *decipher* means "to figure out," you could still understand the meaning of the sentence by the words around it and by considering that students are using something (context clues) in order to do something (decipher) the unfamiliar words. You could deduce, then, that students are making the unfamiliar words more familiar by using context clues. Now, try this sentence:

> It was not until we traveled to Beijing that we realized how *ubiquitous* American fast food was. On every street corner we saw a McDonald's or a KFC restaurant.

If you are not familiar with modern-day Beijing, you may not know that American restaurants are plentiful; in fact, you may believe that China has very little American food. Thus, to understand the meaning of *ubiquitous*, the second sentence provides the context clues. The phrase "On every street corner" from the sentence that follows should help you realize that *ubiquitous* means "everywhere."

Although context clues will allow you to make sense of most unfamiliar words, there will be times when you cannot rely on the other words in the sentence to help you. For example, can you tell what the words *amenable* and *obsequious* mean in the following sentence?

> Charles was *amenable* to going out to eat with Sheila's *obsequious* mother.

In this case, if you don't know what the words mean, the sentence offers little assistance. Does Charles want to go out to eat or doesn't he? Is Sheila's mother someone who is enjoyable to be around or isn't she? To answer these questions, you may need to look up the words. Here is what you would see if you were to look up *amenable* in a dictionary:

a me na ble adj. 1. agreeable 2. open to an activity or idea 3. controllable

Now look up *obsequious* for yourself and see if you can decipher the sentence.

Another way to figure out what words mean is to know some common Latin and Greek root words, prefixes, and suffixes (see Table 6.1). For example, if your professor calls astrology a "pseudoscience" and you know that the Greek root *pseudo* means "false," then you will be able to understand that your professor considers astrology not to be a true science. In order to learn the common roots of words that we use every day, you will need to study word origins. Taking a college reading class or looking up words in the dictionary regularly will help you learn to recognize the roots in many words.

TABLE 6.1 Common Latin and Greek Root Words

Root	Meaning	Example Word	Definition
Ante	Before	Antebellum	Before the war, specifically referring to the American Civil War
Anti	Against	Antibiotic	Against life, specifically against microorganisms
Auto	Self	Autobiography	Writing about the self
Biblio/Bibl	Book	Bibliography	A list of books
Cede	Go, Leave	Secede	Leave an organization or alliance
Chrono	Time	Chronological	Events ordered by the time in which they occurred
Cogn	Know	Recognize, cognizant	To know from before; fully informed
Graph	Write	Autograph	Person's own signature
Inter	Within, Between	Intermission	The period between performances
Phil	Love	Philanthropy	Love of humankind
Photo	Light	Photography	Producing images using light in the process
Pseudo	False	Pseudonym	False name

Tips on Building Vocabulary

- Purchase or borrow discipline-specific dictionaries when you begin a class that contains a large amount of terminology (e.g., medical or scientific dictionaries, foreign language dictionaries, or glossaries for literary terms).
- Before asking your professor or classmate what a word means, look it up.
- Don't be afraid to look up words, even the same word multiple times. You will eventually be able to recall their meanings.
- Use new words in conversation to "try them out." Using them regularly will help you remember what they mean.
- Write new words on 3 × 5 index cards and jot down the book title and page number where they appear. Look up the definitions when you have time and write them on the cards. Take the cards with you and review your new words when waiting in line or stuck in traffic.
- Buy and browse a thesaurus, a book that contains synonyms for words. A thesaurus is handy when you are searching for a word that is similar to another.
- If you have an email account, subscribe to a word-a-day service that sends you a new vocabulary word each day, or buy a word-a-day calendar.
- Subscribe to magazines that challenge your reading skills: *The Atlantic Monthly*, *The New Yorker*, and *Harper's* are examples of print magazines that provide interesting and challenging material.

Increasing Your Reading Speed

Knowing how quickly you read is helpful in planning time for reading and in marking your progress. The goal is to increase your speed *and* your comprehension. In order to calculate your reading speed, time yourself while you read. Go back to the earlier section, "Questioning," and reread it. It is 259 words in length. To calculate your reading speed, divide the number of minutes that it took you to read the passage into 259 to get your reading speed. For example, if it took you 2 minutes to complete the passage, then you read at a rate of 129 WPM (259/2 words per minute).

Number of words   259

Number of minutes   ___

259/___ (number of minutes) = ___ WPM

Average readers read between 200 and 250 words per minute, but that does not reflect their comprehension of the material. Techniques for improving speed are worth learning and practicing. Your college may offer a speed reading class, or you may be able to examine different methods for improving speed through books or websites.

Checking Your Comprehension

The most important aspect of reading is comprehending and remembering what you have read. If your textbook has questions at the end of each chapter that will help you reinforce what you have learned, then get in the habit of answering them when you finish a reading assignment. Even mentally answering the questions will help you understand the material. If your textbook does not have questions, then create your own or write a short summary of the chapter. To reinforce what you have learned, trade summaries with a classmate.

A high WPM reading speed means very little if you do not remember anything that you have read. Your goal should be to improve your reading speed reasonably, to help you keep up with the reading demands of college, and to improve your retention and comprehension of the material.

Improving Your Reading Attention Span

Each semester will get more demanding in terms of reading because as you advance in your degree program, you will be encountering more challenging content. Therefore, the more practice that you have in reading effectively, the easier it will be to complete larger reading assignments. If you find that your "reading attention span" is not long, then you can work on lengthening it. First, you will need to figure out how many pages you can read comfortably without getting distracted or tired. Write down the number in your reading log, a notebook, or in a calendar. Each time that you sit down to read an assignment, notice how many pages it is. See if you can "beat" the number in the previous reading session. The more you read and the more you challenge yourself with reading, the better you will get. Just be patient.

Critical Thinking
EXERCISE 6.3

Of the reading skills discussed, which ones will be most challenging for you to build on? What resources does your college have that will help you strengthen these skills? ■

READING STRATEGIES

As you have read so far, the act of reading is more than just moving your eyes along a page of words. Instead, reading in college requires that you use a reading strategy that

Integrity has been defined as doing what you say you will do even in the face of adversity. Acting with integrity in college includes making a commitment to complete reading assignments in all your classes even if you face challenges to your commitment.

Reading in college is not optional; rather, it is crucial to success. When you make the commitment to enroll in college, you must also follow through with that commitment by tackling the reading that is part of the experience. You will also need to demonstrate integrity when you do not read—be honest with your instructor, if asked, and be honest with yourself that your progress (or lack thereof) is related to how well you are preparing, through active and critical reading, *before* class.

YOUR TURN

Have you experienced the feeling of being confused in class because you did not prepare by reading the assignment beforehand? • What was the experience like? • What did you do the next time you were assigned readings for class? • What did you learn from the experience?

_____

_____

_____

will help you retain the information and think critically about what you have read. The following sections provide different types of proven strategies that can help you read more efficiently and effectively.

Taking Notes While You Read

Taking notes as you read, either in your textbook or in a notebook, is an excellent way to remember what you have read and to begin the process of critical reading. Writing down key ideas, terms to look up later, and questions that you have as you read helps you stay focused and improves comprehension. However, avoid highlighting large sections of text. Excessive highlighting defeats the purpose of noting only key or very important information. If you can write in your textbook, create one- or two-word summaries of each paragraph or section. If you need to keep the text clean, then use your reading log (see Figure 6.1) exclusively. Otherwise, you may want to use it in conjunction with in-text notes.

SQ3R Reading Strategy

One of the most popular reading strategies, called SQ3R, was developed by Francis Pleasant Robinson in 1946 and published in *Effective Study*. Although many books and websites since then have interpreted and expanded the strategy, the overall method works as follows:

(S) Survey: Before reading your text closely, start by examining the headings, subheadings, graphics, charts, and references if included.

(Q) Question: After finding these major organizational signposts, think of questions that you have. One way to generate questions is from headings and subheadings. For example, the subheading "SQ3R Reading Strategy" can be turned into "What is the SQ3R reading strategy?"

(R1) Read: Read each section, making sure you are concentrating on the material.

(R2) Recite: After reading each section, say aloud what the section was about and answer the questions that you asked during the Question stage. You may also want to write your answers on note cards to review later.

(R3) Review: Anytime after you have completed the first four steps, review what you have read. Some experts suggest reviewing within 24 hours of reading, whereas others recommend reviewing what you have read in short sessions over a period of time.

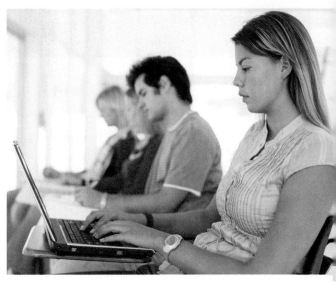

Improving your reading skills includes learning to read on a computer or with other forms of technology.

Thinkstock

Putting the Pleasure Back into Reading

Although not a specific reading strategy, finding pleasure in what you are reading is one way to improve your reading skills. One of the most difficult reading obstacles that every college student faces, no matter how well he reads, is generating interest in the material. A common complaint of students is that the reading was "boring." True, some college reading material will be dry and dull, but you can change how the reading affects you by changing your attitude about the reading itself. Sometimes, you just need to trick yourself into enjoying what you read, and one way to do that is to tell yourself that you will learn something new and useful.

Another way to put pleasure back into reading is to seek out pleasurable reading yourself. If you have favorite authors or types of writing, go to a bookstore or library and get a copy of your favorite book, magazine, or something that may spark your interest. Make an effort to find reading (and browsing through aisles of books will help) that is interesting, stimulating, and even fun. Reading or browsing through a magazine or newspaper a week will help your reading skills. The habit of reading will also make it easier to stick to the schedule you have set for reading class material. If you have a good book on your table, it can serve as a reward for completing less exciting reading assignments. Once you create good reading habits, you will find yourself reading—and enjoying—even after classes are over. You will soon discover that you are curious to learn new things, and reading will satisfy your thirst for knowledge.

Reflection EXERCISE **6.4**

What do you enjoy about reading? What kinds of writing do you like to read and why? ■

PLUS EXERCISE **6.5**

(Personality + Learning Style = Understanding Situations)

Think about Evan's situation regarding how to tackle his reading for the week. The solitary activity of reading seems contradictory to Evan's kinesthetic, outgoing nature. He admits that he is not very interested in what he has to read usually but still needs to read the assignments and also must remember what he has read and respond to it. Using what you have learned from this chapter, what advice would you give him? Once he reads the article and writes his summary and critique of it, what strategies can he use to complete the rest of the reading?

Now, considering your own learning style, personality type, and special circumstances, what can you do to tackle the reading assingments you have for this week? ■

HOW THE READING LOAD AND EXPECTATIONS MAY CHANGE

You have probably noticed that in each chapter's discussion of moving from college to university, the demands always increase, and reading expectations are no exception. Most definitely, the reading load will increase significantly—you may find that you have hundreds of pages a week to read and comprehend. You may also find that you are expected to do more than just recall the information. In addition, you will need to think critically about the reading by asking questions of the author (What does she mean? How does she know? What are the implications of her argument?) and of yourself (Do I agree? Does this argument make sense?). Professors in upper-level classes will also require you to discuss the readings in class. Most definitely, the discussion will move beyond the content of the reading to the formulation of new ideas and opinions about the topic of the reading. The more you are able to contribute, the more you will get out of the reading and the class.

Building Your University Portfolio 6

Find someone you know (or ask your professor for the name of a former student) who has transferred to a four-year university and ask how the reading load has changed, or not, at the four-year university. Is there more to read? Is the material more difficult?

_____

_____

_____

_____

From College to Career

HOW READING SKILLS WILL HELP YOU SUCCEED

There are very few, if any, careers that do not require some level of reading. Jobs in computer programming and networking demand constant reading to stay on top of new developments and trends in the field, as do industrial careers that require you to stay abreast of the latest regulations and laws. No matter how hard you try, there is just no escaping a career without reading.

The good news is that after completing your certificate or degree, you will be a better reader and you will understand the importance of reading regularly. A better vocabulary, improved reading comprehension, and faster reading speed will help you do your job better. An employee who reads well is an asset to a company because she is usually more attuned to the latest trends and ideas. An employee who reads effectively also knows what is happening in the company and can more easily handle challenges on the job.

Building Your Career Portfolio 6

Contact someone in a career that is similar to what you want to do. Ask what reading is involved. Does the career demand daily reading? If so, what kinds of active reading (e.g., skimming or scanning) and what kinds of critical reading (e.g., questioning or evaluating) are expected?

_____

_____

_____

_____

First Voices

STORIES OF SUCCESS FROM COLLEGE GRADUATES

Finding focus and her passion at the community college: University student looks forward to her future

Suzi Garcia,
A.A., Full-Time
University Student

I never really thought about the future while I was in high school; I didn't focus on my studies, nor did I look for colleges after school. After graduation, which I did not even attend, I visited my father's family in Peru. This kind of visit is very typical of Latinos, but I came home six months later just as unfocused as I was before I left. After a year working as a waitress in a chain restaurant, I decided to take a couple of classes at the local community college.

I not only made great friends, both with professors and fellow students, but I also discovered how much more there could be to learning besides taking notes and studying for tests. There are passionate discussions and new ideas. I didn't learn to memorize new information; I learned to think. College showed me there was more to the future than tomorrow. I found myself questioning what it was I wanted to become in life and, with help from my professors, how to accomplish my goals.

Since I have received my associate of arts degree, I have continued on to a university where I am on the road to my bachelor's degree in both Spanish and English with a minor in Creative Writing. I am currently a member of three scholarship and research programs, co-chair for one of my scholarship committees, staff member for the college's literary magazine, and I spent a summer in Europe studying Spanish on a scholarship. They are preparing me for my career and life after school. College has given me opportunities of which I never dreamed, not only for my life now but also for my future.

PATH OF DISCOVERY
Journal Entry

How do you plan to improve your reading skills in college? What do you hope reading well will do for you?

CHAPTER REVIEW QUESTIONS

1. Which reading skills are essential to success in college?
2. What are the differences between active and critical reading?
3. What strategies can you use to make reading more manageable?
4. What types of reading difficulties can a student encounter? What are some strategies for overcoming them?

CHAPTER 6 CASE SCENARIOS

1. Gerry hates to read, and he will do anything to keep from reading in college. He does, though, like to read home improvement magazines. He is working on his associate of arts degree. What can he do to read well and enjoy reading?
2. Meghan thinks she may have a reading difficulty, but she has never been diagnosed. Instead, she has worked extra hard to keep up with and understand her reading assignments. However, as her classes have gotten more difficult, she is worried that she won't be able to keep up. What can she do to stay on top of her reading assignments?
3. Wilson can't remember anything he reads for class, even though he spends hours the night before reading the material. He is also has difficulty remembering what words mean. Although he is building his vocabulary slowly, he still finds himself looking the same word up several times before he can remember. What should he do?

RESEARCH IT FURTHER

1. Interview three people about their reading habits and preferences. Find out what kinds of reading they do for their jobs and what kinds of reading strategies they use to complete their reading. Also, ask if they read for pleasure and what types of reading they enjoy most. Write down your findings and present them to your class.
2. The National Adult Literacy Survey (Kirsch et al., 2004) indicates that over 40% of Americans are functionally illiterate, which means they can function in society but cannot perform complicated reading tasks. Most of these Americans are at a disadvantage socially and economically. Do your own research as to what challenges people who cannot read or cannot read well will face.
3. Create a survey that asks members of the campus community what can be done to encourage students to read more. For example, would they be willing to participate in a book club or to host a local author on campus?

References and Recommended Readings

American Library Association. (2010). Information literacy defined. In *Information literacy competency standards for higher education*. Retrieved from www.ala.org/ala/mgrps/divs/acrl/standards/informationliteracycompetency.cfm#ildef.

International Dyslexia Association. (2009). Dyslexia basics. Retrieved September 18, 2009, from www.interdys.org.

Kirsch, I. S., Jungeblut, A., Jenkins, L., & Kolstad, A. (2008). Executive summary of adult literacy in America: A first look at the results of the national adult literacy survey. National Center for Education Statistics. Retrieved May 15, 2008, from http://nces.ed.gov/naal/index.asp?file=OtherResources/ExecSumAdultLitFirstLook.asp&PageId=156.

Pauk, W. (1984). *How to study in college* (3rd ed.). Boston: Houghton Mifflin.

Pleasant, F. (1970). *Effective study* (4th ed.). New York: Harpercollins College Division.

LISTENING and NOTE TAKING

aura settles in her usual seat in the front row of her world civilization class. After the lesson she learned about writing down important information when she is in class, Laura has gotten better about listening more closely even when distractions compete for her attention.

"The clip we are about to watch," her professor says as she pushes the play button on the television's DVD player, "discusses the ancient library in Timbuktu."

Laura laughs at herself as she tries to spell Timbuktu. She underlines the word so that she can remember to go back and check the spelling when she rewrites her notes. Having dyslexia is frustrating at times, but she has found that laughing about her challenges is a great way to relieve her stress in certain situations.

"I love it when she stops lecturing and shows us these videos," her classmate next to her whispers in her ear. Laura misses some of the information in the video because of the distraction, but makes another note to fill in the missing information later. She loves how engaging the films are, but her dyslexia makes it difficult for her to watch and take notes.

"Hey? Do you have an extra pen?" her classmate whispers again. She knows his name, Franco, because he is a friend of Juanita's, but she hasn't talked to him much. He seems more interested in socializing than paying attention in class.

She hands him a pen and makes another note to fill in any gaps she has from being distracted. Laura is not too worried about the missing information because she has been able to view a few of the clips on her own—the library has a copy of everything her professor uses in class—but even watching them over and over again is sometimes challenging despite her comfort with learning by listening.

As the lights come back on, her professor asks if there are any questions.

"Yeah, I have one. Will that be on the test? I mean, are we responsible for remembering everything that guy said?" asks someone from the back of the room.

"Sure. You have the material that was assigned for reading, the information I cover in the lecture, and then anything else that I bring in. All of this should be studied for the test," the professor says.

"And she's not lying," says Laura to herself. Even with help from her mentor and the tutor in the learning assistance center, Laura has her work cut out for her: The information in the book is arranged chronologically, but her professor lectures on causes and effects in history, constantly referencing other eras, people, and dates in the process. Then there are the tests that cover major themes such as important reformers or federal policies. No one note-taking strategy seems to work for reading, listening, and studying.

"Any other questions?" her professor asks and pauses for a few seconds. "Okay, if you realize you do have questions after class, be sure to email me or come by my office early next week. You have only a week to study for this test. All essay questions. Be prepared to write." She smiles, straightens her papers, and heads for the door.

"I have another question," Franco says to Laura. "Are we going to pass this class?" She knows he is half serious, but Laura is worried about that, too.

Making sense of her notes may be only part of the challenge, but it is the first one she will have to overcome.

In this CHAPTER

Learning to listen and take notes effectively can give you the edge in college because you will be able to take in more information and remember it more easily. Laura can attest to the importance of developing a note-taking system, especially for those who have learning difficulties that prevent them from using just one style. This chapter discusses various note-taking strategies, including the method Laura developed, as well as improving your listening skills.

More specifically, after completing this chapter, you will be able to do the following:

- **Describe ways to listen more effectively.**
- **Discuss basic note-taking strategies.**
- **Explain methods for adapting strategies by type of course.**

THE ART of LISTENING

Listening involves more than just hearing, but is an activity that we often take for granted, an activity that we believe we do well. In fact, John A. Kline (1996), in *Listening Effectively*, reports that people often think they are better listeners than their family members, friends, and coworkers (p. 5). If we believe we are better listeners than others, then we will be less likely to work on the very skill that might prevent so many conflicts, misunderstandings, and hurt feelings—among many other negative effects! It is important to recognize then that, regardless of how you rate yourself as a listener, you will benefit from reviewing basic listening strategies as they relate to gathering information in the classroom. Too often students miss out on crucial information that can help them be successful because of poor listening skills.

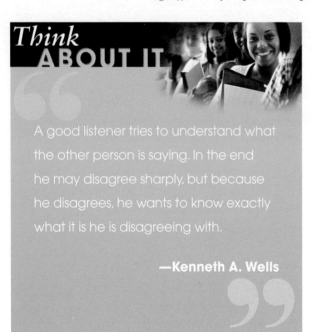

Think ABOUT IT

> A good listener tries to understand what the other person is saying. In the end he may disagree sharply, but because he disagrees, he wants to know exactly what it is he is disagreeing with.
>
> —Kenneth A. Wells

The Listening and Note Taking Connection

First, it will be helpful to examine the connection between listening and college success. Indeed, listening, remembering, and note taking all have something in common: They are necessary in the process of learning.

You will not be able to make it successfully through your classes without doing all three. Retaining and recalling information, however, is only part of the process. This chapter helps you with receiving the information, which will in turn help you with the process of turning the information into a knowledge base that you will build on for the rest of your life.

Preparing to Listen

We have been listening all our lives—to our parents' voices, to our favorite music and television shows, to our friends on the phone. When something is so common in our lives, why would we need to think about how to prepare to listen? Isn't it as natural as breathing? According to Pauline Rowson (2007) in *Communicating with More Confidence,* we would benefit in preparing to listen by considering the reasons that we may not listen well to begin with: We don't agree with the person speaking; we believe strongly in the topic (and therefore cannot "hear" anyone's perspective that differs from ours); we are tired or distracted; or we want to talk ourselves, which is a frequent reason for poor listening (pp. 152–153).

To help prepare for more effective listening, it is important to understand the different types of listening. *Passive listening,* sometimes called casual listening, is characterized by lack of engaged attention. *Active listening,* on the other hand, involves listening that concentrates on what is being said and taking steps to remember the information. To be an active listener, you must decide that listening is a worthwhile activity and that important information will be shared.

The first step to effective listening is to prepare to listen before you get to class. In other words, you will need to read the assigned pages or chapters ahead of time so that you have some knowledge about the lecture or discussion topic. If you have read the chapters ahead of time, you will be familiar with new words and concepts. Preparing to listen also includes reviewing your assigned readings before you get to the classroom. If you have a few minutes between classes or on the bus, pull out your book and skim the major headings, boldfaced terms, and text boxes that appear in the margins.

To listen effectively while in class, avoid distractions. First, you will need to sit up front and put away textbooks for other courses, cell phones, pagers, and other distracting items. Your best defense against interruptions is to clear your desk of anything except your textbook, pen, and paper. Stow other items in your backpack or underneath your desk or table. If you need to get anything out during class, such as a dictionary, minimize the disruption by being as quiet as possible.

If you find yourself next to a chatty classmate or one who likes to write notes to you, simply move. Even if you are only politely listening or reading her messages, you will be guilty of disrupting the class by association. Talkative classmates make it difficult for you and others to listen, and they distract you from taking good notes.

Another aspect of listening effectively is to maintain a positive attitude about the class. If you think the class is boring or a waste of time, you will be less likely to pay attention. Even if your beliefs are true—and others bemoan the class as well—pretend that the class is the only one you have left before graduating and that if you don't pay attention and take good notes, then you will have to spend another semester in the course. In other words, do whatever you need to "psych" yourself up and invest in the class.

Minimizing outside distractions is another way to keep a positive attitude. There will be times when you have to work late, stay up all night with a sick baby, or help a friend who has just had a crisis. If not handled well, these stressful experiences could affect your performance in class. As much as possible, leave your personal life at the door and concentrate on the class that you are sitting in. Even if the lecture for the day

Improving your listening skills in college can translate to improved listening at home. Listening effectively means that you listen with an open mind and without judgment until the speaker is finished. Then you can ask questions of the speaker if there are points that you don't understand. Listening effectively also means that you avoid twisting the person's words to fit what you want to hear.

There may be times that, because you know your family members well, you will assume you know what the other person will say, complete the other person's sentences, or make a decision before the person finishes. You will be a more effective listener (and cultivate better relationships) if you practice the tips for listening in this chapter—and that includes not making assumptions about the speaker or letting your emotions get in the way of listening.

YOUR TURN

In what relationships do you not listen well? • Why do you not listen as closely as you could? • What have been the consequences of assuming what the other person has to say? • How do you feel when a family member assumes what you will say or judges you before you speak?

_____

_____

_____

is overshadowed by a personal problem, remember that you *can* handle both your academic duties and your personal life.

Finally, prepare for class psychologically by preparing physically. Make sure you have eaten something before each class so that you won't be interrupted by a growling stomach. Moreover, dress in layers in case the room temperature is uncomfortable. Nothing is more distracting than being too hot or too cold. Getting plenty of sleep the night before class will also help you pay attention and listen effectively. Although adequate sleep may be a luxury if you work a late shift or you must get up in the middle of the night to take care of a child, be sure to make an effort to get a good night's sleep if possible. You won't be able to maintain high concentration and retention or even good health without adequate rest.

Listening Critically

As previously stated, active listening, much like active reading, involves focusing on the task at hand and concentrating on what is being conveyed, whether words or sounds. Another part of listening effectively is listening critically, or processing what you hear and evaluating it. Listening critically will help you make decisions about what is important and what is not, what is objective and what is biased, and what should be stored for later and what should be discarded.

Listening critically is a skill, one that should be practiced regularly. Your college professors will invite you to think critically and challenge your assumptions (that is learning!). As you get more comfortable with listening actively and critically, you will move from merely listening and taking notes that reflect what your instructors have said to listening to evaluate and ask questions of the notes you have taken. Consider the following questions as you work on listening critically:

- *Speaker.* Is the speaker a credible source? How do I know? What possible biases does he or she have? What is his or her experience with the topic?
- *Message.* What is the speaker's purpose? What are the details he or she uses to convey the message?
- *Details.* Is the speaker using facts or opinions? How do I know? Which type of details work best for what the speaker is trying to convey?
- *Self-knowledge.* What do I already know about the topic? How does what the speaker is saying conflict or support my beliefs and opinions? Do I feel I have learned something new?
- *Larger picture.* How does what the speaker is saying fit into the larger picture? How can I relate the message to something I already know about life or the world at large? Are there any connections between what I have heard and what I have experienced?

Answering these questions will get you started on the right path to listening critically. It is especially important to listen critically and mentally ask questions of what you are hearing, "tuning in" rather than "tuning out," when you hear something that you don't agree with or don't understand.

Remember, too, that *critical* does not mean "negative." If you find that what you are hearing is not holding up to what you know about the subject or the speaker is not credible, you can still ask questions that are respectful and curious. Most people do not mind being politely challenged or debated.

Eliminating Listening Barriers

Despite your efforts to prepare for class, you may find barriers to listening effectively, barriers that you cannot avoid no matter how well prepared you are. For example, what should you do if your instructor talks too fast, uses technical jargon or an advanced vocabulary, is unorganized, digresses from the lecture material (tells stories, allows too many irrelevant questions), or does not explain key concepts? Although you cannot coach your instructor in the art of speaking, you can ask him or her to slow down or define terms. Most professors do not mind repeating information or defining specialized language on the board because they want students to understand the material during lecture or class discussion. It may be a little harder to ask the instructor to be more organized or to stay on topic during a lecture. However, one way to get what you need without offending the professor is to ask if she would mind providing an outline before each class. Another method of getting the professor to stay on the subject is to ask a question about the topic or an upcoming exam or assignment. Your nudging may move the lecture back into focus.

There may also be physical or psychological barriers to listening effectively. If you have an unaccommodated learning disability or a hearing problem, you may not be able to listen productively. Talking to a counselor about learning or hearing difficulties can help you listen more effectively. A more common hindrance to listening is students' insecurities about their ability to do well in the course. It is not uncommon for a new student to feel, at first, intimidated by the course, the instructor, or other students in the class. The reason for the discomfort could stem from a student's feelings that he or she is not good enough or smart enough to be in college. A student also may feel that everyone else, except him or her, knows what to do, what to say, and how to act. This fear is common, and usually it subsides after the first week or two.

Remembering What You Have Heard

Once you adequately prepare to listen in class and you remove any barriers that inhibit your ability to take in information, you will need to turn your attention to remembering what you hear in class. Taking notes, of course, is one way to retain information. However, there are some other methods that will help you recall information at a later date.

Participating in discussion and activities is an excellent way to remember key concepts. In fact, professors consider student participation as part of active, rather than passive, learning. You are more likely to remember a concept if you have incorporated it into your own thinking. There is a reason that the most talkative students are usually the most successful. They have made the material personally relevant, which makes remembering easier. However, participating in class discussion may be difficult if you are shy or feel out of place in the classroom. Some students refrain from asking questions because they don't want to look ignorant in front of their classmates. Then there is the other end of the spectrum from the silent student—the constant questioner. These students dominate the professor's time by asking questions that sideline the discussion or bring up material that has already been covered. Don't be intimidated by a predominantly quiet classroom or by a student who asks the professor excessive questions. If you have a question, ask it. Some instructors believe there are no "stupid questions."

If you don't feel comfortable asking questions during class, visit with your professor after class or during office hours. Some instructors ask students to write questions down and pass them up before class is over. Take advantage of such a practice; you will be able to ask questions without the fear of speaking up in front of classmates.

Another method for remembering, tape recording lectures, is popular with students who have the time to listen. Listening to a tape recording will work best if you have a long commute or if you go over your notes as you listen. Be sure to ask permission before you turn the tape recorder on, and make sure you have fresh batteries with you in case they are needed.

Reflection EXERCISE 7.1

Think about a time when you heard someone speak about a topic that you did not agree with. How did you listen? How did you react to what you were hearing? ■

Tech TIPS

USING TECHNOLOGY TO GET AHEAD

There are many websites that provide tips for listening better and taking good notes. The website YouTube has thousands, if not more, videos of college lectures that you could use as practice for listening and taking good notes. The video of Randy Pausch's "The Last Lecture" provides an excellent opportunity for you to practice listening and note-taking skills.

NOTE-TAKING STRATEGIES

No matter how much you refine your listening skills, they will not be sufficient for taking in and remembering everything that is said in class. That is where your note-taking

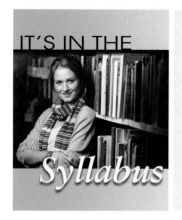

IT'S IN THE *Syllabus*

By looking at your syllabus, can you determine how the information will be presented in the course? Will it be presented by chapters, topics, units?

What are the note-taking expectations for the class? Is that information in the syllabus or did you learn it from your professor or other students?

skills will help you. There are numerous methods of taking notes for a class. Your goal should be to find the note-taking strategy that works best for you. Remember that you may have to adapt your note-taking style to each course, each teaching style, and each learning style strength. For example, outlining may work well in a history course in which the instructor writes key terms on the board and organizes her lecture around key ideas. If your professor prefers unstructured discussion, you will need to adapt your note-taking strategy to make the most of unorganized information.

Whatever you choose for the particular course, your learning style, and the specific situation, there are a few tips that you need to remember when taking notes.

- *Listen for the main ideas.* Instructors will slow down and emphasize certain information, terms, and definitions. They may even use verbal signposts such as "The most important thing to remember," "This may appear on an exam," or "Two crucial points." If the instructor writes or hands out an outline, you can be sure that it contains the main points of the lecture.

- *Leave plenty of "white space" (blank space on paper) when taking notes.* Don't try to fill your page with as much information as possible. You will need the white space to add more notes or to synthesize ideas once you have reviewed.

- *Review your notes as soon as possible after class.* Waiting for two weeks to review your notes will ensure that you won't remember everything that you have written or how it all fits together. Most experts suggest that you review your notes within two days of the class.

How Information Is Presented

Without a doubt, listening effectively is the first step to taking good notes, but you will also benefit from understanding how information can be presented during a lecture. As you attend more classes, you will probably notice that professors have a certain way in which they present their material. Some will follow the textbook information in the same order. Others will lecture only on new material that cannot be found in the textbook or other course materials. Still others will present a combination of the two methods. Reading assigned chapters and materials before you attend class will allow you to determine which information in the lecture is new and which has been covered in assigned reading materials.

As you will learn in Chapter 8 there are many different ways information can be organized. Recognizing the different ways material can be organized will help you stay organized in your notes and will provide you with strategies for revising and reviewing your notes when you begin studying.

Chronological details are arranged in time (first this happened; then this happened . . .). An example of chronological lecture notes can include dates as indicated in the following from a history course:

1801: United Kingdom of Great Britain is created.

1803: Louisiana Purchase is made by Thomas Jefferson.

1815: Battle of Waterloo signals end of Napoleon's career.

Cause/effect details are arranged by presenting a cause and then its effects or an effect and its possible causes. An example of cause/effect lecture notes can look something like the following notes from the same history course:

Cause: Civil War

Effects: (1) slavery ended, (2) industrialism began, (3) the nation was brought back together, (4) the federal government proved stronger than the states.

Compare/contrast details are arranged by similarities and differences. The following is an example of a comparison and contrast of two poets discussed in a literature class:

Robert Frost	Walt Whitman
Similarities	
Male	Male
Used nature in poems	Used nature in poems
"poet of the people"	"poet of the people"
Differences	
Poems are more structured	Poems are open and loose
Speakers more contemplative, solemn	Speakers more upbeat and positive
Life spanned 19th and 20th centuries	Life spanned 19th century

Details are arranged in order of importance with the most important detail coming first and minor supporting details following. Or the important details can start a list that works to a major detail. The following is an example of notes taken from Chapter 1 arranged from most important to least important.

Self-awareness (purpose of education)

Values

Goals

Mission

Personality type

Learning style

Developing a Shorthand

As you take more notes in each class, you will find yourself using a few of the same words over and over again. These words are good candidates for abbreviating or denoting in symbols. You can then create your own shorthand. Shortened words such as "ex." for *example,* "w/" for *with,* and "b/c" for *because* are abbreviations you probably already use in notes and email messages. Symbols that you may already use include % for *percentage,* + for *add* or *and,* and # for *number.* If you use a new abbreviation or symbol for a word, be sure to make a note of what it means; for example, "TR" could mean "Theory of Relativity" in a science course or "Teddy Roosevelt" in a history course.

Here is a list of other commonly abbreviated words and symbols:

At	@
Between	betw, b/w
Decrease	decr
Department	dept
Does not equal	≠
Equals	=
Example	eg, ex
Government	govt
Important	imp
Increase	incr
Information	info
Regarding	re
Significant	sig

Developing a shorthand will allow you more time to concentrate on what is being said. As you get more practice, you will become better at judging which information is worth writing and which is not, and your shorthand will become more efficient. Just remember to read over your notes within a day or two so that your abbreviations are fresh in your mind. It is a good idea also to complete the words or concepts during review so that you won't struggle to remember what all the shortened words mean later in the semester. Moreover, it will reinforce your learning of the material.

Outlining

Using an outline is a good method for taking notes if the instructor is organized and offers information in a logical pattern. Some instructors encourage outlining by writing key words and concepts on the board or an overhead projecting device. If your instructor organizes lectures or class discussions in that manner, you will be able to write an outline for your notes quite easily. The key to making your outlines effective will be to provide plenty of space between the items so that you can fill in the blank spaces with extra information. The following example shows an outline for a lecture on effective listening.

Preparing to Listen Effectively

 I. Listening Critically
 II. Possible Listening Barriers
    A. External
        1. Hunger
        2. Climate discomfort
    B. Internal
        1. Feelings of self-worth
        2. Stress

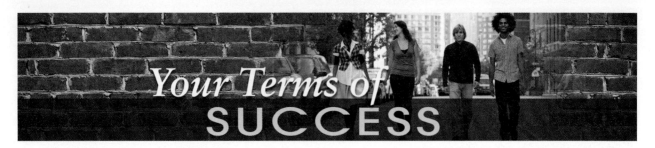

Your Terms of SUCCESS

WHEN YOU SEE . . .	IT MEANS . . .
Active listening	Listening with focus and a purpose.
Annotating	Taking notes within a text.
Cause/effect	An arrangement of information that connects the cause of an event to its effects.
Chronological	An arrangement of information by time.
Compare/contrast	An arrangement of information that connects the similarities and differences of two subjects.
Cornell System	A note-taking strategy that involves dividing your paper into an upside-down T.
Critical listening	Listening to evaluate the information.
Least important/most important	An arrangement of information that lists points based on their importance.
Listening barrier	An obstacle, either physical or mental, that keeps you from listening effectively.
Outlining	An arrangement of information that is ordered by how the information is presented.
Shorthand	A note-taking strategy in which shortened forms of words and symbols are used.
T System	Also known as the Cornell System.

III. How Information Is Presented
   A. Chronological
   B. Cause/Effect
   C. Compare/Contrast
   D. Most Important/Least Important

Taking Notes within the Textbook

Writing in the margins of your textbook, also called *annotating*, can be another effective way to take notes, especially if the reading assignment is lengthy. If you don't mind writing directly in your textbook, you can summarize main points that you have read. Writing brief summaries (two- or three-word summaries) or questions in the margins will help you make sense of and remember what you have read. Brief, marginal summaries will also help you review the material before and after class and when you start studying for an exam.

Annotating in your textbook and writing down critical questions are two methods of further reinforcing what you have read and will help you prepare for listening and note taking in class. Examples of critical questions about a reading include "How do I know this to be true?" and "What else should be considered?" Annotating your textbook with your own notes will help you not only reinforce main ideas, but will also help you synthesize the information in new ways that will produce connections between concepts, making the material more memorable and more relevant.

Critical Thinking
EXERCISE 7.2

What are some drawbacks to using the Cornell System, shorthand, and outlines when taking notes?

If you decide to write in the margins of your textbook, be sure that the book you are writing in is not one that you want to sell back to the bookstore. If you do not want to write in your book but still get the benefits of summarizing the material, you can write your summaries on a separate sheet of paper. Make sure that you label each piece of paper with the chapter title and page number of the book.

Highlighting in your textbook is another method that students use for taking notes on reading material. Mark important concepts for review with a highlighter pen, but be careful that you do not highlight too much information. Over-highlighting the text can defeat the purpose—instead of making it easier to understand key terms and information, too much highlighting can make everything seem of equal importance. Therefore use a highlighter pen sparingly. For example, don't highlight more than two sentences in a row. A better method would be to combine highlighting with written summaries for the greatest effect.

The Cornell System

Cornell University professor Dr. Walter Pauk developed a system for note taking that has become popular among many students. The Cornell System, also known as the T System, is ideal for those who benefit from the visual impact of organized notes, and it can benefit other types of learners, such as Laura, because it is an organized way to take and review notes. The key to the Cornell System is dividing your notebook paper before you begin writing. Draw a horizontal line across your notepaper two inches from the bottom of the page. Then draw a vertical line from the horizontal line to the top of the page about 2 inches from the lefthand margin. The page should look like Figure 7.1.

The largest area, the righthand column, is used for taking notes during class. The lefthand column is used for asking questions as you take notes about material you don't understand during the lecture or to note possible exam questions that you think about as you are writing. The bottom section is reserved for summarizing your notes as you review them. The act of summarizing should help you understand and remember the information.

FIGURE 7.1 Cornell System

Note-Taking Strategies in the Disciplines

The following strategies for note taking in the disciplines are just a sample of what you may encounter in college. Chapter 9 will discuss specific study strategies within disciplines, but here we give some note-taking strategies, grouped by discipline, that will make reviewing your notes and studying easier.

Art

In an art appreciation class, you will need to identify eras (20th century), movements (Cubism), and artists (Picasso) as well as their characteristics, as seen in drawings, paintings, and sculpture. Quickly sketching the works in your notes and listing the characteristic details will help you record the information you are receiving through lectures. You may also notice that in the study of art there are times of intense change (usually coinciding with a world or cultural event) followed by artists who imitate or modify slightly the new style. As you review your notes, look for patterns within groups of artwork and for points of contrast.

Music

In a music appreciation class, use the same suggestions noted for art appreciation when you take notes. Instead of recreating a painting or sculpture in your notes, you may need to write down descriptions of what you are hearing and what the sounds remind you of. Are the sounds fast or slow? Do you hear one instrument or many? Does it sound like a stampede or a trip down a lazy river? "Translating" music samples into written notes as well as reviewing music clips on your own will strengthen your understanding of the material. As with your art notes, during review, look for patterns across movements and eras and denote contrasting ideas and elements.

Literature

Taking notes in a literature class will require you to have completed the assigned readings before class and to have annotated and highlighted your text. Because literature classes, even survey classes, focus more on discussion than on lecture, you will want to be prepared to take notes on the analysis. As with music and art classes, being familiar with basic terminology before you get to class will help you take better notes. As you review your notes, look for ideas that pull the different readings together.

Languages

Foreign language classes center more on speaking and interacting than on listening to a lecture. Taking notes will not necessarily be advantageous, because you will need to focus all your attention on listening actively, processing what is heard, and interacting based on what you have heard. Daily preparation is essential to learning foreign languages; take notes as you encounter new material, and ask questions in class to get clarification on anything you do not understand. Any notes you do take should be reviewed soon after the class. As you review your notes, categorize material such as "irregular verbs" and include any tips for using or remembering the parts of language.

Science

Concepts and processes are key in science classes and should be reflected in your notes. Prepare for class by reading assigned material, making note of new vocabulary words, and studying diagrams and figures in the text and handouts. As with any class, ask questions if you are having trouble following the steps of a process. As you review your notes, consider the different ways that you can represent these concepts and processes visually and physically.

History

History classes are usually presented in chronological order, so using the example for chronological details in the section "How Information Is Presented" will help you take notes in this class. However, you will also be required to move beyond specific dates and events by considering overall themes, ideas, and movements. In addition to chronological order, lectures may also use a cause/effect organization in which you list and elaborate on the effects of a cause or the causes of an effect. An example of a lecture topic in a history class is "The economic and social effects of the end of the Civil War." As you review your notes, look for major themes and be able to recall actions that have led to important events.

Math

Taking good notes in your math classes will require that you prepare for and attend each class meeting. As with foreign languages, studying for math should be an everyday occurrence because the skills you learn in each class build on the ones you learned in the class before. When reviewing your notes, you may want to recopy them and make sure that you understand, line by line of each problem, what you are copying. If you have any questions, you can write them in the margins of your notes and try to get answers during the next class meeting.

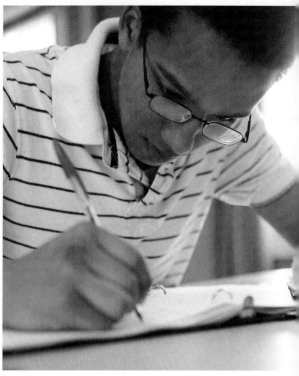

Reviewing your notes regularly is just as important as finding the best note-taking strategy for you.

Thinkstock

Note-Taking Strategies for Learning Preferences

Visual learners benefit from seeing the notes on the page, but they may also benefit from creating images out of the material they have written down. Take, for example, cause/effect information for the increase in electronic communication. An instructor may talk through or write down a few key ideas on the board or in handouts such as the following:

> **In the late 1990s, electronic communication grew at home and in the workplace.
> *Effects: closer relationships with those who are far away, increased productivity, long distance costs decrease, decline in stamp sales, need for communication guidelines at work, problems with sharing too much information or sending junk, bombardment of spam and viruses.

A visual learner may take that same information and create a visual representation of the cause/effect relationship, as in Figure 7.2.

Reading notes aloud, taping lectures, or recording yourself talking through material are all strategies for documenting material. Although "taking notes" implies writing down words and then reading through them, there is no reason that aural learners must suppress their learning style strength during the process. An aural learner like Laura can pair up with someone who is a read/write learner like Juanita and talk

FIGURE 7.2 Visual Learner Note-Taking Strategy for Cause/Effect Information

Need for communication guidelines at work

Long distance costs

Electronic communication increases

Bombardment of spam amd viruses

Increased productivity

through the material presented in a recent class. The read/write learner can then record notes or annotate previous versions and share them with the aural learner.

The act of taking notes by writing or typing them provides kinesthetic learners with a physical activity that makes remembering what has been written easier. Kinesthetic learners like Evan can benefit from using more physical activity or objects when they review their notes shortly after taking them. For example, if you are using formulas to calculate volume in your math class, you may want to review your notes by creating your own volume problems in the kitchen. The act of pouring and measuring water and then calculating your measurements will make it easier to remember the process when you complete homework problems or take a test.

Likewise, a good way for a kinesthetic learner to study for an art class, or any class that uses visual images, is to recreate with paper and colored pencils the artwork you

Integrity MATTERS

There may be a time when you will rely on someone to take notes for you while you are absent, or you may have a learning or physical disability that allows you to ask someone in the class to take notes for you all semester. Student or professional note-takers provide an important service for students with disabilities or unique learners so they can receive the same educational opportunities as other students.

Whether you depend on someone every once in a while or for the duration of your education, you need to consider your own responsibilities in the situation. If possible, review the note-taker's notes with the note-taker or others in the class. Because the physical act of taking notes helps students remember the information, you will need to find other ways to reinforce the material. Don't take your note-taker for granted by missing class or not preparing. The note-taker is not a surrogate student, but a supplement when you are absent or cannot take notes on your own. Act with integrity whether you are borrowing notes from a classmate, relying on a note-taker, or taking notes for someone yourself.

YOUR TURN

How do you feel about taking notes for a classmate or relying on others for notes? • Do you feel a sense of responsibility to take the role of note-taker (or receiver of notes) seriously? • What issues do you need to consider when relying on a classmate for notes or providing notes for someone?

_____

_____

_____

are studying. No need to strive for masterpiece quality when recreating works of art; the physical activity of drawing the wavy lines in the background of Edvard Munch's *The Scream* will help you recall the piece on an exam.

Finding Your Own Note-Taking Style

Laura has developed a special note-taking system for herself because of a learning disability. After taking an introduction to college course, she discovered that the note-taking systems discussed in her textbook did not help her take good notes. Through trial and error, she developed a system that works for her.

To begin with, Laura writes in pencil on her notebook paper. Before class begins, she dates each page and leaves herself plenty of room to write. When taking notes, she writes on only one side of the page; in fact, most of her pages of notes contain less than fifty words. Although she uses more pieces of paper, her notes are easier to read.

Next, she stars words that the instructor says are important. The most important part of her note-taking system is her use of arrows to make connections between ideas. By giving herself plenty of room, she can add connections that are revealed later in the lecture. If her instructor reviews the material before an exam, Laura highlights what she already has and adds notes in the spaces.

One strategy that Laura has developed because of her learning disability is to not worry about spelling. To make connections between ideas, she draws lines between words that relate to each other (see Laura's notes in Figure 7.3). She also makes charts for anything that is compared and contrasted. Finally, she keeps all of

FIGURE 7.3 Laura's Notes

Collaboration
EXERCISE 7.3

Working within a group, determine which classes are the most challenging when it comes to taking notes. Then, choose three strategies that would work best for the selected classes, adapting them if necessary. ■

her notes in a binder with divisions for each class. Staying organized is an important part of her method. Although she uses only one binder during the semester, she keeps her notes easily organized by removing them after an exam. When she takes out notes she no longer needs, she places them in labeled folders at home. Then she carries with her only the notes she needs at the time.

Reviewing Your Notes

Notes are only as good as the extent to which you review them. If you never looked at your notes after you took them, they would serve very little purpose. Therefore, to make the most of your notes, you will need to review them. As stated earlier in the chapter, reviewing should be done within two days of the time you took the notes. With this said, it is easy to be lulled into the sense of "studying" by merely reading over your notes again and again. When reviewing your notes, it is best to reorganize the material, make connections between concepts—even across disciplines—and ask questions about what you are learning.

If you use the Cornell System, then you have a built-in area for adding more information, summarizing, and asking yourself questions. However, if you do not use a particular method, you can still benefit from filling in any blanks or holes in your notes with information you have since learned. As stated earlier, you should also spell out any abbreviations that may cause confusion later. After you fill in any gaps, you should also include questions—either on the same page or a new page—that will help you think about the material on a deeper level. For example, asking "Why is it important to know this?" can help you move beyond demonstrating your comprehension of the material to making it relevant and useful for you.

Freewriting about the material that you are studying is another way of remembering and learning the information that you have listened to. This technique is often used as a way to generate ideas for writing, but it can also be a way to take advantage of all the thoughts you have in your head about the material. For optimum effectiveness, you will need to freewrite within a day or two of the class lecture. With or without your notes, write down (or type into a word processor) all the information that you remember from the class.

The key to freewriting is continuation; in other words, do not stop writing even if you can't spell a certain word or you get stuck on a particular idea. Give yourself 5 or 10 minutes to freewrite; then, go through your freewriting material (some of it you will be able to use and some of it you will scratch out) and highlight or rewrite into complete sentences the information that pertains to

Preparing for class and participating in discussion are two ways that will make taking notes easier.

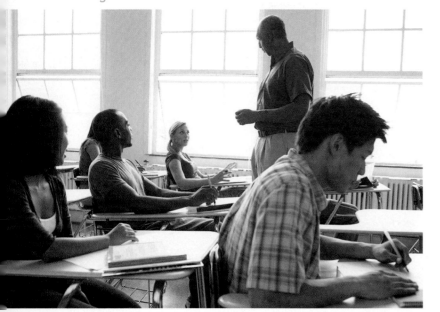

Fancy/Alamy

the lecture. In essence, you will be learning the material in more depth as you write about it.

Finally, reciting notes with a friend can be a useful method for reviewing material. You can do this in person or on the phone. The benefits of reading your notes aloud and discussing them include filling in any gaps of information and reinforcing what you have learned. You can also engage in critical questioning of the material and take turns making connections between major concepts.

Tips for Successful Note Taking

- Prepare for class by reading *all* the assigned material before arriving. If you cannot read all of it, then read as much as you can.
- Prepare to listen actively by removing distractions and bringing supplies.
- Listen actively; concentrate on what you are hearing, seeing, and experiencing.
- Listen critically by asking questions, either on paper or directly in class if your professor encourages questions during class.
- Use a note-taking strategy that takes into account both your learning style strength and the subject matter.
- Go beyond reviewing your notes by only rereading them; instead, focus on concepts and main ideas, make connections between the large ideas, and ask critical questions of processes and ideas.
- Continue the process regularly throughout the semester.

Reflection EXERCISE 7.4

What is your experience so far of listening effectively in college and note taking? What kinds of issues do you encounter in each class with regard to listening? What kinds of issues do you encounter with note taking? ■

PLUS EXERCISE 7.5

(Personality + Learning Style = Understanding Situations)

Think about Laura's note-taking situation in her history class. Because Laura is an introverted person, she finds it hard to ask questions in class or visit her professor one-on-one to get help; she is more comfortable with her mentor or the tutors on campus and is willing to get help from them. Because she has dyslexia, she is very motivated and works hard in her classes, often reviewing and rewriting her notes several times when she studies. However, the variety of ways she needs to arrange and remember information for this class is a challenge. Using what you have learned from this chapter, what advice would you give her? How can she make the most of her note-taking situation and learn the material with confidence?

Now, considering your own learning style, personality type, and special circumstances, what would you do to take notes in a class that requires a variety of ways to organize the material? ■

From College to University

IMPROVING LISTENING AND NOTE-TAKING SKILLS WHEN THERE ARE MORE DISTRACTIONS

When you transfer to a four-year university, the good habits that you have practiced at your community college will help you succeed. However, you may find that you have more distractions. There may be more people on campus and in your classes, more organizations and associations to join, more activities to participate in, and more stress in deciding on a major and getting ready to graduate.

In addition to distractions, you may also find that professors at four-year universities lecture less and rely more on student discussion and presentations. Your ability to organize the material into coherent parts will be vitally important to making sense of the course. If you find yourself at a loss for what to do to take good notes, talk to others who have been at the university longer than you. They may have their own tips. It may also be a good idea, now more than ever, to join a study group or at least find a "study buddy" to review your notes with. Although you may have done well studying by yourself at the community college, you may now realize that group interaction and work is not only encouraged but also necessary for success.

Building Your University Portfolio 7

Find someone you know (or ask your professor for the name of a former student) who has transferred to a four-year university and ask how note taking and listening has changed, or not, at the four-year university. Is there more to listen to and a greater variety of formats (podcasts, video lectures, guest speakers, etc.)? Is more expected in terms of note taking?

_____

_____

_____

_____

From College to Career

PRACTICING CRITICAL LISTENING SKILLS WILL GIVE YOU AN EDGE ON THE JOB

Most of the communication you will do on the job involves listening: to clients' urgent needs, to your employer's plans for the next six months, to coworkers' explanations of how they would complete a project, and to subordinates' questions about how to improve. Being a good listener will involve practicing the critical listening tips that are outlined in this chapter. The reason for cultivating this skill is that you will be bombarded with information from all levels: from your boss above you, from your subordinates below you, and from colleagues around you. Critical listening skills will enable you to filter what you are hearing so that you can act appropriately and avoid making errors in action and judgment. Consider, for example, a coworker who comes to you to complain about a company policy. Without listening actively and critically, you may disregard what the speaker is saying because you don't have time to do anything about it. However, if you took the time to analyze the speaker (Is she a credible source?) and the message (Is the purpose to vent or to change something?) as well as what you know about the situation yourself (Is the policy flawed and in need of change?) and the larger picture (How will this proposed change affect others?), then you are more likely to act appropriately and confidently. On the job, as in life, you will not—and should not—respond the same to all messages you receive from speakers. Practicing critical listening skills will make it easier to determine which messages are critical and which can be acted on later—which will in turn make you a more efficient and effective employee.

Building Your Career Portfolio 7

Contact someone in a career that is similar to what you want to do. Ask that person what kinds of listening and note-taking skills are needed to be successful. Is critical listening an important part of the job? Why or why not? Does this person take notes as part of his or her daily tasks? What is the purpose for the notes and what method is used?

_____

_____

_____

_____

First Voices

STORIES OF SUCCESS FROM COLLEGE GRADUATES

From self-doubt to self-confidence: Determination and encouraging words kept graduate on track for success

Joe Taylor,
A.A., Quality Care/
Appointment Setter

My college experience filled me with anxiety and excitement. Would I succeed? Would I quit? And what would I do after it was all over? I became well known on campus. Professors, staff, administration, and students inspired me with words of encouragement each and every day, which fueled my desire for success.

My classes taught me how to work with diligence, give my all to each assignment, and strive towards advancement, like a desired promotion at work. A professor told me, "Your success is my success," and I held on to those words of inspiration and was very successful in my journey through college; the success continues today. College gave me the tools to achieve satisfaction (happiness, success). I am a winner, not a quitter. Today I help and tutor those preparing for their college placement test and teach basic computer skills. I am employed from home, providing services to over 25,000 customers with satisfactory results: pleasing customers, the corporation, and myself. My best friend for the last 11 years, who is kind hearted, loving, caring, and very beautiful, is now my fiancée.

To those beginning your journey through college, read these words of encouragement and inspiration. I went through college as a disabled student; blind, dealing with screen reading software that did not always work, taking public transportation to and from college, getting my reading materials from tape or CDs, and relying on others for class notes. Like you will be, I was frightened, but I remained focused, calm, and determined and I achieved success. A college education will be the first reward of success in preparing you for the rest of your life. Despite my disability and other challenges, I graduated and so will you. To all future college graduates: Stay focused, remain calm, work diligently because your day is coming soon—graduation and success.

PATH OF DISCOVERY
Journal Entry

Have you ever experienced an important occasion when you did not listen? What happened and what did you learn from the experience?

CHAPTER REVIEW QUESTIONS

1. What preparation should you do to listen effectively in your classes?
2. What listening barriers can interfere and what can you do to eliminate them?
3. How are the Cornell System, shorthand, and outlining different from each other? What are the strengths and weaknesses of each?
4. How would a student who is an auditory learner adapt his note-taking strategy for an art class? How would he adapt for a math class?

CHAPTER 7 CASE SCENARIOS

1. Juan is having trouble making sense of his notes each week for a visual arts class because he has no visuals for the specific artwork being discussed. The instructor does not hand out reproductions of the art, so the students must sketch the pieces during class, but that takes too long. Do you have any other suggestions for Juan besides trying to draw the actual artwork?
2. After borrowing Jon's notes for their college algebra class and promising to return them before the next exam, Theo has instead lost them, and with only two days left before the next test, he is not sure what to do. Jon is a good student who probably doesn't need the notes as much as Theo does, but Theo wants to be able to borrow future notes from Jon. What should he do?
3. Karla has a learning difficulty, and she struggles with taking notes. The counselor has assigned her a note-taker. Now that Karla is getting help with writing down notes, she no longer prepares for class and has stopped listening closely. Sometimes, she doesn't get notes from her note-taker until a week later. If you were Karla's friend or counselor what advice would you give her about using a note-taker?

RESEARCH IT FURTHER

1. Take a survey of the students in one of your other classes as to which of the discussed note-taking strategies they use the most. Create a table of your results and present them to your classmates.
2. Using the key words "note-taking strategies," search the Internet for websites that offer note-taking methods. Choose two or three and review the information to determine which site offers the most practical and complete tips. Present your findings to the class.
3. Create your own note-taking or listening strategy and present it to the class, highlighting the benefits of your method over another method.

References and Recommended Readings

Beglar, D., & Murray, N. (2009). *Contemporary topics 3: Academic and note-taking skills* (3rd ed.). Boston: Pearson.

Kline, J. A. (1996). *Listening effectively.* Maxell Air Force Base: Ala Air University Press.

Rowson, P. (2007). *Communicating with more confidence.* Easy Step-by-Step Guides. Rev. Hayling, England: Summersdale Publishers.

Spears, D. (2008). *Developing critical reading skills.* Boston: McGraw-Hill.

WRITING, RESEARCHING, and PRESENTING

"A 15-page research paper and 5-minute slide show presentation. Due during the last week of class," Juanita repeats to her mother over the phone. She has grabbed a sandwich and is now heading out to a bench in front of the technology center that sits in the middle of campus.

"What do you have to write it on?" her mother asks.

"We get to pick from a list, but I don't even know what some of the topics are, like 'conflict theory,'" Juanita says as she looks over the list again. "I guess that is the point of research."

"Well, you better get started, Juanita. I know how you are about writing papers. Remember when you were taking freshmen composition last year?" her mother asks.

Juanita remembers, for sure, how many nights she stayed up writing papers at the last minute because she thought she worked better under the rush of adrenaline. She thought they were decent papers, but her composition instructor, a professor who taught dual enrollment classes, thought otherwise.

"I guess this is my chance to break those bad habits," Juanita says. "Michael told me that Dr. Kirsey grades hard."

"I thought this was sociology, not English," her mother says.

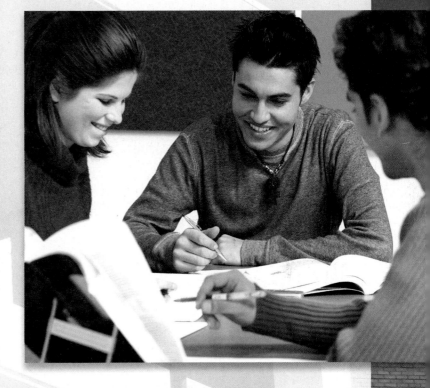

"It is, Mom, but my instructors still expect me to write a good paper. They don't cut you any slack. If it is not written well and uses the right kind of resources, then you can kiss a good grade good-bye," Juanita says.

"You're a good writer, Juanita. You have always loved to write," her mother says. Juanita hears the sound of water in the background, a sign her mother is cleaning up the kitchen.

"I know, but that was when I could write creatively on a topic that interested me. This paper isn't something I can take lightly. I know I can write, but I don't know if I can write 15 pages of research on a topic I don't know anything about right now," she says as she crumples up her napkin and throws away her trash.

Juanita tells her mother she will call later and heads toward the library, with all its information, where there have to be answers for writing a 15-page paper and creating a presentation on a topic that she knows nothing about right now.

Regardless of your major or final career destination, you will be asked to write in college and possibly in your job. As Juanita knows from college classes so far, writing well is an important skill, and you will have the chance to improve your writing while enrolled in college.

Although a discussion of all aspects of good writing is beyond the scope of this chapter, it does provide an overview of the basics of writing well. It will also be a good reference to use when you have completed your composition class and need to refresh your memory about effective writing.

More specifically, after completing this chapter, you will be able to do the following:

■ **Describe the expectations of college writing and the types of writing assigned.**
■ **Identify the steps in the writing process.**
■ **Discuss the stages of research.**
■ **Explain the process for creating an effective presentation.**

COLLEGE WRITING ASSIGNMENTS

Homework has a more complex meaning in college than it did in high school. These assignments are more than just reinforcements of what you learned in class, and they certainly are not the dreaded "busy work" that some high school students suffer; instead, the assignments you are given in college will challenge you to think in ways that you may not be used to, and they will demand much more time than you may have needed to complete assignments in high school. Table 8.1 describes the top ten expectations for college writing. For sure, you will encounter familiar assignments such as extra problem-solving questions in math classes and research papers in English classes, but you may also be required to complete a class multimedia project that involves using slide presentation software or even a community-based project that entails working with various agencies to develop a real-world solution to a problem and then presenting it to local politicians. Other types of writing and presentation assignments include the following:

■ Journals
■ Portfolios
■ Project proposals
■ Essays
■ Research papers
■ Reports
■ Demonstrations (lab work, procedures, etc.)
■ In-class and out-of-class group assignments
■ Formal and informal classroom presentations

Understanding the Assignment

Before you can gloat in the glory of a well-done project or essay, you will have to start with first things first. Understanding the assignment is the first, and sometimes the most crucial step, in succeeding. Too many students jump right in without fully understand-

TABLE 8.1 Top Ten Expectations for College Writing

Expectation for College Writing	What It Means
Fulfillment of the assignment	Your paper faithfully follows the assignment guidelines.
Original thought	Your paper presents your viewpoint of the topic.
Main point or idea	Your paper conveys one major idea.
Organization	Your paragraphs and the details within those paragraphs are presented logically.
Focused paragraphs	Your paragraphs present one minor idea at a time. Each minor idea supports your overall point.
Concrete, specific details	Your concrete details appeal to the reader's senses; your specific details provide a clear picture of your point.
Neat presentation	Your paper is neatly word-processed and printed on clean, quality paper.
Grammatical sentences	Your sentences are complete and error-free.
Correct spelling	All of your words are spelled and capitalized correctly.
Punctual	Your assignment is turned in on time.

ing the directions, the requirements, or the time, equipment, and skills that are necessary to complete the assignment.

Due or Do?

You will often hear two words—*do* and *due*—when your professor discusses a writing assignment with you, and although they sound similar, they have two different meanings. As you learned in Chapter 4, you will "do" your paper, meaning research and write it, well before it is "due" to turn in. Waiting to write an essay the night before or even the day it is due can prove to be much more involved than originally anticipated. Most assignments in college will require hours of reading, understanding, thinking, and then completing. In some cases, you may need the entire semester to work on a large project. You should also consider the effect of a computer failure or printer malfunction if you do not give yourself a time cushion. These factors add to the time it takes to finish a college assignment, so say good-bye to quickly jotting down answers or to writing an assignment the hour before class. Whenever it is D-U-E, you will need to D-O most of the work well before.

Following Directions

Giving yourself the time to complete an assignment will allow you to carefully read and follow the directions. Too often students rush through an assignment sheet only to omit a critical part of the requirements. For example, are you instructed to submit your assignment via email? Will you need to prepare a list of resources you used to complete it? Does it have to be typed? Are you expected to make visual aids? If your assignment has multiple parts, it is important that you complete each part and pay

FIGURE 8.1 Example of Assignment Directions

Topic Proposal

Due: Wednesday, April 18

Before you begin work on your research paper, you will submit a proposal to me for approval. This process is much like proposals that scholars submit to determine if they will be accepted for a conference. Your proposal must be typed and must contain the following, all on one or two pages:

- ■ Your name
- ■ Working title of your research paper
- ■ Working thesis of your research paper
- ■ A 75-word abstract (summary) of your topic
- ■ A 100-word description of how you plan to research your topic

attention to how the parts will be presented. All of these are possible requirements, and if you are unsure of what is expected of you, despite the assignment details, be sure to ask for clarification. Consider the assignment in Figure 8.1 and try to determine the requirements you will need to consider to complete it. Underline, circle, or highlight the important information.

Length, Audience, and Purpose

Length, audience, and purpose are other key factors in understanding writing assignments. For many assignments, you will be given a required length, such as a two-page paper or a 1,500-word essay. Instructors assign lengths to help you gauge the development that you need in order to fulfill the assignment adequately. For instance, if your instructor assigns you a one-page review of a website, then a ten-page paper will not be appropriate because too much information will be included. Conversely, if you have a 2,500-word research paper to write, a 750-word paper will not suffice because there will not be enough information and reflection to fulfill the assignment. If you worry that you cannot meet the length requirement of an assignment, talk with your instructor as soon as possible. He or she will be able to help you narrow or expand your topic so that you will have enough material.

The audience for your assignment includes any potential readers of your paper. When creating a writing assignment, many instructors assume that the audience is your classmates or people who are interested in the subject, but many students assume that the only person who will read their papers is the instructor. If an audience is not specified for your assignment, imagine that you are writing to college students who have been studying the same subject—such as your classmates. How you present your ideas and the words you use should be appropriate for other college students. However, there may be times when you will be assigned a particular audience as part of the requirements for a writing project. The reason that instructors do this is to help you focus your ideas, language, and argument. Consider, for example, an assignment that may be part of a health class:

Writing Assignment for Concepts of Health and Wellness
In a three-page paper, discuss the latest information about sexually transmitted diseases.

This is a straightforward assignment that can be completed by anyone who has access to current information. However, how would the assignment change if your audience were 12-year-old public school students? What information would you add or eliminate? What kind of language would you use? Would you include diagrams and definitions or cartoons? How much detail would you provide? These are all new considerations you will have to make because your audience will have certain limitations. Unfamiliar vocabulary, technical terms, detailed information, and photographs may be inappropriate for these students. Simple terms, diagrams, and personal stories about kids their own age may be a better way to convey the more complicated information.

Now, consider the same topic with a different audience: 70- to 80-year-old men and women who live in a nursing home. Again, you will have the same questions: What information would you add or eliminate? What kind of language would you use? Would you include diagrams and definitions or cartoons? How much detail would you provide? Obviously, this audience will have different needs than young students. Because your audience is more mature, you will need to think about how to approach a topic that they have definite ideas about. Some may be resistant to hearing about the topic because they believe it is not appropriate to discuss, or others may feel they know enough to make their own decisions. Still others will not see the relevance for them. As our two examples show, certain challenges are unique to your audience—changing *who* you are writing for changes *how* you present the information.

A final consideration for your assignment is the purpose. Your purpose for writing will be closely connected to the assignment (see the assignment types discussed in the next section), but there are additional purposes for writing. For example, in addition to evaluating a website, your purpose could also be to make your audience laugh. Or in comparing two popular diet plans in a paper, your purpose could be to persuade readers that one of the plans is a healthier choice. The purposes for writing are endless, but it is important to ask yourself why you are writing and what you want to accomplish besides completing an assignment or getting a good grade. The answers to those questions will be your purpose for writing, and knowing that purpose will help you complete your assignment effectively.

Types of Writing Assignments

Many students underestimate the importance of reading and understanding the writing assignment before they begin writing. Carefully reading and taking note of what you are asked to do will save you time in the long run. The key to fulfilling any assignment is to know what your instructor wants you to do. The following sections discuss different types of writing assignments and how to fulfill each one. Note how the verbs used relate to the type of assignment.

Prompts

No two writing assignments in college will look exactly the same, in part because each professor will have a personal set of *prompts* to describe writing assignments and the kinds of response expected. The following section explores several of the many types of prompts you will encounter in college. Each one asks for a different type of writing product, so be sure to review your instructor's guidelines carefully to make sure you are fulfilling the assignment correctly.

A *summary* is a brief retelling of a subject. In a summary, you will cover the main points of an event or a text without offering your opinion on the subject. An *evaluation* assignment asks for your opinion. You will need to consider the subject's strengths and weaknesses, and you will need to provide specific examples to support your ideas.

Discussion or *description* assignments are usually intended to assess how well you know a topic. The more specific details you can provide, the more likely you will adequately describe or define the subject. An *analysis* is an assignment that breaks a subject apart and looks at its components carefully. Once you have investigated the parts, you must put the subject back together again. When you analyze a poem, you may break it apart into rhyme scheme, language, images, and speaker. To examine each of these parts is to analyze the poem. Once you have completed your examination, you will bring the parts back together again with commentary on how the parts all work together.

The purpose of a *comparison and contrast* essay is to examine two subjects more carefully to make a significant point about them. Before you describe their similarities and then their differences, you will set up the reason for the comparison and contrast. Take, for instance, the cliché "It is like comparing apples to oranges." Well, you *can* compare and contrast them if you have found something significant to express about their obvious differences and their not-so-obvious similarities. Is one more nutritious than the other or are they nearly identical in nutritional content? Is one more popular than the other or do they share the same status in the world of produce? Of course, as part of the comparison and contrast, you will also explore their similarities and differences as they relate to your overall point: Size, color, texture, nutritional composition, popularity, and taste may be details that you use to drive your point home.

Although it may be more complex than reflecting on an experience you have had, a *synthesis* paper sounds scarier than it really is. If you have ever written a research paper in which you used two or more sources to argue an original point about a topic, then you have written a synthesis. The key to a synthesis is that it moves beyond an essay only from one perspective—yours. Instead, a synthesis uses your perspective or argument as the foundation and provides the reader with ideas and support from other sources. When your instructor asks you to synthesize two articles' approaches to understanding the impact of immigration, you will read those two sources, form an opinion about their arguments, and then use information from each source to support your own perspective on the issue.

Persuading an audience and arguing a point demand that you take a stand about a topic. Whether or not you are passionate about an assigned topic, you will need to argue it avidly. A *persuasive argument* is most effective when specific, accurate details are presented. Effective persuasion requires that you treat your readers with respect and you present your argument fairly. Overexaggeration and misrepresentation are not characteristics of a successful argument.

When you are assigned to reflect on a topic, you are being asked for your thoughts about it. *Reflections* are usually informal and allow a professor to get to know more about you. If you are asked to reflect on your progress during the semester or how you have felt about writing a research paper, be sure to provide plenty of details that explain your ideas. The more you move beyond "I have done well" or "I can't wait to get the paper written," the more thoughtful and helpful your response will be.

Formats and Occasions

Research papers and essays will not be the only way you are asked to show your professors how well you write and think. You may also be asked to show your writing ability in other formats and for different occasions. Essay exams and portfolios are the two most popular types of assignments that will require an ability to write well, but you may also need to demonstrate your writing skills in group projects and multimedia presentations. One of the benefits of writing well is that you can easily move from one type of assignment to another. The key to success is to learn what additional writing skills are necessary for these different formats and occasions.

Essay Exams   Essay exams always cause a little more anxiety than any other writing assignments because of the pressure of recalling information and writing with the clock ticking. Because you don't have the luxury of time to write an essay on an exam, you will have to prepare. Students who have trouble producing an essay in a timed environment should be comforted that they can improve their performance by practicing for the exam.

If you know the essay topic beforehand, you can practice writing your response by allowing yourself the same amount of time that you will have when you take the test. The key to writing well under pressure is to simulate the same circumstances when you practice. If you don't know what the topic is beforehand, you can still prepare by going back over your notes and checking to see whether your professor talked about any major issues that would make a good essay topic. Then practice writing responses to questions you think might be on the exam.

Portfolios   A writing portfolio is a collection of your writing throughout the semester. This type of project is popular with instructors because it allows students to work on their writing continuously. Instead of getting a grade on the first draft that is turned in, students can revise papers until they meet the minimal standards for the course. A benefit of the portfolio method is that students can focus on the process of writing instead of the final product—the polished paper.

The best way to handle a writing portfolio is to first review the requirements, including due dates and policies on completing final drafts. If you have questions about expectations, especially if you have never completed a portfolio before, ask your instructor and schedule periodic meetings to make sure that you are completing the components successfully. Finally, take advantage of the opportunity to submit multiple drafts and receive feedback on them. Revising essays for a portfolio takes time, but the rewards are extensive feedback and help with improving your writing.

Evaluation

Your college professors may vary widely in how they evaluate your written assignments. Some professors look for and reward key words and concepts in an essay exam, whereas others mark and count off for grammatical, mechanical, and organizational problems even if the key concepts are easily identifiable. You will soon learn, if you have not already, that each professor has his or her own criteria for grading written assignments, and the sooner you learn what the criteria are, the better able you will be to complete assignments satisfactorily.

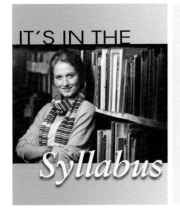

IT'S IN THE *Syllabus*

What are the expectations for writing assignments in your classes? Do the syllabi outline these expectations or provide grading criteria?

If you are unclear about the expectations for writing in your classes, how can you find out more information? What resources are available that can help you determine what to expect?

If your professor does not give you a list of grading criteria, you should ask for a sample assignment or a list of what the professor will be looking for. Talking with the professor before and after the assignment is graded is the best way to know what to expect. Asking other students who have taken classes with the professor is another way to get an idea of how you will be evaluated.

Remember that professors expect you to write at a college level and that your writing assignments will reflect the characteristics that have been discussed in this chapter. You may find that although you received good grades on papers in high school, you have to work much harder for those same grades on college papers. In addition to higher standards, you should be aware that your professors' job is to make you a better thinker and writer, no matter what the subject.

GETTING HELP with WRITING

There may be times when a writing assignment is confusing or overwhelming. If at any time you don't understand what you are supposed to do or you feel stressed about the assignment, contact your instructor as soon as you can. Stressing out about the assignment will only make it seem impossible to complete. Instructors know you have other responsibilities and classes and are often willing to work with you if you have planned ahead and asked for help early.

When getting help with an assignment, be sure to ask your instructor first—he or she is the one who will best know what needs to be done. If your college has a writing center, you should make an appointment with a tutor as soon as you realize you need

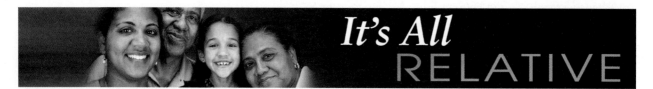

It's All RELATIVE

Sharing with your family what you are writing about and what you are creating for presentations is a great way to connect with those in your family who are not currently in college or who have never attended. Through your writings and presentations, you can connect or reconnect them with the academic world; who knows, you may even inspire them to learn more about a particular subject or even to enroll in college.

Another benefit to sharing your writings and presentations with your family is that they can offer you feedback before you complete your work. They can provide another perspective that you may not get from peer review or a tutor.

YOUR TURN

What assignments have you shared with your family so far? • Why have you or why have you not shared? • What was the reaction to your work? • Are they supportive? • Do they provide critical feedback? • How would you like them to respond to your work?

_____

_____

_____

some help. Writing center tutors will be able to explain what you need to do to complete the assignment.

Other students in the class and friends who are not in the class can be other sources of help, but use their support cautiously. Your classmates may not know much more about the expectations than you. Moreover, your instructor may prohibit any kind of collaboration, even if it is to better understand what you need to do. Getting help from anyone who is not in the class or not taking college courses should be your last resort because they are even further removed from your instructor's expectations.

No matter who helps you with the assignment, be sure that you are doing the assignment rather than letting someone else do it for you. Some students, out of fear or frustration, have found others to complete part or all of their assignments. The most obvious reason to not allow someone else to help too much is that your instructor could penalize you for not doing the assignment yourself. More important, if you do not complete the assignment yourself, you are robbing yourself of an opportunity to learn more about the subject that you are studying and about yourself.

Peer Review

Peer review is a process that you may go through in your composition classes or in classes that have an important group project as part of your grade. Peer review is defined as a procedure in which a classmate evaluates your work. This may occur in a peer review workshop, common in writing classes, in which you and a classmate exchange papers and assess how well each of you has met the assignment requirements. You may also be looking for grammatical and spelling errors, which can be corrected before your final draft or project is submitted. Peer review, especially if assigned as part of your work in a class, can be extremely helpful to you. It can show you what others in the class are writing about and how they are completing assignments, which can in turn help you gauge how well you are doing. It can also help you learn how to correct mistakes, because you may find it easier to see errors in others' papers than in yours. Finally, it can help you get your paper in shape before you complete it for submission.

Tutoring

Another form of assistance available to you as you write your papers is tutoring. Most colleges have a learning assistance center or tutoring lab where other students or professional tutors are available to help those who need it. Tutoring is especially valuable if certain skills, such as grammar or spelling, need to be practiced and refined. The tutors at your college are usually trained to help students with the most common problems, and they have the added benefit of having completed the very courses they tutor in, so they know what to expect in terms of assignments and grading. Tutors, just as peer reviewers, however, cannot assure a good grade on an assignment that is reviewed. They can, though, point out areas that need to be improved and provide resources to help you become more aware of your strengths and weaknesses as a writer.

USING TECHNOLOGY TO GET AHEAD

There are many resources on the World Wide Web that can help you improve your writing, researching, and presentation skills. The website YouTube can provide examples of speeches, both good and bad, that you can evaluate. There are also numerous websites that offer good writing advice for college students. Purdue's Online Writing Lab (OWL) has a vast array of resources for students. Don't forget that your textbooks may also provide technology (e-books, companion websites, etc.) that can help you succeed. Although there are many good websites, be aware that there are also many that provide services, such as writing papers for you, that are not acceptable for use in your classes. Papermill websites, where you can purchase or download free college essays, will not help you achieve excellence.

One major consideration when beginning and completing your writing assignment is maintaining academic integrity; that is, when writing papers that require no research, follow one simple rule: Do the work yourself. Unless your instructor explicitly states that you can work together with a classmate *and* can share answers or help while completing the assignment, avoid collaboration when completing written assignments.

At no time should you copy the answers that another student has written. Just as you would not share answers during a test, it is best not to share your answers on work that is assigned out of class. If you have taken a class in a previous semester, you will also want to keep your assignments from being shared. Instructors may use the same assignments from semester to semester, and you don't want to put a fellow student in an awkward or potentially bad situation.

YOUR TURN

In what ways do students compromise academic integrity, perhaps without even knowing it? • What safeguards do you put in place to ensure academic integrity when working with others, helping classmates with assignments or getting help, or using resources other than those required or suggested by your professors?

_____

_____

_____

How Much Is Too Much Help?

How do you know when you have received too much help on a writing assignment? If someone else writes whole sentences, paragraphs, and pages for you or supplies you with many main ideas and examples that you use in your paper, then you have probably received too much assistance on your writing assignment. Some professors disapprove of editing and proofreading services as well. When in doubt, check with your professor and explain what kind of help you are getting.

Reflection EXERCISE 8.1

How do you feel about your writing skills? What would you like to improve? How will you make those improvements? ■

THE WRITING PROCESS

Prewriting Techniques

Once you have read and understood the writing assignment, it is time to use one or more prewriting techniques to get your ideas down on paper before you start organizing them and writing your rough draft. You probably have your own way of writing, but it is worth investigating some of these proven methods for generating ideas.

There are three common prewriting techniques that you can use to generate details for your paper. *Freewriting* is a simple way to get ideas down on paper. The only rules in freewriting are to start with an idea and stop only after you have filled a page or after a certain amount of time has passed. When freewriting, you can allow your mind to wander off the subject; you must, however, write down everything that comes to mind. Later, when you start organizing your details, you can eliminate anything that does not pertain to your subject. If you are a good typist, you can freewrite by typing into a blank document. Don't worry about spelling, grammar, or punctuation when you freewrite— the purpose is to free your mind of that little voice that censors everything you think.

Clustering is another method of prewriting that works well for those who learn better by visualizing concepts. Clusters, or think links, are visual representations of ideas and their relationship to each other. The key to clustering is to start in the middle of a sheet of paper, write down your topic, and circle it. Draw a line from your subject and write down a related topic that is part of the subject. For instance, "types," "prevention," and "treatment" are all parts of the topic "sexually transmitted diseases." In addition, subtopics branch off "prevention"—for example, "abstinence" and "condoms." The words and phrases that surround a topic or subtopic must be connected to it, both logically and literally, by drawing lines.

Think **ABOUT IT**

"I write entirely to find out what I'm thinking, what I'm looking at, what I see and what it means. What I want and what I fear.

—Joan Didion"

Another effective method for generating ideas is *brainstorming,* a process that involves writing down ideas as they come to you. The goal in brainstorming is to get as many ideas as possible down on paper, no matter how ridiculous or off-topic they are. The more details you generate, the more you have to work with as you begin organizing your paper. To brainstorm, simply write your topic at the top of a sheet of paper, or type it into a new document on your computer, and then start listing any and all ideas that come to mind.

Creating a Thesis and Organizing Details

Once you make a list of details that you would like to use in your paper, give some thought as to what your main point will be, a topic sentence if it is a paragraph or a thesis if it is an essay, before you decide how you would like to organize the details. Your main point will be at least one sentence that tells the reader what the whole piece will present or argue.

There are a variety of ways that you can organize a paper effectively. You can arrange the details from most to least important detail or vice versa. Details can also be arranged chronologically, especially if you are writing about an event that needs to follow a specific time line. Or your points can be arranged from general ideas to specific or specific details to general. It is important to organize your points logically; how you arrange the supporting details will depend on your purpose and audience.

For example, suppose you are writing a paper on the greatest challenges to diversity on your campus, and your details include the lack of cultural appreciation activities, a recent racially motivated incident, the fact that there are few minorities in administrative roles, and the absence of African American literature classes. However, this ordering of the details provides no logical connections among them, so your reader will have a difficult time understanding the magnitude of the problem. Instead, you could order them according to importance. When Juanita chooses a topic and completes her research, she will want to consider the order in which to present her findings. Should she start with the most shocking or the most obvious? These questions will start her on the process of organizing her paper for maximum impact.

Which of the aforementioned details do you think is the most important indication of the challenges to diversity on your campus? Certainly, the most striking is the racially motivated incident. Using it as the first, most important detail in your paper will grab your readers' attention and keep them interested and sympathetic to your thesis. On the other hand, you could start your essay with a least important detail and use the incident as your last, most important point. How you arrange your details, as long as each detail builds on the last and leads to the next while supporting your thesis, depends on your purpose for writing.

Writing Paragraphs

Paragraphs, which are groups of sentences considered as complete units, are the building blocks of an essay. Paragraphs begin with an indentation, known as a tab, on the lefthand side of the page. Well-developed paragraphs can be any length. However, if a paragraph is too short, the reader will think that something is missing; if they are too long, the reader may get lost in what you are trying to say. The key to writing a good paragraph—and you will write many in your college career—is to stay focused on one topic at a time as delineated in each paragraph's *topic sentence*. A topic sentence can appear at the beginning of the paragraph, in the middle, or at the end.

Once you have determined what the paragraph will focus on, you can start putting your details in place. Just as you have considered the overall arrangement of the details in your paper, you will need to give some thought to arranging the details *within* the paragraphs. The same types of organization of details for an entire paper work for paragraphs as well: general to specific or vice versa, order of importance, or chronological. You can use a different method for each paragraph as long as all the paragraphs support your thesis.

Incorporating Transitions

To make your sentences flow smoothly in paragraphs that relate clearly to one another, you will need to use transitions. Transitions are words or phrases signaling to the reader that you are moving from one thought to the next. Imagine describing over the phone how to get from the college to your house. If you didn't use transitions, your listener might be confused as to how to get there. Words such as *First, Next, Then,* and *After* are transitional words that help the listener see how the sentences of the directions relate to one another.

When you move from paragraph to paragraph in your paper, you will definitely need strong transitional phrases or sentences to indicate the introduction of new ideas or that supporting or contradictory points are forthcoming. Phrases such as "In addition to," "Even though," and "Contrary to the point above" are strong enough to slow the reader down to pay attention to your next major point. These words serve as signposts to indicate the beginning of each idea and how each idea connects to the preceding discussion. A paragraph beginning with the words "The first step" is telling you something important: This idea is the first in a series of steps that will follow. "In other words" indicates that the author is restating her first point in case you missed it. "If you have done your reading" ties an idea from the previous sentence. The transition "also" tells you that another point is being made in addition to the one at the beginning of the paragraph. Finally, the phrase "For example" leads to an example for achieving the goal in the previous sentence.

In addition to connecting ideas, transitions improve the readability of the paper. When you read your work out loud and it sounds "choppy" or repetitive in rhythm, you may need to add transitions. Doing so effectively takes practice. If you need help, see your instructor or someone in the writing center at your college. With a little work, the flow of your writing will improve.

Writing Essays

The word *essay* has its origins in French and means "an attempt" or "a trial." For college students, writing essays is an attempt, or a trial, in some sense, to meet the assignment without going crazy! In the context of college, an essay is a written composition on a particular subject that offers the author's view. If, for example, you are asked to write an essay on the death penalty or obesity in children, then you will need to present your viewpoint on the subject. Essays do not usually contain research; instead, they are built on your observations, details, and opinions. They are, in essence, an attempt by you to convey your viewpoint on a subject and perhaps to learn something more of what you think about that subject.

When you are assigned an essay for a class, you need to include some basic components. Without all of them, your essay is simply a piece of writing, just as a few bones do not make up an entire skeleton. At the least, you will need a title, introduction, thesis, body paragraphs, and a conclusion.

Learning how to find and evaluate information is essential to becoming an information literate student.

Thinkstock

Avoiding Plagiarism

No word strikes fear and confusion in academic writers more than *plagiarism*. Simply defined, plagiarism is the use of another's words or ideas without proper acknowledgment. Put another way, if the information or the expression of the information comes from another source besides your own brain, then you must let the reader know what that source is. Proper acknowledgment can be as simple as naming the source or it can be as complex as using a documentation system such as MLA (Modern Language Association) or APA (American Psychological Association). Penalties for plagiarism can range from redoing the assignment to facing expulsion from college. Because most colleges do not distinguish between intentional and unintentional borrowing, it is in your best interest to learn how to avoid plagiarism.

You may ask yourself, "If I don't know what plagiarism is, can I still be penalized if I don't mean to do it?" The answer is that your professors will expect that you already know how to distinguish between your own and others' ideas. If you don't know how to do that, or if you are unsure how you can avoid plagiarism, you should talk with your professors or seek assistance from the writing center.

Critical Thinking
EXERCISE 8.2

Why is writing effectively an important life skill? In what other areas of your life will you use writing? ■

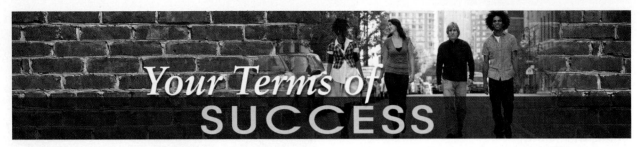

Your Terms of SUCCESS

WHEN YOU SEE . . .	IT MEANS . . .
Analysis	To break apart a subject to examine its parts as they relate to the whole subject.
Audience	The person or persons who will be reading your paper or listening to your speech.
Brainstorming	A prewriting technique that involves writing down everything that comes to mind in a list.
Clustering	A prewriting technique that involves visually representing how a subject is related to other subjects; also called mind mapping.
Conclusion	The last paragraph of an essay, presenting your overall points and final thoughts.
Concrete details	Details or examples that appeal to a reader's sight, taste, smell, touch, or hearing.
Description	Explaining the characteristics of an object, subject, or experience.
Documentation style	The style used to document the sources in your paper; many professors require either MLA (Modern Language Association) or APA (American Psychological Association) documentation and format for papers.
Essay	Literally "an attempt"; a type of assignment that has an introduction, a thesis, body paragraphs, and a conclusion.
Freewriting	A prewriting technique that involves writing freely and without consideration of punctuation, grammar, or spelling.
Organization	How your details for your essay or paper are placed.
Outline	The essential parts of a paper or speech; usually presented in a specific outline format using Roman numerals for each major part.
Peer review	A process in which a peer, or classmate, evaluates your paper or project.
Persuasive argument	Presents a debatable idea in order to convince an audience.
Physical delivery	The bodily and facial movements that enhance or distract from a speech.
Plagiarism	The use of another's ideas, words, or images without proper acknowledgement.
Portfolio	A collection of separate assignments or of drafts of an assignment.
Prewriting techniques	The processes by which details for an assignment are generated.
Reflection	To provide a thoughtful consideration of a topic.
Research	The act of finding, evaluating, and incorporating sources into an assignment.
Rough draft	An unpolished attempt at an assignment.
Summary	To provide an overview of what an entire work or subject is about; does not contain original thought or evaluation.
Synthesis	Combines two or more ideas together.
Thesis	An essay's central idea that is supported throughout the writing.
Transitions	Words or phrases that signal a change in thought or additional ideas.
Visual aid	An object that is used to engage an audience or emphasize a point.
Vocal delivery	How the voice is used in a speech.

THE RESEARCH PROCESS

Research papers differ from essays and other written assignments in that they require you to investigate and incorporate sources to support your ideas. You will have to consider length, audience, and purpose, and you will need to pay close attention to the requirements of the assignment. Instructors may require that you research certain journals or databases, or they may ask for survey results or literature reviews. The steps needed to find and evaluate reliable information before you use it in a paper are included in the definition of information literacy from Chapter 6. As with any writing assignment, you should start early and break it up into manageable parts. For a research paper, you will need to invest a considerable amount of time and energy.

Choosing a Topic

The assignment information you are given may help you determine what your topic will be. In some cases, your professor will be very specific; for example, an assignment may state, "Write a research paper in which you present three methods for teaching preschool children to read." Other professors may be less direct—for example, "Write a paper on an important historical event." If you are ever unsure as to what your topic should be, always ask well before the assignment is due. Oftentimes, you can get ideas for narrowing your topic from the professor or the classmates.

Before you settle on a topic to research, consider the assignment's purpose and length. If you are writing a ten-page paper, your topic will need to be broader than a five-page paper. Also, if you are required to argue a point rather than provide basic information, your topic, and your subsequent research, will be focused differently. Determining your topic first, regardless of what it is, will save you time when you begin to find sources for your paper.

Finding and Evaluating Sources

Once you determine your topic, you can then begin to search for sources for your paper. You will definitely want to learn how to use your library's catalog and databases beforehand. Oftentimes, the library will provide an orientation to students or you can get one-on-one assistance from a staff member. Never waste valuable time by being confused—ask someone for help if you are not sure how to find information.

Your assignment and topic will influence what kinds of sources you need for your paper. If your education class requires that you find websites that provide information on cyberbullying in elementary schools, then you will know to look at online sources for your paper. However, if your education class requires that you write a research paper on the latest studies about cyberbullying, you will most likely need to access journals in your library's databases to find scholarly articles on the subject.

Once you find your sources, you will need to spend time deciding if they are reliable, credible, and useable for your paper. Again, look to your assignment or to your professor for guidance if you are unsure whether a source is acceptable for your paper. Most likely, if it is a source that you have found in the library's catalog or databases, it should be a credible source. Chapter 6 provided specific questions on evaluating sources that can be used in the research process as well.

Incorporating Sources into Your Paper

Deciding what to put into your paper is the next step in the research process. How you do this will depend on the *documentation style* that your professor requires. Two of the most common are MLA (Modern Language Association) and APA (American Psychological Association), but there are more that you will need to be familiar with, such as Chicago Manual of Style (CMS) and Council of Biology Editors (CBE) formats. A documentation style simply means the format in which you acknowledge your sources within the paper and at the end in the references or works cited page.

Regardless of which style you use, incorporating sources into your paper requires that you provide essential information, usually the author's name and the title of the source, whenever you first use it in your paper. This means that whether you are quoting directly or paraphrasing, which is putting the author's ideas into your own words, you will need to let your reader know the origin of the information. Proper acknowledgement and documentation are essential to incorporating your sources correctly. Your professor will certainly want to hear *your* thoughts on the topic, but she will also expect you to have found sources and documented them properly to support your ideas.

Collaboration EXERCISE 8.3

Working in a group, discuss the steps to writing a research paper outlined in the preceding section and determine why students usually have trouble with research papers. What part of the process is most difficult? What can students to do to make the process easier? ■

MAKING SPEECHES and PRESENTATIONS

Learning to speak and present on a topic effectively in college is a skill that will benefit you not only on the job but also in life. For example, you may need to speak on behalf of the parents at your children's school as president of the Parents and Teachers Association, or you may be asked to make weekly announcements at your church. In your college classes, you will more than likely get a specific assignment (Give a 5-minute persuasive speech on a current event) or a specific topic (cloning). However, not all speaking experiences will begin with detailed directions. You may be asked to introduce someone or to "talk for about 10 minutes about whatever you think will interest the audience." Regardless of how you are assigned a speech, the process will be the same: You will need to plan, prepare, deliver, and assess.

Planning a Speech or Presentation

Choosing a topic is the first step to preparing to speak, just as it is in the writing process. At times, you will be provided a topic, but in some of your classes—or for some occasions—you will be allowed to create your own. Topics for speeches can come from your personal experience, current events, or from in-depth research. If you are not sure which personal experience, current event, or research topic you want to explore, it is a good idea to use brainstorming or another method of generating ideas (see the section on prewriting) to determine which topic interests you the most.

Deciding your purpose will be your next step. You may need to inform, persuade, or entertain your audience. If you will be informing them of your topic, you will more than likely use details and language that present the information in an unbiased manner. If you will be persuading your audience, you will probably employ examples and language to change their attitudes or beliefs. Entertaining your audience will involve including information, details, and language that will get a laugh or amuse. Your speech can have more than one purpose—and sometimes all three—but one will be the most emphasized.

Just as writers need to identify their audience before they begin writing, speakers must also consider whom they will be addressing. Audience analysis is the process by which speakers determine who will be the recipients of the message. Audience analysis questions include the following: How many people will be in the audience? What are the characteristics of the audience (gender, ages, race, culture, educational background, learning style, etc.)? What are their attitudes toward your topic? What do they know about the topic?

Occasion analysis questions include the following: When are you speaking? How long will you have to speak? What is the space like (if you can find out in advance)? What else will you need? Visual aids? Handouts? Time for questions or discussion?

Vocal Delivery

What if you crafted a fantastic speech and no one ever heard it because they couldn't understand what you were saying? Sound impossible? It has, unfortunately, happened before: A great speech is lost because the speaker didn't project his voice or mumbled through the words. Vocal delivery, then, is the most important aspect to getting the words out successfully. Consider the following suggestions when practicing and delivering a speech:

- *Pay attention to tone and pitch.* Is the vocal quality of your voice soft or harsh? Do you sound angry or giddy? Audience members prefer voices that are easy to listen to.

- *Speak slowly and deliberately.* Make sure that you are properly pronouncing words (check the dictionary) and using correct grammar (consult a writing handbook). Open your mouth and move your lips to ensure that you are enunciating. Speaker credibility is lost when words are not used properly or poorly pronounced.

- *Use variety when speaking.* Vary volume, pitch, and speed to create interest. Pause between points for effect. Do you remember the monotone teacher in the movie *Ferris Bueller's Day Off?* He didn't vary his volume, pitch, and speed, and his students were either asleep or not paying attention.

Physical Delivery

Appropriate nonverbal communication while you are speaking can mean the difference between an effective and an ineffective speech. Paying attention to and practicing your body movements will help you develop good physical habits when speaking. Here are just a few to consider:

- *Dress appropriately.* If you look professional, you appear more credible. Unless you are making a point by dressing down or wearing a costume, dress up. A neat and clean appearance also suggests attention to detail and understanding the importance of all aspects of presentation.

- *Smile at your audience.* It demonstrates a positive attitude and puts your audience at ease.

Presenting in front of a group gets easier the more you practice and the more you present.
Bill Aron/PhotoEdit

- *Plant your feet.* Place them firmly on the floor and stand up straight. Slouching or slumping lessens your effectiveness.
- *Act naturally.* The more you practice, the more comfortable you will be with your body movements and less likely to use unnatural, mechanical hand gestures and head movements.
- *Move from the waist up only.* Shuffling and pacing are distracting.
- *Step out in front.* Get in front of the podium when speaking to smaller groups of 30 or fewer because it helps create intimacy and connection.
- *Use hand gestures appropriately.* Keep arms and hands close to the body; avoid pointing your finger to emphasize an idea; instead, use a closed fist with thumb slightly up; open hands work well, but avoid banging on the podium or table.
- *Maintain eye contact.* Use the "Figure 8" method of scanning the room so that each area gets your attention throughout the presentation. Think of an 8 lying on its side and trace the curves and lines with your eyes, starting either on the right or left of your audience.

Visual Aids

In addition to considering your delivery methods, both physical and vocal, you may also want to keep in mind how you will use any visual aids. According to Arthur Bradbury (2006), "for a truly powerful *and memorable* presentation you will need to include some form of visual aid" (p. 84). A visual aid can be anything from an object, such as a doll or book, to an elaborate poster or handout emphasizing certain points that the audience can view while you are speaking. Slide presentation software can also provide your audience with a visual representation of your topic.

Reflection
EXERCISE 8.4

What are your experiences with making presentations in front of a class or other audience? What do you fear, if anything, about giving a speech? ■

When using visual aids, remember that they are most effective when they help the audience remember your key points, see a point you are making more clearly, or enliven your presentation without distracting from your words. Here are a few tips for handling your visual aids:

- *Less is always more with visual aids.* They should be simple and easy to understand.

- *Make sure your aids can be seen clearly by a person at the back of the room.* To be seen and not heard was once a virtue, but you will want both in a presentation with visual aids. Clear writing or large font on a slide presentation will help the audience get your point.

- *Be the center of attention even with a visual aid.* You don't want it to take away attention from your speech or dominate your presentation. A well-considered prop or visual aid should enhance rather than become your speech.

(Personality + Learning Style = Understanding Situations)

Think about Juanita's concern over writing a 15-page paper and making a slide show presentation. Because Juanita has a read/write learning preference, she finds writing to be an easy task, although she has procrastinated in the past when it came to writing papers. However, now she is being asked to write on a topic with which she is not familiar and she is worried about creating a presentation to accompany her research. Using what you have learned from this chapter, what advice would you give her? How can she divide her assignment into smaller tasks so that she does not wait until the last minute to complete it?

Now, considering your own learning style, personality type, and special circumstances, what would you do to tackle this major assignment? ■

From College to University

HOW WRITING ASSIGNMENTS AND EXPECTATIONS WILL CHANGE

Most definitely, when you take upper-level courses at the university, you will write more and the expectations will be higher. Your professors who teach at the junior and senior levels will assume that any writing challenges you had in your first two years of college have been overcome. Your professors will be more concerned with the strength and originality of your argument and the depth and breadth of your research than with grammar, punctuation, spelling, and mechanics. Instead, they will expect these lower-level issues to have been mastered, and they will want you to expand on the higher-level issues such as presenting a successful academic argument.

Certainly, you will be writing more to discover what you think about a particular topic. You will also find writing and research more enjoyable as you settle into a major course of study. Most students who transfer and take courses in their major learn that they enjoy writing about subjects that will help them in their careers. This kind of satisfaction comes over time, and although you may not enjoy every writing assignment that you must do in your first two years in college, realize that with each paper you complete, you will become a better writer and thinker, which will help you make your transition to a four-year university that much easier.

Building Your University Portfolio 8

Find someone you know (or ask your professor for the name of a former student) who has transferred to a four-year university and ask how writing expectations have, or have not, changed. Are papers longer? Is more research required? What resources are available to meet the changed expectations at the university?

_____

_____

_____

_____

From College to Career

WHY STRONG SPEAKING SKILLS WILL SET YOU APART AT WORK

Don't think of your speech communication class as the last occasion that you will speak in front of peers and superiors. No matter what career path you take, chances are likely that you will need to use those communication skills to work in groups, relate to your boss, and instruct or present information to your coworkers. Examples of when you will need to rely on what you learned in class include making a presentation to a client, summarizing the company's goals and projects to new employees, or presenting a new idea for efficiency to management. These will all be instances in which you will be able to use what you learned both in class and by frequently practicing your speaking skills for other occasions besides Public Speaking 101. Just as good writing skills are essential to on-the-job success, solid public speaking skills will set you apart from your coworkers as someone who can communicate even the most complicated or mundane aspects of the company's policies. That kind of ability will garner respect and admiration from those who work with you.

Building Your Career Portfolio 8

Contact someone in a career that is similar to what you want to do. Ask that person what kinds of speaking and presentation skills are needed on the job. Does his or her employer provide help in honing those skills? Are there computer skills, such as using slide show software, that are also necessary as part of effective presentation skills?

_____

_____

_____

_____

First Voices

From part-time jobs after a military career to full-time success: Single parent continues to "hustle" after completing two master's degrees

Cheryl Moody,
M.A., Spanish Professor

After serving 10 years in the Marine Corps, I chose to end my military career in order to raise my two children without the constant fear of leaving them for extended periods of time as I had to do in the past. As a single parent, I knew it was my responsibility to make a successful life for my children. One week prior to discharge, I discovered I was pregnant again; yet, I stuck with my discharge decision. Soon after giving birth to my third child, I began a new and rewarding career as a medical transcriptionist, so it never really crossed my mind to return to college. However, many years later, I reached a "glass ceiling" in terms of salary and found myself working additional part-time jobs just to pay my bills. I worked so much that I had very little time to spend with my children. I think the turning point for me was the day I did the calculations and realized I was only averaging a 15 to 20 cents-per-year raise, and at that rate, it would take me years just to make a dollar increase. That is when I considered returning to college full time.

I had many concerns, because I was a 37-year-old single parent with three minor children. I was not receiving child support and had only three semesters of previous college experience, which was 20 years prior. I did not know how I would support my family, nor if I would succeed in school. However, I knew that returning to school would be the only way I could make a positive shift in my circumstance. So, after much thought, I quit my job and returned to school.

The next step was to find employment that would offer me the flexibility I needed as a college student and a single mom. I found two part time jobs—Fun Wash, a laundromat, and Backyard Burger, a fast food restaurant. When I had free time, I went to yard sales, swap meets, and flea markets where I purchased items, restored them, and resold them in order to create additional income for my family.

Now, 10 years later, I have two master's degrees, I am a full-time Spanish professor, and I love teaching my students to love learning. Certainly, my journey was very challenging, but it absolutely changed our lives. When my daughter, who is now 26 years old, comes home to visit, she tells me that her friends often ask, "Is your mama still hustling?" And I proudly tell her, of course I'm still hustling . . . if that means never giving up on my dreams.

PATH OF DISCOVERY
Journal Entry

How have writing and speaking expectations changed for you since high school? What do you expect writing and speaking expectations to be like on the job?

CHAPTER REVIEW QUESTIONS

1. Identify five writing expectations you will encounter in college.
2. What is the writing process?
3. When conducting research, how will you use the information you find?
4. What should you consider when preparing and delivering a speech or presentation?

CHAPTER 8 CASE SCENARIOS

1. Renée is barely passing her literature class. She has not done well on the tests or the writing assignments, so she has asked someone to help her write her final literary analysis paper. A friend of her mother has volunteered to help her write the paper, and when she meets with Renée, offers to write down all of Renée's ideas, organize them, and reword her sentences. The result is an A paper, something that Renée has not been able to achieve all semester. What do you think of the help that Renée has received? Is there some other way that she could improve her writing without this type of assistance?
2. Paul is having a hard time understanding the research assignment that his government professor handed out to the class. He had two months to work on the paper but hasn't done anything yet, with only two weeks to go. Where should he start and what should he do?
3. Pietra is afraid of public speaking and has been postponing taking a speech class until her last semester in college. The professor has lectured about overcoming speaking anxiety and Pietra has read the material in her textbook, but she doesn't think that she will be able to pass the class. What can she do to overcome her intense fear and achieve a passing grade?

RESEARCH IT FURTHER

1. By searching the Internet, create a "hot list" of beneficial writing sites for college students. You may want to focus on a particular aspect of writing such as grammar, or you can create a list for several topics that concern college writers.
2. Interview two people whose careers are in fields other than writing and ask them how writing is important to their jobs.
3. Interview two people whose careers are in fields other than professional speaking and ask them how speaking effectively is important to their jobs.
4. Create a survey of students' attitudes toward and concerns about public speaking. Poll your class and other students and compile your results. Present your findings to the class.

References and Recommended Readings

Bradbury, A. (2006). *Successful presentation skills* (3rd ed.). London: Kogan Page.

Strunk, W., & White, E. B. (2008). *The elements of style* (4th. ed.). Boston: Allyn & Bacon.

Tracy, B. (2008). *Speak to win: How to present with power in any situation.* New York: Amacom Books.

Wilder, L. (1999). *Seven steps to fearless speaking.* New York: John Wiley & Sons.

Zinsser, W. (2006). *On writing well* (30th anniv. ed.). New York: Harper Paperbacks.

STUDYING and TESTS

9

Studying the origins of life in their Biology 101 class is becoming an exercise in their own survival. Juanita, Evan, Michael, and Laura formed a study group early in the semester, on the suggestion of their orientation leaders, and now it has become a precious lifeline. Their professor is great, they all agree, but the mountain of chapters, notes, extra readings, papers, and lab work is killing them.

"So much work for just one class," Michael says. "It's insane."

"Ha," Juanita replies, "I'm taking world literature and psychology. The reading alone takes me hours each night."

Both Michael and Juanita arrived early to the study group so they could find a good booth in the food court before it got crowded. Nervous about the first test, Michael thinks he has studied too many of the wrong things. Juanita has severe test anxiety anytime she takes a test, and studying with a group helps her relax before the big day.

"Are you starting without me?" Laura asks as she drops her heavy backpack on the booth seat by Juanita.

"Of course not," Juanita says. "Michael was just crying about how much work this class is. I had to remind him of my schedule—non-stop reading that will make your eyes cross."

"My mother finished her degree right before I started school and I remember how much she studied. If she can do it, I think I can," Laura says. "But I am *not* ready for this test. Between a sick kid and a paper for history, I couldn't fit it in."

"Does anyone know what the test will cover? I think I have studied all the wrong material," Michael says.

"I have to study everything, even if I don't think it will be on the test," says Juanita. "If I'm not overprepared, I know I will lose it when I get the test. I've been studying since the first week of classes."

"Why am I not surprised?" Evan asks as he slides into the seat next to Michael. "Sorry, I'm late. I had to run by the gym. What have I missed besides Juanita reciting every biology fact from the first day of class?"

The study group laughs at Evan's comment, but they know he usually gets by with little studying. When he does meet with his group, he comes late or leaves early and rarely brings his notes or book.

"Can we get serious now? I have to pass this test," Laura says. Her single parent scholarship requires that she maintain a 3.0 GPA, and Laura works hard to keep it.

"I suggest we start going over everything that we have done since the first chapter," Juanita suggests. "If we work on this for the next four hours, then we can study four more tomorrow. I will probably stay up late tomorrow night to make sure I get it."

Evan, text-messaging while he talks, says, "If we just review our notes, we should be fine. When was the last time you failed a test? They have to give you something for just taking it."

"If I don't know it now, I won't know it in two days and that really scares me," says Laura.

Michael chews on the end of his pen and checks his watch. "I don't have much time to study tonight. My girlfriend needs a ride to work," he says.

"We need to start somewhere even if we can't all stay the whole time or agree on how to do this," says Juanita, the youngest of the group, who has stepped up as the leader.

In this
CHAPTER

As they discuss in their study group, Juanita, Michael, Evan, and Laura have various methods of preparation for their upcoming biology test and different perspectives on how they should study over the next two days. Just as Laura admits to the group and Evan demonstrates by his late arrival, you may also have competing priorities and tasks that keep you from studying, or you may feel anxious about taking a test, as are Michael and Juanita.

Whatever your experience with studying up to this point in your academic career, professors and experienced students alike agree that good preparation will make studying much easier. In fact, you may learn to look forward to studying, especially as you take classes that interest you and apply to your career. This chapter's purpose is to help you improve your study skills, which will in turn help you improve your test-taking strategies. No matter what you have heard, successful students study frequently and effectively. If you have never been "good at" studying, you can improve your skills by following the steps that work best for you.

This chapter provides you with study strategies for preparing for tests effectively as well as tips for taking tests that maximize your success.

More specifically, after completing this chapter, you will be able to do the following:

- **Determine the best study strategies.**
- **Identify and define test question types.**
- **Discuss unique features of different types of tests.**
- **Understand effective test-taking strategies.**

TESTING 1, 2, 3

Although terms are often used interchangeably, a *test* is defined as a set of questions that evaluate one's skills, aptitudes, and abilities on certain topics. Usually, a college test assesses your knowledge and abilities on a part of the course. An *exam*, however, by definition is an assessment of the material for an entire course. Final exams are sometimes called *comprehensive* or *cumulative* exams, which indicate that they will cover what you have studied all semester or term.

Unless your professor tells you directly what will be on the test, assume that anything that was assigned or covered in class might appear. Just about every college student has a story of a test that covered reading assignments and not what was discussed in class. These students were surprised to realize that studying the lecture notes was not enough. The following list shows the variety of items that you may be tested on for any class:

- Material from lectures, discussions, and in-class or out-of-class activities
- Ideas and concepts provided by a guest speaker
- Information from a workshop or field trip
- Multimedia productions such as video or audio
- Assigned readings, including chapters in the textbook
- Handouts, including PowerPoint slides and outlines

You can be assured that you will encounter a variety of test types. Take clues from what you do in class to help determine what kinds of test questions may be used. For example, if your professor spends time applying information from a chapter during class or as an assignment, then you likely have test questions that ask you to apply the information as well. Listen for clues given by the professor, such as "You should write this down" and "This is a really important point." Other cue phrases include "You may see this again on a test" and "If you saw this on a test, how would you answer it?" When you hear these phrases, write down the information being emphasized and review it when studying your notes. A professor who says these things is begging you to take notice!

The best advice to give college students is plain and simple: Study for all tests. No exceptions. Sometimes you will find that you do not need to study as much for some classes; however, remember that studying effectively is a habit. To form the long-term habit, you must do it even when you don't think you have to, which is fundamental to making an activity part of a routine, something Evan may need help establishing for himself.

A Place and Time for Studying

The best time to begin studying is as soon as the semester starts. Be careful of the mindset that because you are not in class every day you don't need to study every day. Some students begin studying the night or day before an exam, which may be too late to review and remember all the material that has been covered over the past several weeks. As stated in Chapter 7, start reviewing your notes within two days of taking them. If possible, you should start studying for future exams right now, today.

If you are a typical college student, then your time will be limited. You may not have the luxury of large blocks of time, so you will need to be creative about studying. Because it is more effective to study for short periods of time, consider studying in between classes, during breaks at work, and on the way to work and school (provided you are not driving). Another way to ensure that you study during the day is to get in the habit of always carrying your notes or books with you—this way you'll be able to take advantage of any unexpected "free" time. You can also get up earlier or stay up later so you can spend a few minutes studying before starting or ending your day.

If you have the luxury of choosing when to study, rather than sandwiching it in between work and family responsibilities, pay attention to what *time of day* you are

It's All RELATIVE

Managing your family obligations and studying may be a challenge unless you have a clear communication plan for making it work. No doubt, you will have family distractions—children who must be cared for and family members who need your time, advice, or help. For sure, you will find yourself balancing school work with family celebrations, get-togethers, and rituals.

Make sure that you talk to your family, even small children, about your studying needs. You may require a quiet place with no distractions or you may have to study away from them—at the library or at a meeting place for study groups—to accomplish your studying goals. Your family may also not realize how *much* time you need. The more you plan for this time—and communicate your plan—the more likely they will be supportive.

YOUR TURN

What studying goals do you have? • What do you need from your family to accomplish your studying goals? • What challenges do you anticipate? • How will you work through those challenges?

_____

_____

_____

most alert and receptive to learning. The best time of day for you to study is dependent on your schedule, your responsibilities, your age, and your personal preferences. Some people identify themselves as "night owls" whereas others claim to be "morning people." Whatever your peak performance time, as you discovered in Chapter 4, be sure to study your most difficult subjects at that time. If you have a predictable schedule all semester, plan to study at the same time each day.

The environment in which you study is just as important as the time of day and the length of time you spend studying. You will need to find the kind of environment that works well for you. Some people need complete silence with no visual distractions, whereas others need a little background noise to stay focused. At the least, create a place that is comfortable, with good lighting, and has space for your supplies and books. It is easier to make time to study when you have a place to do it. If you do not have a quiet and roomy location at home, then search for a place on campus or a local library that offers study space. Some people prefer studying away from home because they are not distracted by the television, phone, or family members.

Small children can pose a particular difficulty in finding quiet time. If you have small children, make a concerted effort to find a quiet spot. You may need to hire a babysitter or arrange to trade child care services with a classmate when you want to study. For example, you could offer to babysit a classmate's kids when he needs to study in exchange for watching yours when you have a paper to write. Some college students who are also parents find time to study only when their children are asleep. Therefore, their best studying takes place late at night or early in the morning at home. Do whatever works best for you.

How to Study Effectively

Studying effectively will include studying with a purpose by setting goals and studying actively, which can entail methods like focusing on what you are studying, reviewing and rewriting notes, or even teaching concepts to classmates. Keeping up with how much you study and understanding *how* you study best will also improve your preparation. If you do poorly on a test, you should review your study methods and make adjustments the next time.

Setting Goals

After determining when, where, and how much you need to study, set study and test-taking goals. Just as you set short-term and long-term goals in Chapter 1, write down the goals you want to achieve when studying and taking tests. Remember the title of Henriette Anne Klauser's book: *Write It Down, Make It Happen* (2001). This also applies to something as short term as studying for and taking a test. Your goals could be as simple as the following:

- I will use my time wisely so that I am able to study all my notes.
- I will ask the instructor questions about any notes that I do not understand.
- I will remain calm before, during, and after the exam by practicing breathing techniques and by relaxing.

Of course, your goals could also include studying with a group or making a high grade. If you have never written down goals for studying or taking tests, then start small. Once you have achieved your first study and test-taking goals, create newer and more challenging ones with each test:

- I will improve my writing skills by practicing the essay questions in a timed environment.
- I will improve my overall retention of the material after the test.

Studying Actively

After setting goals, the next step in preparing for exams is to consider how you approach studying. In order to build a body of knowledge, you will want to study to *learn*, not just to *remember*. In other words, you will want to transfer information from your short-term memory, which only holds information briefly, to your long-term memory, where it can be retrieved long after it is "deposited" there.

One way to improve your memory of learned material is to actively take it in when you study. The goal of active studying is to make connections between concepts and theories so that you can more easily recall the information and write or speak knowledgeably about it. To achieve this kind of mastery, instead of simply rereading notes or passively reviewing the major headings in your textbook, your studying should include activities such as the following:

- Rewriting or summarizing your notes

Think
ABOUT IT

Never regard study as a duty, but as the enviable opportunity to learn to know the liberating influence of beauty in the realm of the spirit for your own personal joy and to the profit of the community to which your later work belongs.

—Albert Einstein

- Rearranging the order of the material from most important to least important or in chronological order
- Making connections between what you have learned in one chapter, unit, or class with material you have learned elsewhere
- Making connections between what you have learned in class and what you have experienced in the real world
- Explaining concepts to someone else who is not familiar with the topic
- Making visual representations of the material

Creating a Study Log

After considering your study goals, you may also want to create a study log that will help you keep track of your tests and preparation steps. The study log in Figure 9.1 provides space for you to capture important information about the class, type of test, and methods for studying. Notice, too, that the study log describes how much the test is worth, an important consideration, especially if the test is worth a significant portion of your grade.

Understanding Course Objectives

To better focus your studying, understand the objectives of the course. You will find the course objectives in the syllabus or in other material that has been handed out to you in class. For example, if one of your course objectives is to identify the processes of cell replication, then you can be sure these processes will appear on tests in some manner. Making sure that you study the material referenced in course objectives will help you focus your time and energy on the right content.

Using Time Wisely

How much time you spend and how many sessions you undertake will depend on the type of learner you are. You could start with 45 minutes of studying three different times a day over the period of a week to see how well you retain and remember the material. Adjust your schedule as needed. Just remember to be conscious of how effective your study sessions are. If they are not helping you meet your study goals, then make

FIGURE 9.1 Study Log

Class	Chemistry
Date	Tuesday, October 27
Material	Chapter 4–7, extra lecture material
Practice/Previous Tests	In library on reserve; answer key for practice test
Question Types	Multiple choice, problem solving
Study Methods	Review notes, work through extra problems, go through practice test, study with group
Time Needed	6–8 hours
Approved Materials for Test	Paper, pencil, calculator
Number of Points	150, 15% of overall grade

changes in your schedule. In Evan's case, his biology study group may not be helping him study in the manner that is most effective for him. If that is the case, he may need to find a different group that fits his study goals better or consider that studying alone may be his best option.

No matter how much time you spend studying, it won't be effective if you are unable to concentrate on the subject. Many times you will find yourself distracted by external and internal commotion. Externally, you may have a noisy or messy house, or people may need or want your time and attention. Internally, you may be preoccupied by illness, stress, self-doubt, or fear. Both internal and external distractions make it difficult to study effectively, so you must take care of them or tune them out. If not, you will find that the time you spend studying is not productive.

For some students, planning ahead to study effectively is not an option. Because of poor time management or procrastination, these students often try to study in one long session of cramming. Such marathon sessions should be avoided when studying for an exam because they usually produce more anxiety than learning. If you do find yourself in a situation in which you must cram, try to maximize the effectiveness of the long hours and loads of material. Organize your time into short periods, no more than one hour at a time, and take many breaks. When you return from your break, review the material you had just been studying before you begin on new material. You may want to try a combination of writing down what you know, drawing pictures to represent the material, reciting key concepts aloud, creating songs with the material, or building a model of a key idea. The more learning preferences you use to understand the material, the better your chance of remembering it all for the test.

Other study tips include making flash cards to quiz yourself or others if you are in a study group. You can also tape-record questions and answers. Instead of playing the tape straight through, stop after each question so you can answer the question aloud. Then, play the answer and see how well you have done. If you can push yourself to enjoy studying, you will be more likely to do it often.

"Cheat" Sheets

Creating "cheat" sheets was once considered an activity only for those who intended to cheat; however, many educators have seen the benefit they can produce. You may have a professor who tells you that you can bring a three-by-five-inch index card to the exam with anything you want written on it. Students who may not have studied much beforehand usually jump at the chance to cram as much information as possible on that tiny white space. The result is that students retain more of the information than they would if they had not created the cheat sheet. Many times, the cheat sheet is not needed because the student has, in effect, studied adequately in making the sheet.

To create an effective cheat sheet, organization is important. One way to organize the card is to divide it into thirds on both sides so that you have six sections (three on one side, three on the other) to work with. Then, at the top of each section write a specific category such as "Formulas" or "Krebs Cycle." Underneath each heading, write the information that pertains to the category. If you are listing formulas, for example, be sure to write clearly and double-check that all elements of the formula are correct.

Even if you are not allowed to bring a cheat sheet—only bring one if you are given permission—you can still reap the benefits of this technique by closing your books and notes and writing down as much information as you can remember about the subject. For example, if you have a test on genetics, take a blank card and write everything you know about DNA on the front and back. In this case, organization is not important; what is important is to see how much you have learned already. Once you have filled up the card, go back through your notes and books to see what you have missed.

Previous Tests and Practice Tests

If allowed by the instructor, study copies of old tests. Your instructor may put them on reserve in the library, post them online in an online learning system, or hand them out in class. Previous exams are an excellent source for the kinds of questions you will probably be asked. If someone offers you old tests from the previous semester, ask your instructor for approval before taking them.

Another beneficial way that some professors help students prepare for tests is by offering practice exams. Some instructors may provide opportunities for you to stop by during office hours to take a practice exam or may offer online practice tests on which you can get instant feedback.

Study Groups

Juanita, Michael, Laura, and Evan took the advice of their orientation leaders early in the semester to create a study group for one of their classes, and they have realized that there are several benefits of studying in groups. First, you have access to more notes and may find that you have missed important information. Second, you experience others' perspectives about the subject, and you may discover that your classmates explain major concepts better than your professor. Third, you have a built-in support group while you take classes, because in the process of studying, you establish friendships.

A key to a successful study group is to limit the number of participants to four or five or fewer. The more members there are, the harder it will be to remain on track. It is also best to study with people who are not close friends to minimize distractions and off-topic conversations. When choosing members of your group, it is a good idea to discuss expectations for the group. If prospective members think they will receive help without contributing themselves, they may not be right for your group. You will need members who will take on specific responsibilities that benefit the whole group.

Once you have chosen your group participants, you should exchange contact information (phone and pager numbers and email addresses) and choose a leader. The leader can change from meeting to meeting, but one person should be in charge of contacting everyone to announce the meeting time and place for the first session. The leader should also be responsible for keeping everyone on task if the group gets off topic and for assigning roles to each person, just as Juanita does for her group when she leads a study session.

When you meet with your group, be sure that each person contributes to the study session and "teaches" his or her assigned part. Periodically, the group should take breaks to keep people focused. To make studying comfortable, try to meet in a quiet location that allows food and drink; this way there will be fewer breaks and fewer distractions from hunger or thirst. Also consider taking turns bringing snacks and beverages or chipping in for a meal. Better yet, go out for a meal *after* you study so that everyone has a goal to look forward to.

Reflection EXERCISE 9.1

What are your experiences with studying? When do you study and for how long? Has it been successful for you? Why or why not? ■

Forming study groups in college is often difficult because many students lead full lives and have very little time to schedule extra activities. They also may not have consistent free time because they work different shifts each week or have different family responsibilities from day to day. To make your study group work, you may need to be creative about how you meet and organize your time. For example, you may want to join a chat

FIGURE 9.2   Tips for Making Study Groups Work

- Start with a small group of three to five people.
- Choose a leader for each meeting.
- Keep a master list of contact information.
- Schedule a time and place that is convenient, comfortable, and conducive to studying.
- Be creative about meeting. Try doing some of the work, such as creating sample test questions, through chat rooms or email.
- Assign each person a role in the group and part of the material to "teach" to the group.
- Do your "homework" before meeting by preparing to "teach" your material.
- Review your notes with each other.
- Quiz each other on the material.
- Be respectful of others' commitments.
- Take frequent breaks.
- Stay on task.
- Meet often for short periods of time rather than "marathon" sessions.

room or use email to create a sample exam and "quiz" each other about the concepts on the exam. See Figure 9.2 for more tips.

TYPES of TEST QUESTIONS

Learning how to take tests will be just as important as learning the material. Knowing how to answer each type of possible test question will make taking an exam that much easier; at least, you will have less anxiety because you will know what to expect.

Question types can be categorized as objective or subjective. Objective questions often require only lower-level thinking because they ask you to recall facts and concepts and usually appear in the form of multiple choice, true/false, fill-in-the-blank, and short answer questions. Subjective questions ask for your opinion about the material or challenge you to apply the material in a new way. Essay and problem-solving (critical thinking) questions are considered subjective because there are a variety of ways the questions can be answered correctly. Students who understand that objective questions usually have only one correct answer often believe that there are no "wrong" answers for subjective questions, and that may be true, but there *are* better ways to answer them.

Sometimes, objective questions are easier to answer because they provide a correct answer within the choices. However, objective questions can also demand significant brainpower, especially when you must recall an answer with very few clues, which is often the case with fill-in-the-blank questions. In the following sections we discuss typical test questions and how to approach answering them.

Multiple Choice

Multiple-choice questions can test your recall of information or they can assess your ability to apply information or analyze situations. Despite their reputation for being easier than other types, expect more difficult and time-consuming multiple-choice questions for college exams, and don't be alarmed if the answers are not obvious.

When answering multiple-choice questions, the first step is to read the question or statement carefully. Then, mark any special words in the question or statement such as *not*, *always*, and *only*. Before looking at the choices, see if you can answer the question yourself. For example, consider the following multiple-choice question:

What should you not do to alleviate anxiety when taking a test? [Notice the word *not* and think in terms of what is not an acceptable answer.]

    A. Arrive early for the exam. [This is something you *should* do, so it is not the correct answer.]

    B. Skip over the directions. [This is something you should *not* do, so it may be the right answer. Keep reading the rest of the choices and lightly mark this one.]

    C. Pay attention to the time limit. [This is something you *should* do, so it is not the correct answer.]

    D. Read all the questions before answering. [Again, this is something you *should* do, so it is not the correct answer.]

After you have read through all the choices, the only correct answer is B.

Consider another multiple-choice question:

When answering an essay question on a test, be sure to

    A. Answer each part of the question thoroughly. [This is something you should do. Keep reading the rest of the choices.]

    B. Organize your essay before writing it by sketching out a quick outline. [This is something you should do. Keep reading the rest of the choices.]

    C. Read the directions carefully. [Again, this is something you should do. Keep reading the rest of the choices to see if "All of the above" appears because all the items so far are good choices.]

    D. All of the above. [This seems the best choice because all the other items are correct.]

After you have read all the choices, D is the correct answer because it includes every response as correct.

When answering multiple-choice questions, read each choice carefully and eliminate any answer that is obviously wrong. If you have to guess, eliminate any answer that is misspelled (usually a sign that the instructor has hurriedly added false answers) or any answer that is shorter than the others. Also, pay attention to choices labeled "All of the above" and "None of the above." If you can determine that at least two of the choices are correct, then "All of the above" is probably the correct answer. Likewise, if at least two of the choices are not correct, then "None of the above" is probably the correct answer.

Matching

A matching section on an exam presents you with two columns: a list of words or phrases that are to be matched with a list of descriptors. Professors who use matching sections are usually seeking basic recall of information, but you will need to read the directions carefully. There may be more than one match for an item in the list or there may be extra descriptors.

To complete matching questions, first read through the entire list and choices to match before beginning. Then, determine if there could be multiple matches to a word in the list. Make sure that you have chosen the correct letter to match with each word in the list. For example, consider the following set of matching questions:

Match the following descriptions of interests and strengths with the appropriate multiple intelligences category. The categories may be used more than once; some may not be used at all.

_____ 1. Enjoy outdoor activities	A. Verbal/linguistic
_____ 2. Know how and why they act	B. Logical/mathematical
_____ 3. Good at design, architecture	C. Visual/spatial
_____ 4. Choose careers in science, computer technology, engineering	D. Bodily/kinesthetic
_____ 5. Use voice or instruments to express themselves	E. Musical/rhythmic
	F. Interpersonal
_____ 6. Enjoy reading and writing	G. Intrapersonal
_____ 7. Can read others' feelings well	H. Naturalistic
_____ 8. Fascinated with pictures	

True/False

True/false questions can be tough even though there are only two possible answer. Guessing or randomly answering true/false questions should only be done as a last resort. It is better to read the statements carefully, noting key words that could point to the correct answer, such as *frequently, sometimes,* and *a few.* These words usually indicate a true statement. Words such as *never, only,* and *always* usually indicate a false statement.

If you have any difficulty answering true/false test questions, try not to confuse yourself with how the statement is worded. Go with your gut instinct. If you are not entirely sure what the statement is expressing, write down a justification of your answer on the test. Sometimes, professors will give partial credit if the wrong answer is clearly justified. Consider the following examples of true/false questions:

Determine if the statements are true or false. Circle the appropriate choice.

T F   1. Howard Gardner's theory of multiple intelligences includes the category Nutritional/Health.

T F   2. OK5R is a test-taking strategy.

T F   3. Priorities are beliefs that can be shaped by experience and are not the same for everyone.

T F   4. A mission statement is important because it declares your beliefs and your goals.

T F   5. A priority is something that keeps you from achieving your goals.

Fill-in-the-Blank/Short Answer

Fill-in-the-blank and short answer questions require that you recall definitions of key terms or items in a series. To complete these types of questions, first read the sentence

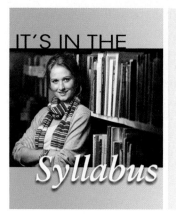

IT'S IN THE
Syllabus

What types of test questions do you anticipate from your classes? What evidence in the syllabus leads you to believe you will have certain types of test questions? (*Hint:* Look at the course description, if included.)

How often will you have tests? How will the tests be organized—around units, chapters, concepts? Will they be online, on-campus, or take-home tests?

or question carefully. Often, points will be lost if you don't answer exactly or misspell the correct term. Consider the following examples of fill-in-the-blank/short answer questions.

1. The T System for taking notes is also known as the _____.
2. Abbreviating words and phrases is called _____.
3. An instructor who is difficult to understand is an example of a listening _____.
4. _____ listening includes making the decision to concentrate on what is being said.
5. _____ is a method of note taking that involves numbering items and organizing them.

Problem Solving

Problem-solving, or critical thinking, questions are used by instructors so that students can demonstrate or apply the concepts or ideas they have learned. When you answer problem-solving questions, read the question carefully, marking multiple steps or parts to the directions. Next, determine what information you will need to solve the problem. Then, break the problem into parts and write down what process or operation you will need to perform. Work through the problem, and once you arrive at an answer, check the question again to make sure you have adequately answered it. Consider the following example of a problem-solving question as well as the explanation providing an approach to answering it:

> Rosa has a scholarship that requires her to maintain a 3.2 GPA while she is in college. During her first semester, she had 4 three-hour credit courses and made two A's and two B's. Now she is taking 1 four-hour course and 4 three-hour courses. If she can make an A in her four-hour course and B's in her three-hour courses, can she keep her scholarship?

In order to answer this question correctly, you will need to know how to calculate a GPA. If we break the steps down further, you will need to know the definition of grade points and quality points and how a GPA is calculated when a student has taken classes for more than one semester. Then, you will need to know how to multiply, add, and divide. These sound like commonsense steps, but writing down every operation that you will need to perform enables you to prepare to answer the question correctly and helps you check the process by which you arrived at the answer.

Now consider the following examples of problem-solving questions.

1. Lenise is taking a history class in which her grade is made up of her results on four exams. She has taken two already, receiving one score of 65% and another of 74%. What are the lowest grades she can make to get a C in the course? Is it mathematically possible for her to earn a B?

2. In Carlos's biology class, the final grade is composed of the following: homework (20%), midterm exam (30%), and final (50%). If Carlos makes an 85% on the final, a 71% on the midterm, and a 68% for his homework grade, what is his final average?

3. Lester needs a 3.63 GPA to be inducted into the Phi Theta Kappa honor society. This semester, he has earned two C's, an A, and two B's in his courses (none of which have labs). Will he be inducted? Show your work below.

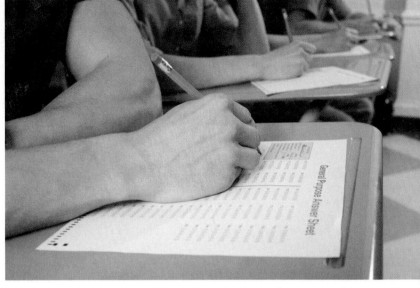

When taking a test, be sure to read directions carefully and pace yourself so that you have plenty of time to finish each section.

Frederick Bass/Getty Images

Essay Questions

Instructors use essay questions to help them measure students' ability to analyze, synthesize, and evaluate the concepts they have learned; this type of question gauges more than students' recall of facts or terms. You can be assured that you will encounter more essay questions in college because they allow students to demonstrate a deeper understanding of the material.

One thing to remember about essay questions is that, although you won't have an enormous amount of time to complete an essay, your professor will still expect you to answer the essay question thoroughly and clearly. Always read the directions carefully. If the essay question has more than one part, be sure to mark each part and answer it in the body of the essay. If the directions specify a length, be sure to meet or exceed it. Before you begin writing, create a brief outline of what you will cover during the essay. Make a short list of transitions and details so that you can refer to the list if you get stuck during the exam.

Finally, because your professor will be reading and grading many essays, a clearly organized essay will stand out and make it easy for her to tell that you have discussed the key points. Just be sure to give yourself plenty of time to write the essay and use any remaining time to proofread and edit your work. Chapter 8's information about putting the finishing touches on writing can also help you with essay questions. Consider the following examples of essay questions:

1. Do you think that colleges should strive, at whatever cost, to ensure that their campuses are diverse?

2. Do you think that colleges should prohibit personal and/or intimate relationships

Critical Thinking
EXERCISE 9.2

What types of questions are most challenging for you? What strategies can you employ to master them? ■

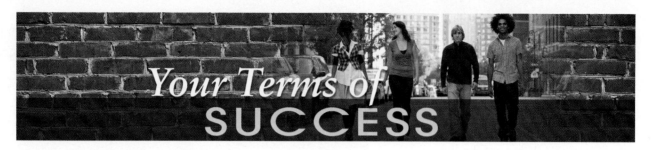

Your Terms of SUCCESS

WHEN YOU SEE . . .	IT MEANS . . .
Academic integrity	Refraining from cheating or using unapproved resources for a test or an assignment; completing a test or an assignment on your own.
"Cheat" sheet	A studying method that includes recording information, outlines, or formulas on a small card or sheet of paper; sometimes allowed by instructors to be used while taking a test.
Comprehensive exam	An exam that covers an entire semester's worth of material; usually given as a final exam.
Course objective	A goal that the instructor has identified for the student to meet once the course is completed.
Essay test question	A test question that requires a student to answer in the form of an essay.
Final exam	An exam that is given at the end of a semester.
Matching test question	A test question that provides one column of descriptors and another column of words that must be matched with the appropriate descriptor.
Multiple-choice test question	A type of test question in which an incomplete sentence or a question is given and the correct response must be chosen from a list of possibilities.
Objective test question	A question with only a limited number of possible answers; includes matching, multiple choice, true/false, and short answer.
Online test	A test that is taken through the Internet or through a course management system such as Angel or Blackboard.
Open-book test	A test for which one is permitted to look up answers in a textbook or in one's notes.
Short answer test question	A test question or prompt that requires a brief answer. The answer can be one word, one sentence, or a couple of paragraphs.
Subjective test question	A test question that requires a student to provide a personal answer. Usually, there are no "wrong" answers to subjective questions.
Take-home test	A test that can be taken home to complete.
Test anxiety	The fear one has when thinking about or taking a test.

between professors and students? Explain your response and refer to the college's policy regarding student–professor relationships in your essay.

3. How have your relationships at home and at work changed since you have entered college?

TYPES of TESTS

Just as important as knowing the types of questions you will encounter is understanding the kinds of tests you can expect in different classes. For example, a math test will look quite different from a music test, and the study strategies used to prepare for them and the experience of taking them will be different. Here we discuss a few different types of tests you may encounter in college. You may be able to apply the same tips to exams in other disciplines.

Math and Science Tests

For math and science tests, it is best to work through the problems you know first. Then complete the problems that you do not know as well. If you complete your test early, consider reworking the test questions again on another sheet of paper and comparing your answers. If you discover two different answers for the same problem, figure out which answer contains the error. Always show your work and complete as many parts of a multiple-part problem as possible. You may receive partial credit for completing the process correctly even if you have not arrived at the right answer.

When answering questions on science tests that involve processes or major concepts, draw a picture to create a visual of the process and to help you answer questions about the steps. Regardless of what question types you encounter, you will need to recall terms and definitions.

Fine Arts and Literature Tests

When taking exams in fine arts and literature classes, it is as important to explain the significance of the selected work as it is to identify key passages, authors, terms, and eras. In either discipline, work through the easier questions first and save plenty of time for the writing portions. Think about the major themes and historical importance of the works and look for those themes to be part of the questions on the test. Although recall of facts about eras, dates, and creators of works will be part of the exam, there should be a significant emphasis on synthesizing the material.

Open-Book and Take-Home Tests

There will be occasions when you are given an open-book or take-home test. Although they sound like the easiest kinds of test to take, professors who hand out open-book tests make sure that you work hard to answer the questions correctly—in other words, with harder questions than in-class, closed-book exams. Even if you know ahead of time that the test will be an open-book exam, you will still need to study for it so you can avoid spending too much time looking through your book and notes for the answers to the questions. With preparation, you should be able to find the answers quickly. Speed will matter because

Tech TIPS

USING TECHNOLOGY TO GET AHEAD

Taking online tests can be very different than taking them in a face-to-face format. You may find that online tests have time limits to them; you may also find that you cannot use outside sources (such as notes, your book, or the Internet) to complete the work. You will have to be careful, especially if you are new to online tests, that you mark the correct answers and save them before completing your test—you won't be able to go back to make changes once you hit "Submit."

you will probably have many questions to answer on an open-book exam, thoroughly testing how much you know about the subject. Likewise, take-home exams are often more difficult and time-consuming than a regular test. At the least, your instructor will expect more from you on a test completed at home. Because expectations are higher, you will need to give yourself plenty of time to formulate your answers and to check your work. Even though you will be unsupervised when writing the exam and probably expected to use a variety of resources for help, you will still need to maintain integrity. In other words, unless you receive permission from your instructor, do not accept or give help to other classmates.

Online Tests

Even if you do not take online classes, you may be required to take a quiz or test on an online learning system or through a website, such as a publisher's site that supports your textbook. Online tests are usually timed, which means you will need to keep an eye on how much time you take to answer the questions. Instructors often set a time limit for online exams to discourage students from reviewing notes, going through the text, or surfing the Internet for answers. If your professor offers a practice test, taking it can provide a good feel for how much time you will have and what types of questions you will answer. Additional considerations include revisiting questions if possible to check your answers for multiple-choice questions, ensuring that you have saved your answers before submitting your exam, and not sharing information about the exam with other students who have not taken it yet.

Comprehensive Exams

Comprehensive, or cumulative, exams are usually given during a week dedicated for "finals." Not all final tests are comprehensive—some professors choose to give their students shorter tests instead. However, most of the finals you take in college will reflect what you have learned all semester. Taking comprehensive exams at the end of the semester can be a daunting task if you have several classes, but there are some tips that will help you manage the challenge. First, it is important that you study for all your classes regularly. Reviewing notes daily will help you keep the information fresh. Second, make sure that you keep your notes and course materials organized so that you can easily find what you have covered throughout the semester. When you get closer to the date of your final exam, begin studying more intensely by reviewing the most current material and working backward toward the material that was covered at the beginning of the semester.

Collaboration
EXERCISE 9.3

Working within a group, brainstorm a list of tips that could help students study and take tests effectively. Divide your tips into categories that would help visual, aural, and kinesthetic learners. ■

TEST-TAKING STRATEGIES

Preparing for the Test

Before you begin to think about what is on a test and how you should study, you must make sure that you are taking care of yourself. Eating and sleeping are fundamental to doing well on tests. If you are not healthy, then you cannot perform at your highest

Numerous recent studies have reported that nearly 75% of college students have admitted to cheating at least once. The reasons students give for cheating are many: Some don't believe that their professors notice or care about their work; some believe that they can justify their cheating because the class or test is unfair; others believe that getting a good grade is the most important goal if scholarships and program admissions (such as nursing school) demand high standards.

No matter what the reason, cheating—and getting caught for cheating—can ruin your college experience. Colleges do take cheating seriously and often have no tolerance for those who cheat. Penalties can range from an F in the course to expulsion from the college.

YOUR TURN

Why do *you* think such a high percentage of college students have reported cheating? • Do you think colleges create environments in which it is hard to maintain academic integrity? • Why or why not?

_____

_____

_____

level. Just as athletes prepare for performance days in advance by eating carbohydrates and resting, you should focus on getting regular sleep and eating well days before the exam. At the least, get a good night's rest the night before the test and avoid refined sugar (candy, cakes, and cookies) and caffeine. For more specific information on staying healthy, refer to Chapter 10.

Maintaining a good attitude as you prepare for the exam is another effective strategy. Monitor and eliminate any negative self-talk about your ability to do well on exams. Instead, visualize yourself taking the test successfully and earning a good grade.

Taking the Test

Once you have prepared for the test, both physically and mentally, you should be ready to take it. Before you leave for class, be sure that you have the appropriate supplies: Will you need a watch, paper, pen, pencil, a calculator, or a dictionary and thesaurus? Are there any approved test-taking aids that you need to bring as well? Will you be able to use your textbook or a cheat sheet with formulas on it?

Once you arrive in class, take a seat away from distractions and where you feel comfortable to spread out and get to work. If you are not wearing a watch, sit somewhere you will be able to see a clock. Cell phone access, which many students use to keep track of time, may be restricted during tests, so be sure to keep track of time some other way. When taking tests that use a Scantron or bubble form in which you have to pencil in your answers by filling in circles, be sure to bring at least two sharpened pencils.

When you first get the test, read through all the questions, noting which ones will take longer to answer than the others. Taking that time to read all the questions is actually a time saver, because you will know what to expect and how to pace yourself.

Unless guessing will count against your grade, answer or attempt to answer each question on a test. Do not leave an item or question blank.

Bill Aron/PhotoEdit

Turn the paper over and check out the back. Your instructor may have made two-sided copies of the test, which means you will have questions on the back and front of the paper.

As you read through the test, make note of the types of questions and use the tips in this chapter to answer them. Read the directions for each section carefully and mark any special instructions. For example, in a matching section, there may be more than one match for an item in one of the columns; in an essay writing section, there may be a choice of topics. Also, be aware of how many points each section is worth. If one section is worth half the points for the entire exam, you will need to spend a majority of your time working that part.

Pacing yourself during the exam is very important. Before you begin the test, you should determine how much time you need to spend on each section based on the types of questions, your comfort level with the questions, and the amount of points it is worth. As a general rule, you should spend less than a minute per multiple choice and true/false question and 15 minutes or more to answer essay questions. For the other types of questions, you will need to spend somewhere in between 1 and 5 minutes. If you get off track and spend too much time on one section, don't panic. You will just need to work quickly and carefully on the rest of the exam.

Working the easiest questions first, mark questions that you can't answer quickly or that you find confusing. Don't come back to them until you have completed all the questions that you can easily answer. If you are unsure of an answer, mark that question as well and plan to review it before turning in your exam. If the question or problem has multiple parts, work through as many of the parts as you can. Do not leave questions unanswered. Partial answers may receive partial credit unless you have been instructed otherwise.

Finally, leave yourself 5 to 10 minutes to check your work. If you finish an exam early, always go back through the questions and go over your answers to ensure that all questions are answered and that all parts are completed. If you have written an essay, read through your response and check for grammatical, spelling, and punctuation errors. Initial each page and number the pages of your essay, if appropriate. Turn in your exam and any paper on which you worked problems or drafted an essay.

Maintaining Integrity during the Test

You may have recently read about the new lengths that students go to in order to cheat on exams or to plagiarize. Advances in technology have made cheating easier and seemingly more widespread, although there is no clear evidence that more students are cheating now than were 30 years ago; however, there does seem to be more confusion about what constitutes cheating. For example, some professors require group presentations and collaboration on projects; however, very few offer guidelines on who should do what and how to document the part that each student does. In addition, collaboration on homework assignments, which was encouraged in high school, may now be prohibited in college. When in doubt about how you should complete homework or group projects, ask your instructor for specific guidelines.

The integrity rules are a little clearer when taking a test. Unless otherwise stated, do not use notes, books, or classmates as references for the exam. Most instructors will ask you to clear your desk of any material except paper and a pen or will ask you to move away from the nearest person. These precautions are to ensure that there are no questions about the originality of the work. Other instructors are more trusting of students and may leave the classroom or give the class a take-home test. An instructor who allows such freedom is sending you a message about integrity: He trusts that his students will act maturely, responsibly, and honestly. Violating that trust can have grave consequences, because not only does the cheating student create problems for herself, but she has also damaged the relationship of trust for the entire class.

To ensure that you act with integrity when taking an exam, whether supervised or not, do your own work and keep your work surface clear of books, papers, folders, cell phones, pagers, and even drink bottles. If possible, distance yourself from other students so that they are less likely to cheat off you. If you are ever in doubt, however, about your actions or the requirements for an exam, be sure to ask your professor.

Beating Test Anxiety

All of the information in this chapter is difficult to put into practice if you have overwhelming anxiety about taking tests. It is not unusual to experience nervousness, anxiety, and fear before or during a test, but extreme anxiety accompanied by excessive sweating, nausea, and crying is not normal. If you are experiencing conditions that make taking and completing tests impossible, you should see a college counselor or other professional. However, if you occasionally experience very mild reactions, there are some techniques that can help minimize your anxiety and fear. Remember that some degree of nervousness is normal and can actually give you an adrenaline boost.

Basic relaxation techniques such as deep breathing and visualizations can take the edge off the tension of taking a test. Taking the time to breathe deeply whenever you feel overwhelmed will help you stay in control. Also, visualizing yourself relaxing or succeeding at a test can help you get beyond self-defeating doubt and stress.

Reflection EXERCISE 9.4

What studying mistakes have you made before or while taking a test? ■

PLUS EXERCISE 9.5

(Personality + Learning Style = Understanding Situations)

Let's revisit the study group's discussion. Juanita, the youngest, learns best by writing but has severe test anxiety, whereas Michael is visual and needs more direction in what to study. Evan, a kinesthetic learner, has gotten by with little studying in the past, whereas Laura learns best when she hears information, but has been distracted with other obligations. What study strategies and test-taking tips can each use?

Now, considering your own learning style, personality type, and special circumstances, what would you do if you were studying with fellow students whose learning styles and levels of preparation differed from your own? ■

From College to University

HOW STUDYING AND TESTING MAY DIFFER AFTER TRANSFER

As you take upper-level classes, you may find that tests and papers seem to get fewer and farther between, but their importance to the overall course is greater. Your reading load will increase and the subject matter will get more technical. You may also find yourself reading a variety of material: textbooks, journal articles, lab manuals, dissertations, novels, surveys, charts, graphs, and statistics.

Your critical thinking skills will be essential to making it through these courses. Your professors will also expect you to have strong study skills and solid test-taking strategies because they will provide few clues as to what you will be tested on and how you will be tested. This is not to say that university professors are cold and uncaring about your learning; instead, because they are concerned with pushing your abilities in terms of thinking and learning, they may have little time for helping you improve your study skills.

If you have a solid foundation of skills and strategies, then you will be successful. You will just need to monitor your progress and make adjustments as necessary. For instance, although you may not have studied with a group before, at the university you may find that study groups are essential for covering the massive amounts of material. Your goal should be finding what works best for you and what continues to help you succeed.

Building Your University Portfolio 9

Find someone you know (or ask your professor for the name of a former student) who has transferred to a four-year university and ask about his or her experience with taking tests at the university level. Are the tests harder? Are there more or fewer tests? What advice can this person give you about taking tests and studying?

_____

_____

_____

From College to Career

PREPARATION COUNTS

Just as you prepare for exams and presentations in college, you will use the same skills on the job. Time management, attention to detail, and careful preparation will be necessary for success in your career. Depending on your career choice, you may have to pass proficiency tests or certification exams, sometimes annually. Failing an exam in college may not mean the end of your academic career, but failing a licensing exam or a certification test could very well be the end of your job. Thus, the stakes—and the stress—will be much higher on the job.

Although the pressure to pass will be greater, chances are good that your college experience with multiple tests has sharpened your test-taking skills sufficiently to get you through exams on the job. In addition to reviewing the test-taking strategies outlined in this chapter, you should also take advantage of any test preparation seminars that your employer offers. Also, now is the time to demonstrate your ability to study with others. There is no better study group than your coworkers because they all have the same investment as you: They want to pass the exam in order to keep their jobs or advance to a higher position.

Building Your Career Portfolio 9

Contact someone in a career that is similar to what you want to do. Ask what tests are required in the field and about the challenges for passing the tests. For example, is there a test to enter the field? Is there a test after one reaches a certain level? Are there tests to help one advance in the career? What advice would this person give about studying for those tests and passing them?

_____

_____

_____

_____

First Voices

STORIES OF SUCCESS FROM COLLEGE GRADUATES

From leading his college class to leading a university: First-generation student still in college after all these years

Charles Welch,
Ed.D.,
University President

I was fortunate to have the ideal college experience. However, because I was the first member of my family to ever attend college, I entered college with very limited knowledge about what it takes to be a successful college student. Through hard work, self-discipline, and extensive involvement in extracurricular activities, I was able to fully absorb the comprehensive educational experience. I was a member of a Greek organization where I made lifelong friendships, I was involved in countless student activities where I learned the importance of teamwork and communication skills, I was able to graduate in four years, and I even had the privilege of serving as president of the student body.

My life, and the life of my entire family, has been forever altered because of my college experience. I have traveled to places, met people, and experienced opportunities that I could have only dreamed about as a child. My wife, closest friends, and professional mentors are all relationships I made in college. Because of the impact that higher education had on me personally, I have now committed my professional life to providing opportunities to other young people to attain a life-changing college degree.

Professionally, I have worked at the White House and on Capitol Hill for multiple members of Congress. I have also served as an academic dean, college vice president, and I accepted two college/university presidencies before the age of 35, making me one of the youngest university presidents in the United States. Perhaps my greatest success, however, is my family and my two daughters. Fortunately, because I was able to receive a college degree, my daughters face a bright future with limitless opportunities for success.

My advice to a student beginning their educational journey would be to always remember that it does not matter where you start in life, what matters is where you finish. It does not matter where you come from, what matters is where you end up.

PATH OF DISCOVERY
Journal Entry

How do you study best for tests? How did you develop these study habits? What do you want to change, if anything, about how you prepare for exams?

CHAPTER REVIEW QUESTIONS

1. What kinds of study strategies will benefit visual, aural, read/write, and kinesthetic learners?
2. What kinds of questions can you expect on science tests? On literature tests?
3. Compare studying in a group with studying on your own. What are the benefits of both? What are the drawbacks?
4. In what ways can a student beat test anxiety?

CHAPTER 9 CASE SCENARIOS

1. Sylvia's accounting professor has announced to the class that he allows students to study from old tests. In fact, he keeps a folder of previous exams in the library for students to access. At a study session for the test with a classmate, the student pulls out a copy of a test with the current semester's date on it. Sylvia questions her classmate, who says that the professor gave her a rough draft of a test that he decided not to use. When Sylvia gets to class, she recognizes every question because it is the same test that her classmate had. What should Sylvia do?
2. Ryan does not think he knows how to study well. He glided through high school without cracking open a book. Now he is in college and taking five classes: Intermediate Algebra, Reading Improvement, Introduction to Sociology, Speech Communication, and Concepts of Health and Wellness. He is struggling through his health and math classes. What can you tell him about studying for those subjects that will help him get back on track?
3. Betty gets sweaty palms and wants to throw up each time she takes a test. She has failed classes before because she couldn't calm herself down enough to take a major test. This semester, though, Betty must do better because she cannot keep dropping or failing her classes. What advice can you offer that will help ease her fears? What can she do and what kind of help can she get so that she can be successful?

RESEARCH IT FURTHER

1. Investigate methods of cheating that have occurred with "high-stakes" testing such as licensure and college entrance exams. Write a report about these methods and the effects that they have had on how organizations test.
2. What are the most popular ways that students study at your college? Create a questionnaire that asks students how, when, and where they study. Once you tally the results, determine whether the students at your college need a one-page reminder of how to study effectively. If you think they do, create one based on the shortcomings of their methods of studying.
3. Using the material in this chapter, create two or three games that can help students remember and understand the material.

References and Recommended Readings

Klauser, H. A. (2001). *Write it down, make it happen: Knowing what you want and getting it!* New York: Simon & Schuster.

Paul, M. A., & Paul, K. (2009). *Study smarter, not harder.* Bellingham, WA: Self Counsel Press.

Roubidoux, S. (2008). *101 ways to make studying easier and faster for college students: What every student needs to know explained simply.* Ocala, FL: Atlantic Publishing Group.

10

STRESS and HEALTH

Evan is a student by day and a kickboxer by night, usually competing several times a semester. At 20 years old, he can already tell that it takes him longer to see the results of regular strength training than it did three years ago. Even if he is a little slower in the ring, he has made up for it with smarter moves, the result of years of training both his body and his mind.

Because he is dedicated to the sport, he spends hours each afternoon and evening working as hard, or sometimes harder, than he does for his college classes. Sometimes he wonders if he can do both and be successful in and out of the ring. A few years ago, he saw a doctor because of depression, and he feels the symptoms creeping up on him again.

When he steps out of his car to enter the metal building that he calls his second home, a strong hand squeezes his shoulder.

"Evan, man, you're a little late today," his coach says. "What gives? You are usually early to practice."

"Hey, Coach. I hit some heavy traffic on the way in because I didn't leave at the time I usually do. Had too much homework to do," Evan replies.

"Evan, I know you are committed to college. That's great, but you have to do your time at the gym. If you don't, you won't be ready for your next fight. No offense, but I don't train second place."

The words sting Evan. He is highly competitive—you have to be, in this sport—and he prides himself on his athletic ability. True, he isn't getting any younger, but a winning title is still possible for an "old geezer" like him.

Then there is college—another goal that he wants to achieve. When he registered for college, he really thought he could do both kickboxing and college and succeed at both. Most definitely, his workouts at the gym provide him with the energy release he needs. What better way to relieve stress and stay in shape than to box every day?

Evan packs his sweatshirt into his gym bag, stretches, and thinks about the homework he still has to complete before going to bed tonight, which will be around 2 A.M. if he gets home by 11:00. A few energy drinks and a protein bar will be needed to keep him awake to get his work done.

"I've got some extra drills we need to work on tonight," his coach says. "Can you stay another hour after you get your workout in?"

Evan hesitates. He has to finish a paper, and now he will need to stay up all night to get it done even though that will mean "sleepwalking" through his classes and maybe even his workout tomorrow.

"Sure, Coach," Evan says, and reassures himself that worrying about what he has to do won't make it any better.

For most of us, minimizing the negative effects of stress and maximizing good health is a matter of making appropriate choices. How to decrease stress, how to increase energy, what to eat, how much to exercise, and how to reconnect with ourselves are judgments we make every day, yet so many of us make inappropriate choices. The choices we make now are decisions that we will literally have to live with for decades to come. We will be living longer than our ancestors did, but will our lives and our health be better? Some experts are seriously worried that we are making decisions about our health without thinking through the consequences.

The purpose of this chapter is to provide you with information so that when you know better, you will make better choices for your physical, mental, and sexual health, which will in turn help you handle stress more effectively.

More specifically, after completing this chapter, you will be able to do the following:

■ **Define stress and where it can appear in your life.**
■ **Describe methods for reducing stress and minimizing any stress-related illnesses.**
■ **Determine which health issues are important to consider while you are in college.**
■ **Identify methods to make better choices about your overall health.**

UNDERSTANDING STRESS

Stress is a physical and psychological response to outside stimuli. In other words, just about anything that stimulates you can cause stress. Not all stress, however, is bad for you. For example, the stress you feel when you see someone get seriously hurt enables you to spring into action to help. For some students, the stress of an upcoming exam gives them the energy and focus to study. Without feeling a little stressed, these students might not feel the need to study at all.

What? Me Worry?

Not everyone, however, handles stress the same way, and a stressful situation for you may not produce the same reaction for someone else. How we handle stress depends on our genetic makeup, past experiences, and the stress-reducing techniques that we know and practice. There are ways to reduce stress or change our reaction, both physically and psychologically. First, though, it is important to be able to identify causes of stress. The list in Figure 10.1 is not exhaustive, but it can start you thinking about different ways that you experience stress.

Each of us has certain triggers, such as the ones listed in Figure 10.1, that stress us out. Usually, however, the same situation doesn't stress us out the same way each time it occurs. Take waiting in line at the bank. One day, you might be extremely angry at waiting 15 minutes in a line to cash a check because you are late for a job interview. The next time that you are in the same line waiting the same amount of time, you may be calm and relaxed because you are enjoying a little quiet time to think while your mother waits in the car. Thus, it is not necessarily the situation or action that causes negative stress, but more likely other factors that are involved.

FIGURE 10.1 Possible Causes of Stress

- Self-doubt
- Fear of failure or the unknown
- Congested traffic
- Uncomfortable situations
- Life experiences such as the death of a loved one, having a child, getting married, or moving
- Waiting in lines
- Pressure to succeed (from yourself or others)
- Speaking in public
- Lack of support—financial, physical, or psychological
- The demands of a job such as a promotion or demotion, deadlines, and evaluations
- Too many activities and not enough time to complete them
- Computer problems

When you are suffering from lack of sleep, you may be more likely to react negatively to people and situations that usually would not bother you. When you are feeling unsure of your abilities to be successful in college, you may take constructive criticism as a personal attack. Being aware of times and situations that cause you the most stress is one step to helping manage stress better. If you realize that you are sensitive to others' feedback because you are feeling insecure, then you may be less likely to react negatively.

In Figure 10.2, place an X next to situations that are negatively stressful for you. Consider other situations or people that cause you to react negatively. The goal is to recognize a pattern of stress and then work to overcome it.

FIGURE 10.2 What Stresses You Out?

Situation	Stresses Me	Does Not Stress Me
Starting a big project		
Paying bills		
Being in a messy environment		
Receiving graded papers and exams		
Not getting enough sleep		
Taking a personal or professional risk		
Getting out of bed		
Not getting feedback on my work		
Being distracted by other people		
Thinking about the future		
Taking tests		

Stress in College

Because you will encounter stress at college, work, and home, it is important to be able to identify the different stressors in each environment and work toward minimizing the negative stress in each area. Some weeks, you will have to contend with negative stress in only one area, but there will be times when it seems as though each part of your life is making you miserable. The more you understand what you can and cannot control, the more likely you will be able to work through stressful times and stay on track with your goals.

Stress in college is inevitable, but it doesn't have to be overwhelming if you know what you can do to minimize negative stress in the first place. There are several ways that students unknowingly cause themselves stress: failing to read the catalog and student handbook about course prerequisites and descriptions as well as degree program requirements; registering for more hours than they can handle; trying to do too much at work and home; missing deadlines; arriving late for class or appointments; and keeping the same social schedule despite more academic demands.

The information in this chapter and throughout this book should help you minimize your stress in college by providing you with information and strategies for accomplishing your goals. Even if you avoid the stress-producing behaviors just noted, you may still find that things don't go your way in college. If you accept that there will be times that you or others will make mistakes, then you will be more likely to bounce back from problems. Minimizing the negative effects of stress can include commonsense activities such as reading all information that you receive from the college; paying attention to flyers on doors, bulletin boards, and tables; and talking to your advisor, instructors, and counselor on a regular basis.

You will also want to regularly check the college's website for announcements and updates. Be sure, too, to read publications such as newspapers and newsletters that the college sends to the community. As always, ask questions when you are not sure of something, and make an effort to get involved with campus organizations and clubs because people in these groups often know what is going on around campus.

Stress at Home

Reducing stress at home will, no doubt, be the first step for minimizing your overall stress. Because your family and friends are likely to be your most important supporters, what they think of you and the demands they place on you will need to be discussed. Some family members may be unsure of what you are doing or worried that your schoolwork will leave little time for them. Your friends may feel the same way, especially if they are used to hanging out with you after work and on the weekends. The key to minimizing stress at home is to communicate your needs. Talk to your loved ones about what you and they can expect when you are taking classes

Some other tips for making your home life a sanctuary rather than an asylum include telling your family when you have exams or major projects due and informing them of your breaks and vacation time. They may be excited to count down the days until you are finished with the semester. Remember to explain how your responsibilities will change when you are in college. Also, be aware that you are a role model for your family—you may be inspiring other family members to go to college.

Stress at Work

For some, stress on the job can be the most difficult to deal with because of the fear of performing poorly and being fired. Stress on the job can also be particularly tough to manage because you may feel uncomfortable confronting coworkers and being honest about your feelings. There are ways, though, to cope with the negative effects of stress at work. To help minimize the amount of stress at your job, consider talking to your employer about your educational goals. Your boss may be very encouraging about your determination to increase your knowledge and improve your skills. Your employer may allow you flextime to take classes, which means you may be able to arrive at work early, skip a lunch break, or stay late in order to take classes during the day.

As you would with your family, let your boss know when you have finals or other activities that may interfere with your regular workday, but avoid studying on the job. Be sure to handle any conflict that may arise from your schedule as soon as possible. Coworkers may be jealous of your success or they may misunderstand the arrangements you have made to work and go to school. If you have any concerns, address them to the appropriate person.

There is no cure-all for stress. It is an integral and important part of life and can actually be thrilling and exciting. Nonetheless, preventing unnecessary stress in the first place can keep you happier and healthier, which will make you better able to achieve your goals.

Integrity MATTERS

Have you ever promised someone that you would do something for her, only to break your promise? Have you ever offered to help someone, only to let him down when he needed you most? We all have had moments in our lives when we were not true to our word about what we would do. No matter why we fail to see our promises through, the end result always causes us some stress in our lives because such actions, or inactions, can damage our relationships with others.

One way to eliminate stress and anxiety is to make integrity a top priority in your life. Only promise what you know you can deliver. Tell someone no or do not even offer in the first place if you know you won't be able to keep your word. Even though it may seem less stressful to take the easier path, in the long run, your negative stress will decrease when you maintain your integrity.

YOUR TURN

When have you let someone down by not delivering on a promise or an offer to help or when has someone let you down? • How did you feel about not honoring your word or about the other person's broken promise? • In what ways did your relationship change?

_____

_____

_____

Stress-Related Illnesses

Stress can cause a variety of health-related problems, such as sleep deprivation. Stress-related illnesses can vary from person to person, but there is one common denominator: With information and techniques for reducing stress, you can decrease the negative health effects. Although some of the following illnesses can be caused by other factors such as heredity and environment, they can be signs that stress is making you ill:

- Digestive problems including upset stomach, heartburn, constipation, diarrhea, and ulcers
- Severe headaches and migraines
- High blood pressure, heart attack, and stroke
- Muscle and joint pain
- Cold, flu, respiratory, and sinus infections

Reflection
EXERCISE 10.1

In what ways have you experienced stress this semester? Is stress more of a problem at home, work, or college? What can cause you the most stress in those areas of your life? ■

Staying healthy by eating well, exercising, and getting adequate sleep are all ways to help prevent stress-related illnesses. Be careful, especially at stressful times such as the beginning and end of the semester, that you do not neglect both your physical and mental health, for you will be more susceptible to stress-related illnesses that could keep you from doing well in college.

HANDLING STRESS

No doubt you have felt stress since enrolling in college. You wouldn't be human if you didn't at least worry at the beginning of the semester how you will manage it all—family, work, college, and personal life. Stress is normal, but it can seriously derail college students from achieving their goals if they cannot manage it successfully. Looking for ways to minimize—not eliminate, because you can't—stress and to maximize balance in your life will make your college experience more enjoyable, if not completely stress free.

Reducing the Negative Effects of Stress

Because you cannot eliminate all stress, you will need to develop methods for reducing the negative effects that your body and mind experience when they are stressed out. One of the quickest, easiest ways to reduce the negative effects of stress is to take a deep breath. You may have even told someone who was upset to breathe deeply in order to calm down. Proper breathing is, as many cultures have known for thousands of years, an important part of life; for example, in yoga, the ability to control the breath is essential to controlling the mind and body and to bringing fresh air to the lungs and other organs.

Visualization is another method for reducing the effect that stress has on the mind and body. In order to visualize a more relaxed time and place, all you need to do is to find a quiet, comfortable spot, sit down, and close your eyes. Relaxation experts suggest that you visualize a place that makes you feel warm and relaxed. Many people think about a beach because the mood there is often relaxed and the sound of the ocean is comforting. You will need to find your own special place.

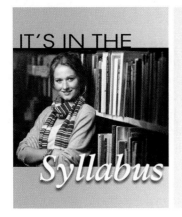

IT'S IN THE Syllabus

What parts of your professors' syllabi will cause you the most stress in terms of meeting the expectations? What will be easiest for you to manage?

If you find yourself overwhelmed or confused by the expectations in your courses, what can you do to help minimize your stress?

Once you decide where you want to go mentally, you should start noticing the details in your chosen place. If you are at the beach, then you should feel the sunshine's heat. Next, listen to the waves crashing on the surf and smell the salty air. Depending on how long you need to visualize this special place, you may want to stick your toe in the water or lie down on the beach and soak up the rays—leave your stress in those designated beach trash cans. The goal in this method of relaxation is to stay there as long as you need to; when you mentally return to your present location, you should feel refreshed and renewed.

Sometimes physical activity can be a better stress reliever than mental exercises. Getting outside or to the gym to work out your frustrations and stress is an excellent way of maintaining your health. By exercising, you can eliminate the physical side effects of stress while you take your mind off your troubles. If you do not usually exercise, take it slowly. Start with a 15-minute walk around the block or do some simple stretching exercises on the floor. Overdoing exercise can lead to more stress, so start small and increase the time you spend getting your blood circulating as you get stronger.

If you happen to exercise too much, you can look toward massage therapy to reduce all your stress. Although it is a little less conventional than other methods of reducing stress, a massage can improve circulation and alleviate muscle soreness. You can seek professional massage therapy or ask a family member to rub your neck, shoulders, or feet. Massage therapy can give you the rejuvenation you need to tackle the rest of the week.

The cliché "Laughter is the best medicine" is another way of saying it is an ideal way to eliminate stress. Have you ever been in a very stressful situation when someone made you laugh and you thought, "Boy, I needed that"? You probably felt all the tension melt away as you doubled over giggling. Surrounding yourself with people who make you laugh is one way to keep stress at a minimum. Other ways include renting comedies or reading funny books. Of course, good, old-fashioned acting silly can relieve stress and anxiety as well.

Last, you can comfort yourself with familiar favorites to eliminate the negative effects of stress. A special meal or a visit with your best friend can put you at ease. Looking at old photographs, reminiscing about family trips, and watching your favorite movies can be great stress relievers. If you have enrolled in college in a new town or you have moved out on your own for the first time, you may find comfort in the familiar, whether an old pillow or a favorite movie. Make sure, though, that your methods of reducing negative stress are healthy. Drugs and alcohol may temporarily relieve stress, but they cause more problems in the long run.

Making good food choices is the foundation for overall good health.

Justin Sullivan/Getty Images

Staying Flexible

An important method of managing stress is to remain flexible. If you try to control too many aspects of your life, you will quickly discover you can't do it all. Although it is important to manage your time and mark progress toward your goals, you still need to plan for the unexpected and be willing to make adjustments. Good time managers plan for problems by keeping their schedules loose enough to make room for adjustments. For example, if you have a doctor's appointment at 2:00, you shouldn't schedule a job interview at 3:00. Delays in the doctor's office or traffic problems could keep you from your interview and cause more stress, just like with Evan. Instead, you should give yourself plenty of time in between scheduled tasks, especially if you will have to rely on others' time management skills.

Knowing When to Get Help with Stress

If you ever feel as though you cannot cope with the amount of work and responsibility that you have—despite attempts to reduce your stress—seek professional help. Excessive crying, difficulty breathing, inability to get out of bed, and suicidal thoughts are severe reactions to stress. Knowing when to reach out to other people will be crucial in your recovery.

Critical Thinking EXERCISE 10.2

What stress-relieving techniques are most helpful to you and why? How will you make sure to find time to relieve stress while you are in college? What possible effects will *not* managing your stress have on you? ■

When asking for help, find someone you trust who will be objective about your experiences. Sometimes, close friends and family members can be your best allies to combat stress, but other times an outside party, who will listen to what you have to say without judging, can be extremely helpful. When you talk to someone, be honest about what you are feeling. Don't try to minimize any fear or anxiety. The more the person knows about what you are experiencing, the better able he or she will be to help.

WHAT'S GOOD for YOU

Think about this scenario: You have just bought a brand-new car and are about to drive it off the lot. Before you do, the salesperson provides you with an owner's manual and begins to tell you how often you will need to fill the tank, replace the oil, check the brakes, and rotate the tires. You tell the salesperson you don't need to know any of that stuff, and you drive the car off the lot. Besides, you know that the car needs to be filled up whenever the light on the dashboard comes on. What else is there to know?

For those who own and drive cars, you can imagine what will happen next. One day, maybe in a few months or a few years, you will find the car stops working regularly or stops working at all. In some cases, the repairs are minimal; in other cases, major repairs must be made to get the car into shape. The costs could be astronomical, so much so that you find yourself without a car and without hope for getting another one anytime soon.

Now, consider that the car is your body. You know when you are hungry and when you are tired, when you feel happy and when you are stressed, but do you know how to take care of yourself? Maybe you do know that exercising will improve your health and help you manage your stress, but you won't make the time to include fitness as a part of your weekly routine. Just as a car will eventually have problems without regularly scheduled maintenance, there will come a day when the neglect will keep your body from running properly or at all.

Learning to take care of your physical and mental health is crucial to getting where you want to go. To continue the car analogy, you won't be arriving at your destination if the vehicle is not in proper working order. One of the benefits of higher education, as stated earlier in this book, is that you must learn to make better choices, including better choices about your health. You can do that by understanding what you can control and how to get information to stay physically and mentally healthy.

Eat Well

One key to living a healthy life is making it a priority to eat nutritious food. Getting the recommended daily allowances of fruits, vegetables, whole grains, proteins, and fats is a commonsense approach to healthy eating, but as a society, we are choosing less healthy foods that are quick and easy—and loaded with calories, fat, salt, and sugar. Some of the reasons for poor nutritional choices include lack of time, information, and access to healthy alternatives. Increased stress is another reason that students make poor food choices; they may choose comfort food over nutritious alternatives.

To make healthier choices, arm yourself with information. As with any aspect of your health, the more you know, the better choices you can make. Learn what healthy foods are and seek them out. Read about and pay attention to serving sizes; too much of even a healthy food can add unneeded calories and contribute to weight gain. Read and learn to interpret food labels and ingredient lists that provide information about what is in the food and how much of it represents recommended daily values. The U.S. Food and Drug Administration (2004) provides detailed information on their Web page, titled "How to Understand and Use the Nutrition Facts Label," which can be accessed at www.cfsan.fda.gov/~dms/foodlab.html.

Another way of getting nutritional information is to talk with a physician or a nutritionist to get a better idea of what kinds of food will be best for you to consume. Regular doctor visits will determine if you have any potential health risks, such as high blood pressure or diabetes, which will make your food decisions even more crucial to good health. Keeping chronic illnesses in check with monitoring and medication will not only help you feel better, but it will also keep you healthy for the long term.

Eating healthy means eating regularly. Most experts recommend eating smaller meals more frequently rather than heavy meals 5 to 7 hours apart. At the very least, as nutritionists recommend, start the day with a healthy breakfast, even if you don't have enough time to sit down and eat a full meal. You will feel more alert and energized throughout the early morning. However, what you eat for breakfast is just as important as whether you eat at all. Powdered doughnuts and a sugary, caffeinated soda will not provide you with the nutrients you need to be at your best. A piece of fruit and a cup of yogurt, for example, would be a better choice if you have to eat on the run. In addition to smaller, frequent nutritious meals, drinking plenty of water throughout the day has numerous health benefits, including regulating body temperature and assisting digestion.

FIGURE 10.3 Tips for Healthy Eating in College

- Find and read reliable information about health issues.
- Eat consciously and take time to appreciate the nourishment you are receiving from healthy foods.
- Plan your meals *and* snacks ahead of time so that you are not susceptible to last-minute poor choices.
- Take bottled water in your backpack and drink it throughout the day.
- Take healthy snacks with you to eat between classes to avoid making unhealthy choices at the vending machines or at the student union.
- Pay attention to serving sizes and eat what you need to stay healthy, not the amount that you want to eat.
- Make wise choices at vending machines by avoiding food that is high in fat, caffeine, sugar, or salt content.
- Make any changes gradually. Think long-term health, not short-term results.

Avoiding fad diets is another strategy for staying healthy. Although they may promise increased energy and weight loss, the results may be short lived and potentially harmful. A better approach to eating healthy is to stick to the recommended guidelines from the Food and Drug Administration or a health expert. Be aware, too, of the potential for eating disorders such as anorexia and bulimia. Anorexia, a condition in which people strictly control how much food they eat, and bulimia, a condition in which people cycle between overeating (binge eating) in a short amount of time and then purging (through vomiting or abusing laxatives), are two eating disorders that can cause serious physical and psychological harm. Students who suffer from anorexia or bulimia, or believe they do, should see a health professional as soon as possible.

Why should you be concerned about what you eat and how much? One benefit of eating healthy is that it improves your body's functions. You may find that eating better enhances your ability to sleep or reduces the fatigue you feel by the end of the day. Eating well also improves your mental abilities. Studies have shown that eating certain foods, such as fish, can improve your test-taking abilities. Finally, eating healthy without overeating helps keep stress under control, which in turn keeps stress-related illnesses at a minimum. See Figure 10.3 for more tips.

Get Moving

We all know that making good choices about nutrition and exercise is part of a healthy lifestyle, but busy students often find it difficult to squeeze in time to work out. Take into consideration that as a student, you will spend many hours sitting down studying or working on the computer. Even if you previously had a regular exercise routine, you may find that you have to make studying a higher priority.

Because you may have less time for exercise, it will be even more important that you find time to include some physical activity in your busy schedule because of the numerous health benefits. At the very least, getting regular exercise will help you relieve stress.

Regular exercise can lower blood pressure, increase your metabolism, improve muscle tone, and lessen your chances of suffering diseases that are directly related to a sedentary lifestyle. It can also improve your mood and self-confidence. Experts vary

FIGURE 10.4 Tips for Exercising in College

- Take a physical education class at your college.
- Use the exercise facilities and equipment on your campus.
- Take advantage of walking trails or paved walkways on your campus.
- Park farther away from the buildings and get extra steps in.
- Join a gym and go regularly.
- Ask a friend to exercise with you.
- Incorporate short sessions of exercise into your studying routine by taking walking or stretching breaks in between reading or writing papers.
- Learn how to play a new sport or investigate a new form of exercise.

on how much exercise is ideal, but most agree 30 minutes of sustained activity three or four times a week will provide you with health benefits.

If you have trouble getting started or staying in an exercise routine, consider setting fitness goals that are reasonable and achievable. Reward yourself whenever you meet your goals, and don't get discouraged if you fall short now and then. Regular physical activity should be a lifestyle, not a short-term effort, so think of your progress as part of a long-term plan to live better. See Figure 10.4 for tips, but as with any exercise program, see a doctor before you begin and start gradually if you are not usually physically active.

Sleep Soundly

Getting an adequate amount of sleep each night is as important to maintaining good health as what you eat and how often you exercise, but most Americans, especially college students, do not get enough sleep to maintain their health. Experts say that adults should get 7 to 9 hours of sleep a night to function normally throughout the day, but millions regularly get 6 hours or less. While you are in college, you may believe that 6 hours a night sounds like a luxury as you juggle your multiple responsibilities. For sure, there will be times that, because of circumstances, you will not be able to get enough sleep, but those times should be few and far between. Maintaining a regular schedule of going to bed and getting up will help you get the amount of sleep you need. Despite the myth of what college life is like, pulling "all-nighters" to study for tests or complete assignments is strongly discouraged, because it will make you less likely to perform well the next day.

For some students, the idea of keeping a regular sleeping and waking schedule seems impossible because of other factors that limit their ability to sleep. The reasons for sleep deprivation are varied, but include health problems such as breathing obstructions and stress. If you believe your lack of sleep is the result of medical problems, consider seeing a health care professional. For stress-related sleep problems, practicing the stress-relieving strategies discussed early in this chapter will help alleviate the symptoms; however, if you find that relaxation techniques do not improve your ability to sleep well, then consider seeing a general practitioner or mental health professional for issues regarding stress.

What you put into your body can affect your sleeping habits. Eating high-fat and high-sugar foods near bedtime can slow you down, even if they seem to speed you up at first. Good sleep can also elude you if you consume alcohol and caffeine—even in small amounts—close to the time that you go to bed. Drugs, including medications for common illnesses, can deprive you of sleep or make you feel sluggish after you take them. Avoid consuming food, drink, or medications that overstimulate or make you drowsy right before bedtime. Never abuse prescription, over-the-counter, or illegal drugs to stay awake.

In addition to what you put into your body, what you do to it will affect your ability to get a good night's rest. Exercising too close to your bedtime will make it harder to fall asleep. However, too little physical exertion during the day can also contribute to difficulty falling and staying asleep. Experts suggest exercising early in the day—an activity as easy as walking for 30 minutes will suffice—in order to sleep more productively at night. Regular exercise will also help you alleviate the negative effects of stress. If you find, though, that you cannot "shut off" your mind because thoughts overwhelm you, consider writing down your worries—anything you may stay up thinking about after the light is off—in a journal, which will help you unwind and put away your day's thoughts.

Because sleep deprivation can contribute to irritability, depression, and physical health problems, it is important to make getting enough sleep a priority throughout the semester. If you have difficulty sticking to a regular sleep schedule, treat it like any other goal and write down what you want to do. Make it easier to achieve your goal by keeping your bed and bedroom free of clutter and by avoiding using your bed as a place to do homework or watch television. In other words, creating a sanctuary in your bedroom, a place where you can truly relax, may alleviate stress and anxiety that contribute to sleeplessness. Finally, avoid taking naps during the day, even on weekends, because they can throw off your sleep schedule. If you have an irregular schedule because of working different hours each day of the week, find a system that is relatively regular and that works for you. You may have to be creative about how you get enough sleep each evening or day.

The bottom line is that sleep deprivation can be dangerous and deadly. How little sleep you get should not be a medal of honor that demonstrates how much you work or how dedicated you are to meeting your goals. Getting enough sleep is a necessary part of living well, enjoying what you *do* accomplish, and being enjoyable to be around when you are awake.

Drugs and Alcohol

There are some habits that we know are potentially hazardous to our health, and yet some people still indulge in them. Smoking and using tobacco products, taking drugs, and consuming too much alcohol are known risks, but college students sometimes pick up these poor health habits because of peer pressure, a desire to fit in, and a need to find a way to relax or escape.

According to the American Heart Association (2009), about a quarter of Americans smoke, and people with the least education (9 to 11 years in school) are more likely to smoke than people with more education (more than 16 years in school). Smoking or chewing tobacco carries with it increased risks of heart disease, stroke, high blood pressure, cancer, and emphysema. The more educated you become about the health risks that are associated with smoking and using smokeless tobacco, the more it will be obvious that using tobacco products can cause serious health consequences. There are a variety of methods for quitting. It is worth investigating what your college and community offer if you are a smoker or a user of smokeless tobacco. Your college may provide information, support groups, or physician referrals for students who want to quit.

Alcohol and drugs are two other health issues that often affect college students—sometimes even before they get to college. Having parents, partners, or friends who have abused drugs or alcohol is one way students can be affected. They may feel that they have to take care of others who drink too much or take drugs, which can take a toll on their time and emotional well-being. Students may also suffer from abusing

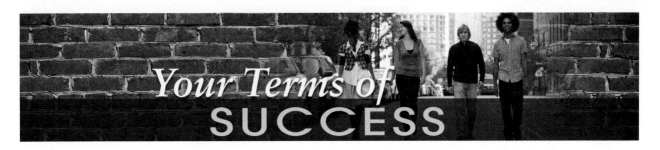

Your Terms of **SUCCESS**

WHEN YOU SEE . . .	IT MEANS . . .
Acquaintance rape	See date rape.
Active lifestyle	Maintaining regular exercise.
Alcohol abuse	Using alcohol excessively or to the impairment of your senses.
Balanced living	Finding balance in one's personal, academic, and professional life that provides a sense of well-being.
Date rape	Rape, or forced sexual contact, between two people who know each other or who are dating.
Mental abuse	Harmful treatment of the mind or intellect.
Mental health	The condition of one's mind or mental processes.
Physical health	The condition of one's body.
Sedentary	Sitting in one place, not active.
Sleep deprivation	The condition of not getting enough sleep.
Spiritual health	One's religious or spiritual outlook on life.
STDs	Sexually transmitted diseases.
Stress	A physical and psychological response to outside stimuli.
Stress-related illness	An illness that is caused by the body's reaction to stress.
Verbal abuse	Harmful treatment of someone through yelling, name-calling, or insults.

drugs and alcohol while in college—and the effects can be far reaching. According to Facts on Tap (2009), a website that offers drug and alcohol education and prevention information, 159,000 first-year college students will drop out of college because of issues related to drug and alcohol abuse.

Being drunk or high can have grave consequences, the least of which is that you will do something you later regret. You increase your risk of having an unwanted sexual experience and causing physical harm to yourself and others. Death from overdosing on drugs and alcohol can happen even for those who are first-time users. Whether they are consumed for recreational purposes or because of other, more serious health reasons, abusing drugs and alcohol should not be a part of your college career because you will find it more difficult to reach your educational and personal goals. See Figure 10.5 for tips on avoiding drugs and alcohol.

In addition to abusing alcohol and illegal substances, taking medications for purposes other than their prescribed uses can have grave consequences, including death.

FIGURE 10.5 Tips for Avoiding Drugs and Alcohol in College

- Educate yourself about the effects of abusing drugs and alcohol.
- Cultivate relationships with people who have healthy habits.
- Avoid situations in which you know drugs and alcohol will be present.
- Take walking breaks instead of smoking breaks.
- Find other ways to relax that are healthy, free, and legal.
- Talk with a counselor or health care professional if you feel you are about to make a poor decision regarding the use of drugs and alcohol.
- Appeal to your vanity, if all else fails: Drugs, alcohol, and tobacco make you look and smell bad.

Excessive consumption of medications that contain amphetamines and narcotics may seem like a good idea at first if you have trouble staying awake or going to sleep, but continued use beyond the prescribed period can lead to dependency.

Sex

A discussion of health issues would not be complete without talking about sexual health. Most colleges and universities strive to educate their students, especially those who are recently out of high school, about sexual responsibility and common sexually transmitted diseases (STDs). Gary Gately (2003) reports the alarm of many experts and college officials at recent statistics showing that 73% of students report having unprotected sex while they are in college. More disturbing is that 68% of those having unprotected sex do not consider themselves at risk (Gately, 2003), pointing to a major reason why students, despite sex education in high school or elsewhere, continue to engage in risky sexual behavior. Students, especially those 18 to 24 years of age, believe they are immortal and that nothing they do will have negative consequences. Because most STDs lack immediate visible or physiological symptoms, students who are at risk for contracting a sexually transmitted disease rarely ask to be screened for signs of infection.

Risky behavior, which includes having sex with multiple partners and having unprotected sex, opens the door to possible infections and illnesses such as chlamydia, gonorrhea, genital herpes, HIV, and AIDS (see Table 10.1). Some diseases can be transmitted in ways other than sexual intercourse. Hepatitis B and C are both diseases that can be contracted through shared razors or toothbrushes, body piercing, or tattooing.

If you are sexually active, it is important to be screened regularly for STDs even if you do not have symptoms. Your long-term health and the health of those you come in contact with are at risk if you do not. As with any health issue, educate yourself with the facts about risk factors and symptoms. Then, monitor your behavior, practice safe sex, and see a doctor regularly to maintain good health.

Depression and Suicide

The pressures to succeed while juggling multiple priorities can lead to negative stress and feelings of being overwhelmed. Often, feeling a little stressed during the semester is normal, but there are times that students can feel as though they are in over their heads, with no hope of getting out. It is no wonder that one of the most common mental health issues on college campus is depression.

TABLE 10.1 Common Sexually Transmitted Diseases

STD	Symptoms	Treatment
HIV and AIDS	May have no symptoms; extreme fatigue, rapid weight loss	No cure, but prescribed medication can keep the virus from replicating
Chlamydia	May have no symptoms; abnormal discharge, burning during urination	Antibiotics
Genital herpes	May have no symptoms; itching, burning, bumps in the genital area	No cure, but prescribed medication can help treat outbreaks
Gonorrhea	Pain or burning during urination; yellowish or bloody discharge; men may have no symptoms	Antibiotics
Hepatitis B	Headache, muscle ache, fatigue, low-grade fever, skin and whites of eyes with yellowish tint	No cure, but prescribed medication can help guard against liver damage

In an online article about college students and depression, Neil Schoenherr (2004) reports that Alan Glass, M.D., the director of student health and counseling at Washington University–St. Louis, claims problems students face often start before they enroll in college: "Students arrive already having started various medications for depression, anxiety and attention deficit disorders." Signs of depression include loss of pleasure in activities, feelings of hopelessness, inability to get out of bed, increased use of alcohol or drugs, changes in appetite or weight gain or loss, altered sleep patterns (sleeping too little or too much), extreme sensitivity, excessive crying, lack of energy or interest in participating in activities, and indifference to taking care of oneself.

Suicide is another mental health issue associated with depression. With the startling statistic that 25% of college students have contemplated suicide, it is no wonder that college health and counseling centers strive to educate students about the signs of severe depression that may lead to suicide attempts. Thoughts of ending your life should always be taken seriously and you should seek help immediately. Call a college counselor, an advisor, a hospital emergency room, or 911 if you are thinking about committing suicide.

Collaboration EXERCISE 10.3

Studies have shown that community college students have higher rates of depression and suicide than students at four-year universities. Working in a group, record the various reasons that this may be true and create a list of local resources that could help such students. ■

HEALTHY LIVING for LIFE

There is more to life than just eating well and exercising. Healthy living is a practice that involves all parts of your well-being: physical, mental, and spiritual.

Living a Balanced Life

Living a balanced life means paying attention to and improving all areas of your life—from relationships to cardiovascular health to your inner peace. If one area is overdeveloped,

USING TECHNOLOGY TO GET AHEAD

The Internet provides many quality resources for maintaining your health and wellness. Look for government-sponsored sites, such as the Food and Drug Administration's website, and other reliable sites that are affiliated with organizations that are truly trying to provide the most accurate health information. If you have a serious health issue, do not, though, try to diagnose yourself using website information. Seek sound face-to-face medical advice from your physician.

then the other areas will suffer from the lack of balance. There will be times that you will need to put in more hours at work and school, throwing the balance off slightly, but be careful that you make some time for the other areas that have been neglected.

A great way to stay balanced is to strive to create relationships with people on campus. Having healthy relationships with professors, advisors, and classmates will not only enable you to stay connected with your college work, but it will also provide you a personal support network in case you feel as though you need help with the stresses of being in college.

Balancing your life to eliminate stress also entails evaluating your values and priorities whenever you begin to feel stressed. You can then identify areas in your life that are getting out of balance and put those areas higher up on your list of priorities. For example, if you value exercise and are stressed because you realize that you have been spending most of your time at work or at school, you can make working out a higher priority, creating better balance in your life.

Maintaining Healthy Relationships

Maintaining healthy relationships is as much a part of your good health as eating nutritious foods and exercising, but relationships can also be unhealthy and even dangerous. One sign of an unhealthy relationship is abuse: physical, mental, verbal, and sexual. Being in a relationship with someone who is abusive is not healthy. Although the previous statement seems like common sense, take time to think about it. No one deserves to be hit, controlled, or humiliated, *ever*.

Although we know that someone who makes us feel bad physically or emotionally can prevent us from being our best, studies find that abused men and women find it difficult to

Incorporating regular exercise into your routine will help you alleviate some of the negative effects of stress.

Shutterstock

It's All RELATIVE

Sometimes one of the most important activities to promote good mental health is communication. Keeping feelings bottled up inside can lead to unhealthy thoughts and expectations. Learning to express fear, anger, and disappointment can have the effect of lessening the negative stress from carrying those feelings bottled up inside.

If you do not feel comfortable saying what is on your mind to family and friends, you may start by talking with a counselor or therapist who can help you learn to communicate more openly with others. You can also learn effective communication techniques as well as conflict management methods that will help you deal more successfully with strong feelings by reading books and articles and watching others who model effective behavior.

YOUR TURN

What communication techniques do you use when you have to talk to your family about a difficult issue? • Do you feel your techniques are effective? • Why or why not? • What would make your communication with family stronger?

_____

_____

_____

get out of abusive relationships. One reason people stay with abusive partners is that the abusers often are—at first—charming, attentive, and loving. It is only later that abusers begin to show subtle signs that something is not right; they may be extremely jealous, verbally insulting, and focused on your every move. Victims may also be dependent financially or emotionally on their abusers, which makes eliminating their influence difficult at best.

One particular type of unhealthy relationship that occurs most frequently among traditional college students is date or acquaintance rape. Simply defined, *rape* is a forced sexual act in which one party does not actively consent; often, the two people involved are not complete strangers—hence the terms *date rape* and *acquaintance rape*. Although men and women can be victims of date rape, women make up most of the victims. Alcohol or a "date rape drug" such as Rohypnol may be involved in the incident. Many experts warn college-age women and men about the risk factors for date rape and encourage them to get to know whom they are going out with, avoid getting intoxicated, make sure their food or drinks are not handled by others, and communicate loud and clear if they find themselves in an uncomfortable situation.

Maintaining a healthy relationship takes time and energy, but there are many ways to make sure your relationships are positive experiences. For example, get to know people well before spending time alone with them. Learn to communicate your wants and needs effectively. Say no loud and clear when you do not want something to happen. Watch for signs of abusive and controlling behavior; sometimes, people show you signs of their true selves in

Reflection EXERCISE 10.4

How do you maintain balance while taking college classes? Do you schedule certain times during the week to take care of yourself? What do you do to maintain balance? ■

PLUS

EXERCISE 10.5

(Personality + Learning Style = Understanding Situations)

Let's revisit Evan's situation. He is extroverted, with a kinesthetic learning preference; getting regular exercise and working out with others helps him stay healthy and release stress. However, his dedication to kickboxing has been taking away time and energy from college, and his coach doesn't seem very supportive of his competing activities. What advice can you offer that would help him be successful in college? Can he devote enough time to both parts of his life and expect to do well?

Now, considering your own learning style, personality type, and special circumstances, what will you do to stay focused on college when you find yourself challenged by competing priorities? ■

smaller, subtler ways early in a relationship. If a situation makes you uncomfortable, get out of it immediately. Last but not least, do not abuse alcohol and drugs, which can impair your ability to judge situations. If you feel as though you have no options in removing yourself from an abusive relationship, seek professional help.

Getting Help When You Need It

An important part of making good choices and staying healthy is to get regular checkups and to see a health professional whenever you experience pain, difficulty, or even uncertainty about a health issue. Your college may provide access to a health clinic or health fairs. Free screenings, health seminars, and dispensing of over-the-counter medications are possible services that your college clinic may offer. Take advantage of these types of services, such as blood pressure checks or information about handling diabetes, because they may provide you with life-improving or life-saving information. If your college provides only limited access to health services, then you will need to find other ways to monitor your health. Regular checkups are part of taking care of yourself both in the short and the long term.

From College to University

HOW YOUR STRESS WILL CHANGE AND HOW TO HANDLE THE NEW PRESSURES

There are many possible stressors awaiting you when you make that move from your community college to university. Increased tuition, higher expectations, more difficult workload, impending graduation, and goal realization are all reasons to feel anxious about the transition, but remember that you have already succeeded in college by getting this far.

To meet the challenges that await you, be honest about them. For example, your professors will be asking more from you academically. In addition, recognize the fact that you will be graduating in just a few semesters and that you should plan for life after school. These realities, while daunting, do not have to be defeating if you are honest about them. With some work—and the good habits you form at your community college—you can handle them with the same success.

Regardless of the new challenges, once you transfer, it will be even more important to have a solid support structure at work and at home. In addition, you will be making connections with people whom you hope will help you get a job after college. All of these relationships can provide you with a system for handling the demands of a four-year university. You will also need to be mindful of the stress-reducing strategies that work best for you. Practice them regularly and seek assistance in achieving your goals; you will then be more relaxed and more confident in your abilities.

Find someone you know (or ask your professor for the name of a former student) who has transferred to a four-year university and ask him or her to identify the top three stressors and what resources are available at the university to help. Record the answers below.

From College to Career

MAKING HEALTHY LIFESTYLE CHANGES IS A GOOD LONG-TERM STRATEGY

Making healthy choices in college certainly has short-term results in that you will feel better and handle the negative effects of stress more effectively. However, the purpose of making better choices should be a long-term strategy to create a better life for you and your family. Therefore, when you complete your certificate or degree and enter into or return to the workforce, you may need to revise or reinforce your health goals. For example, you may have had time after classes to work out or play a sport as part of your exercise routine, but after graduation, you may have to change the time or place that you work out.

In addition to finding time to continue your positive health choices from college, you may also need to consider making your mental well-being part of your overall health plan. Maintaining healthy relationships with those who have positive influences on your life is one way to keep stress levels at a minimum and to create a safety net of friends and family when you may need them. Avoiding drugs, alcohol, and other poor health choices will be crucial to performing your best on the job. Some employers have strict policies about the use of drugs and alcohol on or off the job.

Because of the importance of good health, some employers have made keeping their employees healthy a top priority—it saves time and money in the long run when employees do not miss work because of illnesses. Talk with the human resources department about what your company offers employees to support healthy habits. They may provide free screening, free or reduced-cost vaccinations, time off for doctors' appointments, health insurance, discounted gym memberships, and planned physical activities such as softball or basketball games.

Contact someone in a career that is similar to what you want to do. Ask what kinds of health insurance and activities are part of his or her job. Also inquire whether there are any improvements in terms of health-related issues needed in the career field that the person's employer could institute to make employees healthier.

First Voices

From a textile mill town to a life helping others: First-generation student finds a long road and a small school changed his life

Kevin Todd Houston,
Ph.D.,
Assistant Professor

I graduated from one of the smallest two-year colleges in America. In a good semester, the college enrolled no more than 250 students. I was raised in Chester, South Carolina, a very small textile town. Each day, I drove over 60 miles round trip to attend classes. My parents were textile workers for most of their lives. I am a first-generation college student coming from a home where education was not a top priority. Little did I know how much my college education would change my life. I did not know how a small drive each day would change the way I looked at the world. That is what my college education did for me: It gave me a perspective of the world far beyond my little hometown and the views I held growing up.

My road to college teaching has been a long and rewarding journey. My first degree was in photojournalism. However, after completing this degree and taking my first position, I found that my true calling was working with the deaf and hard of hearing. I returned to college to obtain a master's degree in speech pathology. My first professional position in this field was with the North Carolina School for the Deaf. I later returned to college to work toward my Ph.D. at the University of South Carolina where upon completion of my doctorate, I taught for several years.

From there I held a joint position for the Department of Health and Human Services Early Intervention Program and UNC–Chapel Hill. Later, I was recruited to become the Executive Director of the Alexander Graham Bell Association for the Deaf and Hard of Hearing in Washington, DC. I held this position for five years before joining the faculty at Utah State University.

My advice to you as a first-year, first-generation college student would be this: Never give up on yourself. Never stop believing that you have the power, the knowledge, and the capability to succeed. You may have family issues, money problems, child care problems, and troubles due to a poor educational background. None of this matters. What matters is how badly you want your degree and the career of your dreams and how hard you are willing to work for it. It can be yours.

PATH OF DISCOVERY
Journal Entry

According to the categories listed in the chapter, evaluate how well you are improving or maintaining healthy habits.

CHAPTER REVIEW QUESTIONS

1. What are the different ways students can incorporate exercise into their busy schedules?
2. What are the major health issues that college students face?
3. What can students do if they find themselves in unhealthy relationships?
4. Predict the effects for a student who makes poor health choices during a semester.

CHAPTER 10 CASE SCENARIOS

1. Vin-Singh has been having trouble sleeping since he started college. He shares an apartment with another student who likes to stay up late and play loud music. Vin-Singh eats well and avoids caffeinated drinks, but he does not exercise regularly and often feels anxious when he tries to sleep. What advice can you give him for improving his sleep?
2. Wanda has not exercised since she was in high school, and now, 20 years later, she sees the importance of improving her health. In fact, she wonders if the 30 pounds she has gained since high school is keeping her from feeling her best when she juggles the demands of college. She is about to start her last year in college, one that will be stressful for her as she takes classes that will help her pass a licensing exam and get a good job. She also wants to lose weight and start an aggressive exercise program. In light of what she is about to face, what advice can you give her?
3. Ever since D. J. started college, he has focused on his studies and has cut out all activities that do not help him achieve his educational goals. He has told his friends that he won't be able to hang out with them; he has cut back on his hours at work; he has stopped playing basketball and running; he has even stopped attending religious services so that he can have time to take as many class hours as possible each semester. He wants to graduate with a degree as fast as he can and start working, and his grades are good. However, after a few semesters, he feels depressed and isolated but is not sure why. What advice can you give him?

RESEARCH IT FURTHER

1. Interview three people about their health habits. Find out what they do to maintain good health. Write down your findings and present them to your class.
2. Search the Internet for national statistics regarding violence against college students. Determine what groups are more likely to experience physical and sexual abuse. Inform the class of your findings.
3. What does your college offer in terms of health care for its students? Create a list of services and events along with contact numbers for community services that students may need. Present the list to your classmates.

References and Recommended Readings

American Heart Association. (2009). Cigarette smoking statistics. Retrieved September 6, 2009, from www.americanheart.org/presenter.jhtml?identifier=4559.

Facts on Tap. (2009). Alcohol and student life. Retrieved September 6, 2009, from www.factsontap.org/factsontap/alcohol_and_student_life/index.htm.

Gately, G. (2003, August 23). College students ignoring risks of unprotected sex. *Health Day News*. Retrieved August 29, 2005, from www.hon.ch/News/HSN/514968.html.

Schoenherr, N. (2004). Depression, suicide are the major health issues facing college students, says student health director. *News & Information*. Washington University–St. Louis. Retrieved September 6, 2009, from http://newswustl.edu/tips/page/normal/4198.html.

U.S. Food and Drug Administration. (2004). How to understand and use the nutrition facts label. Retrieved May 16, 2008, from www.cfsan.fda.gov/~dms/foodlab.html.

NEXT SEMESTER

11

Juanita and Laura's Story

"Hey, Laura, who are you taking for world history?" asks Juanita as she squints in the bright sun outside the library. Laura pulls out a sheet of paper with her schedule for next semester. Her brightly painted nails catch the sunlight and look like twinkling stars.

"I have Dr. Franks," she says. "I interviewed him and Professor Martinsen last week to see which one would be a good fit for me." Laura takes off her jacket and stuffs it in her backpack while Juanita checks her phone to see if her mother has called, still a daily ritual though decreasing as she takes classes on the college campus. When Juanita was in high school, she talked to her mother four or five times a day.

"Really? I just checked out that website where you can write about your instructors," Juanita says. "I think I am going to get Mr. Bernstein. He makes you do a group project rather than an exam—at least that is what they say about him."

"It's hard to get a good picture just from an Internet site, don't you think? Maybe you should go talk to him first. How do you know what he is like as a person?" asks Laura, frowning at her friend. Because of Laura's dyslexia, she spends much more time rewriting her notes and working on assignments than her fellow students. Getting professors that she feels comfortable with is important to her. She knows she is not as technologically savvy as the younger students, but sometimes she thinks finding things out the "old fashioned way" is best.

"Maybe I need to find someone who can also help me with my degree plan. I am still unsure about what I want to major in. I know I am only 18, but I need to get this decided soon," Juanita says. Her phone vibrates. She has a new message, but it is from her cousin, not her mother.

"Are you still worried that your parents are going to be upset if you choose something other than engineering or medicine?" Laura asks. She feels lucky that even at her age, her mother encourages her to do what she wants.

"Probably, but now that I am 18, I guess I don't have to worry about my mom calling my advisor to tell him what I should major in," she says, smiling at Laura and shading her eyes from the sun.

"I tell you what. Pick up your things and come with me. I need to go to counseling anyway. I am worried about my scholarship for next semester and I need to know if I bomb our final in biology what I should do," says Laura.

Juanita gathers her books and stuffs them in her backpack. She follows Laura to the campus center, hoping to get some answers to her questions about how she should plan not only her next semester, but also her life. As they walk across campus, Juanita's phone rings again, and she sees that it is her mother this time.

In this CHAPTER

The purpose of this chapter is to help you navigate the last few weeks of classes and plan your semesters to come. As both Laura and Juanita remind us, these last weeks will be filled with decisions to make about finances and coursework, but once you have successfully completed a certificate or degree program you will be able to say, "I did it!"

More specifically, after completing this chapter, you should be able to do the following:

- **Determine the steps to complete your education at this college or another.**
- **Understand how to prepare for the end of the semester as well as what to expect.**
- **Identify methods of paying for college.**
- **List the benefits for both staying in college or returning after a break.**

PLANNING for YOUR EDUCATIONAL FUTURE

It is never too early to begin thinking about your educational future, especially if it involves completing a certificate or degree at your current college. Understanding what you need to do—in addition to passing your courses—may mean the difference between graduating on time and staying another semester to finish just one class. Visiting your advisor regularly can help you stay on track; so can reviewing the college catalog and reading the college's website and other information for updates.

A Difference of Degrees

You probably discovered when you enrolled that colleges offer a variety of certificate and degree options, but you may not be entirely clear about the differences between programs. Certificate programs, offered at community and technical colleges, usually last a semester or two semesters (sometimes referred to as "one year" programs) and require about 15 to 30 credit hours. Students enroll in certificate programs either to gain skills to enter the workforce or to complete training requirements for a job. Most certificate programs are not transferable, which means they do not necessarily meet the requirements of an associate's or bachelor's degree. Instead, they usually serve a specific purpose of providing graduates with a set of skills that they can readily use on the job. If you plan to use a certificate program as a stepping stone for an associate's or bachelor's degree, be sure that you check with the department or college (if it is not the same as the one in which you are currently enrolled) where you will complete your final degree plan. For example, if you want to pursue a bachelor's degree in nursing, but you are thinking about completing a nursing certificate first, talk to an advisor in the bachelor's program to determine what, if any, courses they can take from your certificate program. Although you may choose, for personal or professional reasons, to earn a certificate

TABLE 11.1 Program Types

Program Type	Length/Requirements	Purpose
Certificate	One semester or two; 15–30 credit hours	To obtain skills necessary for a job-related or personal goal or for direct entry into the workforce; not intended to fit into a higher degree
Associate of Applied Science	Four semesters; about 60 credit hours	To obtain knowledge and skills for direct entry into the workforce; usually not intended to fit into a higher degree
Associate of Arts/ Science	Four semesters; about 60 credit hours	To obtain knowledge and skills for transfer to a higher degree program or for direct entry into the workforce
Bachelor of Arts/ Science	Eight semesters; about 120 credit hours	To obtain knowledge and skills for transfer to a graduate degree program or for direct entry into the workforce
Master's Degree	Number of semesters depends; about 30 credit hours beyond bachelor's	To obtain knowledge, skills, and mastery of a field or discipline for further graduate study or entry into the workforce.
Doctoral Degree	Number of semesters depends; about 60 credit hours beyond bachelor's	To obtain knowledge, skills, and mastery of a field for research in that field and/or entry into the workforce.

first and then take additional classes to complete another degree, knowing what will be accepted and what will not can help you make the best educational decisions now.

In addition to certificate programs, community and technical colleges offer associate of arts (A.A.), associate of science (A.S.), and associate of applied science (A.A.S.) degrees (see Table 11.1). An associate of arts and an associate of science degree closely mirror the first two years of a bachelor's degree program and are often transferable to a four-year university with little problem.

The associate of applied science degree is different because it is a 60-hour (at least) program that is intended for students who plan on entering the workforce after graduation; it is not usually intended for students who want to transfer to complete a bachelor's degree, although some four-year universities are beginning to accept courses that are completed in this degree program. An associate of applied science in accounting degree, for example, is meant for students who want an entry-level job in bookkeeping. Bachelor's degrees are most often offered at four-year colleges and universities, although some community colleges may offer one in addition to their associate degrees. A Bachelor of Arts (B.A.) and Bachelor of Science (B.S.) are the basic degrees that are considered the final stopping point for most students. However, earning a bachelor's degree does not mean you have to stop there. You may also want consider a graduate degree, often called master's degrees (M.A., M.S.) and doctorates (Ph.D., Ed.D.). These degrees often require that you complete a four-year degree and usually contain at least 30 additional credit hours beyond a bachelor's degree for a master's and at least 60 additional credit hours for a doctorate.

Tech TIPS
USING TECHNOLOGY TO GET AHEAD

Your college website, as well as any other college website, can give you information about different types of degrees and their requirements. You may also find valuable information about when classes are offered and what you have to do to complete your degree and graduate on time. Be sure to begin your search of college websites with those colleges in your area (or that offer online degrees) to get a good idea of your options.

Choosing the right certificate or degree program will take some thought and discussion with college advisors, people in the career you want or already have, and your instructors. Ultimately, your career and life goals will determine which program to choose. With fluctuations in job requirements, changes in industry, and longer lifespans, you may find yourself back in college again at some point in your life to learn a new skill, change your life's direction, or dabble in a hobby.

Figure 11.1 shows an example of a degree program that Laura may consider. Although relatively simple to follow, the degree plan may confuse Laura if she must complete prerequisites before she can take some of the courses. For example, before Laura entered college, her ACT test scores placed her below college entrance requirements; thus, she had to complete her developmental courses before she could take some of the college-level courses that are part of her degree program.

So how does Laura plan for next semester? If in her first semester Laura completes Introduction to College (a three-credit-hour course), Developmental Reading (no college-level credit), Developmental Writing (no college-level credit), Introduction to Sociology (a three-credit-hour course), and Psychology and the Human Experience (a three-credit-hour course), she will meet two of the requirements for an associate of applied science degree in early childhood education. She would check those courses off her degree plan and start working toward the remaining courses.

Having met the developmental requirements for her degree plan, Laura's schedule for next semester might look like the following:

ENGL 1311	English Composition I	3 hours
ECD 1103	Child Development	3 hours
ECD 1003	Foundations of Early Childhood Education	3 hours
PSYC 2300	Psychology and the Human Experience	3 hours
ECD 1203	Healthy, Safe Learning Environment	3 hours
		15 hours

If Laura takes 15 hours her second semester and 15 hours each semester after that, she still will need an extra semester because in her first semester she earned only 6 hours toward her degree. Even though the early childhood associate's degree plan maps out four semesters, some students may need more time because of taking fewer hours a semester or from having to complete developmental classes. These are things you will need to consider as you map out your degree program.

Transferring to Another Institution

You may find that you want to complete a degree at a different institution. Even if you feel sure that it's possible, investigate what you need to do for a successful transfer. There may be special scholarships for transfer students, and there will certainly be admissions requirements such as completing an application, providing transcripts of your work at your current college (and any other college you have attended), and submitting financial aid forms (if you are receiving financial aid). To make sure of a smooth transfer, it is strongly encouraged that you visit the campus and speak with an advisor in the department in which you will ultimately get a degree.

Deadlines and Important Dates

Once you decide on your schedule and the classes you want to take, you should take advantage of early registration periods and due dates. If there is even a small chance you will return next semester, consider registering for courses just in case. Depending on your college's

FIGURE 11.1 Degree Plan

Early Childhood Development [*the department*]

Associate of Applied Science [*type of degree—usually completed in four semesters*]

Option: Early Childhood Education [*the emphasis within the degree*]

This option is for early childhood caregivers and paraprofessionals who wish to improve their skills and credentials. Early childhood curriculum is the focus. This option is also appropriate for supervisors, for curriculum coordinators, and for CDA renewal. [*description of how this degree will benefit you*]

[*Suggested schedule for each semester. It is usually not mandatory that you take the courses in the order suggested, unless one is a prerequisite for another.*]

First Semester		Credit Hours
ECD 1003	Foundations of Early Childhood Education	3
ECD 1103	Child Development	3
ECD 1203	Healthy, Safe Learning Environment	3
ECD 1303	Practicum I	3
ENGL 1311	English Composition I	3
	Total Credit Hours	15

Second Semester		
ECD 2003	Child Behavior	3
ECD 2103	Preschool Curriculum OR	
ECD 2403	Infant/Toddler Curriculum	3
ECD 2503	Nutrition for the Young Child	3
ECD 2303	Practicum II	3
MATH 1301	College Business Mathematics	3
	Total Credit Hours	15

Third Semester		
ECD 2703	Language Arts	3
ECD 2803	Special Needs	3
ENGL 1312	English Composition II	3
PSYC 2300	Psychology and the Human Experience	3
HLSC 1304	Concepts of Lifetime Health and Wellness OR	
MUSC 2300	Introduction to Music OR	
ARTS 2300	Introduction to Visual Arts	3
	Total Credit Hours	15

Fourth Semester		
ECD 2903	Trends in Curriculum	3
BUS 1303	Introduction to Computers (or higher-level computer course)	3
SOCI 2300	Introduction to Sociology	3
SPCH 1300	Speech Communication	3
ANTH 2310	Cultural Anthropology OR	
PSYC 2300	Developmental Psychology	3
	Total Credit Hours	15
	Total Hours for A.A.S.	60

Reflection
EXERCISE 11.1

Which degree best fits your goals? Why is it the best type of degree for what you want to do or become? ■

policies, you should be able to drop courses by a certain date without penalty, and it will be easier to drop classes than build a schedule from classes that are still open. In addition to being aware of registration periods, take note of payment due dates. Some colleges require that you pay soon after you register, even if that means paying for tuition and fees a few months in advance. If you do not pay on time, your classes may be dropped, and you will have to start all over right before the new semester, which could mean that you don't get the classes for which you originally registered.

COMPLETING the SEMESTER

The end of the semester is a good time to start assessing how you have done and where you want to go. Begin planning for next semester while not neglecting any loose ends from your current classes. You should now know what to expect at the beginning of next semester, and with that additional information, you should be able to make better choices and prepare yourself for what lies ahead.

Course Evaluations

Course evaluations (sometimes called "student evaluations" because students provide the assessment of courses and instructors) are an integral part of taking a college class. Each semester you may be asked to complete an evaluation form for your instructor. Because evaluations are anonymous and not given to the instructor until grades have been posted, you should feel comfortable being open and honest about the course when answering the form's questions.

The purpose of course evaluations is to provide the instructor as well as the administration with a description of how students feel about the instruction they received in the course. Some colleges look very closely at course evaluations and determine raises and promotions based in part on the scores that instructors receive. Other colleges merely use them as a discussion tool to improve the instructors' teaching. No matter how your college uses the information, you should try to be honest about your instructors' abilities. Providing constructive criticism, rather than general comments, is most helpful to the instructor.

Phrases such as "Professor Banks is not a good instructor" or "Dr. Wright is perfect" do not provide specific information that will help your instructor improve or continue doing what you think works very well. Instead, you may want to offer concrete examples, such as "The instructor graded fairly and handed back exams in a timely manner" or "The professor rarely explained the assignments." Specific statements allow your instructors to pinpoint exactly what worked for you and what didn't.

Most student evaluation forms contain questions that you answer by checking a box or filling in a bubble as well as questions that you answer by writing a narrative response. The following examples show two types of questions that you may see on a course evaluation form:

1. My instructor uses class time effectively.
   A. Strongly Agree   B. Agree   C. Strongly Disagree

2. My instructor grades fairly.
   A. Strongly Agree   B. Agree   C. Strongly Disagree

3. What can your instructor do to improve the course? _____

4. What does your instructor do well? _____

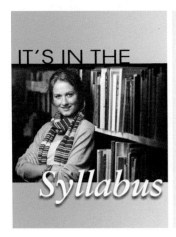

IT'S IN THE *Syllabus*

What information is in the syllabus regarding the final exam? Will it be comprehensive? Will it count more toward your overall grade than other tests and assignments? What will the exam cover and what day and time is it scheduled?

It is never too early to start asking questions about the final exams in your classes. You may want to consider the following questions to ask your instructors: What will the final exam cover? How long do we have to take it? Are there previous exams we can use for studying? How much time do you recommend for students to spend studying?

When answering questions such as these, take time to reflect on the instructor's performance during the semester. Create a list of activities that you did in class during the semester and think about the results. Then consider the overall performance of your instructor. Did he come to class on time? Was she easy to contact when you needed her? Did he act professionally? Did she seem to have a good knowledge of the subject matter? Remember that the objective of student evaluations is to provide feedback that will help instructors improve, so the more information you provide, the better.

Preparing for Final Examinations

Another traditional "ending" to the semester is final exams. Surviving "finals week" is often considered a well-earned badge for a college student. The reasons that finals are so stressful for some college students is that they often carry more weight than any other tests during the semester, they contain questions about material from the entire semester, and they are all scheduled around the same time.

To help you survive finals, go back to Chapter 9 and review the material about taking tests. There are additional steps you can follow to get ready for them quickly in these final weeks of the semester. First, be sure to note the day, place, and time of each final and write it down on your calendar. Double-check this information a week before the exam. Be aware that where and when you take your finals may differ from where and when you took your classes during the semester.

A few weeks before the final, ask questions about the exam. What will you be allowed to use? What do you need to bring? What should you study? Is photo identification required? Get plenty of rest during the days that lead up to the exam. When you take the exam, use your time wisely. Final exams usually take longer to complete than regular tests, so be sure you use the entire time that you are allotted (one to three hours). Be prepared by bringing ample writing supplies and any approved items such as a calculator or dictionary.

CHOOSING CLASSES
for NEXT SEMESTER

Even if you have not completed your classes this semester, you can start planning for next semester. By now, you should be familiar with the college catalog and can identify the courses that you may want to take by reading their descriptions and checking your

FIGURE 11.2 Catalog Description

DEVE 0336. Elementary Algebra

This course includes, but is not limited to, the following concepts: operations on integers and rational numbers; solving linear equations and inequalities in one variable; graphing linear equations and inequalities in two variables; operations on exponents and polynomials; and problem-solving techniques. Prerequisite: DEVE 0334 with a grade of C or better, or a COMPASS Algebra placement test score from 23 to 32, or a score of 16 or 17 on the mathematics section of the ACT. Final grade will be A, B, C, or NC (no credit). (3 credit hours)

degree plan. Both the description and your plan will help you determine which classes you need to take in what order. Figure 11.2 is a typical catalog description for a developmental math course.

In addition to reviewing the catalog descriptions for a course, you will also want to determine whether there is a required course you must take beforehand. In the example of Elementary Algebra in Figure 11.2, a student will need to either provide a test score that meets the minimum requirement or she will need to complete successfully the *prerequisite,* or the course required before it. Courses may have *corequisites,* which are other courses that must be taken before or at the same time as the course. For instance, a Chemistry I course may have a corequisite of Intermediate Algebra, which means a student can complete the course before enrolling in Chemistry I or can take the course during the same semester.

Course Formats

In addition to which courses to take, you may also want to research your options for the design of courses. Many colleges are now offering classes in a variety of formats. You may have the opportunity to take classes in a *learning community,* which means that two or more classes are linked together by a certain topic. The students in the learning community classes stay together for each course. For example, a class of 25 students may take a morning speech communication class and then the same students take an afternoon college writing. Even though each class is taught by a different professor, they may study similar topics or the students in the learning community may be required to work on a project that links both courses together.

Web-enhanced classes are another format that you may want to consider when registering for next semester. The term *web-enhanced* usually means that some part of the class will be online and that you will be required to complete work via a computer. *Hybrid* is another common name for a class that requires computer work. In the case of hybrid classes, though, you may only meet once a week on campus, instead of two or three times, and then do the rest of your coursework online. Good computer skills and access to a computer will be requirements for this type of class.

Among the numerous types of course formats, a popular option involves *alternative pacing.* These courses can also be called *accelerated* classes, in which you are able to complete your work at a faster pace than a regular 16-week semester. There can also be *self-paced* classes in which you work at your own speed, whether over a semester or more than one. Usually, accelerated and self-paced classes require online work and testing to ensure you are mastering the material. Finally, *intersession* classes, as the name implies, are offered during the period between semesters, functioning much like accelerated classes in that a large amount of material is covered in a short period of time.

Learning Formats

As if a course's presentation is not enough to consider when building your schedule for next semester, you may also want to think about how classes may require you to learn. *Service learning* is gaining popularity at many colleges, and it involves community service as part of the learning process. The course's service learning project may involve working at a homeless shelter, designing a neighborhood playground, or testing area drinking water. The project will depend on the course and the hours needed to complete the project will depend on the instructor's assignments, but such a course offers a unique opportunity for students to apply the concepts they learn in class to help solve a community issue. *Cooperative learning* is another type of format that requires students to work in small teams to learn the material in a course. Cooperative learning groups work all semester to help their teammates learn concepts and complete projects. Different from small group work that you may participate in for other classes, cooperative learning is sustained and deliberate—the teams work together for the entire semester.

Professors

Just as important as which classes you take next semester, and in which formats, is with whom you take those classes. By now, you should realize that choosing the right instructor could make the difference in how much you enjoy and learn in a class. If you have the option of choosing an instructor, then you should start talking with other students about them. Ask specific questions of a variety of people. Remember that each student has his or her own view of what makes a good instructor, a view that might not match your own. Questions you should ask need to move beyond "Is she a good teacher?" Instead, you should ask about her teaching style, the types of assignments she gives, and how available she is during office hours. Be wary of Internet sites that rate professors. They are not reliable because anyone can post just about anything they want without regard to accuracy, or sometimes decency. There is no mechanism to keep the same people from posting multiple positive or negative comments, which can present only part of the picture.

An even better way to determine which instructors are the best for you is to talk with them before enrolling. Make an appointment with a potential instructor and ask pertinent questions: How much reading is involved? How do you teach the course? Do you require a research paper? What do you expect students to know when they complete the course? The benefits of interviewing your instructor before signing up for the class include determining whether the instructor is a good fit with your learning style and making a good impression by demonstrating your maturity and interest in your education.

Building Your Schedule

What worked this semester and what didn't? Why? What will change for you next semester? Did you have enough time in between classes? Did you waste time that could have been spent more productively? All of these questions will need to be answered before you set your schedule for next semester.

When planning your next semester (and beyond), consider five factors: how many hours you need to take, how many hours you need to work, what support is available, what other obligations (planned trips for work or with family, for example) you have, and how much stress these factors will cause.

- *Number of credit hours.* To determine how many credit hours you need to take, be sure to review your financial aid, scholarship, and degree plan information. If you are receiving financial aid, you may be required to take a full load, which often means at least 12 hours. As you can see in the previous example, Laura needed to take 15 hours each semester in order to finish her degree in four semesters. However, because she had to take developmental classes her first semester, she only met 6 hours of the required courses for her associate's degree.

- *Number of work hours.* If you will not be working next semester, you can skip this section. However, even if you are only working a few hours a week, you will need to schedule your work hours so that they do not overlap with the times you are in class. You also need to allow plenty of time to get to and from work and school. Be realistic when calculating this time and plan for delays. An accurately planned schedule will help keep your stress levels at a minimum.

- *Amount of learning support and learning opportunities.* If you know or anticipate a need for learning assistance or tutoring, be sure to build that time into your schedule. You may also need to see each of your professors on a regular basis, some more than others, which should also be a consideration when creating a schedule. If you leave little time for meeting with your instructors, it will be difficult to get the help and advice you need. Good time management and a flexible schedule will allow plenty of time for visits to the computer lab to get help with technology issues, to the library for assistance in using the databases or locating material, and to the tutoring lab at the hours and locations that are most convenient to you.

- *Other obligations.* Working, going to school, taking care of a family, and participating in social and community activities all require your time and energy.

When planning for next semester, consider the obligations that you have and how you will balance college with those obligations.

Thinkstock

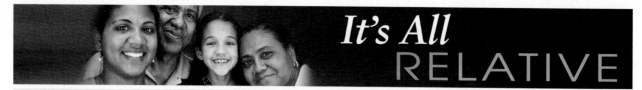

It's All RELATIVE

Letting your family know the certificate or degree plan you have chosen and how much time it will take to complete the plan will be essential in maintaining the lines of communication. Although they may be supportive of your goal—a college degree—they may not realize the amount of time it takes to complete.

Be sure that you share the plan with them. Consider posting it in a prominent location and checking off the classes you take each semester. They can then participate in your accomplishments.

YOUR TURN

How many semesters will it take for you to complete your educational goal? • What can you do to help your family understand the length of your commitment? • What can you do to help them participate in your accomplishment of each step in the process?

_____

_____

_____

_____

To balance all your activities, you will need to keep an eye on upcoming events and make sure you plan accordingly. For example, if you are thinking about registering for the fall semester and you know that you must take a weeklong trip for work in October, you should contact potential instructors to see what their policies are for missing class. Likewise, if you like to participate in your child's school activities, you will need to consider how much time you can give if you are also studying for classes. You may find that you need to cut back on social and volunteer commitments or at least postpone them until after the semester.

- _Stress levels._ Your work schedule, course load, and other responsibilities can lead to high levels of stress. For example, if you have to take 15 hours of courses to maintain your financial aid and you have to work 40 hours to pay your bills, but you feel overwhelmed and anxious about balancing it all, then you are not likely to handle both well. If you find yourself in this situation, you will need to reconsider your plans before you get in over your head. Getting locked into a rigid schedule that doesn't allow you to drop a course that is too difficult or to decrease your hours at work will lead to frustration and high levels of negative stress.

On the other hand, you may thrive on such a schedule because you work better when you have to manage your time carefully. You may be the type of person who cannot study well if you have unlimited amounts of time to do it. If this is the case, you may feel excited about having so much activity in your schedule. Still, you could encounter a problem in which having flexibility (being able to drop a class or reducing your work hours) will help you cope. If you don't have this flexibility, then you need to pay extra attention to staying on top of your work. For example, if you find on the first day of the semester that one of your classes will be much more demanding than you had anticipated, you will need to be more careful about keeping up with assignments and managing your stress effectively. Planning ahead and managing your time will help you cope with a stressful schedule.

What should you do if you cannot work a schedule out despite your efforts to make it all fit together? There may be a semester that a course you need is not offered or the class is filled before you can register. Should you throw up your hands and quit when faced with these problems? Of course not. Instead, you should take advantage of the relationships you have cultivated at college. Now is the time to talk with fellow students, instructors, and advisors. They may be able to offer solutions that you have not considered. If, however, there is an academic need for you to get into a class or rearrange your schedule, you should point that out. Some college officials are willing to bend the rules if you need one more class to complete your degree and transfer on time.

Critical Thinking
EXERCISE 11.2

What do you need to consider before registering for classes next semester? What will you need to work around (e.g., family obligations, work schedule, or degree requirements)? How will you manage your schedule in light of your other obligations? ■

FINANCING YOUR EDUCATION

When thinking about your financial future, most likely paying for college will be at the top of your list. Even if you have a solid plan for paying tuition, fees, and books, it will be worth your time to investigate other methods in case your current approach falls through. Regardless of where you choose to go to school, it is likely that you will need to decide how you will pay for the costs you incur.

Scholarships

Winning a scholarship is by far the most rewarding (financially and psychologically) way to pay for college because it is literally free money—you don't have to pay it back. There are thousands of scholarships out there for needy and accomplished students. All you have to do is find them. To find which ones match your profile, you will need to get the word out that you are looking. Talking with friends, family, employers, and college officials is a great way to start the process. They may know of obscure scholarships that will fit your needs perfectly.

Another way to get information about scholarships is to talk with the financial aid officers and counselors at your college. They have access to and knowledge of scholarships that fit the college's student profiles such as single parent and transfer scholarships that will pay your tuition and fees at a four-year university. Other effective methods for finding scholarships include investigating sources at the library and searching the Internet. Searching print and Web-based databases will provide you with more than enough information; the only problem will be narrowing your focus.

Whatever information about scholarships you find—whether in books, in counselors' offices, or on the Internet—don't pay for it. There are services that claim to match your qualifications with scholarship qualifications but charge a fee to do so. You can get free help from high school and college counselors as well as libraries and Internet searches. No reputable scholarship will demand a fee to apply, and very few scholarship services will require payment. There are legitimate scholarship searching services out there, but be careful. The website FinAid! (www.finaid.org) provides information about different types of financial aid for college students as well as tips for avoiding scholarship services scams. According to this site, any service that guarantees to match you with a scholarship or that offers you an award that you did not apply for is likely to be a scam. Many colleges recommend www.fastweb.com as a great starting point for finding scholarships that match your accomplishments.

Grants

By definition, grants are financial assistance that does not need to be paid back. A common federal grant is the Pell Grant, which can be awarded for full-time or part-time enrollment. To determine your eligibility, talk with your financial aid counselor or visit any of the various websites that provide governmental information about financial aid. When you research Pell Grants, you will find that there is a limit to the amount of the award ($5,550 for July 1, 2010–June 30, 2011) and that your college will receive the money and then disburse it to you once classes start. Because of recent federal requirements about grants and student loans, colleges may wait several weeks before paying students. If you are expecting to receive your grant the first day or week of classes, you should make alternative arrangements to pay bills (including your bookstore bill).

Another type of grant that a student can receive is the Federal Supplemental Educational Opportunity Grant (FSEOG), which is available to those who demonstrate an exceptional need. According to the U.S. Department of Education (2008), the difference between a Pell Grant and an FSEOG is that "each participating school will receive enough money to pay the Federal Pell Grants of its eligible students. There's no guarantee every eligible student will be able to receive an FSEOG." The procedure for receiving an FSEOG is similar to that for receiving a Pell Grant; your eligibility will determine the amount that you receive, and your college will disburse the money to you after the semester begins.

In addition to payment schedules, you will need to maintain good academic standing at your college to remain eligible to receive grant money. If you apply for a grant, be sure to make note of the minimum GPA that you must have in order to ensure your eligibility to receive future grant money. One last tip for continuing to receive grant funding: Make sure that you adhere to the college's attendance policy. You may be penalized (and lose your grant funding or have to pay it back) for missing too many classes or for dropping a class. As always, check with your financial aid officer to make sure that you clearly understand the expectations for receiving grants.

Student Loans

In the event that you are not eligible for grants, you should investigate student loans. The idea of taking out a loan to attend college makes many students shudder with fear because they don't want the added pressure that they must pay back what they borrow. If you can avoid a student loan, then by all means do so. However, receiving a student loan sometimes makes more financial sense in the long run.

Federal student loans typically carry low interest and can be paid back over 10 years. For families that would otherwise have to deplete their savings or borrow against

Student loans, because they are low interest and have a long-term payment plan, are often a good way to pay for college if you do not have the financial means to do so otherwise. However, there are serious consequences if you do not pay them back when required to do so. Defaulting on student loans can make you ineligible for future federal aid and can have negative consequences on your credit rating.

Before you sign to receive a student loan, be sure that you have a plan to pay it back after you graduate. If you find yourself unable to make a payment after your loan payments become due, notify your lender immediately. Sometimes, the lender can work out a repayment plan for you if you have an unusual hardship.

YOUR TURN

What are your concerns about paying for college? • What would be your plan for repaying a loan should you take one out? • What is your back-up plan if you were to find yourself unable to pay it back when it came due?

_____

_____

_____

retirement or their mortgages to pay for college, a low-interest student loan is a good option. Most loan programs allow you to defer payment (but you may accumulate interest) until after you graduate, or you can sometimes defer payment if you remain unemployed after you graduate.

One type of loan is the Stafford Loan, which comes in subsidized and unsubsidized versions. A subsidized loan is one in which the government pays the interest for you while you are in college. Once you graduate and start making payments on your loan, you will accrue interest as well. The government does not make interest payments for an unsubsidized loan; however, you may, instead, pay the interest while you are in college (usually a small amount), or you can wait until after you graduate to make any payments, although your interest will be capitalized. In other words, the interest will be added to the principal amount of the loan, which makes your monthly payments higher.

A federal Perkins Loan is a loan between you and your college. According to the website Student Aid on the Web (2009), the Perkins Loan currently allows you to borrow $5,500 per year up to $27,500 for 5 years, and you don't have to start repaying it until 9 months after you graduate or drop below at least part-time status. One benefit of a Perkins Loan is that you may be able to cancel up to 100 percent of the debt if you meet certain criteria. For example, on graduation, if you choose to teach in a "teacher shortage" area or if you serve as a full-time nurse, you may be eligible for cancellation of your loan. As you would for any type of federal financial aid, check out their websites (they usually end in ".gov") for the most current information.

PLUS, which stands for Parent Loan for Undergraduate Students, is another method for receiving money to help pay for college. If you are fortunate enough to have parents willing to take out a loan to help you pay for college, PLUS is a possible option. To qualify, you must be a dependent student, which means your parents support you financially. A PLUS can be provided by the government or by private lenders. Parents who take out a PLUS are usually trying to make up the difference between the cost of tuition and the financial aid package that their children receive. Nonetheless, it is the parents who are ultimately responsible for repaying the loan, which can begin as early as 60 days after they receive it.

Military and Veterans Financial Aid

Being a member of the military can be especially helpful when you are paying for college. There are numerous benefits for active members and veterans as well as their dependents, one of which is the Montgomery G.I. Bill. To find out about military benefits, talk with a financial aid officer or a special counselor at your college or at a Veterans Affairs office for specific information. According to the United States Department of Veterans Affairs website, the Post-911 G.I. Bill, which went into effect on August 1, 2009, provides benefits for qualified applicants to help pay for tuition and some expenses related to attending an accredited and approved institution of higher education. There are differences between the Montgomery G.I. Bill and the Post-9/11 G.I. Bill, and you can find a benefits comparison as well as a form to complete on the website www .gibill.va.gov.

Work-Study

Work-study is a program that allows students to earn money while they work on campus. The reason it is called "work-study" is that the job may allow for you to study when you work, although most work-study positions are similar to office assistant jobs and will keep you busy for the majority of the time you work. To work in such a program, you must be eligible for federal work-study money, and you will be limited to a certain number of hours you can work per week. Not everyone who is eligible for work-study will be able to find a position on campus, however. Each department and area of the college advertises, hires, and manages work-study positions; sometimes, hiring can be competitive. There may be specific requirements (such as computer skills) that a candidate must meet before being hired. Because some positions require working with students' personal information, work-study students must also abide by the college's privacy standards.

The benefits of participating in work-study include earning some money that will help pay your expenses and also working closely with college employees. By getting to know professors and administrators better—and by working for them—you may have access to valuable advice and information. To investigate whether or not work-study is available for you, talk with your financial aid officer. He or she will review your eligibility and help you apply for on-campus employment.

Tuition Waivers for Employees

Another source of financial help is your employer. Large corporations sometimes offer financial assistance for employees, although there may be stipulations that you work for a certain amount of time after graduation. If your employer doesn't offer scholarships to employees, you should still ask if he or she is interested in doing so; employers will benefit from employees who further their education. Finally, your college may offer tuition

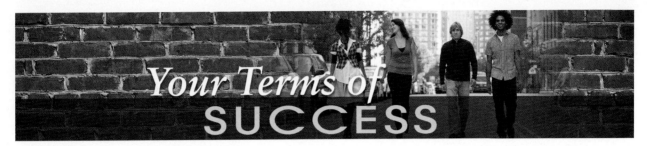

Your Terms of SUCCESS

WHEN YOU SEE . . .	IT MEANS . . .
Accelerated classes	Classes conducted at a faster pace than regular semester-long classes. May require more time per week to complete, but may also allow you to complete sequences of classes more quickly than if you took classes during a traditional term.
Cooperative learning	Arrangements in which students work in small groups or teams to complete class assignments. Goals of the group work will vary, but usually cooperative learning requires that all members contribute to the learning process.
FASFA	Free Application for Student Federal Aid.
Hybrid classes	Classes that are held on campus for part of the semester and that also use an online learning system to supplement learning on the days students are not in class. Will require access to a computer and the Internet.
Intersession classes	Classes that are scheduled in between regular semesters. Sometimes offered in January or May before or after a spring semester or term. Usually faster-paced but limited to only one or two classes available to take.
Learning communities	Taking classes with a "cohort" or the same group of students for two or more classes. Classes often share similar assignments and course content.
Perkins Loan	Low-interest loan that helps students pay for undergraduate education.
PLUS loan	Parent Loan for Undergraduate Students.
Self-paced classes	Course requirements completed at student's own pace. If you need more time than a traditional semester, you are allowed to continue in the classes until you have successfully mastered the course content.
Service learning	Requirement to participate in a community project as part of a course. The project will reinforce the concepts and content of the course and may also include an opportunity for you to reflect on what you have learned.
Web-enhanced classes	Using the World Wide Web to supplement learning in a class. Will require access to a computer and the Internet. Sometimes *Web-enhanced* is used interchangeably with *hybrid*.
Work-study	A financial aid program that allows students to earn money while working on campus. Depending on the position's job duties, you may be able to study when you are not engaged in a task.

waivers for its full-time employees. Some students seek jobs offered at colleges so that they can take classes for free or at a reduced cost. If you need a part-time or full-time job while you are in school, you may want to check out the openings at your college.

Applying for Financial Aid

Each college is different in how they handle the application process, but it is worth talking generally about what to expect when applying for financial aid. Even if you receive financial aid for this academic year, there may be some information that you need to know before applying again. The first step in the process is obtaining a Free Application for Federal Student Aid (FAFSA), which can be picked up from the financial aid office of your college or can be accessed online at www.fafsa.ed.gov. The website provides particularly helpful information that is broken down in steps, which can make the process less intimidating.

Be sure to remember that financial aid applications must be renewed each academic year; the time line for receiving aid for a year starts in August and ends in July. Thus, if you applied for financial aid in November and received it for classes that started in January, you will have until July to use that aid; then, you will need to reapply for aid for the fall semester.

As part of the FAFSA application process, you will need to determine whether you are considered "independent" or "dependent." The federal government defines a student's independence by certain criteria such as age, marital status, or whether both parents are deceased. Students who fit the definition for dependent status, but with extenuating circumstances, may be able to appeal that their status be changed to independent.

In addition to determining your ability to pay for college, you will also be asked to provide an Estimated Family Contribution (EFC) amount; for example, if you receive child support payments or Social Security payments, you will have to report that income as part of your EFC. One other consideration when applying for financial aid is that each year a certain percentage of loan applications get identified for verification. This means that a number of student financial aid applications may take longer to process because of the requirements of verification.

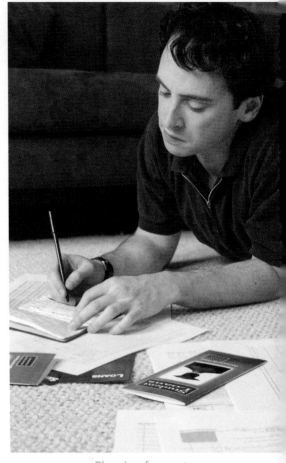

Planning for next semester includes taking into account how you will pay for both college and living expenses.

Thinkstock

Renewing Financial Aid and Paying It Back

In order to continue receiving financial aid, you will need to make sure that you understand and follow the requirements of your college. Many colleges maintain a satisfactory academic standing policy that states you will need to stay enrolled in a number of credit hours and maintain a minimum grade point average to continue to receive grants and loans. Sometimes, the required GPA is higher than the GPA to remain in college. For example, you may have to maintain a 2.7 GPA to continue to receive financial aid but need only a 2.0 GPA to stay in college.

If you do not meet the requirements for a semester, your college may place you on financial aid probation, which means you must meet the college's requirements for the next semester to be removed from probation. Failing that, the next step after probation can be suspension from financial aid, in which you no longer receive financial aid, although you may still be able to enroll in classes as long as you pay for them yourself. If your suspension involves extenuating circumstances, some colleges have an appeals process. This means you may file an appeal and appear before a committee who will determine whether you can reapply for financial aid.

Whenever applying for loans, you need to consider how you will pay them back after completing your degree or otherwise leaving college. Student loan default is a common problem nationwide and there are stiff penalties for failing to pay back the federal government. On the other hand, loan forgiveness programs are often available for students who major in fields that are in high demand in their community. To find out more about these types of programs, be sure to talk to someone in the financial aid office at your college.

QUESTIONING YOUR DECISION to CONTINUE

There is tremendous pressure on those who do not have higher degrees to get them. Frequently high school students hear this pitch from parents, counselors, and teachers: Success in life is dependent on obtaining a college degree. People who have been in the workforce know, as well, that a college degree can be the difference between doing the same job until retirement and being promoted.

But does everyone need to go to college? College is a great place to continue your education and to make your career dreams a reality. There are also indirect benefits to pursuing higher education, such as improving your health and financial well-being because you know more about yourself and the world around you. Nonetheless, going to college is not the only key to success. There are many vibrant, intelligent, successful people who have not completed a college degree.

Is College Right for You?

How will you know if college is not right for you? It may be difficult to tell, but you shouldn't quit going if you are unsure. The best way to discover how you feel about being in college is to ask yourself a series of questions. Then talk about your responses with a college counselor, advisor, or trusted friend who can give you good advice.

Think **ABOUT IT**

"Perseverance is not a long race; it is many short races one after another."

—Walter Elliott

- Who wants me to be in college?
- Do *I* want to be in college?
- How do I feel when I am in class?
- How do I feel when I am studying?
- How do I feel after I take an exam?
- What do I want to major in? Why?
- What do I want to do with my life? Do I need a college degree to do it?
- What do I value about higher education? What can it do for me?
- What is my passion?

Take your time answering these questions. You may find that your discomfort about being in college is really a fear about a new beginning and the unknown. Being apprehensive about a new program or a new environment is perfectly normal and does not necessarily indicate that you are not right for college. On the other hand, you may know very clearly that you do not want to be in college at this point in your life. College may not be the best choice for you *right now*, which means that you should consider returning when you are certain it will be your top priority.

Benefits of Continuing Your Education

If you are considering whether or not to continue your education next semester, it may be helpful to think about the benefits of going on. First, you will be that much closer to finishing a degree. More completed classes mean more degree requirements checked off the list. Second, if you have to take courses in a sequence (e.g., Writing I and Writing II), then you are more likely to remember what you learned in the first course. Staying out too long between courses that need to be taken close together may lead to forgetting important concepts, which could make that second course more difficult for you. Finally, staying in college now will mean you are more likely to stay friends with classmates. Even taking a semester break may result in losing touch with people you know and rely on now.

Benefits of Taking a Break

If you decide you need a break before completing your degree, be sure you make the most of the time away from college. Some students use that time to earn extra money, take care of personal issues, or work on their academic skills outside of college. A much-needed break can help you stay focused; instead of burning out by continuing a stressful pace, you may find yourself able to reenergize so that you can return with more focus and enthusiasm. A break can be a time to clarify your goals, and it can also help you recommit to the degree path you started on. Of course, during your break, if you decide to change degrees or career directions, you can return with a renewed sense of purpose.

Reflection EXERCISE 11.4

How do you feel about being in college? Have you had any thoughts about quitting? If so, what is keeping you motivated to continue? If not, what would have to happen for you to consider seriously not continuing your education? What can you do to help stay motivated? ∎

PLUS EXERCISE 11.5

(Personality + Learning Style = Understanding Situations)

Think about Juanita's dilemma regarding whom to take next semester and what degree plan to follow. Juanita is an independent read/write learner who is usually shy in social situations. Because she still lives at home, although she is 18, she feels some obligation to consider her parents' opinions about her future. Using what you have learned from this chapter, what advice would you give her? How can she gain confidence in mapping her future for herself?

Now, considering your own learning style, personality type, and special circumstances, what would you do to choose the right classes, professors, and degree plan in spite of your uncertainties about which choices to make? ∎

From College to University

PREPARING FOR UNEXPECTED HIGHER COSTS

It is very likely that you will see a change in college costs when you transfer to a university. You may be paying twice as much for tuition at the four-year school as you did at your local community college. In addition to tuition, you may see added fees that you didn't have at your community college: Fees for athletic facility use, sporting events, campus organizations, and labs are possible additional expenses. Be sure to read the college catalog carefully and add the fees to the cost per credit hour to get an accurate picture of what you will be spending per class.

Despite the increase in tuition and fees, you may notice that your bookstore expenses stay the same. Although the price of books can be a significant portion of your overall college expenses, it is unlikely that you will experience an increase in cost. However, upper-level science and computer classes require weighty textbooks and additional software. These books can cost as much as $100. Multiply that by four classes, and you will be paying at least $400 for the semester. An advantage, however, to transferring to a larger school is that there are more people from whom you can buy used books. Take notice of special discounts for used books in the bookstore and look for flyers on bulletin boards that announce books for sale.

Building Your University Portfolio 11

Find someone you know (or ask your professor for the name of a former student) who has transferred to a four-year university and ask him or her if the costs are different. How much difference is there in tuition costs? Are there additional fees (such as athletics) that are new? What other costs should someone anticipate when transferring?

_____

_____

_____

_____

From College to Career

THE BENEFITS OF RETURNING TO WORK BEFORE CONTINUING YOUR EDUCATION

There may be a time when you must interrupt your college career to return to your job full time. Balancing financial and educational goals may become too difficult to handle, which may mean that your financial needs take precedence. If this happens to you, there are some ways of dealing with the transition back to the world of work while still keeping your eye on returning to college.

First, realize that going back to work doesn't have to be forever. Just because you are unable to return for more than one semester doesn't mean you never will. Be sure to talk with your employer about your desire to get a degree. You may be surprised by his or her support of your goals. There may even be financial assistance for employees who take college classes. Remember to also discuss with your family and friends your need to further your education. Someone may be willing to help you with finances, scheduling, and family duties. Set a time line for returning to college. If you need to work a semester to earn more money to pay for tuition, then be sure to keep up with registration periods and college announcements.

Finances will be another consideration, so be sure to save your money. Even if expenses were not the reason you returned to work, putting aside money in a "college fund" will make it easier to re-enroll in college. You won't have any excuses for not being able to afford the increased costs. Look for scholarships and financial aid for working adults. Some states are creating grant programs for nontraditional students who work full time in order to increase the number of college graduates in their states. Finally, keep connected with former classmates and instructors. If you are aware of what is going on at the college, you are more likely to return because you will feel as though you had never completely left.

Building Your Career Portfolio 11

Contact someone in a career that is similar to what you want to do. Ask whether it would be better to stay and finish a degree or instead to work in the field awhile before completing a degree. What are the advantages and disadvantages of each decision?

_____

_____

_____

_____

First Voices

STORIES OF SUCCESS FROM COLLEGE GRADUATES

Honor student in high school hits rough patch in college: Juggles family and work while succeeding the second time around

Richard Moss,
Ph.D.,
Student Success Coach

Graduating from high school in 1990 with a 3.2 GPA, a member of the National Honor Society, and taking what are now known as AP courses, I assumed I would breeze through college. I was in for a rude awakening. I began the Spring 1991 term with 15 hours, but finished with only 9. At the end of my first semester of college, I had a GPA of 0.9. Yes, 0.9. When my mother saw my grades, she asked where my GPA was. I replied "Right there." Her next statement was, "No son, there is no number in front of the decimal point." I eventually "flunked out" of my first university. After getting married and maturing, I transferred to a local university in 2000 and began work to finish my bachelor's degree. I completed my degree in two years and graduated with a B.A. in political science and 3.0 GPA to boot, while working a full-time job.

While in the final two terms of my bachelor's degree, I was encouraged by two faculty members to shoot for a master's degree. After a lot of thought and prodding, I applied to the master's program for public administration at the same university. My acceptance was contingent on my graduation from my bachelor's program. I graduated with my B.A. August 13, 2002, and began work on my master's degree two weeks later. While still working a full-time job, I was able to complete my master's degree in December 2004, after 2½ years, with a 3.91 GPA.

In August 2005, on the same day that Katrina hit no less, I began work on a Ph.D. in public policy. What made this even more challenging than my first two degrees was the fact that my school was three hours away. So, while working a full-time job, I traveled with another coworker 400 miles round trip, one day a week to school. We would leave around 10 A.M. headed for classes and return home around midnight, ready to be at work by 8 A.M. the next morning. I am now taking qualifying exams, with an anticipated graduation date of December 2010.

PATH OF DISCOVERY
Journal Entry

What degrees are you interested in pursuing? Why do these degree plans appeal to you?

CHAPTER REVIEW QUESTIONS

1. What do you need to consider before registering for classes next semester?
2. In what ways can you prepare for the end of the semester?
3. What are four ways a student can pay for college? What are the benefits of each method?
4. What are the benefits of staying in college? What are the benefits of not finishing a degree?

CHAPTER 11 CASE SCENARIOS

1. Anja is considering transferring to the university nearby after she graduates with her associate's degree. She is very nervous and is not sure what she needs to do to plan a successful move once she completes her degree. What advice would you give her about making the move and getting involved in the transition now?
2. Ramielle has paid for her first semester of tuition from her savings, but she is looking for other ways to pay for the rest of her college. She doesn't qualify for any grants and is not sure what her options are. Explain to her what choices she has to pay for college without incurring too much debt.
3. Riley has had a difficult time getting used to the expectations in college. He has not had a successful semester so far, and he is getting pressure at work to quit college and take a promotion. It means more money, but less time to get the degree that he wants. He could always come back, he knows, but at 25 years old, he is afraid that if he doesn't go to college now, it will be even harder when he earns a bigger paycheck. What would you tell him about quitting college?

RESEARCH IT FURTHER

1. As an individual, or within a group, research the qualifications and requirements for the different loans and grants that your college offers. With the information, create a one-page sheet for each type of financial aid that can help students remember the differences between each type.

2. Investigate the entrance requirements of two four-year universities in the area. Find out GPA requirements, available types of scholarships and financial aid, and what kinds of degree programs they offer. Make a brief presentation to your class.
3. What, if any, alumni services does your college offer? If they provide very few or none at all, brainstorm a list of ideas that you would like to see implemented and present them to an administrator at your institution who can give you feedback on what is possible. Then, report to your class on which suggestions can be implemented and which cannot.

References and Recommended Readings

The College Board. (2009). *Getting financial aid 2010*. Plano, TX: Author.

Cress, C. M., Collier, P. J., & Reitenauer, V. L. (2005). *Learning through serving: A student guidebook for service-learning across the disciplines*. Sterling, VA: Stylus.

Lipphardt, D. (2008). *The scholarship and financial aid solution: How to go to college for next to nothing with short cuts, tricks, and tips from start to finish*. Ocala, FL: Atlantic Publishing Group.

"Perkins Loans." (2009). *Student aid on the Web*. Retrieved October 12, 2009, from http://studentaid.ed.gov/PORTALSWebApp/students/english/campusaid.jsp.

Schlacther, G., & Weber, R. D. (2009). *Kaplan scholarships 2010: Billions of dollars in free money for college*. New York: Kaplan Publishing.

U.S. Department of Education. (2008). Types of Federal Student Aid. Retrieved May 14, 2008, from http://studentaid.ed.gov/students/publications/student_guide/2006-2007/english/typesofFSA_grants.htm.

U.S. Department of Veterans Affairs. (2009). What Is the Post-911 G.I. Bill? Retrieved October 12, 2009, from www.gibill.va.gov/GI_Bill_Info/CH33/Post-911.htm.

12

A CAREER
and a LIFE

The big red arrow points to the ballroom. The smell of popcorn fills the large space, and the red and yellow balloons wave back and forth when students walk through the double doors. Evan and Michael feel as though they have walked into a carnival instead of a career fair.

"Hey, Michael. Did you see that clown in the corner juggling bananas?" Evan asks.

"Where?" Michael asks as his head swivels around to find what he has missed.

Evan bends forward, places his hands on his chest, and starts laughing.

"All right, all right. You got me," Michael says, softly punching Evan in the shoulder.

Instead of people with red rubber noses and big shoes, there are dozens of booths inviting students to leave their résumés and learn more about a variety of local and national businesses and industries. The only jugglers are students who are picking up flyers, business cards, and chocolate candy from the bowls on each table.

Fresh from class, in jeans and a college sweatshirt, Evan stops to pick up a piece of candy. "I'm planning on going to all the booths. Are you?" Evan asks.

Michael has done a little research and knows the two booths he wants to visit. He runs his fingers down his pressed khakis and checks his crisp white dress shirt for the tenth time since he put it on this morning.

"No," he says, "I plan on finding the two companies I checked out on the Internet last night. The plan is simple: Introduce myself, tell 'em what I know about the open positions, and leave with them with my résumé."

"Man, aren't you afraid you will be cutting yourself short? Shouldn't you hit every one of the booths just in case? You can't be *that* sure of what you want to be when you grow up," Evan asks in rapid fire.

"I don't know. I guess with all my time in the military, I have a lot of experience doing different jobs. I definitely know what I *don't* want to do," Michael replies. "Besides, I am applying for that internship at the nursing home. My advisor says I will learn a little something about the nursing field and get to know some people."

"But there are so many options," Evan says. "How do I know that I am going to make a lot of money with whatever I choose? I don't want to waste any time doing something that will get me nowhere."

"Well, what degree can you earn that will get you a job that pays well?" asks Michael.

"That's my problem. I don't quite know. I mean I know what I like to study, but how do I know that is going to get me a job where I don't have to wear a coat and tie?" Evan says.

"I am certain you won't be landing any jobs like that the way you are dressed today!" Michael says. He slaps Evan on the back and laughs.

Evan looks down at his jeans and shrugs when he notices a spot on the left leg. He pulls out 30 copies of his résumé from his backpack and starts with the booth near the door.

"Watch this! They will all remember Evan," he says. He strolls to the first table and introduces himself.

"I am Evan. It is a pleasure to meet you," he says to the woman representing an aeronautic firm. He gives her a firm handshake and a broad smile.

"So tell me what your company does and what I would do if I worked for you," Evan says. The woman pulls Evan closer and shows him photos of aircraft interiors.

Michael walks straight to one of the two health care companies at the fair. Because his girlfriend works in health care, he already knows what he needs to do to get a good entry-level job. He also knows how to progress in the field.

"Here goes nothing," Michael says to himself. He looks over his shoulder to see that Evan is working his way down the line of booths and wonders if he should do the same.

In this CHAPTER

Deciding where you want to go and what you want to do, as both Michael and Evan demonstrate, can be characterized by uncertainty. After reading this chapter, you will have a better understanding of your choices *after* you have taken courses at your college. Even though you have just begun your journey toward a certificate or a degree, you may want to keep in mind your options and the different paths you can take. Ideally, you should read this chapter thoroughly and then refer to it as you complete each semester, ensuring that you are on the right track and reminding yourself of the different choices you have.

More specifically, after completing this chapter, you will be able to do the following:

■ **List the opportunities available for career exploration.**
■ **Identify the steps to writing a résumé and cover letter.**
■ **Discuss the importance of networking effectively.**
■ **Describe the processes for creating a life beyond college.**

CAREER EXPLORATION

Whether you know exactly what career you want or are still exploring the possibilities, your college experience can help you focus on what you want out of your professional life. After reading the section below about getting ready for a career, remember that the people you meet at your college can help you in many ways: they can help you decide what career is a best fit for you and they can help you prepare to find and secure that job.

Career Values and Goals

Before you begin delving into the resources and services available at your college, take some time to reflect on your career values and goals. They may not be much different than the ones you recorded when you read Chapter 1. However, it is worth consider-

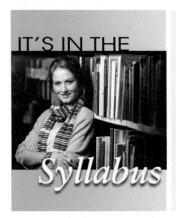

IT'S IN THE *Syllabus*

Your syllabus may help you in your career exploration (if you don't already know what you want to do when you complete your degree). Look at the course content, or what is covered during the semester. Do any topics really interest you? Do you find yourself drawn to certain subjects? What are they?

Your syllabus may also contain contact information for your instructor, which can be helpful when you need career advice or a recommendation letter. Which instructors do you have now who will be helpful to you in the future?

ing what you value in a career and what kinds of experiences you want to have. For example, do you value working with others in projects with strict deadlines or would you prefer to work alone with little supervision? Your answer to that question and others can help you determine what you value and what careers work best for you. If, for instance, you have a strong interest in writing, but you prefer working with others, you may decide to choose a career that has many opportunities for collaboration when writing.

In addition to considering your values as they relate to your career, you may also want to consider your career goals—it is never too soon to think about them! For example, is your goal to move up quickly in a company or would you rather find a business that will allow you to indulge in a preferred lifestyle, such as traveling and meeting a diverse group of people? For sure, when you get to the point of creating clear, realistic, and reachable career goals, your values will inform what you write down or tell others, just as values and goals will influence your discussions with a career counselor or your search for a job and the resulting interviews.

If you are not sure where to start when considering your career values and goals, then you may want to check out the various career assessment programs, such as DIS-COVER or Kuder, at your career counseling center.

Career Counseling

Long before you think about graduating and finding a job, you should visit the career counselors at your college. Preparing for a career takes longer than a few weeks, and the more planning you do, the smoother the process will be. Each college offers different services in its career center, but most provide access to interest inventories, which can help you pinpoint which fields you are best suited for. Most career services also provide "career libraries" that include information about different occupations as well as their responsibilities and pay potential. In addition, career centers may offer help with writing a cover letter and résumé and tips for interviewing for a job. Evan could spend some time in his college's career library to learn more about his opportunities before he hits all of the employers at the career fair.

Don't forget that your professors can also be great career counselors because they often have connections

Think ABOUT IT

Volunteer—not so you can build your résumé, but so you can build yourself.

—Anonymous

with people in the field (or have friends or relatives working in different industries). You never know when your welding instructor may have a contact at an accounting firm or a biology instructor may have a connection with the human resources department at an advertising firm. Tell professors what you want to do as a career whenever you have a chance. They may be likely to remember you and your goals when they meet someone in your field of study.

Career Fairs

Career fairs are another way to get information about jobs and employers in your area. If your college sponsors a fair off campus or provides one to students on campus, then be sure to take advantage of it. Whether or not you are graduating next month or next year, it will pay to approach a career fair with the goal of making contacts and learning more about area businesses.

When you attend a career fair, there are several steps you can follow to make the most of your visits with potential employers. This list is just a start; you can get even more tips from your college counselors about how to maximize your time at a career fair.

- *Dress professionally.* Also, carry a professional-looking bag (no backpacks!) and a folder with copies of your résumé. Neatness counts.
- *Do your homework.* Find out what companies will be present at the fair and research the ones that interest you. You can find out more about them through their websites or through searching in the library.
- *Avoid asking what a company does.* Your research should tell you what the company does.
- *Choose a few booths to attend.* Instead of blanketing the fair and hitting every representative, be selective and limit yourself only to companies that you would like to work for.
- *Write and practice a standard introduction.* Then use it when you meet someone at the fair. Make sure the introduction is brief (state your name, your interests, and any relevant experience you may have) so that you maximize your time at the fair.
- *Be energetic and positive.* Recruiters and employers want to meet eager, exciting potential employees.

If you cannot make your college's career fair, you may be able to participate in a virtual career fair, which allows job seekers to "meet" participating companies and send résumés. Virtual career fairs are usually linked to a college's website and coincide with the actual fair. For example, the Virtual Career Fair link may only be available while the on-campus fair is open. Some colleges and organizations, however, provide a continual virtual career fair so that students can investigate potential careers and companies at any time. One such website is www.careersinoilandgas.com, which offers an abundance of information and resources for anyone interested in a career in the oil or gas industries. Other sites, such as www.collegegrad.com/careers, offer more general information about careers as well as advice and preparation for job seekers.

Internships

Another work option for college students is an internship. This is a supervised position that allows a student to receive on-the-job training. Usually, internships are unpaid, which makes them less attractive to students who need to work. However, even if you need to make money while attending college, think about an internship anyway. Your college may offer course credit for internships, or you might even get paid for your work. This may be a good way to get closer to your degree *and* explore careers. Another idea is to volunteer once or twice a week at a place of business. If you have a few extra hours a week or can trade college credit for an internship, then you should investigate the benefits of interning.

Why are internships such a good opportunity for college students? One reason is that they allow you to work closely in a field that you may be interested in pursuing. In addition, internships can help you explore different ways that a major can be used in the workforce. For example, an English or journalism major may want to participate in an internship at a newspaper or as a proofreader at a company. A networking major may want to intern at a small business to get practical experience with computer networking issues on a small scale. These opportunities can give you firsthand experience with using your degree.

Internships also allow you to network with others who can help you find a job once you graduate. Even if you decide that you don't want to work in the same area as your

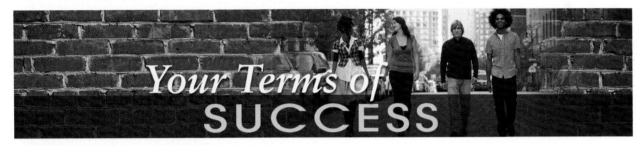

Your Terms of SUCCESS

WHEN YOU SEE . . .	IT MEANS . . .
Career fair	An event that brings various employers together into one place to meet job seekers.
Cover letter	A letter that "covers" a résumé and provides a more detailed description of a job applicant's qualifications.
Internship	A supervised position that allows a student to receive on-the-job training.
Networking	Creating connections among people for the purpose of helping them or having them help you.
Objective	A statement in a résumé that explains your career goals.
Recommendation letter	A letter written to provide a recommendation of your abilities and skills.
References	People listed on a résumé who can provide a recommendation of your abilities and skills.
Résumé	A document that provides information about you, your education, and your work experience.
Résumé padding	The act of exaggerating or lying about educational or work experience on a résumé.
Social networking	Creating connections, usually through websites, for the purpose of communicating with others.

internship, you will have contacts that may help you find a job in other fields. If you decide to intern, you should treat it as a job. Some employers rely on interns to complete certain projects each year, and they will expect you to be serious about the position, even if you don't get paid. Keeping a good attitude and being self-motivated are excellent ways to shine during your internship. In addition, you should meet regularly with your supervisor to ask questions and get guidance on projects. Most of all, make the best of your unique opportunity, and add that experience to your résumé.

Reflection EXERCISE 12.1

At your college and in your community, what kinds of resources are available for you to explore careers? Which ones are you planning to use? ■

JOB PREPARATION

In addition to educating or training you for a career, your college may also include services that help you land the job you want. Many specialized programs, such as nursing, culinary arts, and welding, provide job placement as well as a degree or certificate. Other degree programs, such as fine arts or health sciences, may offer fewer career services, but the instructors and advisors in those programs can still be valuable resources as you prepare for the workforce. At the very least, you will need to know the basics for finding a job after you graduate. Writing résumés and cover letters, as well as polishing your interviewing skills, will be necessary for you to move into your career of choice. As you get more education, the jobs you apply for will require that you present yourself more professionally.

Writing a Résumé

Learning to write a résumé is an essential skill for new graduates, and there is no time like the present to begin honing that skill. According to John J. Marcus (2003) in his book *The Résumé Makeover: 50 Common Résumé and Cover Letter Problems—and How to Fix Them,* a résumé is "no place to be modest. Prospective employers and recruiters will be looking for exciting accomplishments, and if they don't see them, your résumé will pale in the face of the competition" (p. 9).

There are actually two parts to an effective résumé: the résumé and the cover letter. A résumé is a page or two that lists your qualifications and accomplishments. A cover letter, on the other hand, provides information to a specific person that highlights your strengths that may not be apparent in the résumé. Both should be printed on high-quality paper using a good printer. A résumé, as well as any other document you send to a potential employer, should be carefully proofread for errors.

When writing a résumé, the first item you will include is your name, address, phone number, and email address. Make sure your voicemail has an appropriate message on it and that your email is professional as well: ejcantu@abcmail.com is preferred over bananafreak72@chunkymonkey.com. Double-check that there are no errors in your address, phone number, or email address—one misplaced number or letter can cost you an interview because you won't get the message. Michael's résumé contains a new email address to replace his more personal one that he uses for friends and family because he wants to separate career email from more casual correspondence.

A successful résumé will also contain a clear objective, or statement, that tells others what your career goals are. Think of it as a mini mission statement for your career. Objectives are not always written in a complete sentence. For example, your objective may

Although you may be excited to include accomplishments on your résumé, you will need to be sure that you do not go overboard in describing what you have done in the past. A good rule to follow is to always provide accurate, truthful information in your résumé and cover letter. Highlight your accomplishments without overexaggerating them.

Lying on a résumé is called "résumé padding," and it can get you in serious trouble. At the very least, you may not get the job; at the very worst, you could be fired after you are hired if the company finds out that your résumé contains false information.

YOUR TURN

Where is the line between making your accomplishments noteworthy and exaggerating them? • What steps will you take to ensure that all of your information for a résumé or a cover letter is accurate?

_____

_____

_____

be "To join an aircraft maintenance team at a highly rewarding company" or "To use my knowledge and skills to manage employees in the retail industry effectively." Writing a good objective takes time and consideration, and you may need to develop more than one if you plan to apply for different types of jobs or jobs in different industries. At least, be sure that your objective matches the job for which you are applying. If, for example, your objective is "To have a fulfilling career working with infants and toddlers in an accredited daycare" and you are applying to teach classes at a nursing home, then you may not get a second glance, much less an interview. Counselors and professors can help you craft an appropriate objective as you build your résumé.

Once you include an appropriate objective, you will need to include information about your educational accomplishments and job history. If you have not completed your degree at this point, you can write down the anticipated date: "Associate of Arts, May 2012." Be sure to include any other certificates or degrees that you have earned. The most recently earned certificate or degree should be listed first. Information about your work history may be placed either before or after the information about your education. Again, list most recent job first and include the date you worked, your position title, the name of the company and location, and a bulleted list of job responsibilities. The following is a very basic format for reporting your work experience on a résumé. Depending on what kind of format you use, the order of the information may vary.

2008–2010   Dental Assistant   No Worry Dental Group   Tacoma, WA

- Cleaned clients' teeth and identified problem areas.
- Took x-rays of clients' teeth and updated their charts.
- Provided guidance for preventing tooth decay and improving gum health.

Depending on how much experience you have had, the first few parts of a résumé may be easy to complete. Many students have previous or current work experience and know what educational experiences they have had. However, a part of the résumé that is sometimes more difficult is the section on extracurricular activities, organizations, or awards. If you are early in your college career, you may not feel as though you have been able to participate in extracurricular activities worthy to add to your list of accomplishments. Nonetheless, with just a little creative thinking, you may be able to create a list of activities and endeavors. For instance, if you received a college scholarship, you can list it as an award. If you volunteer regularly with your child's school, you can list that. If you have participated in a fundraising event, organized a community meeting, coached a sport, or sat on a committee at your church or synagogue, you can list those accomplishments. You may not realize all the ways you have been involved with others that can show you have other interests than college and work.

Your college will also provide you with future opportunities to add to a résumé, so be sure to keep your eyes and ears open for chances to participate in a one-day event or a semester-long program. The key is to get involved at any level and record your involvement so that you can remember it when you need to develop your résumé. Here are just a few opportunities for students to get involved that colleges often provide:

- Dean's list or president's list for specified grade point averages
- Student ambassadors organization for promoting the college in the community
- Student government association for representing the voice of students
- Honor societies such as Phi Theta Kappa and Phi Beta Kappa as well as honor societies for specific disciplines such as Sigma Kappa Delta, an English honor society
- Special events such as fundraisers, cultural events, political or community rallies, or celebrations

One last part of the résumé that you will want to include is a list of references or a statement that says references are available upon request. As you meet people in college, you may want to create a list of potential references. A professor whom you got to know well, your advisor whom you see each semester as you plan your degree, or a campus official with whom you have worked closely on a project are good candidates for letters of recommendation or references. People you have worked with—either on the job or through a community project—are other excellent possibilities for references. Make sure these people know you well enough to speak of your strengths and potential in the workplace. Getting their permission before you list them is essential to getting a good reference.

Figure 12.1 is an example of a résumé showing one way you can list information. There are many ways to grab an employer's attention, and résumé books will provide you with examples of the various formats. However, a format that is concise, easy to read, and professional is usually best.

Creating a Cover Letter

A cover letter accompanies a résumé and explains in detail how your qualifications match what the employer is looking for. As with a résumé, keep a cover letter brief and to the point, usually no more than a page unless you have enough work experience that you believe needs to be detailed in the letter. Often, the reason that cover letters should be short and to the point is that many employers simply scan these documents to see whether candidates meet the minimum qualifications and then decide, pretty quickly, whether or not to interview them. The more concise your résumé and cover

FIGURE 12.1 Sample Résumé

Juanita Cook
1234 Broadway Street
Anyplace, US 01234
555-555-1234
jrcook@anyplace.edu

Objective	To use my experience and education to work as an accounting manager.
Education	Associate of Applied Science in Accounting, Juno College, May 2011
Experience	Bookkeeper, Mays and Associates, August 2009–present

- Send invoices to clients
- Pay invoices from clients
- Maintain general ledger
- Supervise one staff member

Work-Study, Financial Aid Office, Juno College, January 2008–July 2009

- Filed financial aid applications
- Maintained communication with students through newsletter

Honors and Awards	Accounting Award for Outstanding Student, May 2010 President's Scholarship, August 2009–May 2011 Volunteer of the Year, Humane Society, October 2008

References Available Upon Request

letter, the easier it will be for potential employers to determine whether you are right for the job.

When writing a cover letter, be sure to address a specific person. Avoid starting your letter with "Dear Sir or Madam" or "To Whom It May Concern." If you do not know to whom to address the letter, call the company and ask for the appropriate person's name, along with the correct spelling. If you are responding to several different job advertisements, double-check that you have correctly matched each letter with its corresponding addressed envelope. Also be sure that you have not made any references to people or companies other than to whom you are sending the cover letter.

The basic format of a cover letter is simple; once you type in your address, the date, and the potential employer's name, company name, and address, follow this outlined format:

1. Introduction Paragraph
   a. Introduce yourself
   b. Tell where you learned about the job (Internet, newspaper, person at the company)
2. Background Paragraph
   a. Tell more about yourself and how you are qualified
   b. Relate your education and skills to what the company is looking for
3. Closing Paragraph
   a. Tell potential employer how to contact you
   b. Thank the person for her time and say you are looking forward to hearing from her

Figure 12.2 is an example of an effective cover letter that could accompany the résumé in Figure 12.1.

FIGURE 12.2 Sample Cover Letter

1234 Broadway Street
Anyplace, US 01234

June 1, 2011

Dr. Judy Pile
Ingram Enterprises
6789 Levi Lane
Anyplace, US 09876

Dear Dr. Pile,

I am responding to your advertisement in the *Tonitown Times* for an accounting specialist at your company Ingram Enterprises. As you will see from my résumé, I have earned an Associate of Arts degree in accounting from Juno College, and I have experience working as a bookkeeper for a local company.

My additional experience as a work-study in the financial aid office at Juno has allowed me to improve my people skills as well as to understand how an organized and efficient office works. I have also learned to use the following computer programs effectively: Microsoft Word, Microsoft Excel, and QuickBooks.

I am sure that you will find both my education and experience fit the position that was advertised. If you would like to interview me, I can be reached during the day at 555-555-1234. I look forward to hearing from you.

Sincerely,

Juanita Cook

Interviewing

Another important component to a successful career, if not the most important, is interviewing for a job. If your winning résumé gets you an interview, you are about halfway to getting a job. The tips in this section will help you maximize your performance at the interview. Do a little research by checking out the company's website or search for other company information that may have appeared with the job advertisement. The goal is to find out what the company does and where it is going.

Don't forget to practice interview questions with your friends or family. Try to simulate the interview process by sitting across from the person who is practicing with you. Ask that person to make note of any fidgety habits and unclear answers. When you interview, you will want to dress professionally and pay attention to the details. Keep your fingernails clean and short. Check out hems and cuffs for tears. Make sure your clothes are clean and pressed and your shoes are polished. For women, be sure that there are no runs in your hose and that your heels are not scuffed.

When you score an interview, be sure to arrive early. Introduce yourself to the receptionist and prepare to wait. If you are offered a drink, decline; you may end up spilling it on your clothes. During the interview, listen carefully to the interviewer's questions, pause before answering, and speak slowly and carefully. Be sure, too, to look all of the interviewers in the eye when speaking, sit up, and lean forward slightly. Show by your body language that you are interested and relaxed, even if you are nervous. And speaking of nervous, if you are that is normal, but be sure to avoid fidgeting with a pencil or paper and tapping your fingers or feet.

When you are speaking of what you can do, be sure to highlight your strengths. Even if you don't meet all of the job's qualifications, you may be able to persuade the employer that you can do the job. It may be a good idea, however, to avoid inquiring about the salary at the beginning of the interview. Instead, ask about the job responsibilities and benefits—the interviewer may provide a salary range as part of the information. As a last question, you may want to ask about the time line for filling the position. Knowing when the company will be making the final decision will help you prepare for the next step.

As you leave, thank everyone you meet and follow up with a thank-you letter to each interviewer (see Figure 12.3). If you do not know how to spell their names, call the receptionist the next day to get the correct spellings.

Interviewers want to hire people who are energetic, polite, professional, and appreciative. Put your best face forward and try to relax and enjoy the process.

Cyber Considerations

The Internet has made it much easier to find and apply for jobs, communicate with potential employers, and network to improve your contacts and connections. However, it can also be a potential hazard if it is not used appropriately and professionally. Most people are aware that posting messages, information, and photos can be risky—even dangerous—to your professional "health," but they may not be aware how much potential employers look for—and find—before they interview candidates. Many employers and company recruiters search for potential candidates online to see what kinds of information and images are out there. In some career fields, the more a candidate exposes (literally and figuratively) himself, the less likely it is he will get the job.

What can you do to protect yourself? Deleting your accounts is your best defense, but you can also change your account settings to private. Be aware, though, that if you have a large network of "friends," people who want to find out about you may still be

FIGURE 12.3 Sample Thank-You Letter

Juanita Cook
1234 Broadway Street
Anyplace, US 01234
555-555-1234
jrcook@anyplace.edu

July 12, 2011

Dr. Judy Pile
Ingram Enterprises
6789 Levi Lane
Anyplace, US 09876

Dear Dr. Pile,

Thank you for interviewing me yesterday. I enjoyed meeting you and your colleagues and learning more about how your company works.

After speaking with you, I am more firmly convinced that I would be a good person for the job. My education and experience would be a great match for what the position demands. I enjoy professional challenges, and I think your company provides the type of opportunities I am looking for.

Please feel free to contact me at 555–555–1234 or jrcook@anyplace.edu. I look forward to hearing from you.

Sincerely,

Juanita Cook

---

able to do so. It is best not to post or put into writing anything that you think may be questionable to a potential employer, and if you have posted anything, delete it if you feel it may jeopardize your ability to get the job you want.

Troubleshooting

All college career counselors want students to walk into high-paying jobs the day after graduation, but the reality is much different. Students who major in sought-after fields, such as information technology and health services, sometimes do not find the jobs that they thought were plentiful. Fluctuations in the economy are usually the cause for changes in the job market. Being prepared in case the job market has changed is your best defense.

To keep yourself grounded, formulate a plan for what you will do if you don't waltz into a dream job immediately. When writing your plan, be sure to answer the following questions:

- Are you willing to take less money if the opportunity is good?
- Are you willing to relocate for a better job?
- Are you willing to take a job in a different field than you expected?
- Are you willing to repackage your skills and knowledge to be considered for different types of work?

These are all questions that both Evan and Michael would do well to ask themselves. Even though Michael is very sure of the kind of job he wants, he may want to have an alternate plan in case those jobs are not readily available when he graduates. Evan can ask himself these questions also, to focus on what is most important to him in a job.

In addition, start building up your network of friends, family, coworkers, classmates, and acquaintances, if you have not already been working on it. Let them know that you are about to graduate and will be looking for a job.

Finally, consider the process that you must go through if you are to be successful in finding the right job for you. Getting a job, then, requires you to prepare in the following ways:

Practice interviewing with a fellow student or a career counselor before going out there for real.

Rubberball/Getty Images

- Consider which field best suits your skills, personality, and dreams.
- Attend workshops and information sessions that provide assistance with résumé writing, interviewing, and networking.
- Prepare a solid résumé.
- Network with friends, family, and acquaintances.
- Actively look for work.
- Respond to job advertisements by sending out your résumé and cover letter.
- Follow up job interviews with a thank-you letter.
- Remain positive and flexible but stick to your goals.

Collaboration
EXERCISE 12.2

Working in a group, discuss and list all the types of activities and events your college provides for students to get involved with that could be included on a résumé. ∎

NETWORKING

Diane Darling, in her book *The Networking Survival Guide* (2003), defines *networking* as "sharing of knowledge and contacts; getting the help you need when you need it from those from whom you need it . . . ; [and] building relationships *before* you need them" (p. 16). Now, even more than ever, networking is an essential part of staying connected with others, especially because social networking sites on the Internet have made it so easy (and addictive) for us to keep up with each other.

Networking Online

One of the largest trends in networking is using online websites such as LinkedIn and Facebook to create networks of friends, family, and special-interest groups. The possibilities seem endless as to how you can use the Internet to connect with others who have special interests and activities or problems to solve. With this said, if you decide to join a network that focuses on an interest of yours, such as auto body repair, be sure to investigate who runs the group, what kinds of information are shared, and how active the group is. Some networks will be more active than others, which will make it easier to connect with people and get involved; networks or groups that are less active won't help you if you are using them to get to know others as potential contacts in the future. Because creating networks of your own is so easy, you may want to consider creating an interest group if you cannot find one to join. Networking sites such as Facebook allow you to set up groups that can be used for professional, educational, or social purposes.

Networking Face to Face

Another way to get to know others is to network with them face to face. Finding active groups who share similar interests may be easier than you think. Look to clubs on campus that share your interests. Even if they are not career related, such as a drama club, you will meet people who may be future contacts for jobs. You can also get involved with your community through volunteer programs or civic groups such as your city's chamber of commerce. They may sponsor community-building, fundraising, and social events that allow you to meet other people in career fields that you are interested in. Additionally, involvement in such groups can provide you with more experience to record on your résumé. The more people you get to know, the more likely you will be able to use those contacts when you need them—in finding a career or in anything else.

Recommendation Letters

Recommendation letters and letters of reference are part of the job-finding process. If you have taken the time to cultivate a good relationship with a professor or an administrator at your college, you will have an easier time asking for and receiving a recommendation letter that is full of specific information about the quality of your work and your character.

When considering someone to ask, choose a person who has had the chance to see you at your best. If you worked closely with a professor or spent many hours talking with a counselor, ask him or her to write a recommendation letter for you. The better the person knows you, the better the recommendation let-

Collaboration EXERCISE 12.3

Working in a group, discuss the drawbacks and benefits of networking exclusively online. What can be lost in not networking face to face? What can be gained? ■

ter will be. In addition, give this person plenty of time to think about the quality of your work or recall specific examples in order to write a polished letter. If you are on a tight deadline, such as a week, be honest with the person and give him or her a chance to decline the opportunity. If the person does agree to write a recommendation letter on such short notice, be sure to provide him or her with all the necessary materials to complete it properly, including an addressed, stamped envelope and the correct forms. You may want to include a brief résumé so that the person can speak specifically about your accomplishments.

Once your recommendation letter has been written, write a thank-you note and show your appreciation for the favor. Consider a handwritten note that expresses your gratitude rather than a verbal or email message of thanks. Finally, when requesting a recommendation, you should take the necessary steps to ensure that you do not read the recommendation letter. If you must hand deliver the letter, ask that it be sealed in an envelope first. Maintaining the confidentiality of the recommendation ensures a more honest appraisal from the individual who has written it. Committees that evaluate recommendation letters want truthful descriptions of your abilities and strengths; if they know that you have seen the recommendation letter, they may doubt the accuracy of the description.

Giving back to the community is one way you can serve as a role model for others.
Bob Daemmrich/PhotoEdit

CREATING a LIFE

It has now become a cliché to say that "commencement"—the ceremony marking graduation—means "a beginning" rather than "an ending." Many graduation speakers address that point each year: When you graduate from college, you are not just ending your academic career; you are beginning the rest of your life. For college students, however, the difference between being in college and going off to a career may not be that clear. In fact, career and college, for most college students, are very much intertwined. Therefore, it may seem that there is no distinct beginning and ending for you. However, once you do graduate with a certificate or degree or even a group of credits, you can think about a brighter future as a beginning.

What will be left for you once you graduate? Beyond transferring, there is always graduate school or a professional school. Why not go as far as you can with your degree? With each semester, you are getting closer. Once you meet your goal of graduating with an associate's degree or certificate, you will see that all it takes is goal setting, time management, and a desire to meet your goals.

Another "beginning" as you complete a degree at your college is lifelong learning. Not only will you be able to use the research and information literacy skills that you have learned in college, but you will also have access to materials through alumni

FIGURE 12.4 Goal Achievement and Goal Setting

Goals I Have Met

1. Completed my courses with above-average grades.
2. Created a study group with classmates.
3. Kept up with my commitments on the job.
4. Paid my tuition.

New Short-Term Goals

1. Get registered for next semester.
2. Speak with a counselor about career possibilities.
3. Make at least two A's in my classes.
4. Take more time to relax.

borrowing privileges at the library. In addition, you may be more interested in and informed about guest speakers and community events that are sponsored by your college. At the very least, you will have a network of instructors, counselors, and advisers to call on when you need advice and information.

Mission, Values, and Goals Revisited

In Chapter 1, you wrote down your values, goals, and mission statement. Do you still have that information in a convenient location? If so, get it out and reflect on how well you have met your original short-term goals and how far you have come to reaching your long-term goals. Have your values changed any? Or have they been strengthened by your achievements? Have you followed your mission statement? Is there anything that you would change about it?

To answer these questions, you will need to reflect on your achievements over the past semester. Your mission and values should not have changed much in the past weeks, but if they have, you can make a new list of values and rewrite your mission statement. Most definitely, some of your short-term goals should be met, and you have no doubt moved on to a new list as you make your way to your long-term goals. Now is the time, then, to revisit your long-range plans and make adjustments if you need to. Keeping up with what you have accomplished will serve as a reminder of your success if you ever feel unsure about your progress. Figure 12.4 is an example of a new list you can make.

Once you revise your short-term goals, you may notice that your time line for reaching your long-term goals needs adjusting as well. Keeping your list in a convenient location and looking at it every day or week will help you stay on track.

Reflection EXERCISE 12.4

In what ways have you already mentored others who want to attend college or are just starting their college careers? How have you influenced others to value education? ■

Engaging in the Community

Although your focus during college will be on yourself and either moving on to another degree or to a new job, consider looking for opportunities to enhance your community. One of the purposes of higher education is to improve the lives of individuals so that the community benefits as well, and it is essential that educated community members give back and make improvements.

Professional clubs, social and civic groups, churches, and volunteer organizations are other ways you can get involved in the community after college, if you have not done so already. The people you meet in these groups and the connections you make, both professional and personal, can enrich your life and career. If you are not part of a community group, seek out one whose interests are similar to yours; also, look for ways to participate in events in your community, whether in a 5K run or a recycling drive. Participating in strengthening your community will allow you to give back to those in need, improve your surroundings, and gain friendships and business connections that may last a long time.

Achieving your goal of getting a college degree will be a proud moment for you and your family.
Shutterstock

It's All RELATIVE

As you know, first-generation college students are a special group of people. They often have overcome overwhelming personal and financial obstacles to attend college, and some get lost along the way, thinking that college is too difficult for them. Many of them may need a mentor to help them stay on track. Once you are confident that you can manage college or once you graduate, you may want to seek out others who need a mentor.

Some obvious candidates are people in your family who could benefit from enrolling in a certificate or degree program. These family members may be apprehensive about returning to school because they don't know if they can handle the responsibilities, or they may believe they cannot afford to go to college. As a mentor, you can share what you know about how to manage going to school with other obligations. You are proof that others can do it and do it successfully.

YOUR TURN

Who in your family can you mentor? • What will you tell them about going to college? • What kind of support can you offer them?

_____

_____

_____

_____

**(Personality + Learning Style =
Understanding Situations)**

Let's consider both Evan and Michael's career fair adventure. Evan is a kinesthetic learner who is very outgoing, which may be why he is visiting every booth. Michael, however, sees an opportunity to make his time count, which is why he only chooses two booths to visit. Evan seems to lack focus and confidence in what he wants to do. What advice would you give him before he hands out his résumé to all the attending companies? Michael, on the other hand, knows exactly what he wants to do and how to get there, but he lacks the confidence to go for his dream. Taking into consideration his personality type and learning style, what is the best course of action for him?

Now, considering your own learning style, personality type, and special circumstances, how would you approach a career fair and making a decision about what you want to do with your degree? ■

Now may not be the time to encourage you to help financially, but think about how you can continue to support your school after you have left. In order for a college—or any educational institution—to be successful in improving the lives of the people in its community, it must depend in part on its graduates to make a good name for themselves and to give back with their time, talent, and financial resources. There are a variety of ways that you can contribute to the education of those who will surely follow in your footsteps.

By being a productive, educated member of society, you are already giving back to your college. Because higher education's mission is to improve a community by increasing the knowledge of its population, we all benefit from students who complete graduation requirements for degree and certificate programs and go on to lead productive, happy lives. The skills and knowledge you have obtained in college are a good advertisement for the school. Alumni who make a difference in the lives of others through their jobs and community service fulfill the college's mission to not only provide education to strengthen the local economy, but to also graduate people who demonstrate the ideals of higher education.

From College to University

HOLD OFF ON STARTING YOUR CAREER UNTIL YOU HAVE MET YOUR EDUCATIONAL GOAL

It will be very tempting to head back to work before you have completed your certificate or degree because of changes in your family or financial situation. However, remember that if you can hang in there and go further toward your ultimate educational goal, the better opportunities you will have in the workforce and the easier it will be to go back if you do find yourself "stopping out" of college for a while as you work.

Another idea for helping you stay in college before returning to work is to look for ways to break your ultimate educational goal into achievable, realistic shorter-term goals that will move you in the right direction. For example, if you need to return to work before completing your registered nursing (RN) degree, which is often a two-year degree, you may be able to complete a licensed practical nursing (LPN) program in a shorter amount of time. Completing a shorter program first, working in the field, and then returning to complete a longer program may be a good fit for your educational and financial needs. Be sure, though, that you speak with an advisor to make sure you avoid taking too many classes that will not fit into your longer-term educational goal.

Building Your University Portfolio 12

Find someone you know (or ask your professor for the name of a former student) who has transferred to a four-year university and ask what kinds of career services are available for students. Are there specific clubs that you can join to help you get to know others in the same career field? Are there career fairs to participate in?

_____

_____

_____

From College to Career

PRACTICING WHAT YOU HAVE LEARNED TO EARN THE JOB

Time management, goal setting, and long-term planning are all skills that you have learned during your college career, and these skills will take you far in the workplace. If anything, knowing that you can juggle multiple responsibilities, such as taking care of family, job, and college, as well as yourself, should give you the confidence to tackle other challenges that you will face in the workforce. For sure, practice those skills on the job, but also know that you may need to improve on those skills as you complete new tasks, take on more projects at work, or change positions.

Don't forget that your college, even long after you have graduated, can help you while you are in the workplace. You may still have, for example, access to their career services as a graduate of the college. You may also be able to use the library to do research. For sure, you will have the connections that you made while in college, people you can call on for advice and friendship. Look into what services they offer for you before you graduate, services that you can utilize as a successful graduate.

Building Your Career Portfolio 12

Contact someone in a career that is similar to what you want to do. Ask how he or she landed the job. How did the résumé, cover letter, and interviewing help in winning the position? Are there any tips that he or she can give you to be successful at getting hired?

_____

_____

_____

First Voices

A "window to opportunity" opened doors to her professional dream: Professor had family support in accomplishing her goals

Rosa Maria Abrero,
Ph.D., Assistant
Professor, College
of Education

I knew from an early age that I was going to college. My mother would always talk about the "windows of opportunity" that would allow me to attend school, although we did not have the money for college. My first experience away from home was exciting, but at the same time I knew it would also bring difficulties because I would have to work to make ends meet. But this is what I wanted. I knew I was going to be a teacher.

The National Defense Student Loan (NDSL) allowed me this opportunity. I chose to teach in the poorest district in San Antonio, Texas: Edgewood ISD. I knew that if I was successful there, I could teach anywhere. I taught in Edgewood 4 years and married; then, I left for Dallas, Texas, where I started a bilingual program in Garland, Texas. While teaching for 12 years for the Garland schools, I again felt the calling to return to school. I attended a nearby university and earned a master's degree in 1981. Coming to live in Austin, Texas, was the culmination of my dream. I taught while going at night for my doctorate degree. I feel fortunate that my family, my two boys, Robert and David, together with my husband supported me in what I wanted to accomplish for my life.

I have been transformed from a quiet student to a more self-assured woman who knows that an education is the means to achieve goals. My mission now is to help others achieve their goals by being there for them and inspiring them to continue just like I did. Never give up your dreams. Continue to work and fulfill your plan.

PATH OF DISCOVERY
Journal Entry

What if anything would keep you from completing your degree? What keeps you motivated to continue?

CHAPTER REVIEW QUESTIONS

1. How can you explore different kinds of careers?
2. What are the differences and similarities between a cover letter and a résumé?
3. Identify the different types of networking and explain the costs and benefits of each.
4. How will you build a life beyond college?

CHAPTER 12 CASE SCENARIOS

1. Rudy is getting a degree in business management, but doesn't have any idea how to look for a good job. He is not really even sure if that is what he needs to break into financial planning. What advice can you give him to make sure he is starting his career planning on the right foot?

2. Brian's dream is to own a horse farm, but he doesn't think he can afford his ambition, so he is in his second semester as a radiology technician because it is a job with a steady income. Also, Brian doesn't want to quit school to follow his desire because he values an education. What advice can you give him about following his dreams?

3. Lawrence is ready to graduate with a degree in networking, and he has been circulating his résumé with the hope that he can roll right into a job after graduation. Because of his lack of experience in his field, Lawrence has decided to exaggerate some of his responsibilities as a work-study student in the Information Technology Department and as an intern at a local advertising company. What should you tell Lawrence before he sends his résumés out to prospective employers?

RESEARCH IT FURTHER

1. Search for a website that is devoted to helping you discover the right career for you, such as www.solutionskills.com/index.html. Research a career that interests you and collect information about the education needed, the pay you can expect, and the potential for advancement. Present your findings to your class.

2. Individually or within a group research the qualifications and requirements for the different loans and grants that your college offers. With the information, create a one-page sheet for each type of financial aid that can help students remember the differences between each type.

3. Investigate the entrance requirements of two four-year universities in the area. Find out GPA requirements, available scholarships and financial aid, and what kinds of degree programs they offer. Make a brief presentation to your class.

4. What, if any, alumni services does your college offer? If they offer very few or none at all, brainstorm a list of ideas that you would like to see implemented and present them to an administrator at your institution who can give you feedback on what is possible. Then, report to your class on which suggestions can be implemented and which cannot.

References and Recommended Readings

Darling, D. (2003). *The networking survival guide: Get the success you want by tapping into the people you know.* New York: McGraw-Hill.

Farr, M. J. (2004). *Same-day résumé: Write an effective résumé in an hour.* Indianapolis, IN: Jist Publishing.

Leider, R. J. (2005). *The power of purpose: Creating meaning in your life and work.* San Francisco: Berrett-Koehler Publishers.

Marcus, J. J. (2003). *The résumé makeover: 50 common résumé and cover letter problems—and how to fix them.* New York: McGraw-Hill.

Safko, L., & Brake, D. (2009). *The social media bible: Tactics, tools, and strategies for business success.* San Francisco: Wiley & Sons.

VARK Learning Styles

The VARK inventory, developed by Neil D. Fleming and Charles Bonwell, uses the categories Visual, Aural, Read/Write, and Kinesthetic to help you determine your learning style preference. They also provide learning strategies based on your strengths determined by the information that you provide about how you would best act or react in certain situations. If you have strong preferences in more than one mode, you are considered multimodal (MM).

VARK INVENTORY*

Choose the answer which best explains your preference and circle the letter. Please select more than one response if a single answer does not match your perception. Leave blank any question that does not apply.

1. You are helping someone who wants to go to your airport, town centre or railway station. You would:

    a. go with her.
    b. tell her the directions.
    c. write down the directions.
    d. draw, or give her a map.

2. You are not sure whether a word should be spelled *dependent* or *dependant*. You would:

    a. see the words in your mind and choose by the way they look.
    b. think about how each word sounds and choose one.
    c. find it in a dictionary.
    d. write both words on paper and choose one.

3. You are planning a holiday for a group. You want some feedback from them about the plan. You would:

    a. describe some of the highlights.
    b. use a map or website to show them the places.
    c. give them a copy of the printed itinerary.
    d. phone, text or email them.

4. You are going to cook something as a special treat for your family. You would:

    a. cook something you know without the need for instructions.
    b. ask friends for suggestions.

    c. look through the cookbook for ideas from the pictures.

    d. use a cookbook where you know there is a good recipe.

5. A group of tourists want to learn about the parks or wildlife reserves in your area. You would:

    a. talk about, or arrange a talk for them about parks or wildlife reserves.

    b. show them internet pictures, photographs or picture books.

    c. take them to a park or wildlife reserve and walk with them.

    d. give them a book or pamphlets about the parks or wildlife reserves.

6. You are about to purchase a digital camera or mobile phone. Other than price, what would most influence your decision?

    a. Trying or testing it.

    b. Reading the details about its features.

    c. It is a modern design and looks good.

    d. The salesperson telling me about its features.

7. Remember a time when you learned how to do something new. Try to avoid choosing a physical skill, e.g. riding a bike. You learned best by:

    a. watching a demonstration.

    b. listening to somebody explaining it and asking questions.

    c. diagrams and charts—visual clues.

    d. written instructions—e.g. a manual or textbook.

8. You have a problem with your knee. You would prefer that the doctor:

    a. gave you a web address or something to read about it.

    b. used a plastic model of a knee to show what was wrong.

    c. described what was wrong.

    d. showed you a diagram of what was wrong.

9. You want to learn a new program, skill or game on a computer. You would:

    a. read the written instructions that came with the program.

    b. talk with people who know about the program.

    c. use the controls or keyboard.

    d. follow the diagrams in the book that came with it.

10. You like websites that have:

    a. things you can click on, shift or try.

    b. interesting design and visual features.

    c. interesting written descriptions, lists and explanations.

    d. audio channels where you can hear music, radio programs or interviews.

11. Other than price, what would most influence your decision to buy a new non-fiction book?

    a. The way it looks is appealing.

    b. Quickly reading parts of it.

    c. A friend talks about it and recommends it.

    d. It has real-life stories, experiences and examples.

12. You are using a book, CD or website to learn how to take photos with your new digital camera. You would like to have:

    a. a chance to ask questions and talk about the camera and its features.

    b. clear written instructions with lists and bullet points about what to do.

    c. diagrams showing the camera and what each part does.

    d. many examples of good and poor photos and how to improve them.

13. Do you prefer a teacher or a presenter who uses:
    a. demonstrations, models or practical sessions.
    b. question and answer, talk, group discussion, or guest speakers.
    c. handouts, books, or readings.
    d. diagrams, charts or graphs.

14. You have finished a competition or test and would like some feedback. You would like to have feedback:
    a. using examples from what you have done.
    b. using a written description of your results.
    c. from somebody who talks it through with you.
    d. using graphs showing what you had achieved.

15. You are going to choose food at a restaurant or cafe. You would:
    a. choose something that you have had there before.
    b. listen to the waiter or ask friends to recommend choices.
    c. choose from the descriptions in the menu.
    d. look at what others are eating or look at pictures of each dish.

16. You have to make an important speech at a conference or special occasion. You would:
    a. make diagrams or get graphs to help explain things.
    b. write a few key words and practice saying your speech over and over.
    c. write out your speech and learn from reading it over several times.
    d. gather many examples and stories to make the talk real and practical.

Scoring

For each question, mark your answer below and then add up how many V's, A's, R's, and K's you have. The largest number of V, A, R, or K indicates your learning style preference. For example, if you marked "A" for question number 2, your learning style preference for that question is V. If you have more V's than any other letter, your learning style preference is Visual.

Question	Choice A	Choice B	Choice C	Choice D
1	K	A	R	V
2	V	A	R	K
3	K	V	R	A
4	K	A	V	R
5	A	V	K	R
6	K	R	V	A
7	K	A	V	R
8	R	K	A	V
9	R	A	K	V
10	K	V	R	A
11	V	R	A	K
12	A	R	V	K
13	K	A	R	V
14	K	R	A	V
15	K	A	R	V
16	V	A	R	K

Calculating Your Score

Add the number of each letter and write the totals in the spaces below.

Total Number of V's circled _____

Total Number of A's circled _____

Total Number of R's circled _____

Total Number of K's circled _____

Look at your calculated score. If you have more V's than any other letter, then you have a strong visual learning preference. You may also have another learning style preference that is the same or close to your dominant learning style preference. For example, if you recorded 8 R's and 7 K's, you have both a read/write learning style preference as well as a kinesthetic learning style preference. Record your preference(s) in the space below.

My VARK Learning Style Preference is _____.

As you read each student story and consider the situations presented at the beginning of each chapter, think about these students' learning style preferences and how they affect their experiences and choices. Consider, too, how your learning style preference would affect you in a similar situation. You will be able to answer specific questions related to learning styles with the PLUS (Personality + Learning Style = Understanding Situations) Exercises within each chapter.

Now that you know your learning style preference, you have made that first step. May the rest of the journey move you closer to your educational and personal goals.

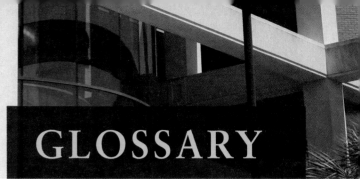

Academic calendar—A list of important dates. Included are vacation breaks, registration periods, and deadlines for certain forms.

Academic probation—A student whose GPA falls below a designated number can be placed on academic probation. If the GPA does not improve, then the student may be prohibited from registering for classes for a designated number of semesters.

Articulation agreement—A signed document stating that a college will accept the courses from another college.

Associate of Applied Science—A degree that consists of about 60 credit hours of courses. Not intended to serve as a transferable degree to a four-year university.

Associate of Arts—A degree that consists of about 60 credit hours of general education courses. Often considered as the equivalent of the first two years of a four-year degree.

Audience—In essay writing, the audience is the person or persons whom you are addressing.

Bachelor's degree—A degree that consists of about 12 credit hours of both general education courses and major courses.

Catalog—A book that provides students with information about the college's academic calendar, tuition and fees, and degree/certificate programs.

Corequisite—A course that you can take at the same time as another course. For example, if intermediate algebra is a corequisite for physical science, then you will take both courses during the same semester.

Cornell System—A note-taking system in which a student draws an upside-down "T" on a sheet of paper and uses the space to the right for taking notes, the space to the left for adding questions and highlighting important points, and the space at the bottom for summarizing the material.

Course objective—A goal that the instructor has identified for the student to meet once the course is completed. For example, a course objective could be to use MLA documentation properly.

Cover letter—A letter accompanying a résumé that describes how a person's qualifications match the advertised requirements for the job.

Creative thinking—Thinking that creates or generates ideas.

Critical thinking—The ability to use specific criteria to evaluate reasoning and make a decision.

Curriculum—A term used to refer to the courses that a student must take in a particular field, or it can refer to all the classes that the college offers.

Developmental classes—Sometimes referred to as remedial classes, developmental classes focus on basic college-level skills such as reading, writing, and math. Students who earn scores below a certain number on standardized tests such as the ACT and COMPASS exams may be required to take developmental classes before enrolling in college-level courses.

Doctoral degree—A degree that consists of about 60 credit hours beyond the bachelor's degree.

Family Educational Rights and Privacy Act (FERPA)—A federal law that ensures that a student's educational records, including test grades and transcripts, are not accessed or viewed by anyone who is not authorized by the student to do so.

Full-time student—A student who is taking at least 12 credit hours of courses per semester.

Full-time worker—A person who is working at least 40 hours per week.

Grade point average (GPA)—The number that is used to determine a student's progress in college. It refers to the number of quality points divided by the number of hours a student has taken.

Knowledge—The product created from taking in information, thinking about it critically, and synthesizing one's own ideas about what one has read or seen.

Long-term goal—A goal that takes a long time to complete (within a year or more).

Major—The area that a student is focusing on for his or her degree. If a student wants to teach third grade, his or her major can be elementary education. (*See also* Minor.)

Master's degree—A graduate degree that consists of about 30 credit hours beyond a bachelor's degree.

Matching question—A test question that provides one column of descriptors and another column of words that must be matched with the appropriate descriptor.

Minor—A second area that a student can emphasize in his or her degree. A minor usually requires fewer classes and is not as intensive as a major. For example, if a student majors in marketing but also wants to learn more about running his or her own business, the student may want to minor in business or accounting.

Mission statement—A declaration of what a person or an institution believes in and what that person or institution hopes to accomplish.

Multiple-choice question—A type of test question in which an incomplete sentence or a question is given and the correct response must be chosen from a list of possibilities.

Objective question—A question that presents a limited number of possible answers.

Part-time student—A student who is taking less than 12 credit hours per semester.

Prerequisite—A required course or score that must be completed or achieved before enrolling in a course.

Priority—Something that is important at a particular moment.

Purpose—What a student hopes to accomplish with his or her writing assignment.

Quality points—The number that is assigned each grade. For example, an A is worth four quality points and a B is worth three quality points.

Remedial classes—*See* Developmental classes.

Résumé—A page or two that provides a person's educational and work experience, career objective, and contact information.

Short-term goal—A goal that can be accomplished in a short period of time (within a week or a few months).

SQ3R—A reading method that consists of the following elements: survey, question, read, recite, and review.

Stress—A physical and psychological response to outside stimuli.

Student handbook—A publication of the college that outlines what the college expects of the student.

Subjective question—A test question that requires a student to provide a personal answer. Usually, there are no "wrong" answers to subjective questions.

Syllabus—A document that contains an overview of the course, including objectives, assignments, and required materials as well as the instructor's policies for attendance, exams, and grading. It may also contain the college's policies on disability accommodations and academic dishonesty.

Time management—Strategies for using time effectively.

Topic—The subject of a piece of writing.

Transcript—A record of the courses a student has taken and the grades the student has earned. Transcripts also note the student's grade point average.

Transfer—Refers to moving from one school to another. Students who transfer must apply for admission to the second school and must request that their transcripts be sent to the new school.

T system—*See* Cornell system.

Values—Part of a person's belief system that provides the foundation of what the person does and what the person wants to become. If a person values financial stability, then the person will look for opportunities to earn money and provide a secure future.

Work-study—A federal program that allows students to work at their college while taking classes. Students must qualify for work-study money and must meet college department requirements for work.

INDEX